W9-CNM-046

Love Hina

By

Ken Akamatsu

Los Angeles • Tokyo

Translator – Nan Rymer
English Adaptation – Adam Arnold
Retouch and Lettering – Dolly Chan
Graphic Designer – Anna Kernbaum
Editor – Paul Morrissey
Associate Editors – Robert Coyner and Trisha Kunimoto

Senior Editor – Jake Forbes
Pre-production Manager – Fred Lui
Art Director – Matthew Alford
Brand Manager – Kenneth Lee
VP Production – Ron Klamert
Publisher – Stuart Levy

Email: editor@TOKYOPOP.com
Come visit us online at www.TOKYOPOP.com

A  book

TOKYOPOP® is an imprint of Mixx Entertainment, Inc.
5900 Wilshire Blvd. Ste 2000, Los Angeles, CA 90036

©1999 Ken Akamatsu. First published in 1999 by Kodansha Ltd., Tokyo.
English publication rights arranged through Kodansha Ltd., Tokyo.

English text © 2002 by Mixx Entertainment, Inc.
TOKYOPOP is a registered trademark and the
Robofish logo is a trademark of Mixx Entertainment, Inc.

All rights reserved. No portion of this book may be reproduced or
transmitted in any form or by any means without written permission
from the copyright holders. This graphic novel is a work of fiction.
Any resemblance to actual events or locales or persons, living or dead,
is entirely coincidental.

ISBN: 1-931514-97-6

First TOKYOPOP® printing: June 2002

10 9 8 7 6 5 4 3 2 1

Printed in Canada.

CONTENTS

Love Hina

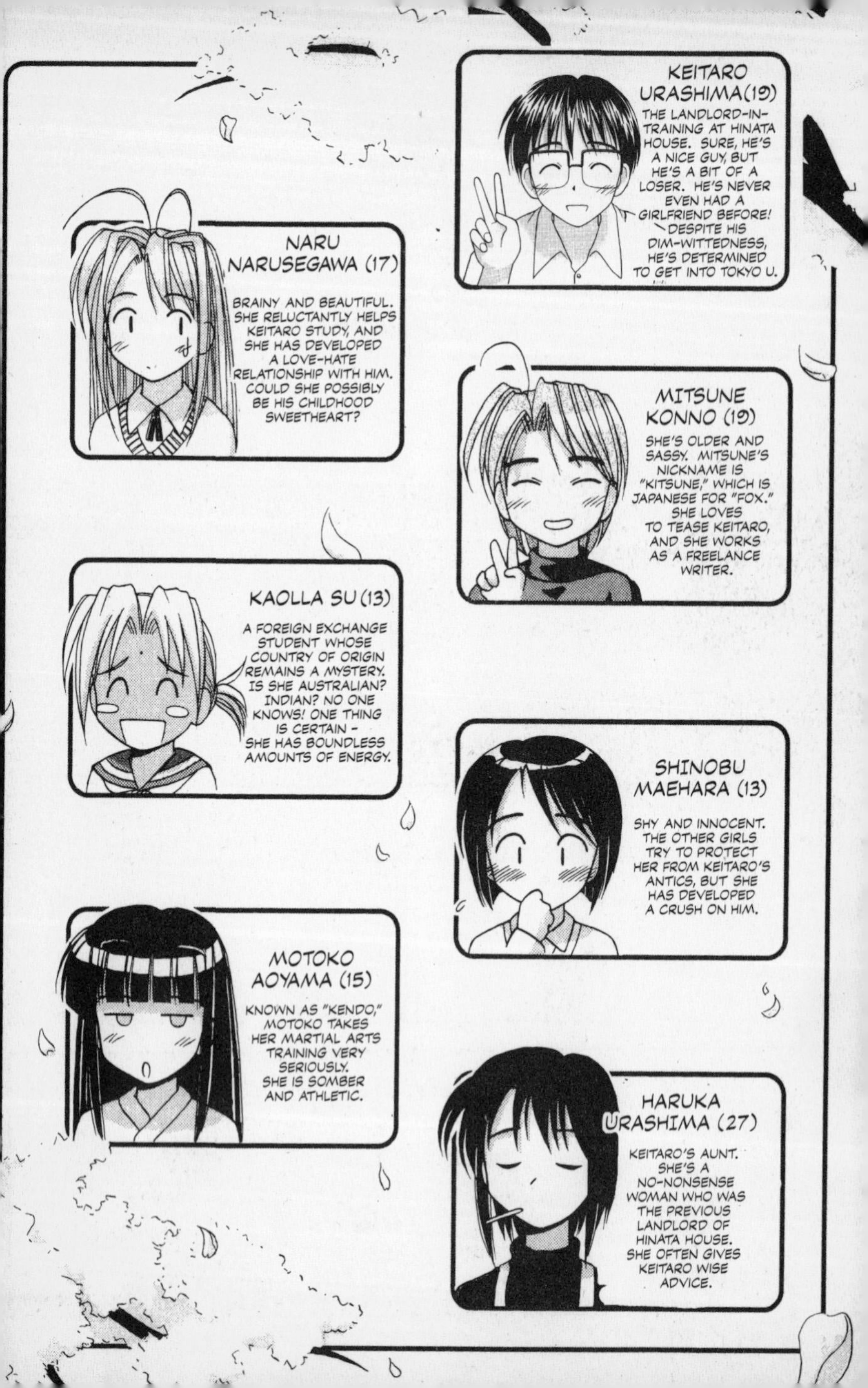

KEITARO URASHIMA (19)
THE LANDLORD-IN-TRAINING AT HINATA HOUSE. SURE, HE'S A NICE GUY, BUT HE'S A BIT OF A LOSER. HE'S NEVER EVEN HAD A GIRLFRIEND BEFORE! DESPITE HIS DIM-WITTEDNESS, HE'S DETERMINED TO GET INTO TOKYO U.
NARU NARUSEGAWA (17)
BRAINY AND BEAUTIFUL. SHE RELUCTANTLY HELPS KEITARO STUDY, AND SHE HAS DEVELOPED A LOVE-HATE RELATIONSHIP WITH HIM. COULD SHE POSSIBLY BE HIS CHILDHOOD SWEETHEART?
MITSUNE KONNO (19)
SHE'S OLDER AND SASSY. MITSUNE'S NICKNAME IS "KITSUNE," WHICH IS JAPANESE FOR "FOX." SHE LOVES TO TEASE KEITARO, AND SHE WORKS AS A FREELANCE WRITER.
KAOLLA SU (13)
A FOREIGN EXCHANGE STUDENT WHOSE COUNTRY OF ORIGIN REMAINS A MYSTERY. IS SHE AUSTRALIAN? INDIAN? NO ONE KNOWS! ONE THING IS CERTAIN - SHE HAS BOUNDLESS AMOUNTS OF ENERGY.
SHINOBU MAEHARA (13)
SHY AND INNOCENT. THE OTHER GIRLS TRY TO PROTECT HER FROM KEITARO'S ANTICS, BUT SHE HAS DEVELOPED A CRUSH ON HIM.
MOTOKO AOYAMA (15)
KNOWN AS "KENDO," MOTOKO TAKES HER MARTIAL ARTS TRAINING VERY SERIOUSLY. SHE IS SOMBER AND ATHLETIC.
HARUKA URASHIMA (27)
KEITARO'S AUNT. SHE'S A NO-NONSENSE WOMAN WHO WAS THE PREVIOUS LANDLORD OF HINATA HOUSE. SHE OFTEN GIVES KEITARO WISE ADVICE.

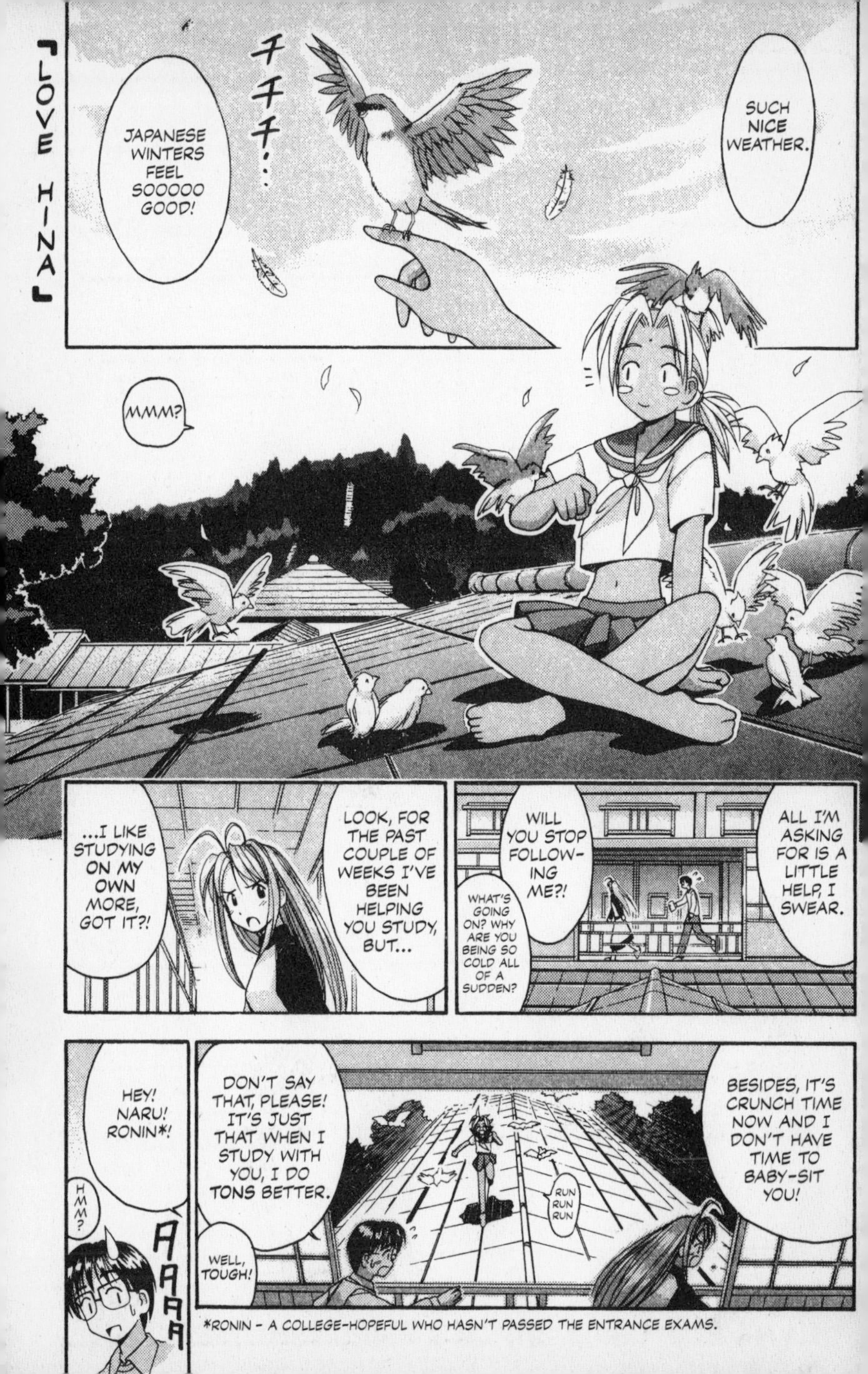
「LOVE HINA」
SUCH NICE WEATHER.
チチチ…
JAPANESE WINTERS FEEL SOOOOO GOOD!
MMM?
ALL I'M ASKING FOR IS A LITTLE HELP, I SWEAR.
WILL YOU STOP FOLLOW-ING ME?!
WHAT'S GOING ON? WHY ARE YOU BEING SO COLD ALL OF A SUDDEN?
LOOK, FOR THE PAST COUPLE OF WEEKS I'VE BEEN HELPING YOU STUDY, BUT...
...I LIKE STUDYING ON MY OWN MORE, GOT IT?!
BESIDES, IT'S CRUNCH TIME NOW AND I DON'T HAVE TIME TO BABY-SIT YOU!
DON'T SAY THAT, PLEASE! IT'S JUST THAT WHEN I STUDY WITH YOU, I DO TONS BETTER.
RUN RUN RUN
WELL, TOUGH!
HEY! NARU! RONIN*!
HMM?
AAAA

*RONIN - A COLLEGE-HOPEFUL WHO HASN'T PASSED THE ENTRANCE EXAMS.

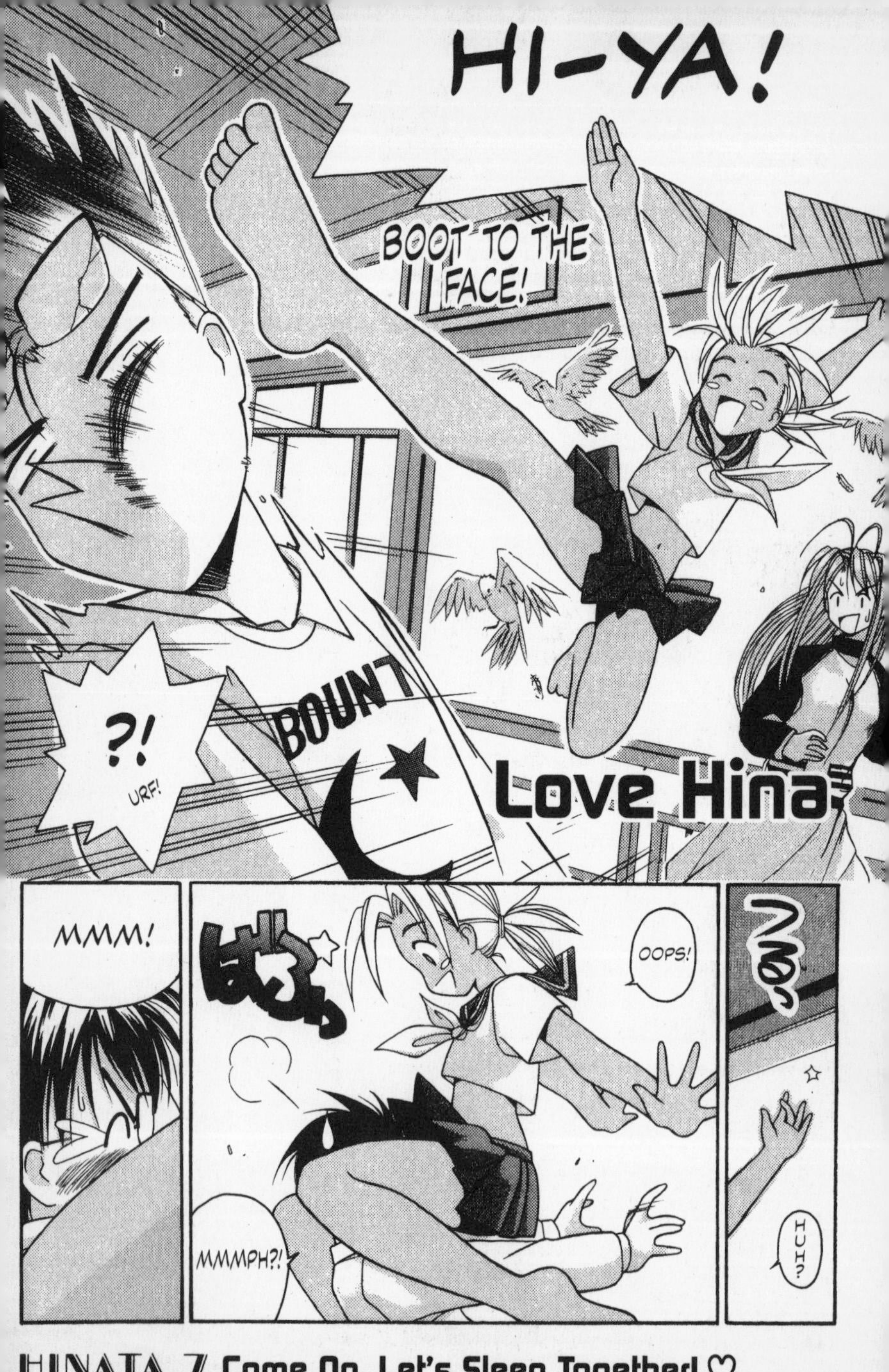
HI-YA!
BOOT TO THE FACE!
Love Hina
BOUN
?!
URF!
HUH?
OOPS!
MMMPH?!
MMM!

HINATA.7 Come On, Let's Sleep Together! ♡

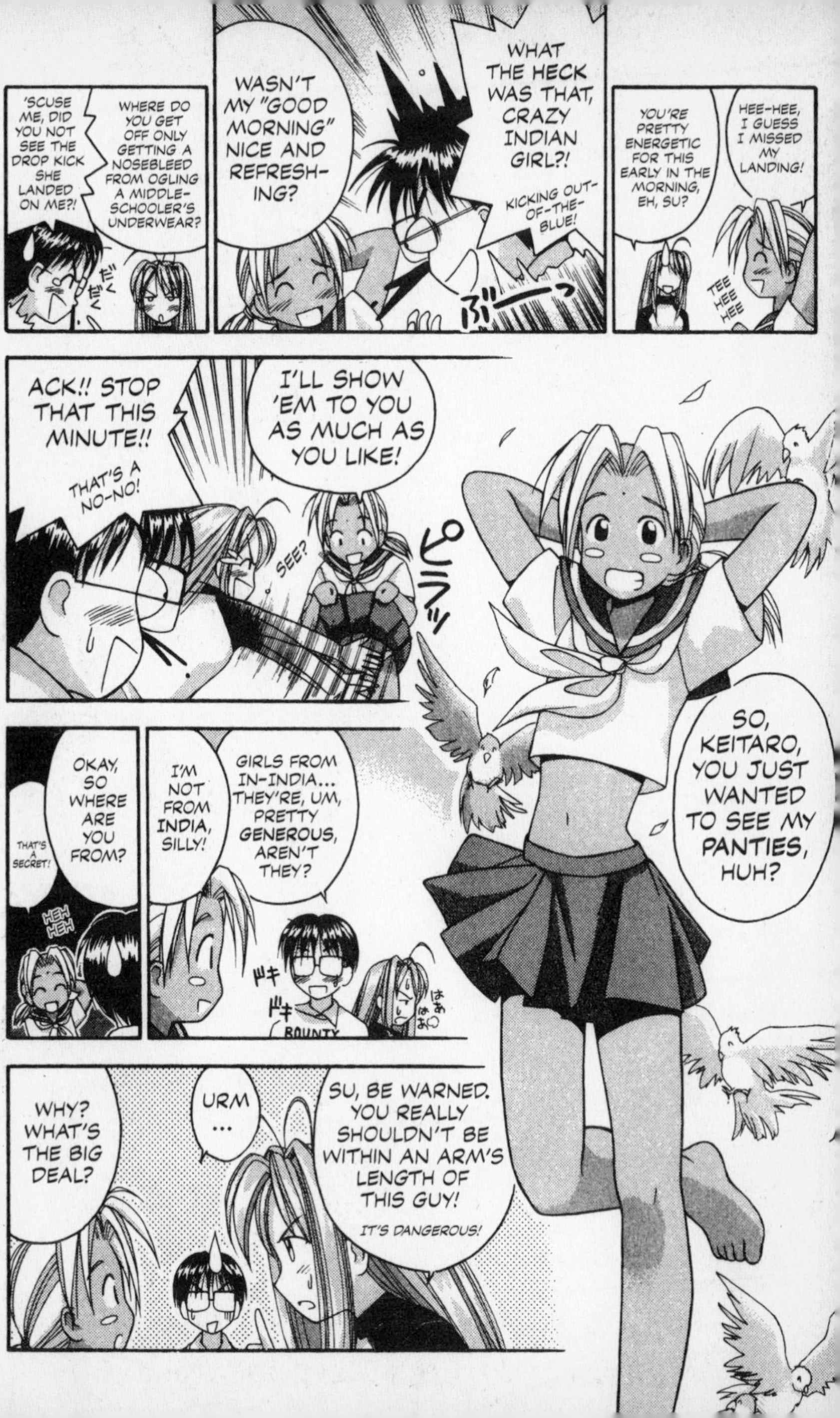
HEE-HEE, I GUESS I MISSED MY LANDING!
YOU'RE PRETTY ENERGETIC FOR THIS EARLY IN THE MORNING, EH, SU?
TEE HEE HEE
WHAT THE HECK WAS THAT, CRAZY INDIAN GIRL?!
KICKING OUT-OF-THE-BLUE!
WASN'T MY "GOOD MORNING" NICE AND REFRESH-ING?
ぶーっ
WHERE DO YOU GET OFF ONLY GETTING A NOSEBLEED FROM OGLING A MIDDLE-SCHOOLER'S UNDERWEAR?
'SCUSE ME, DID YOU NOT SEE THE DROP KICK SHE LANDED ON ME?!
だくだく
SO, KEITARO, YOU JUST WANTED TO SEE MY PANTIES, HUH?
I'LL SHOW 'EM TO YOU AS MUCH AS YOU LIKE!
ピラッ
SEE?
ACK!! STOP THAT THIS MINUTE!!
THAT'S A NO-NO!
GIRLS FROM IN-INDIA... THEY'RE, UM, PRETTY GENEROUS, AREN'T THEY?
I'M NOT FROM INDIA, SILLY!
ドキドキ
BOUNTY
OKAY, SO WHERE ARE YOU FROM?
THAT'S A SECRET!
HEH HEH
SU, BE WARNED. YOU REALLY SHOULDN'T BE WITHIN AN ARM'S LENGTH OF THIS GUY!
IT'S DANGEROUS!
URM ...
WHY? WHAT'S THE BIG DEAL?

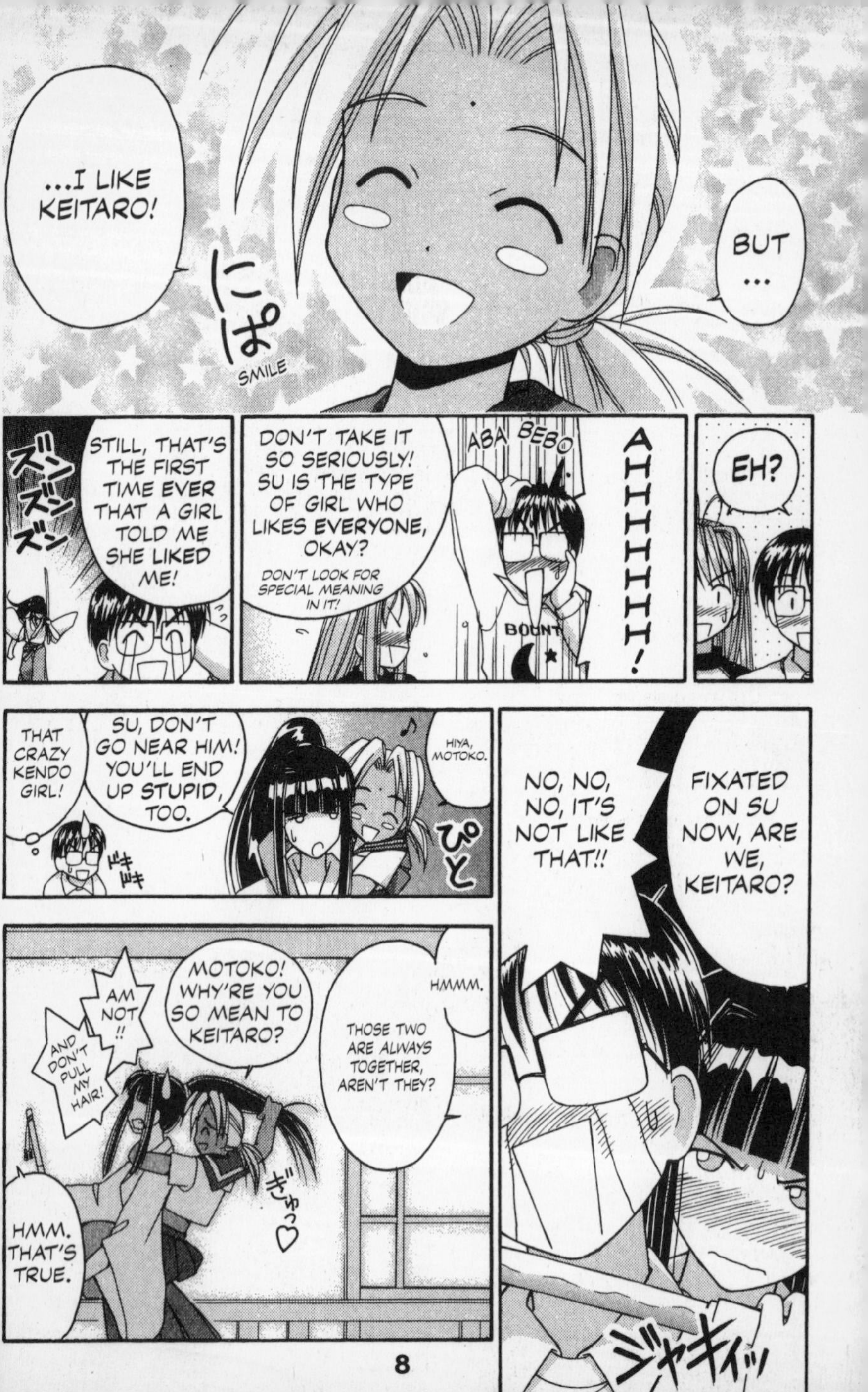
BUT ...
...I LIKE KEITARO!
にぱ
SMILE
EH?
AHHHHHHH!
ABA BEBO
DON'T TAKE IT SO SERIOUSLY! SU IS THE TYPE OF GIRL WHO LIKES EVERYONE, OKAY?
DON'T LOOK FOR SPECIAL MEANING IN IT!
STILL, THAT'S THE FIRST TIME EVER THAT A GIRL TOLD ME SHE LIKED ME!
ズーンズーンズーン
FIXATED ON SU NOW, ARE WE, KEITARO?
NO, NO, NO, IT'S NOT LIKE THAT!!
ジャキイッ
HIYA, MOTOKO.
ぴと
SU, DON'T GO NEAR HIM! YOU'LL END UP STUPID, TOO.
THAT CRAZY KENDO GIRL!
ドキドキ
HMMM.
THOSE TWO ARE ALWAYS TOGETHER, AREN'T THEY?
MOTOKO! WHY'RE YOU SO MEAN TO KEITARO?
AM NOT!!
AND DON'T PULL MY HAIR!
ぎゅっ♡
HMM. THAT'S TRUE.

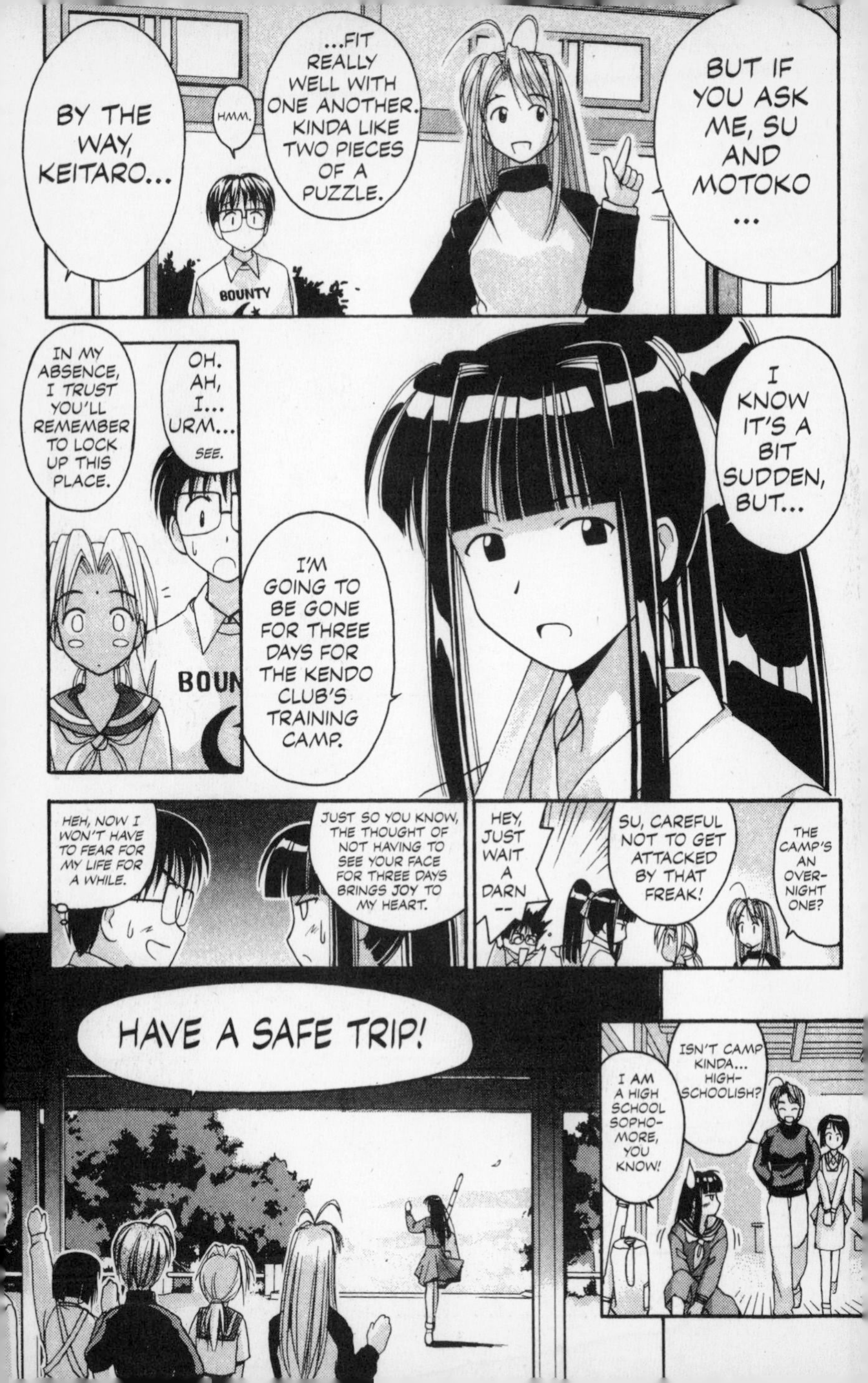
BUT IF YOU ASK ME, SU AND MOTOKO ...
...FIT REALLY WELL WITH ONE ANOTHER. KINDA LIKE TWO PIECES OF A PUZZLE.
HMM.
BY THE WAY, KEITARO...
I KNOW IT'S A BIT SUDDEN, BUT...
I'M GOING TO BE GONE FOR THREE DAYS FOR THE KENDO CLUB'S TRAINING CAMP.
OH. AH, I... URM... SEE.
IN MY ABSENCE, I TRUST YOU'LL REMEMBER TO LOCK UP THIS PLACE.
THE CAMP'S AN OVER-NIGHT ONE?
SU, CAREFUL NOT TO GET ATTACKED BY THAT FREAK!
HEY, JUST WAIT A DARN --
JUST SO YOU KNOW, THE THOUGHT OF NOT HAVING TO SEE YOUR FACE FOR THREE DAYS BRINGS JOY TO MY HEART.
HEH, NOW I WON'T HAVE TO FEAR FOR MY LIFE FOR A WHILE.
ISN'T CAMP KINDA... HIGH-SCHOOLISH?
I AM A HIGH SCHOOL SOPHO-MORE, YOU KNOW!
HAVE A SAFE TRIP!

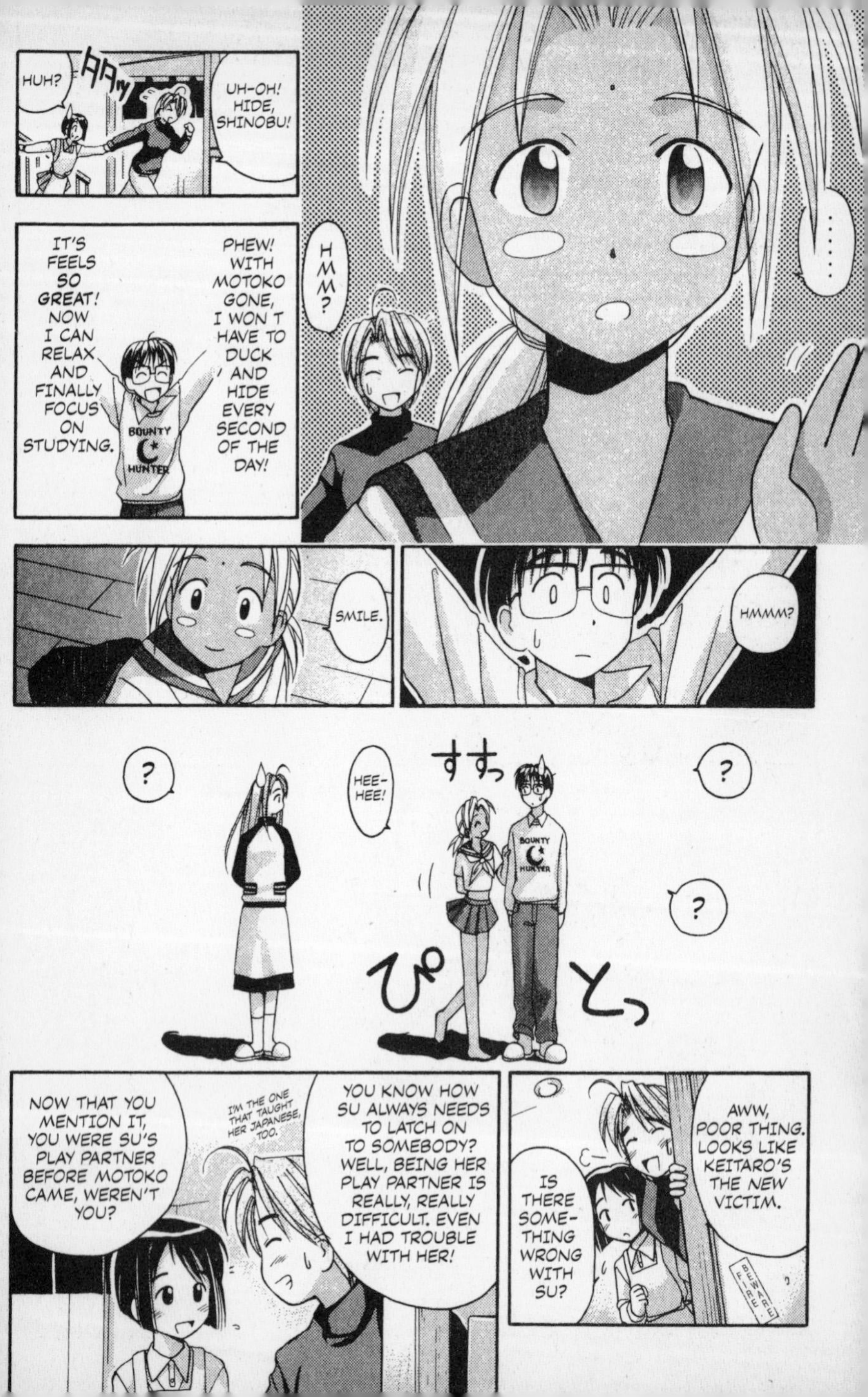
......
HMM?
UH-OH! HIDE, SHINOBU!
タタッ
HUH?
PHEW! WITH MOTOKO GONE, I WON T HAVE TO DUCK AND HIDE EVERY SECOND OF THE DAY!
IT'S FEELS SO GREAT! NOW I CAN RELAX AND FINALLY FOCUS ON STUDYING.
BOUNTY HUNTER
HMMM?
SMILE.
?
すすっ
HEE-HEE!
?
?
BOUNTY HUNTER
ぴとっ
AWW, POOR THING. LOOKS LIKE KEITARO'S THE NEW VICTIM.
IS THERE SOMETHING WRONG WITH SU?
BEWARE FIRE
YOU KNOW HOW SU ALWAYS NEEDS TO LATCH ON TO SOMEBODY? WELL, BEING HER PLAY PARTNER IS REALLY, REALLY DIFFICULT. EVEN I HAD TROUBLE WITH HER!
I'M THE ONE THAT TAUGHT HER JAPANESE, TOO.
NOW THAT YOU MENTION IT, YOU WERE SU'S PLAY PARTNER BEFORE MOTOKO CAME, WEREN'T YOU?

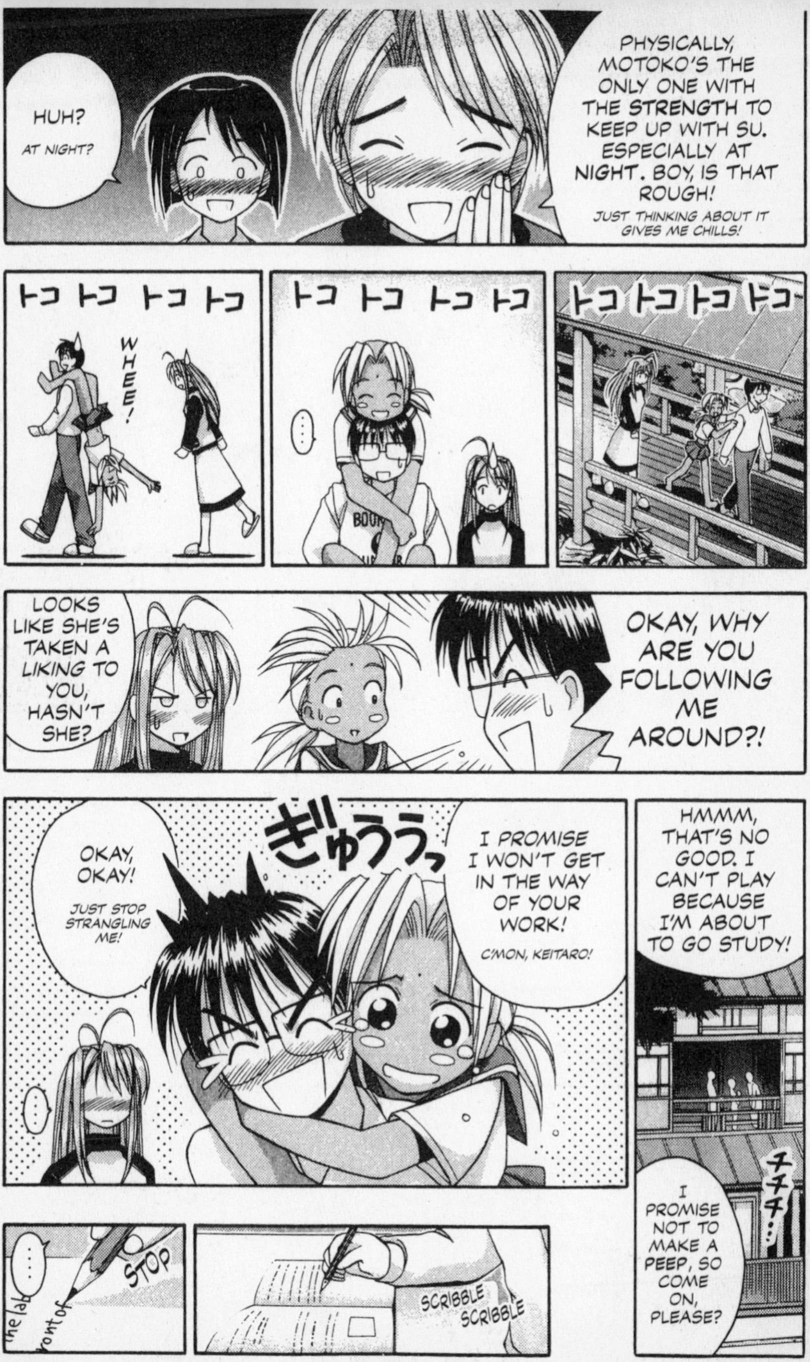
PHYSICALLY, MOTOKO'S THE ONLY ONE WITH THE STRENGTH TO KEEP UP WITH SU. ESPECIALLY AT NIGHT. BOY, IS THAT ROUGH!
JUST THINKING ABOUT IT GIVES ME CHILLS!
HUH?
AT NIGHT?
トコトコトコトコ
トコ トコ トコ トコ
...
トコ トコ トコ トコ
WHEE!
OKAY, WHY ARE YOU FOLLOWING ME AROUND?!
LOOKS LIKE SHE'S TAKEN A LIKING TO YOU, HASN'T SHE?
HMMM, THAT'S NO GOOD. I CAN'T PLAY BECAUSE I'M ABOUT TO GO STUDY!
チチチ...
I PROMISE NOT TO MAKE A PEEP, SO COME ON, PLEASE?
I PROMISE I WON'T GET IN THE WAY OF YOUR WORK!
C'MON, KEITARO!
ぎゅううっ
OKAY, OKAY!
JUST STOP STRANGLING ME!
...
SCRIBBLE SCRIBBLE
STOP
...

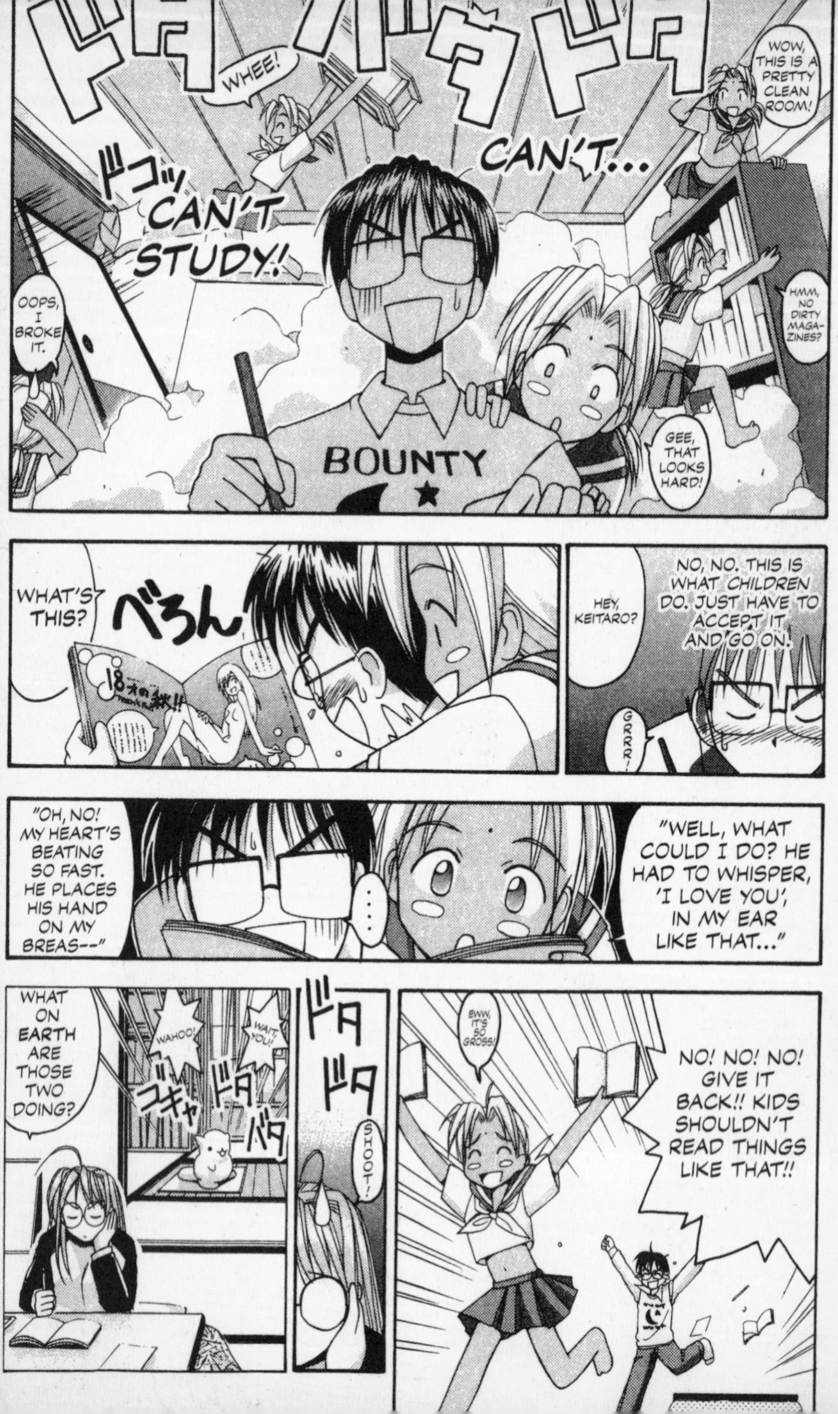
ドタ バタ ドタ
WOW, THIS IS A PRETTY CLEAN ROOM!
WHEE!
CAN'T...
HMM, NO DIRTY MAGAZINES?
ドコッ
CAN'T STUDY!
GEE, THAT LOOKS HARD!
BOUNTY
OOPS, I BROKE IT.
NO, NO. THIS IS WHAT CHILDREN DO. JUST HAVE TO ACCEPT IT AND GO ON.
HEY, KEITARO?
GRRR!
べろん
WHAT'S THIS?
18才の秋!!
"WELL, WHAT COULD I DO? HE HAD TO WHISPER, 'I LOVE YOU', IN MY EAR LIKE THAT..."
...
"OH, NO! MY HEART'S BEATING SO FAST. HE PLACES HIS HAND ON MY BREAS--"
NO! NO! NO! GIVE IT BACK!! KIDS SHOULDN'T READ THINGS LIKE THAT!!
EWW, IT'S SO GROSS!
ドタ ドタ
SHOOT!
WAIT, YOU!
WAHOO!
ドタ バタ
ゴキャ
WHAT ON EARTH ARE THOSE TWO DOING?

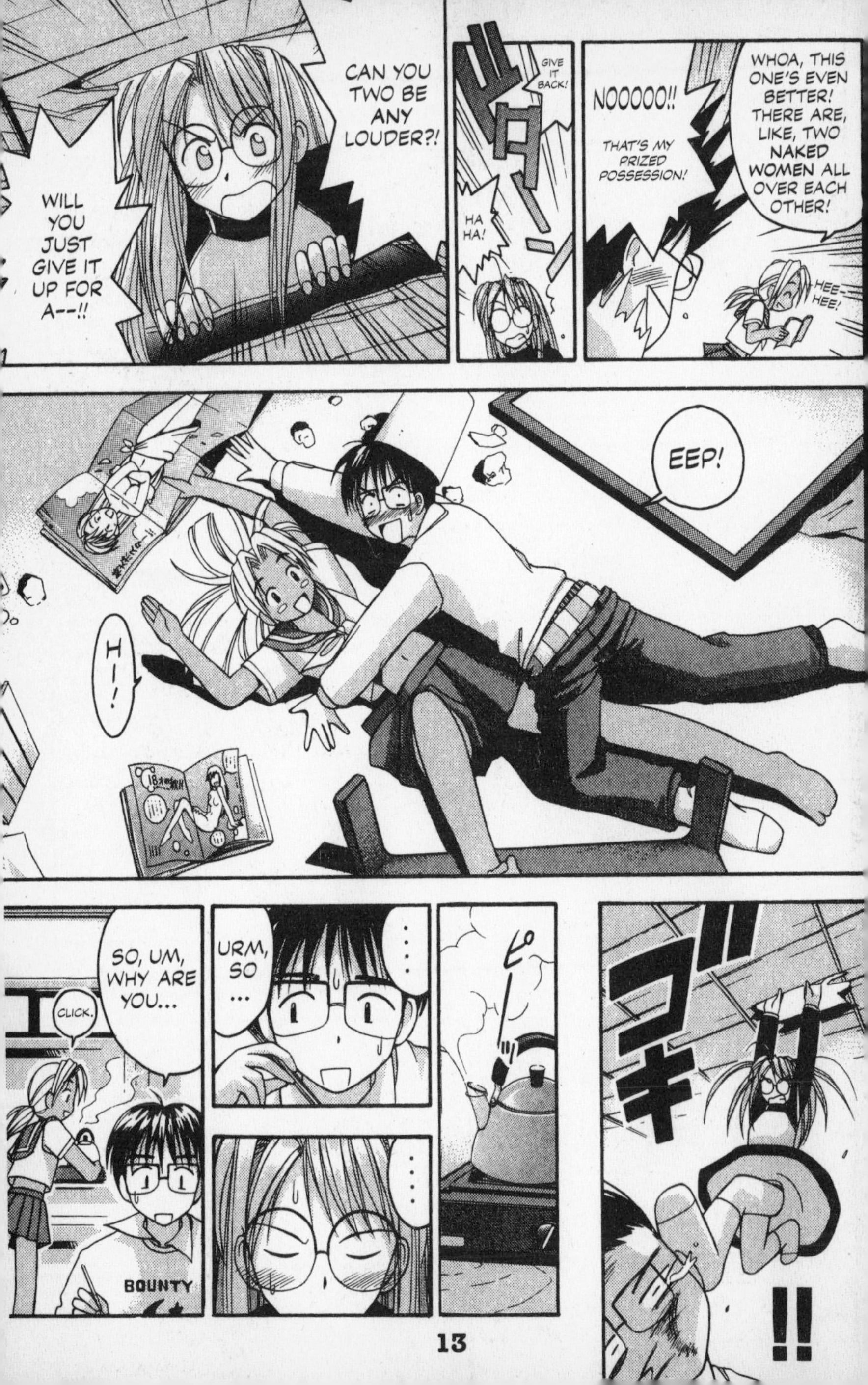

WHOA, THIS ONE'S EVEN BETTER! THERE ARE, LIKE, TWO NAKED WOMEN ALL OVER EACH OTHER!
NOOOOO!!
THAT'S MY PRIZED POSSESSION!
HEE-HEE!
GIVE IT BACK!
HA HA!
CAN YOU TWO BE ANY LOUDER?!
WILL YOU JUST GIVE IT UP FOR A--!!
EEP!
HI!
!!
URM, SO ...
....
....
SO, UM, WHY ARE YOU...
CLICK.
BOUNTY

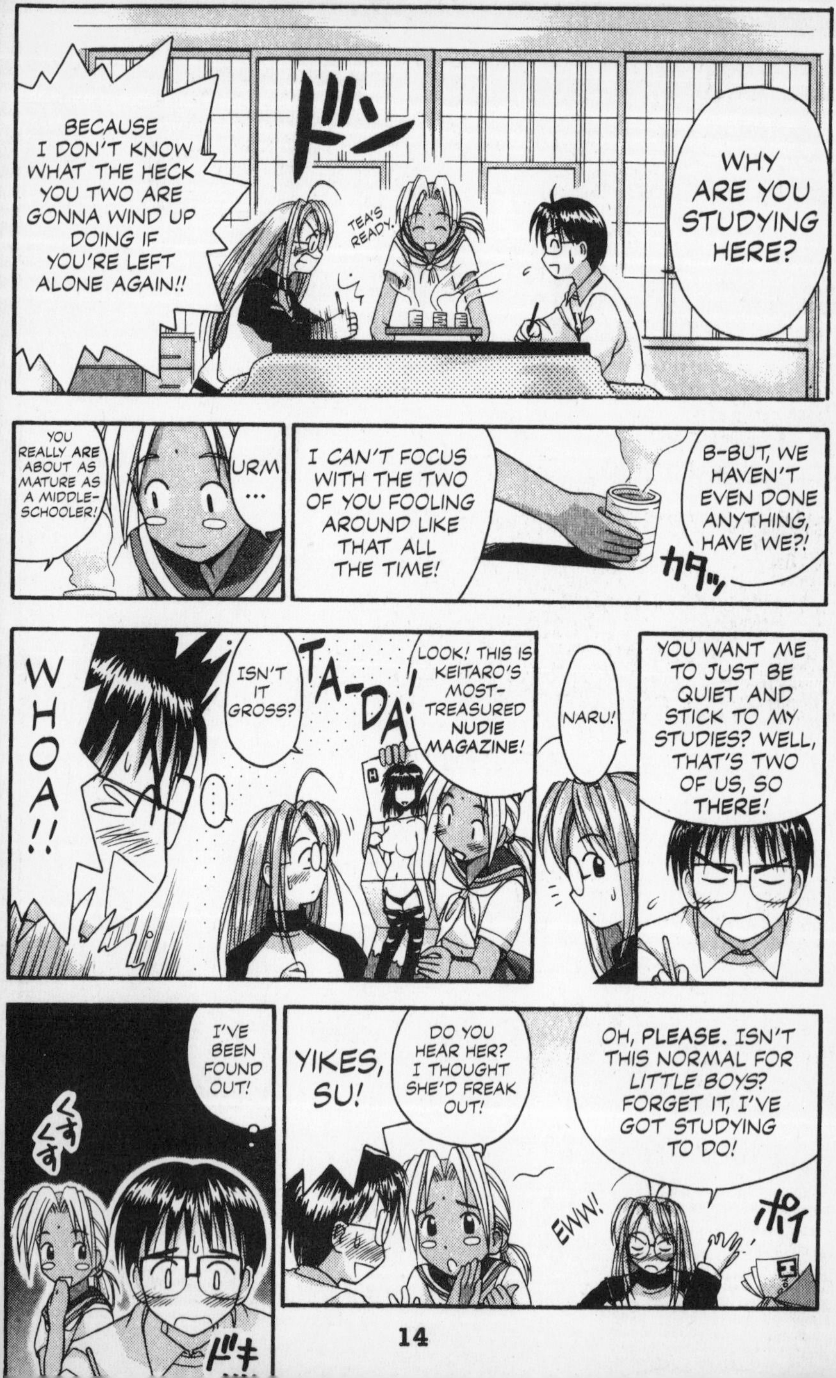
WHY ARE YOU STUDYING HERE?
ドーン
TEA'S READY!
BECAUSE I DON'T KNOW WHAT THE HECK YOU TWO ARE GONNA WIND UP DOING IF YOU'RE LEFT ALONE AGAIN!!
B-BUT, WE HAVEN'T EVEN DONE ANYTHING, HAVE WE?!
カタッ
I CAN'T FOCUS WITH THE TWO OF YOU FOOLING AROUND LIKE THAT ALL THE TIME!
URM ...
YOU REALLY ARE ABOUT AS MATURE AS A MIDDLE-SCHOOLER!
YOU WANT ME TO JUST BE QUIET AND STICK TO MY STUDIES? WELL, THAT'S TWO OF US, SO THERE!
NARU!
LOOK! THIS IS KEITARO'S MOST-TREASURED NUDIE MAGAZINE!
TA-DA!
ISN'T IT GROSS?
...
WHOA!!
OH, PLEASE. ISN'T THIS NORMAL FOR LITTLE BOYS? FORGET IT, I'VE GOT STUDYING TO DO!
ポイ
EWW!
DO YOU HEAR HER? I THOUGHT SHE'D FREAK OUT!
YIKES, SU!
I'VE BEEN FOUND OUT!
くすくす
ドキ

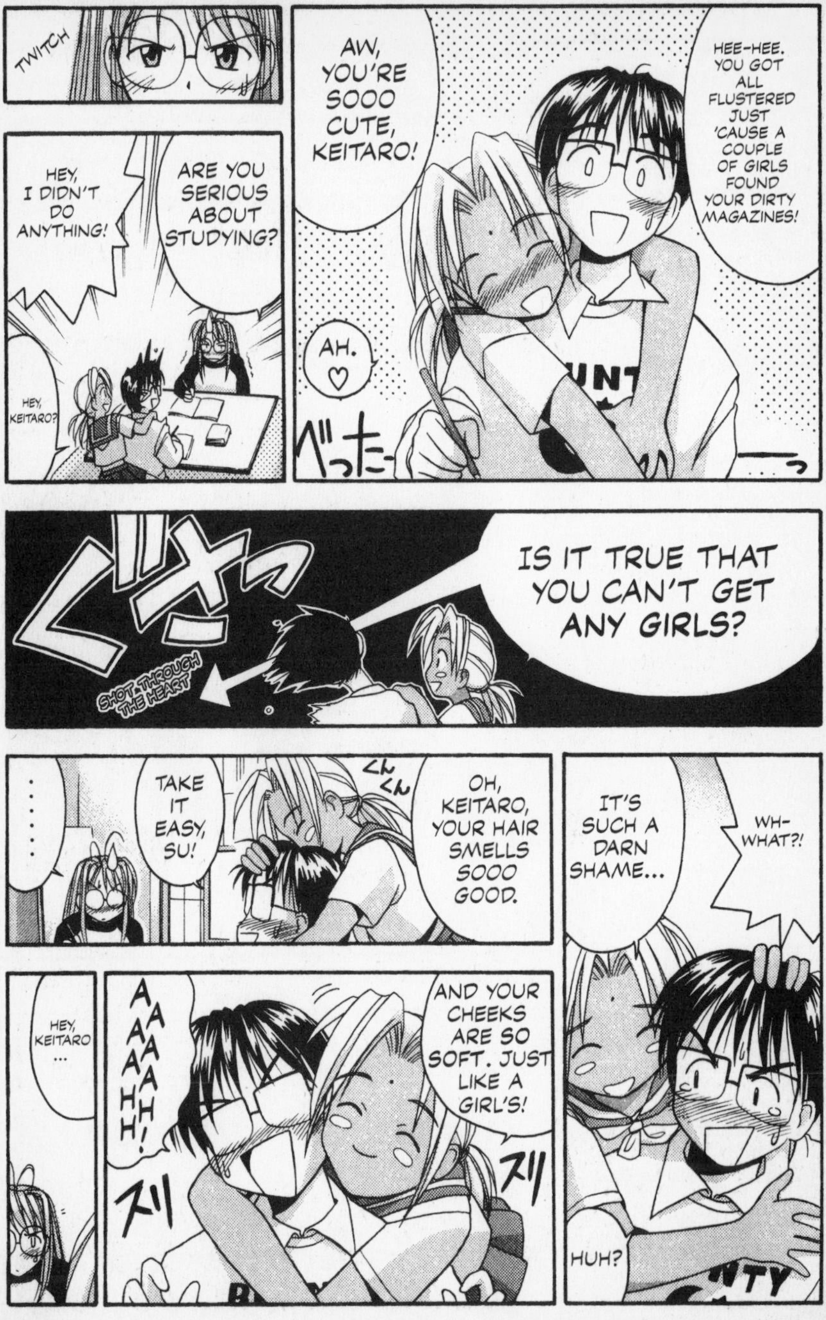
HEE-HEE. YOU GOT ALL FLUSTERED JUST 'CAUSE A COUPLE OF GIRLS FOUND YOUR DIRTY MAGAZINES!
AW, YOU'RE SOOO CUTE, KEITARO!
AH. ♡
べったー
TWITCH
ARE YOU SERIOUS ABOUT STUDYING?
HEY, I DIDN'T DO ANYTHING!
HEY, KEITARO?
IS IT TRUE THAT YOU CAN'T GET ANY GIRLS?
ぐさっ
SHOT THROUGH THE HEART
IT'S SUCH A DARN SHAME...
WH-WHAT?!
HUH?
くんくん
OH, KEITARO, YOUR HAIR SMELLS SOOO GOOD.
TAKE IT EASY, SU!
......
AND YOUR CHEEKS ARE SO SOFT. JUST LIKE A GIRL'S!
スリ
AAAAAAAAHH!
スリ
HEY, KEITARO ...

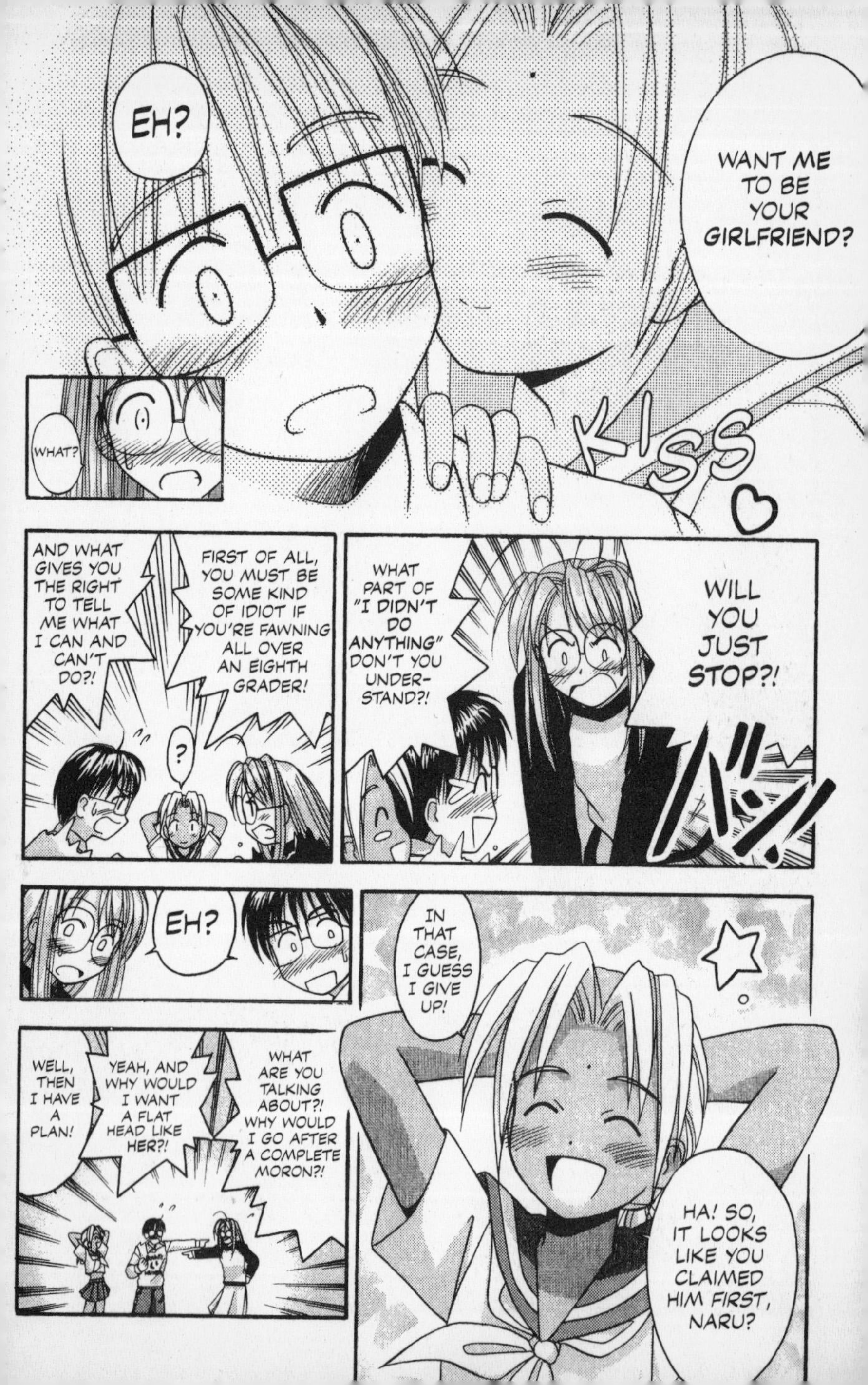
WANT ME TO BE YOUR GIRLFRIEND?
EH?
KISS
WHAT?
WILL YOU JUST STOP?!
WHAT PART OF "I DIDN'T DO ANYTHING" DON'T YOU UNDERSTAND?!
バン!
FIRST OF ALL, YOU MUST BE SOME KIND OF IDIOT IF YOU'RE FAWNING ALL OVER AN EIGHTH GRADER!
AND WHAT GIVES YOU THE RIGHT TO TELL ME WHAT I CAN AND CAN'T DO?!
?
IN THAT CASE, I GUESS I GIVE UP!
HA! SO, IT LOOKS LIKE YOU CLAIMED HIM FIRST, NARU?
EH?
WHAT ARE YOU TALKING ABOUT?! WHY WOULD I GO AFTER A COMPLETE MORON?!
YEAH, AND WHY WOULD I WANT A FLAT HEAD LIKE HER?!
WELL, THEN I HAVE A PLAN!

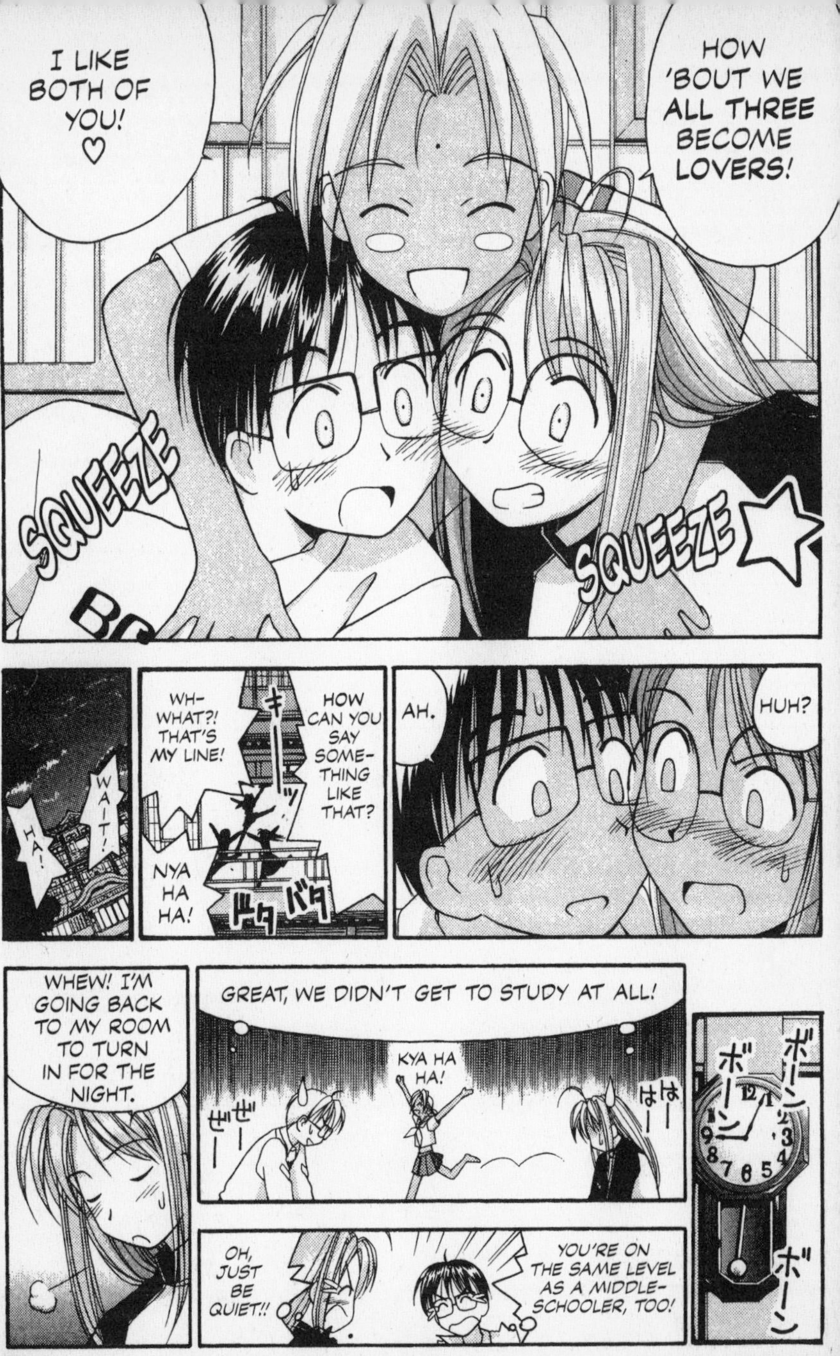
HOW 'BOUT WE ALL THREE BECOME LOVERS!
I LIKE BOTH OF YOU! ♡
SQUEEZE ☆
SQUEEZE
HUH?
AH.
HOW CAN YOU SAY SOME-THING LIKE THAT?
WH-WHAT?! THAT'S MY LINE!
キーッ
NYA HA HA!
バタ
ドタ
WAIT!
HA!
ボーン
ボーン
ボーン
GREAT, WE DIDN'T GET TO STUDY AT ALL!
はー はー
KYA HA HA!
ぜー ぜー
YOU'RE ON THE SAME LEVEL AS A MIDDLE-SCHOOLER, TOO!
OH, JUST BE QUIET!!
WHEW! I'M GOING BACK TO MY ROOM TO TURN IN FOR THE NIGHT.

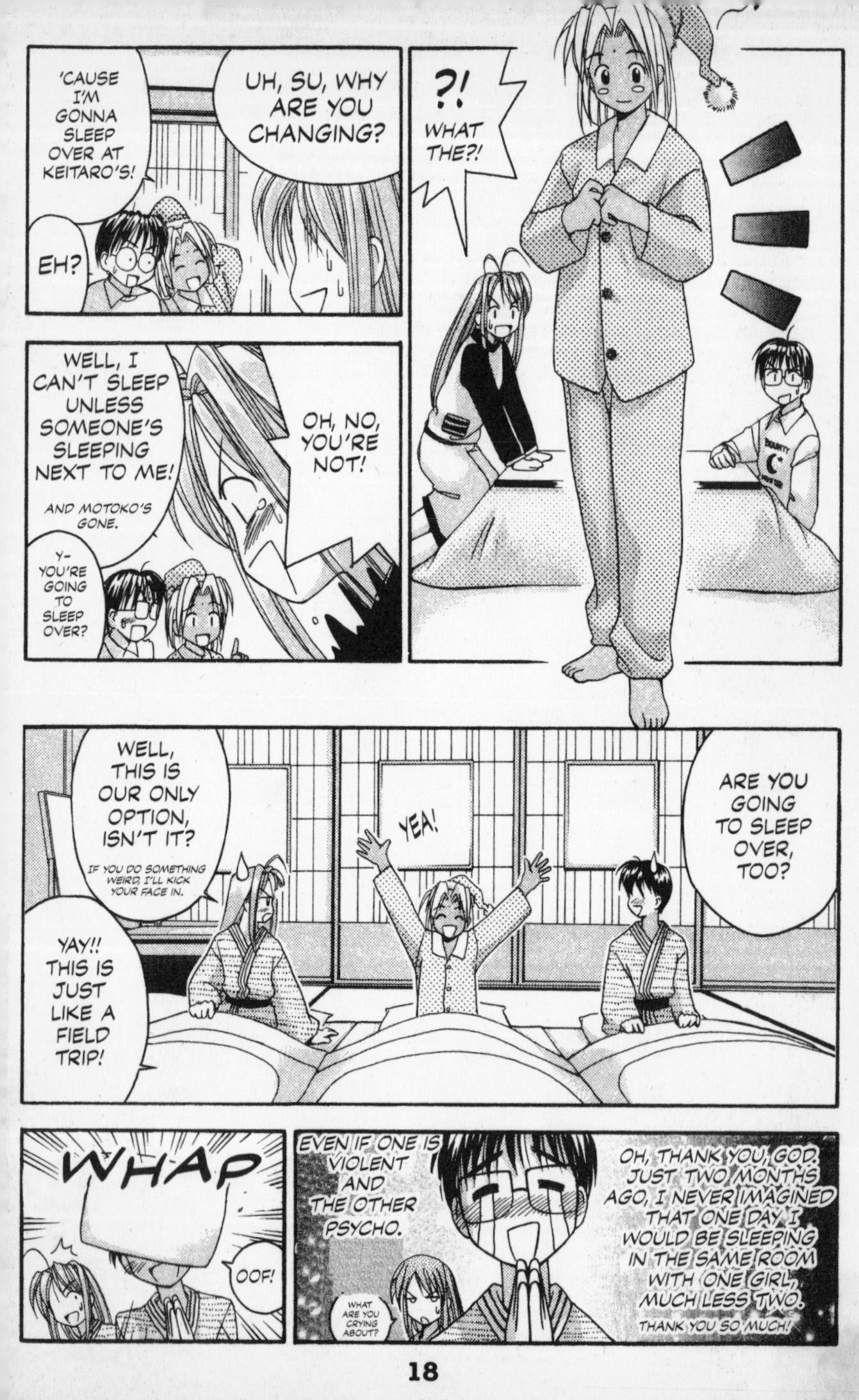
?!
WHAT THE?!
UH, SU, WHY ARE YOU CHANGING?
'CAUSE I'M GONNA SLEEP OVER AT KEITARO'S!
EH?
OH, NO, YOU'RE NOT!
WELL, I CAN'T SLEEP UNLESS SOMEONE'S SLEEPING NEXT TO ME!
AND MOTOKO'S GONE.
Y-YOU'RE GOING TO SLEEP OVER?
ARE YOU GOING TO SLEEP OVER, TOO?
YEA!
WELL, THIS IS OUR ONLY OPTION, ISN'T IT?
IF YOU DO SOMETHING WEIRD, I'LL KICK YOUR FACE IN.
YAY!! THIS IS JUST LIKE A FIELD TRIP!
OH, THANK YOU, GOD. JUST TWO MONTHS AGO, I NEVER IMAGINED THAT ONE DAY I WOULD BE SLEEPING IN THE SAME ROOM WITH ONE GIRL, MUCH LESS TWO.
THANK YOU SO MUCH!
EVEN IF ONE IS VIOLENT AND THE OTHER PSYCHO.
WHAT ARE YOU CRYING ABOUT?
WHAP
OOF!

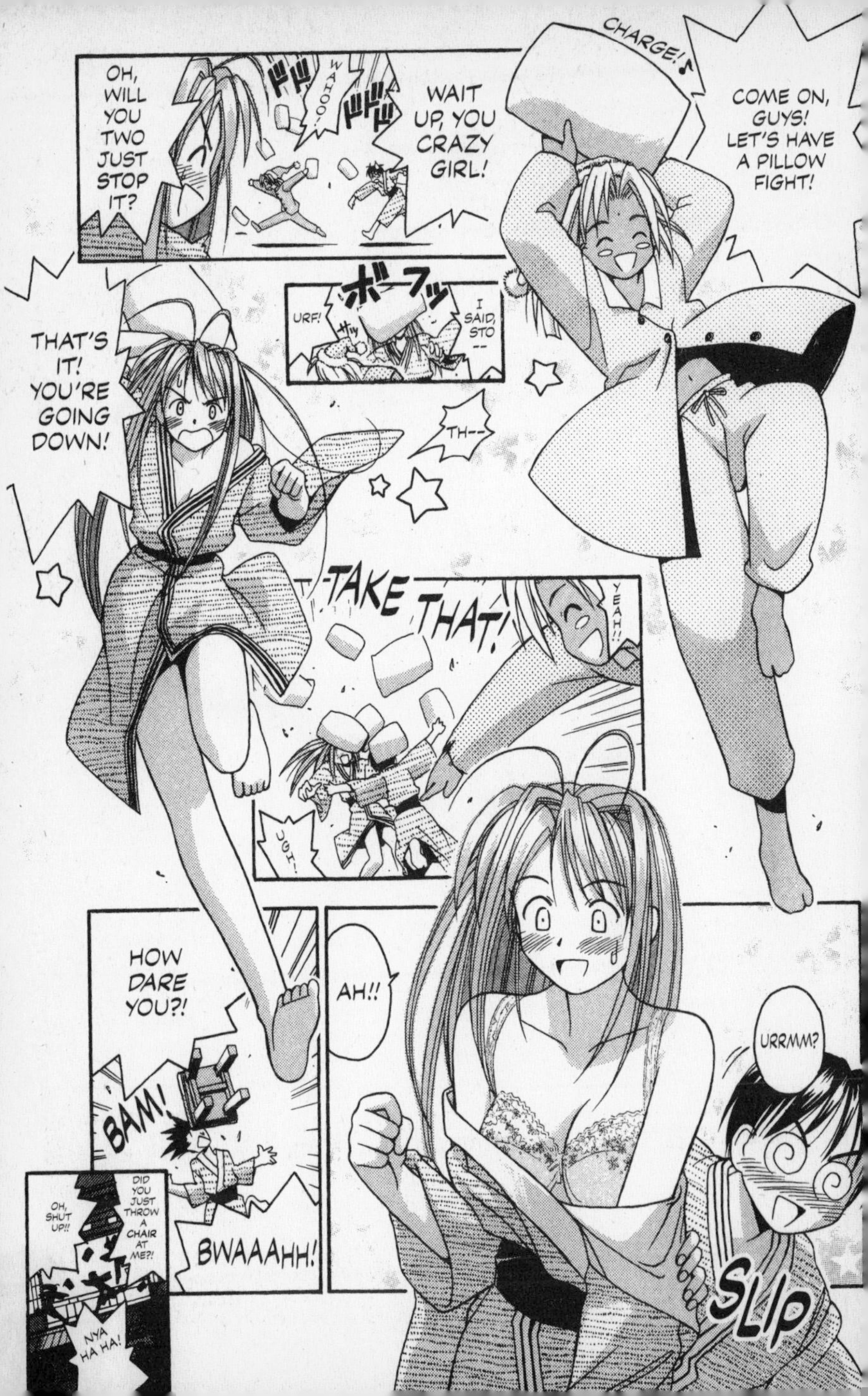
CHARGE!♪
COME ON, GUYS! LET'S HAVE A PILLOW FIGHT!
WAIT UP, YOU CRAZY GIRL!
WAHOO!
OH, WILL YOU TWO JUST STOP IT?
I SAID, STO--
ボフッ
URF!
THAT'S IT! YOU'RE GOING DOWN!
TH--
YEAH!!
TAKE THAT!
UGH!
URRMM?
AH!!
SLIP
HOW DARE YOU?!
BAM!
BWAAAHH!
DID YOU JUST THROW A CHAIR AT ME?!
OH, SHUT UP!!
NYA HA HA!

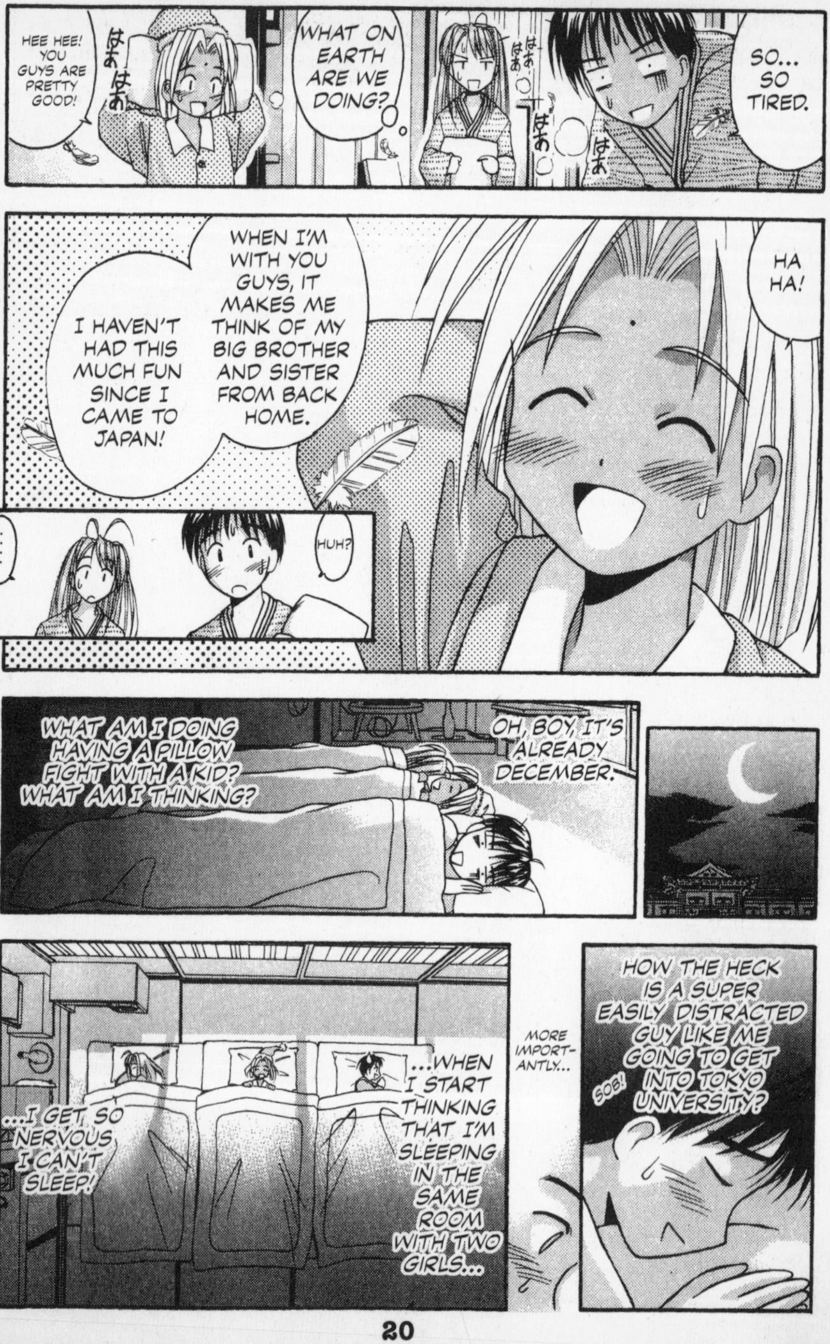
SO... SO TIRED.
はあ はあ
WHAT ON EARTH ARE WE DOING?
はあ はあ
HEE HEE! YOU GUYS ARE PRETTY GOOD!
はあ はあ
HA HA!
WHEN I'M WITH YOU GUYS, IT MAKES ME THINK OF MY BIG BROTHER AND SISTER FROM BACK HOME.
I HAVEN'T HAD THIS MUCH FUN SINCE I CAME TO JAPAN!
HUH?
...
OH, BOY, IT'S ALREADY DECEMBER.
WHAT AM I DOING HAVING A PILLOW FIGHT WITH A KID? WHAT AM I THINKING?
HOW THE HECK IS A SUPER EASILY DISTRACTED GUY LIKE ME GOING TO GET INTO TOKYO UNIVERSITY?
SOB!
MORE IMPORTANTLY...
...WHEN I START THINKING THAT I'M SLEEPING IN THE SAME ROOM WITH TWO GIRLS...
...I GET SO NERVOUS I CAN'T SLEEP!

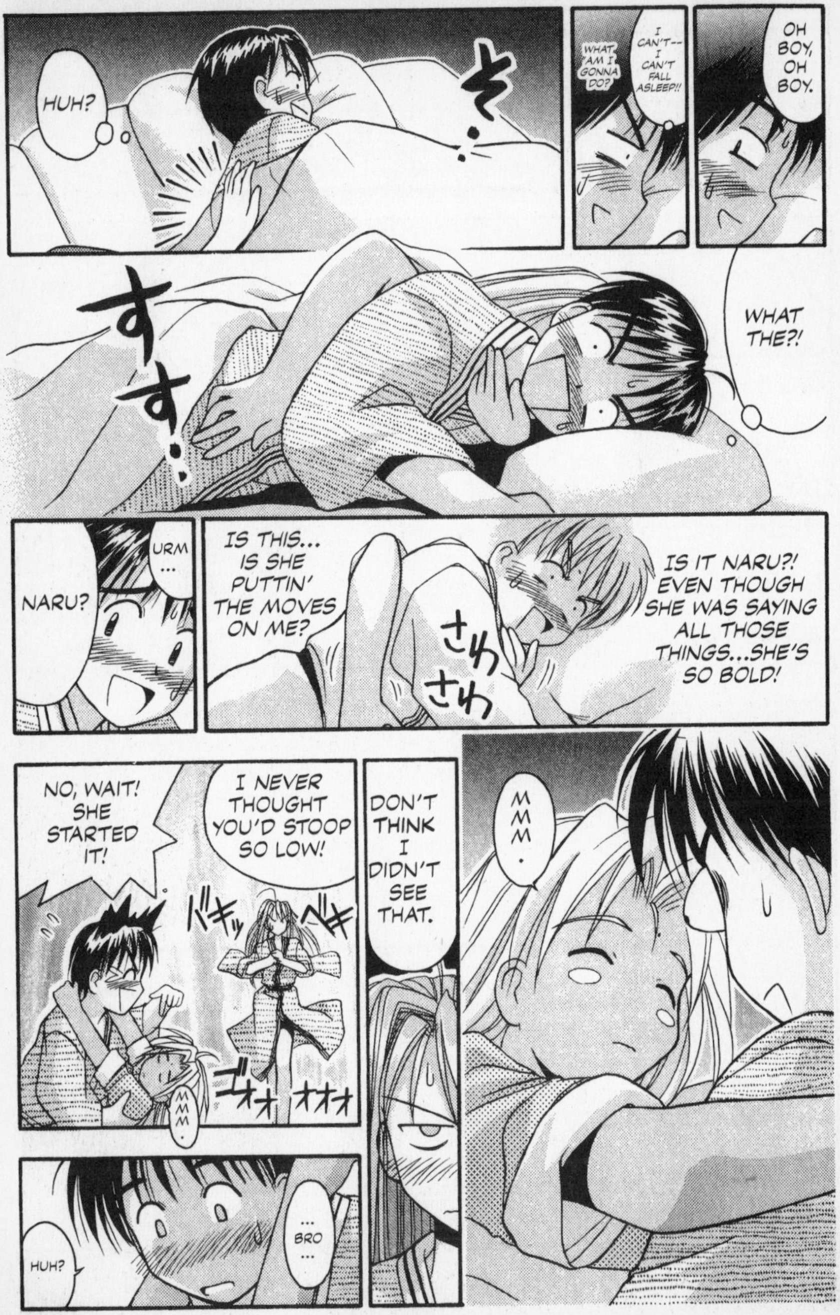

OH BOY, OH BOY.
I CAN'T-- I CAN'T FALL ASLEEP!!
WHAT AM I GONNA DO?
そ…!
HUH?
WHAT THE?!
すす…
IS IT NARU?! EVEN THOUGH SHE WAS SAYING ALL THOSE THINGS...SHE'S SO BOLD!
IS THIS... IS SHE PUTTIN' THE MOVES ON ME?
さわさわ
URM...
NARU?
MMM.
DON'T THINK I DIDN'T SEE THAT.
I NEVER THOUGHT YOU'D STOOP SO LOW!
NO, WAIT! SHE STARTED IT!
バキッ
ベキ
ゴオオ オオオ
MMM...
...BRO...
HUH?

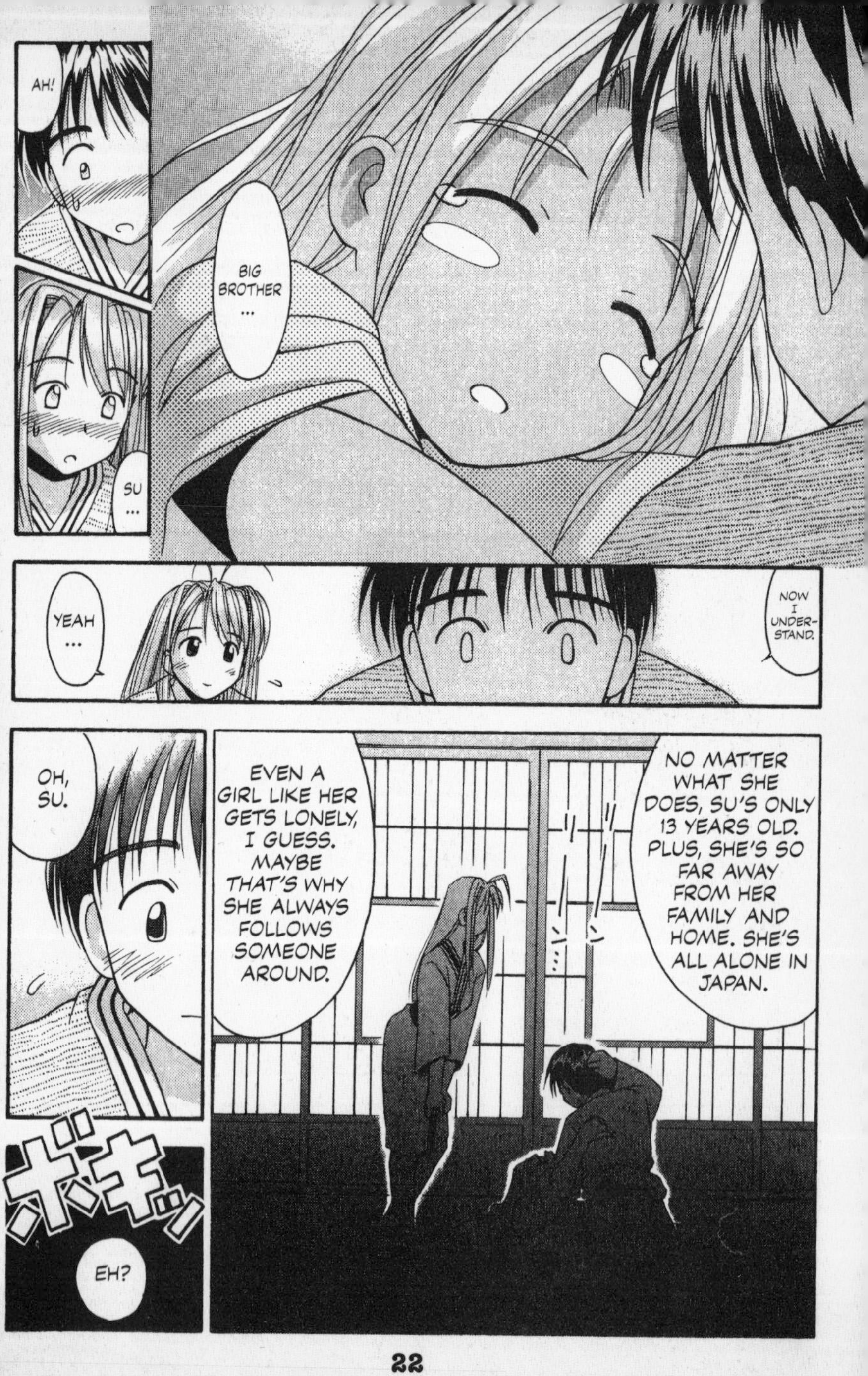
BIG BROTHER ...
AH!
SU ...
NOW I UNDERSTAND.
YEAH ...
NO MATTER WHAT SHE DOES, SU'S ONLY 13 YEARS OLD. PLUS, SHE'S SO FAR AWAY FROM HER FAMILY AND HOME. SHE'S ALL ALONE IN JAPAN.
EVEN A GIRL LIKE HER GETS LONELY, I GUESS. MAYBE THAT'S WHY SHE ALWAYS FOLLOWS SOMEONE AROUND.
OH, SU.
EH?

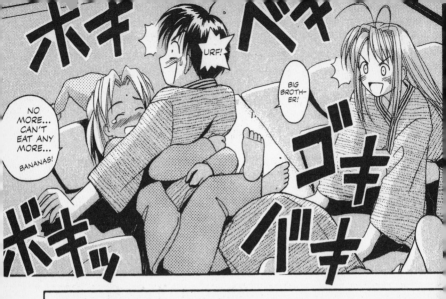

BIG BROTHER!
URF!
NO MORE... CAN'T EAT ANY MORE... BANANAS!
GYAAAHHHHHHHHHHHHHHHHHHHHHHH!!!
WAH?
CRIK CRACK CRUSH
SO, SHE FINALLY POUNDED HIM!
AND I SAID I WAS ROUGH!
THE NEXT MORNING.
SLEEPY!
WASN'T IT SO MUCH FUN SPENDING THE NIGHT TOGETHER?
CAN I GO SLEEP OVER AT YOUR PLACE TODAY, NARU?
COME BACK SOON, MOTOKO, DEAR! PLEASE! ANYONE WHO CAN PUT UP WITH THAT GIRL ON A DAILY BASIS DESERVES MY RESPECT.
HE'S IN BAD SHAPE.
OH, BOY.
...

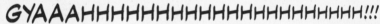

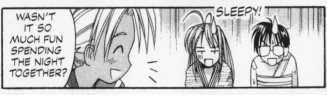

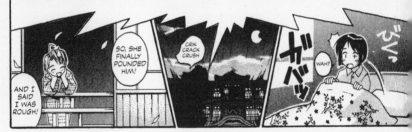

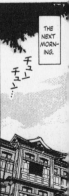

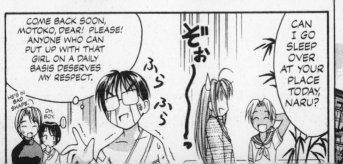

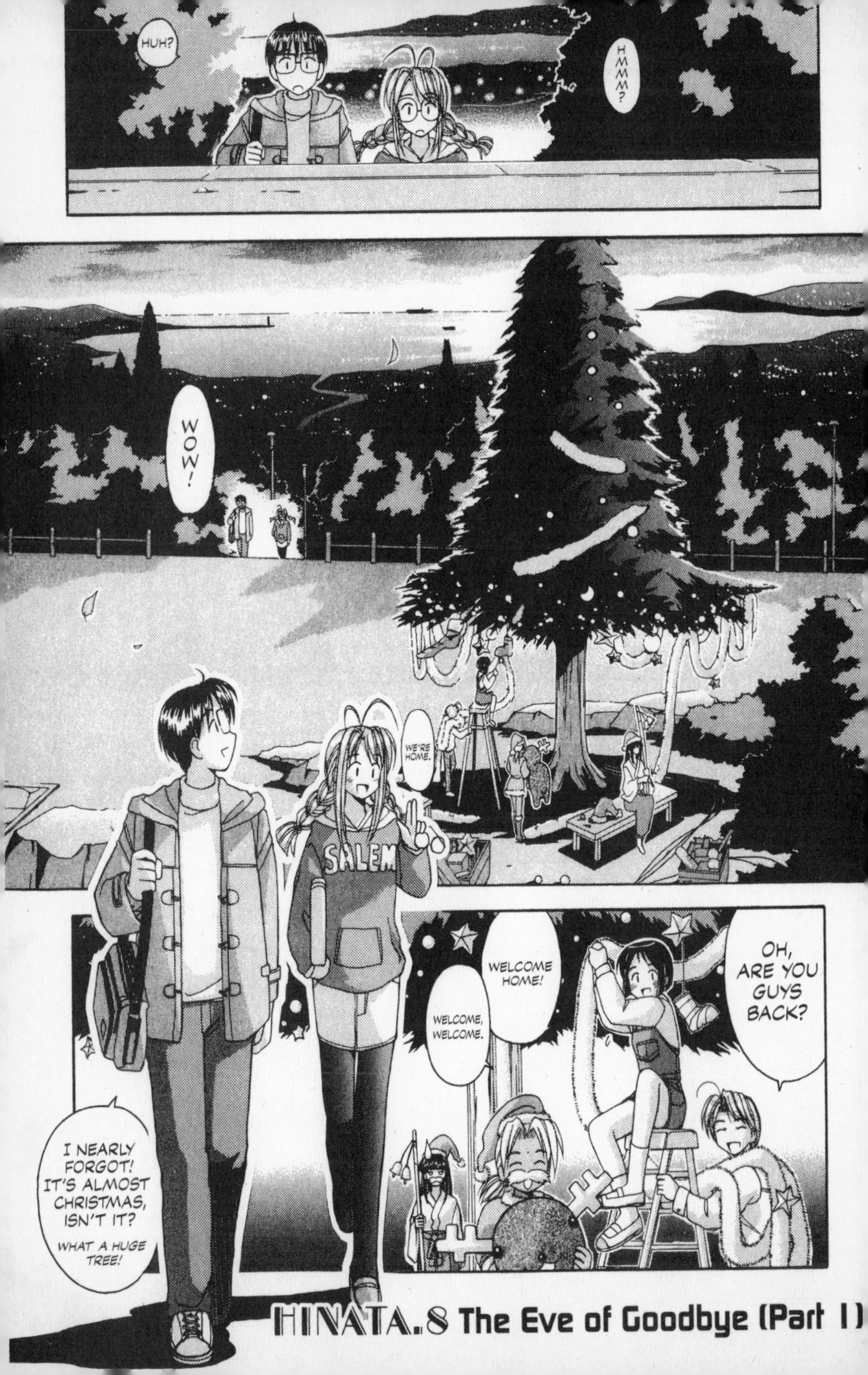
HMMM?
HUH?
WOW!
WE'RE HOME.
OH, ARE YOU GUYS BACK?
WELCOME HOME!
WELCOME, WELCOME.
I NEARLY FORGOT! IT'S ALMOST CHRISTMAS, ISN'T IT?
WHAT A HUGE TREE!
HINATA.8 The Eve of Goodbye (Part 1)

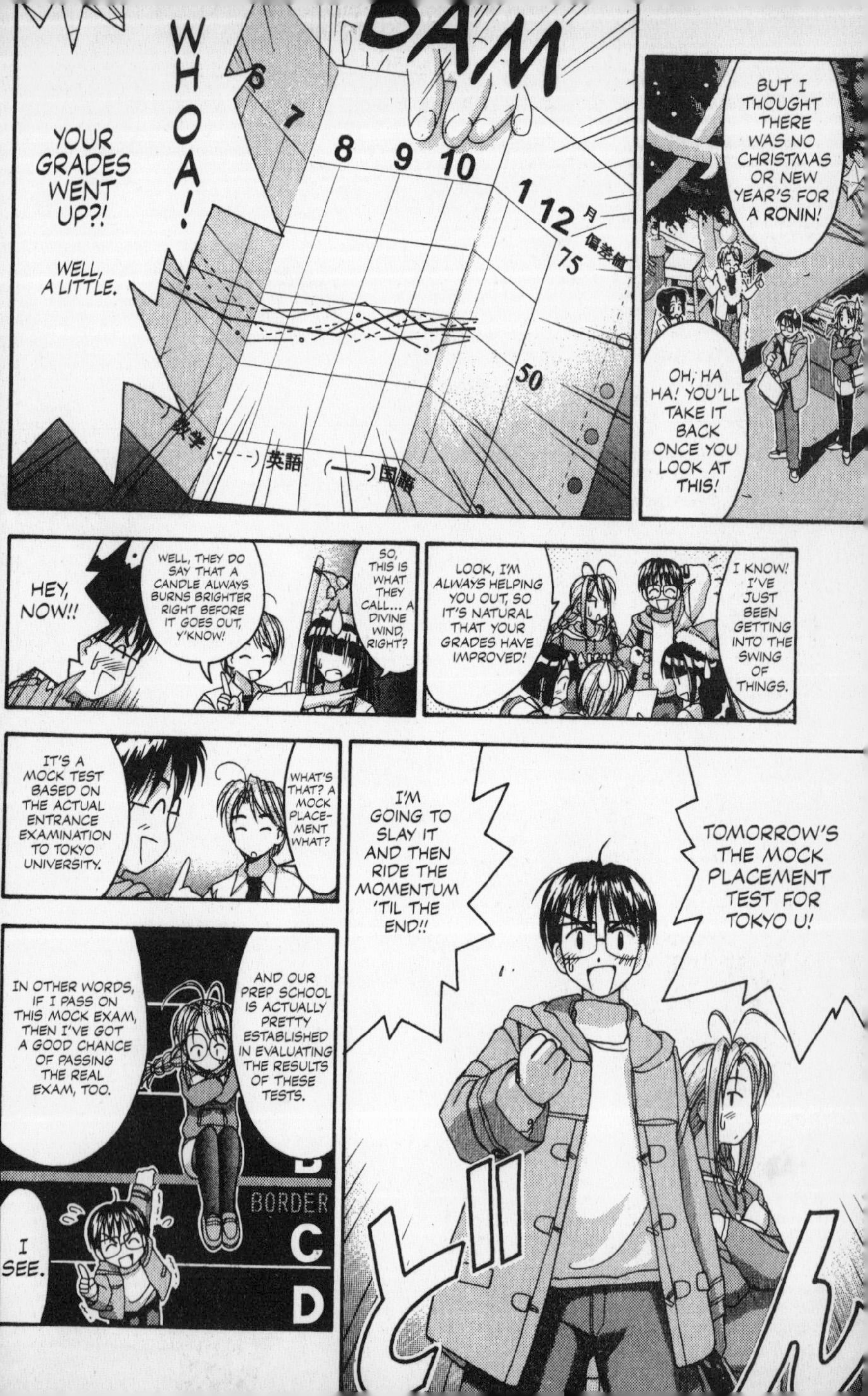
BUT I THOUGHT THERE WAS NO CHRISTMAS OR NEW YEAR'S FOR A RONIN!
OH, HA HA! YOU'LL TAKE IT BACK ONCE YOU LOOK AT THIS!
BAM
WHOA!
6 7 8 9 10 11 12月
偏差値
75
50
数学
(- - - -) 英語
(——) 国語
YOUR GRADES WENT UP?!
WELL, A LITTLE.
I KNOW! I'VE JUST BEEN GETTING INTO THE SWING OF THINGS.
LOOK, I'M ALWAYS HELPING YOU OUT, SO IT'S NATURAL THAT YOUR GRADES HAVE IMPROVED!
SO, THIS IS WHAT THEY CALL... A DIVINE WIND, RIGHT?
WELL, THEY DO SAY THAT A CANDLE ALWAYS BURNS BRIGHTER RIGHT BEFORE IT GOES OUT, Y'KNOW!
HEY, NOW!!
TOMORROW'S THE MOCK PLACEMENT TEST FOR TOKYO U!
I'M GOING TO SLAY IT AND THEN RIDE THE MOMENTUM 'TIL THE END!!
WHAT'S THAT? A MOCK PLACE-MENT WHAT?
IT'S A MOCK TEST BASED ON THE ACTUAL ENTRANCE EXAMINATION TO TOKYO UNIVERSITY.
AND OUR PREP SCHOOL IS ACTUALLY PRETTY ESTABLISHED IN EVALUATING THE RESULTS OF THESE TESTS.
IN OTHER WORDS, IF I PASS ON THIS MOCK EXAM, THEN I'VE GOT A GOOD CHANCE OF PASSING THE REAL EXAM, TOO.
B
BORDER
C
D
I SEE.

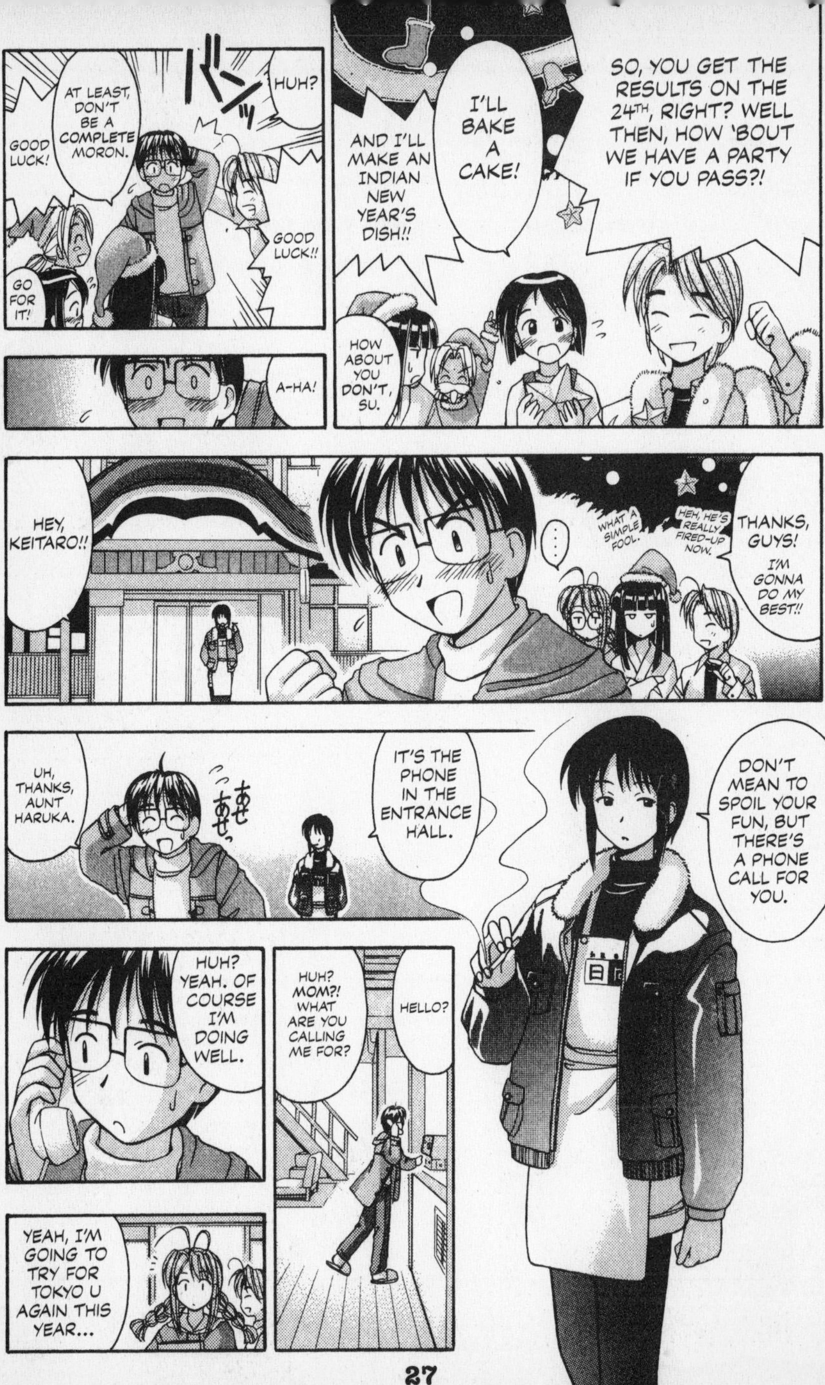
SO, YOU GET THE RESULTS ON THE 24TH, RIGHT? WELL THEN, HOW 'BOUT WE HAVE A PARTY IF YOU PASS?!
I'LL BAKE A CAKE!
AND I'LL MAKE AN INDIAN NEW YEAR'S DISH!!
HOW ABOUT YOU DON'T, SU.
バンッ
HUH?
AT LEAST, DON'T BE A COMPLETE MORON.
GOOD LUCK!
GOOD LUCK!!
GO FOR IT!
A-HA!
THANKS, GUYS!
I'M GONNA DO MY BEST!!
HEH, HE'S REALLY FIRED-UP NOW.
WHAT A SIMPLE FOOL.
...
HEY, KEITARO!!
DON'T MEAN TO SPOIL YOUR FUN, BUT THERE'S A PHONE CALL FOR YOU.
IT'S THE PHONE IN THE ENTRANCE HALL.
あせあせ
UH, THANKS, AUNT HARUKA.
HELLO?
HUH? MOM?! WHAT ARE YOU CALLING ME FOR?
HUH? YEAH. OF COURSE I'M DOING WELL.
YEAH, I'M GOING TO TRY FOR TOKYO U AGAIN THIS YEAR...

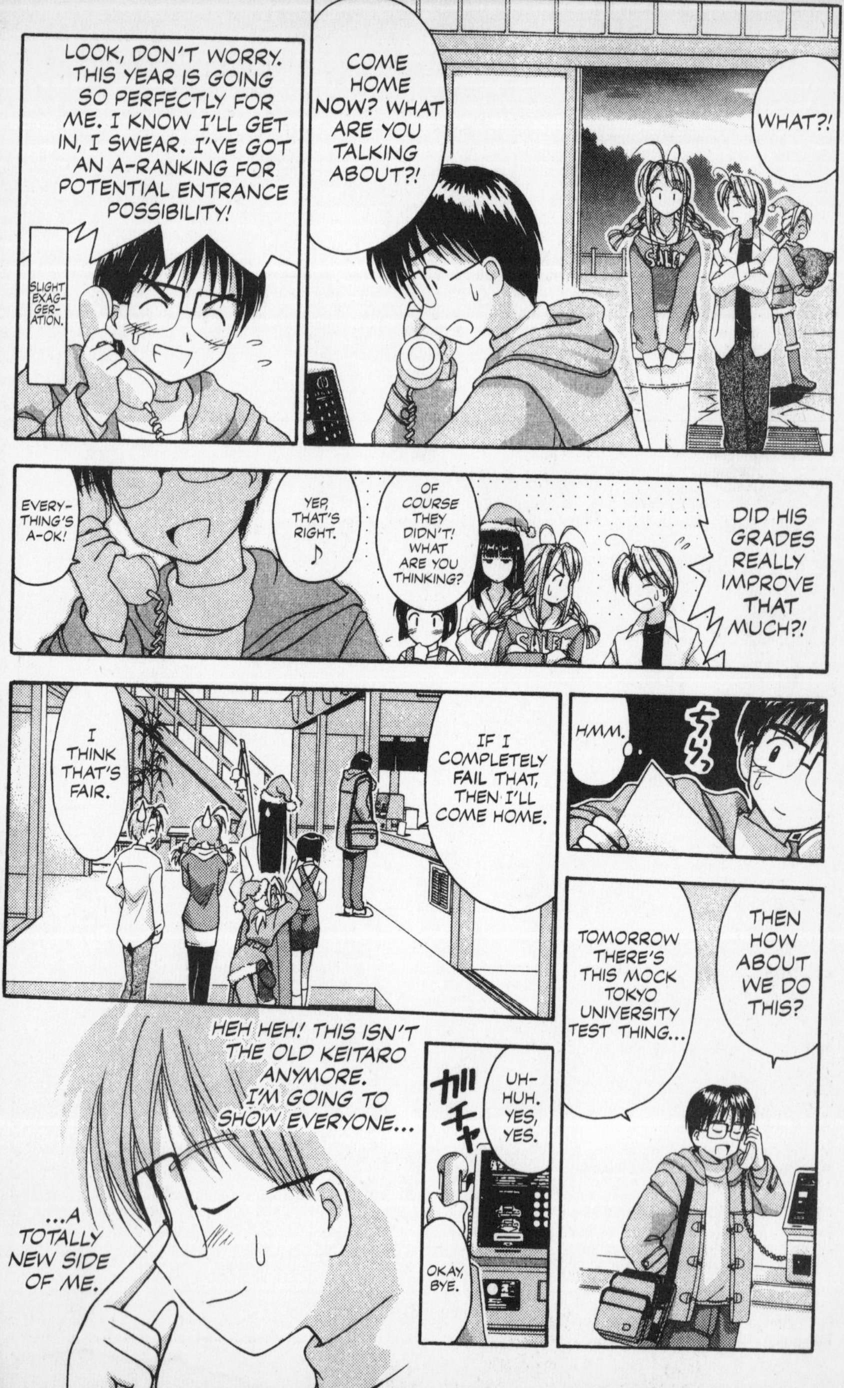
WHAT?!
COME HOME NOW? WHAT ARE YOU TALKING ABOUT?!
LOOK, DON'T WORRY. THIS YEAR IS GOING SO PERFECTLY FOR ME. I KNOW I'LL GET IN, I SWEAR. I'VE GOT AN A-RANKING FOR POTENTIAL ENTRANCE POSSIBILITY!
SLIGHT EXAGGERATION.
DID HIS GRADES REALLY IMPROVE THAT MUCH?!
OF COURSE THEY DIDN'T! WHAT ARE YOU THINKING?
YEP, THAT'S RIGHT. ♪
EVERYTHING'S A-OK!
HMM.
THEN HOW ABOUT WE DO THIS?
TOMORROW THERE'S THIS MOCK TOKYO UNIVERSITY TEST THING...
IF I COMPLETELY FAIL THAT, THEN I'LL COME HOME.
I THINK THAT'S FAIR.
UH-HUH. YES, YES.
OKAY, BYE.
HEH HEH! THIS ISN'T THE OLD KEITARO ANYMORE. I'M GOING TO SHOW EVERYONE...
...A TOTALLY NEW SIDE OF ME.

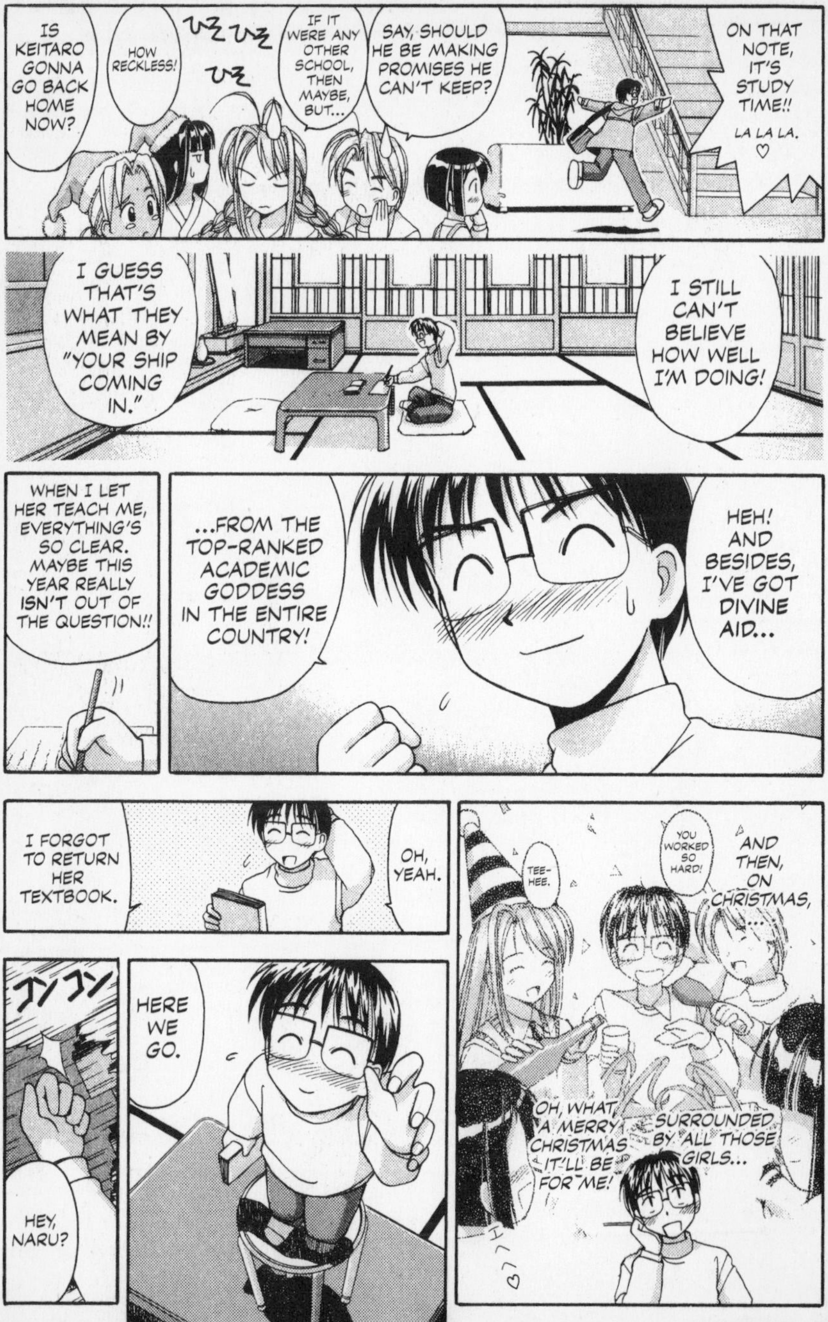
ON THAT NOTE, IT'S STUDY TIME!!
LA LA LA. ♡
SAY, SHOULD HE BE MAKING PROMISES HE CAN'T KEEP?
IF IT WERE ANY OTHER SCHOOL, THEN MAYBE, BUT...
ひそひそ
ひそ
HOW RECKLESS!
IS KEITARO GONNA GO BACK HOME NOW?
I STILL CAN'T BELIEVE HOW WELL I'M DOING!
I GUESS THAT'S WHAT THEY MEAN BY "YOUR SHIP COMING IN."
HEH! AND BESIDES, I'VE GOT DIVINE AID...
...FROM THE TOP-RANKED ACADEMIC GODDESS IN THE ENTIRE COUNTRY!
WHEN I LET HER TEACH ME, EVERYTHING'S SO CLEAR. MAYBE THIS YEAR REALLY ISN'T OUT OF THE QUESTION!!
AND THEN, ON CHRISTMAS,
YOU WORKED SO HARD!
TEE-HEE.
...
SURROUNDED BY ALL THOSE GIRLS...
OH, WHAT A MERRY CHRISTMAS IT'LL BE FOR ME!
OH, YEAH.
I FORGOT TO RETURN HER TEXTBOOK.
HERE WE GO.
コンコン
HEY, NARU?

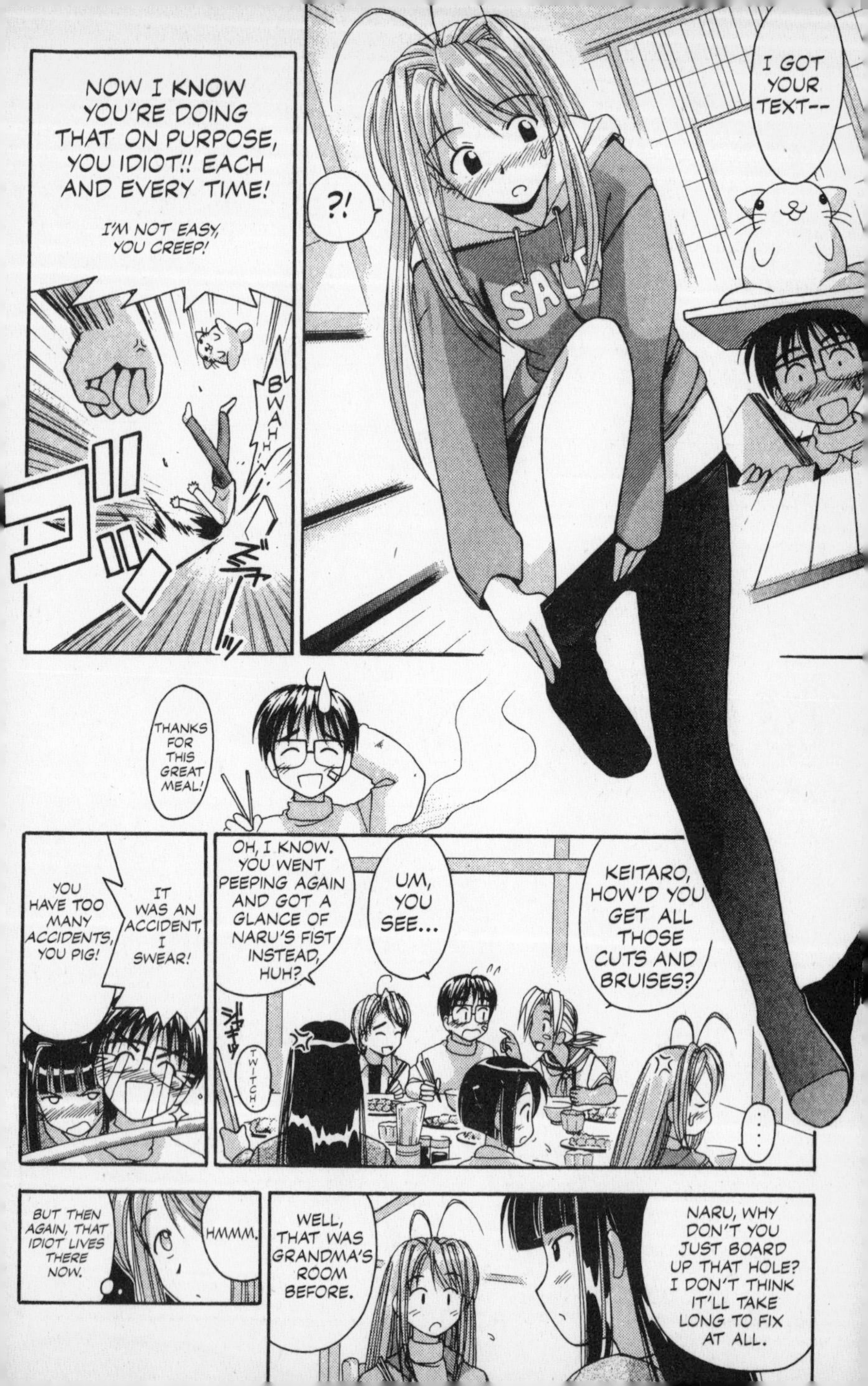
I GOT YOUR TEXT--
?!
NOW I KNOW YOU'RE DOING THAT ON PURPOSE, YOU IDIOT!! EACH AND EVERY TIME!
I'M NOT EASY, YOU CREEP!
BWAH!
THANKS FOR THIS GREAT MEAL!
KEITARO, HOW'D YOU GET ALL THOSE CUTS AND BRUISES?
UM, YOU SEE...
OH, I KNOW. YOU WENT PEEPING AGAIN AND GOT A GLANCE OF NARU'S FIST INSTEAD, HUH?
TWITCH
....
IT WAS AN ACCIDENT, I SWEAR!
YOU HAVE TOO MANY ACCIDENTS, YOU PIG!
NARU, WHY DON'T YOU JUST BOARD UP THAT HOLE? I DON'T THINK IT'LL TAKE LONG TO FIX AT ALL.
WELL, THAT WAS GRANDMA'S ROOM BEFORE.
HMMM.
BUT THEN AGAIN, THAT IDIOT LIVES THERE NOW.

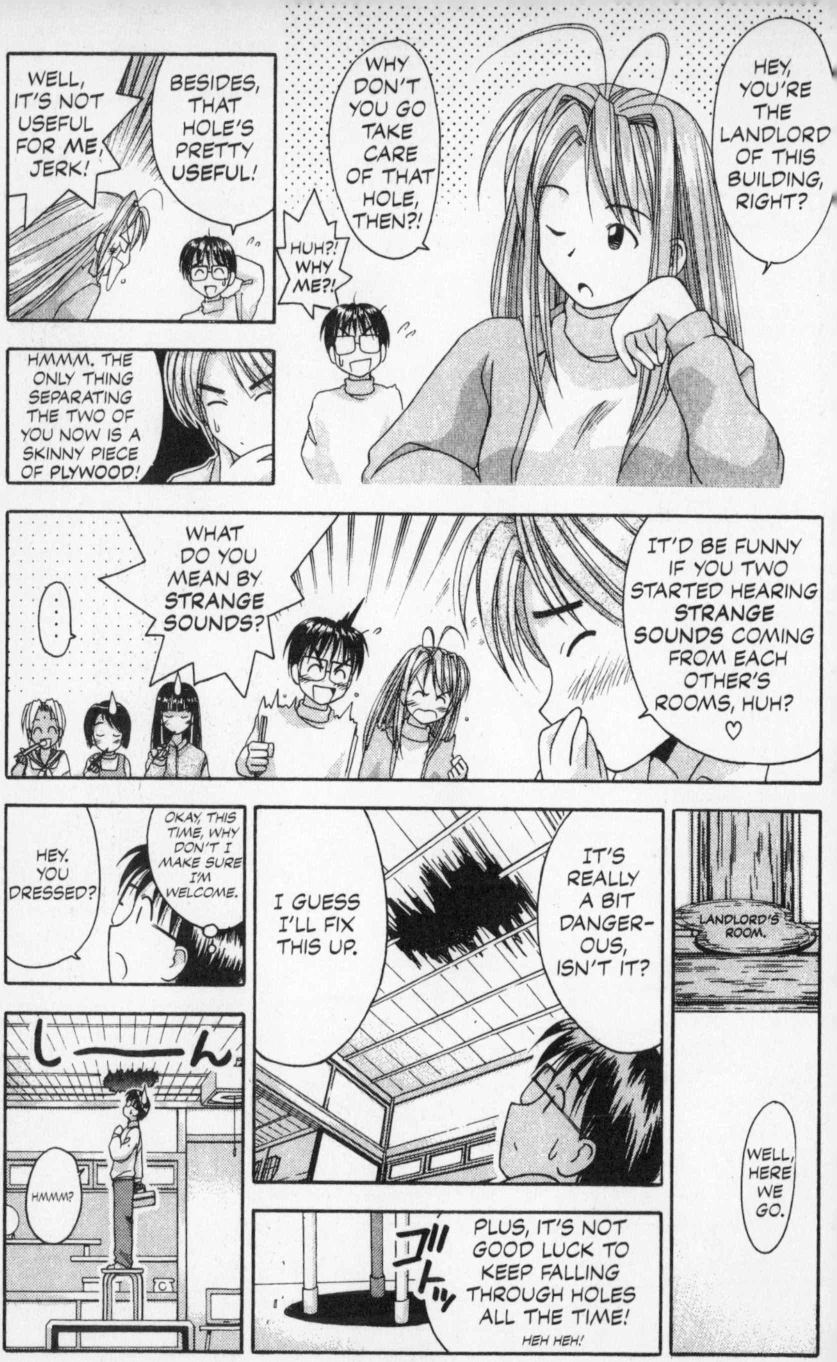
HEY, YOU'RE THE LANDLORD OF THIS BUILDING, RIGHT?
WHY DON'T YOU GO TAKE CARE OF THAT HOLE, THEN?!
HUH?! WHY ME?!
BESIDES, THAT HOLE'S PRETTY USEFUL!
WELL, IT'S NOT USEFUL FOR ME, JERK!
HMMM. THE ONLY THING SEPARATING THE TWO OF YOU NOW IS A SKINNY PIECE OF PLYWOOD!
IT'D BE FUNNY IF YOU TWO STARTED HEARING STRANGE SOUNDS COMING FROM EACH OTHER'S ROOMS, HUH? ♡
WHAT DO YOU MEAN BY STRANGE SOUNDS?
...
LANDLORD'S ROOM.
WELL, HERE WE GO.
IT'S REALLY A BIT DANGER-OUS, ISN'T IT?
I GUESS I'LL FIX THIS UP.
ゴトッ
PLUS, IT'S NOT GOOD LUCK TO KEEP FALLING THROUGH HOLES ALL THE TIME!
HEH HEH!
OKAY, THIS TIME, WHY DON'T I MAKE SURE I'M WELCOME.
HEY. YOU DRESSED?
しーーん
HMMM?

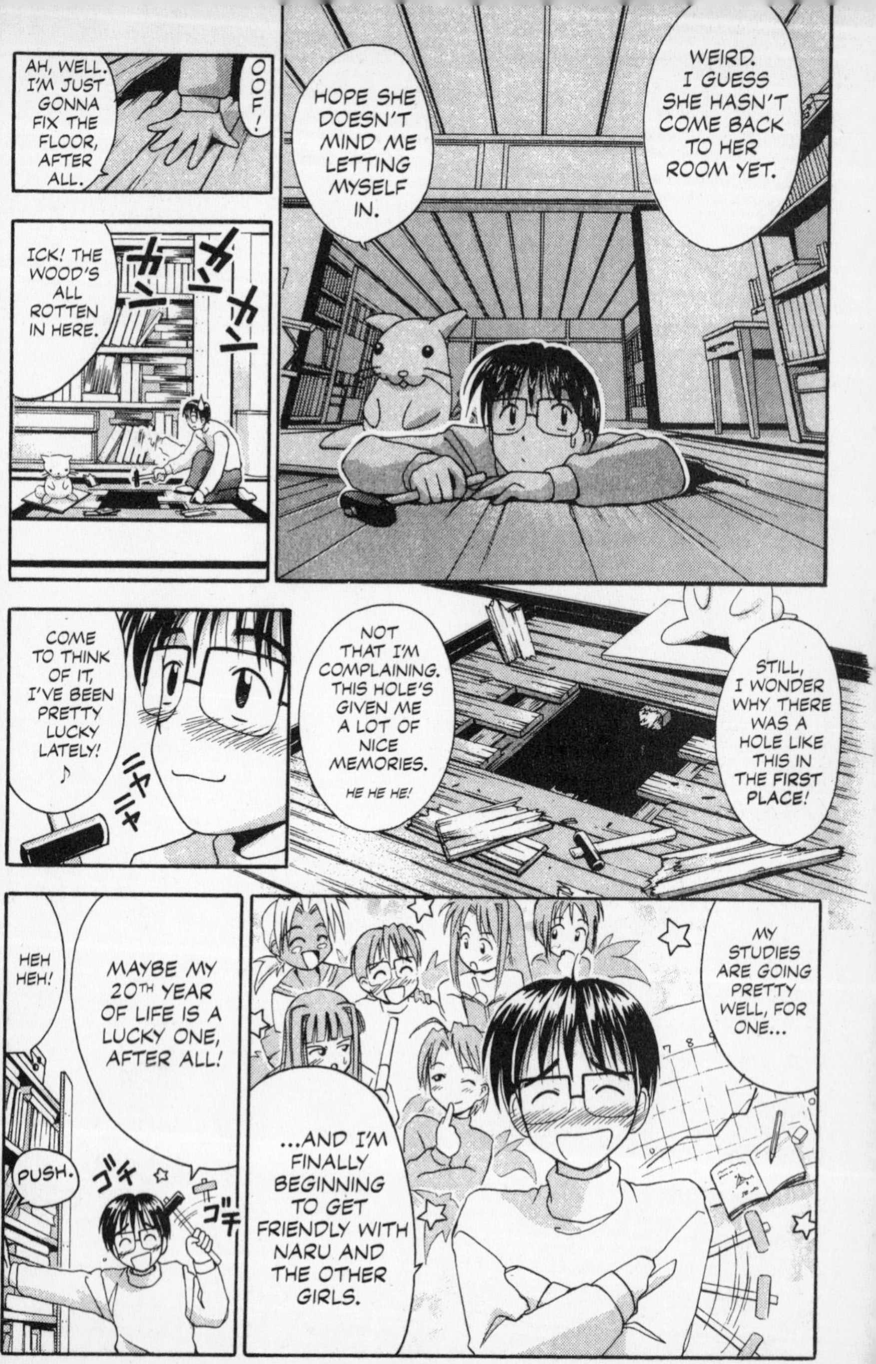
WEIRD. I GUESS SHE HASN'T COME BACK TO HER ROOM YET.
HOPE SHE DOESN'T MIND ME LETTING MYSELF IN.
OOF!
AH, WELL. I'M JUST GONNA FIX THE FLOOR, AFTER ALL.
ICK! THE WOOD'S ALL ROTTEN IN HERE.
STILL, I WONDER WHY THERE WAS A HOLE LIKE THIS IN THE FIRST PLACE!
NOT THAT I'M COMPLAINING. THIS HOLE'S GIVEN ME A LOT OF NICE MEMORIES.
HE HE HE!
COME TO THINK OF IT, I'VE BEEN PRETTY LUCKY LATELY! ♪
ニヤニヤ
MY STUDIES ARE GOING PRETTY WELL, FOR ONE...
...AND I'M FINALLY BEGINNING TO GET FRIENDLY WITH NARU AND THE OTHER GIRLS.
MAYBE MY 20TH YEAR OF LIFE IS A LUCKY ONE, AFTER ALL!
HEH HEH!
PUSH.
ゴチ
ゴチ

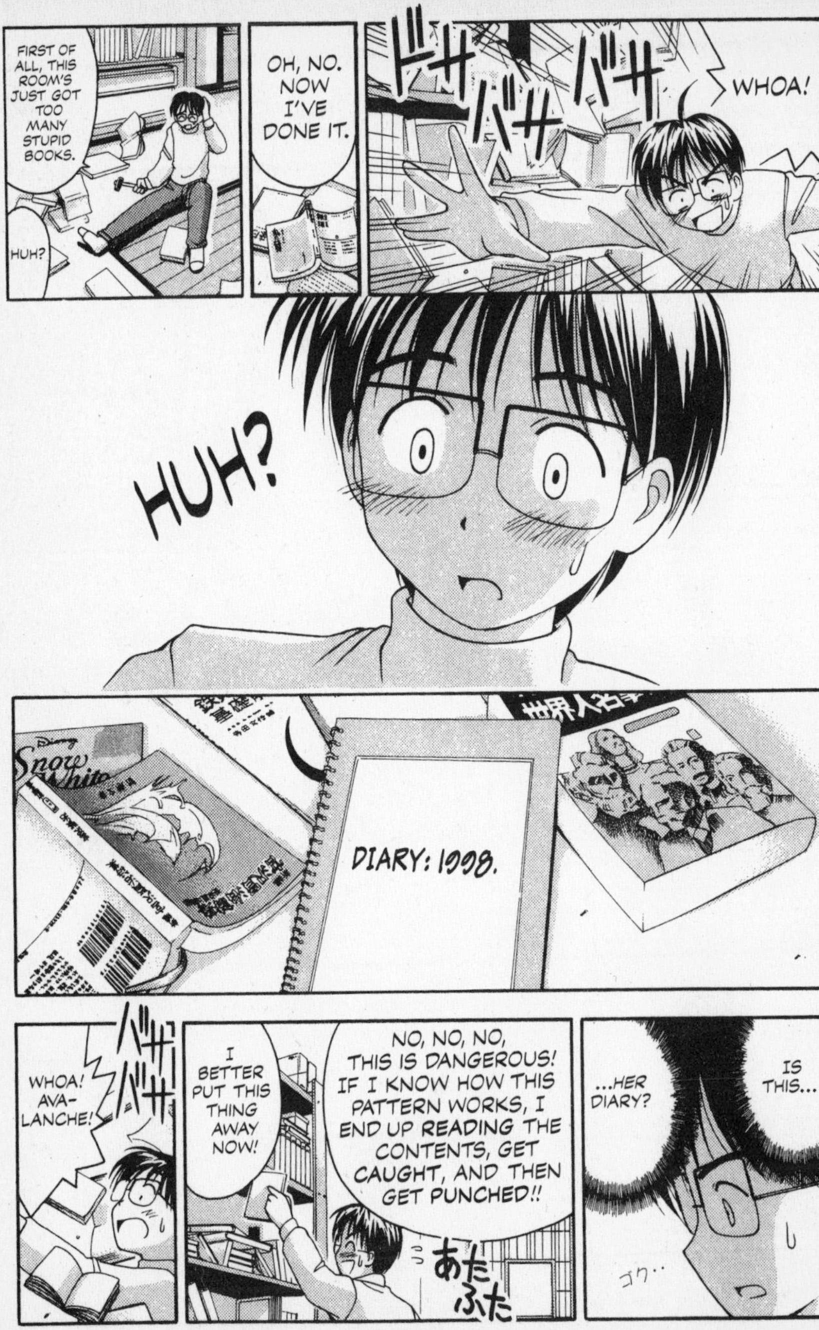

ドサ
バサ
バサ
WHOA!
OH, NO. NOW I'VE DONE IT.
FIRST OF ALL, THIS ROOM'S JUST GOT TOO MANY STUPID BOOKS.
HUH?
HUH?
DIARY: 1998.
IS THIS...
...HER DIARY?
ゴク‥
NO, NO, NO, THIS IS DANGEROUS! IF I KNOW HOW THIS PATTERN WORKS, I END UP READING THE CONTENTS, GET CAUGHT, AND THEN GET PUNCHED!!
I BETTER PUT THIS THING AWAY NOW!
あたふた
バサバサ
WHOA! AVA-LANCHE!

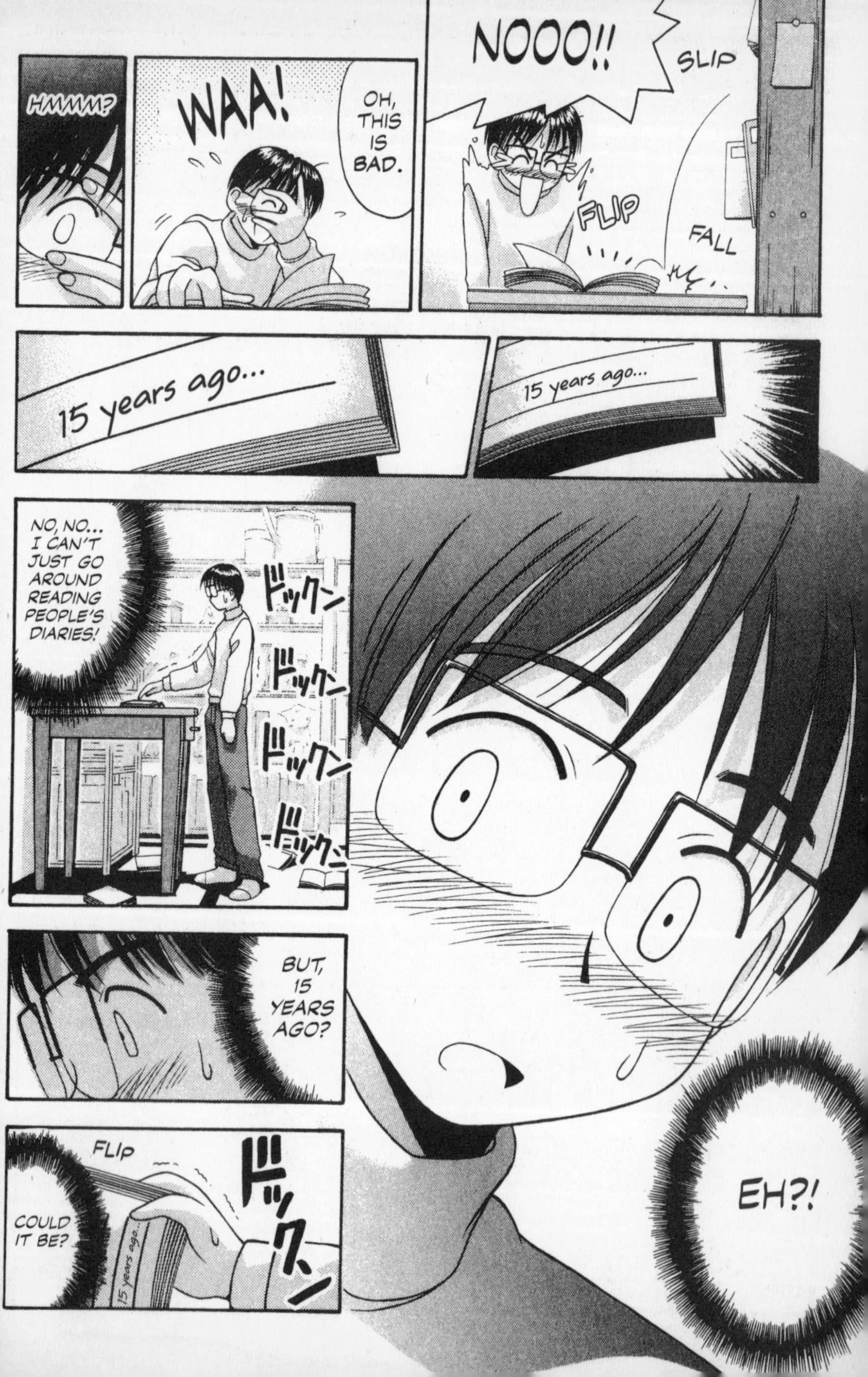
NOOO!!
SLIP
FLIP
FALL
WAA!
OH, THIS IS BAD.
HMMM?
15 years ago...
15 years ago...
EH?!
NO, NO... I CAN'T JUST GO AROUND READING PEOPLE'S DIARIES!
ドックン
ドックン
ドックン
ドックン
BUT, 15 YEARS AGO?
ドックン
FLIP
COULD IT BE?
15 years ago...

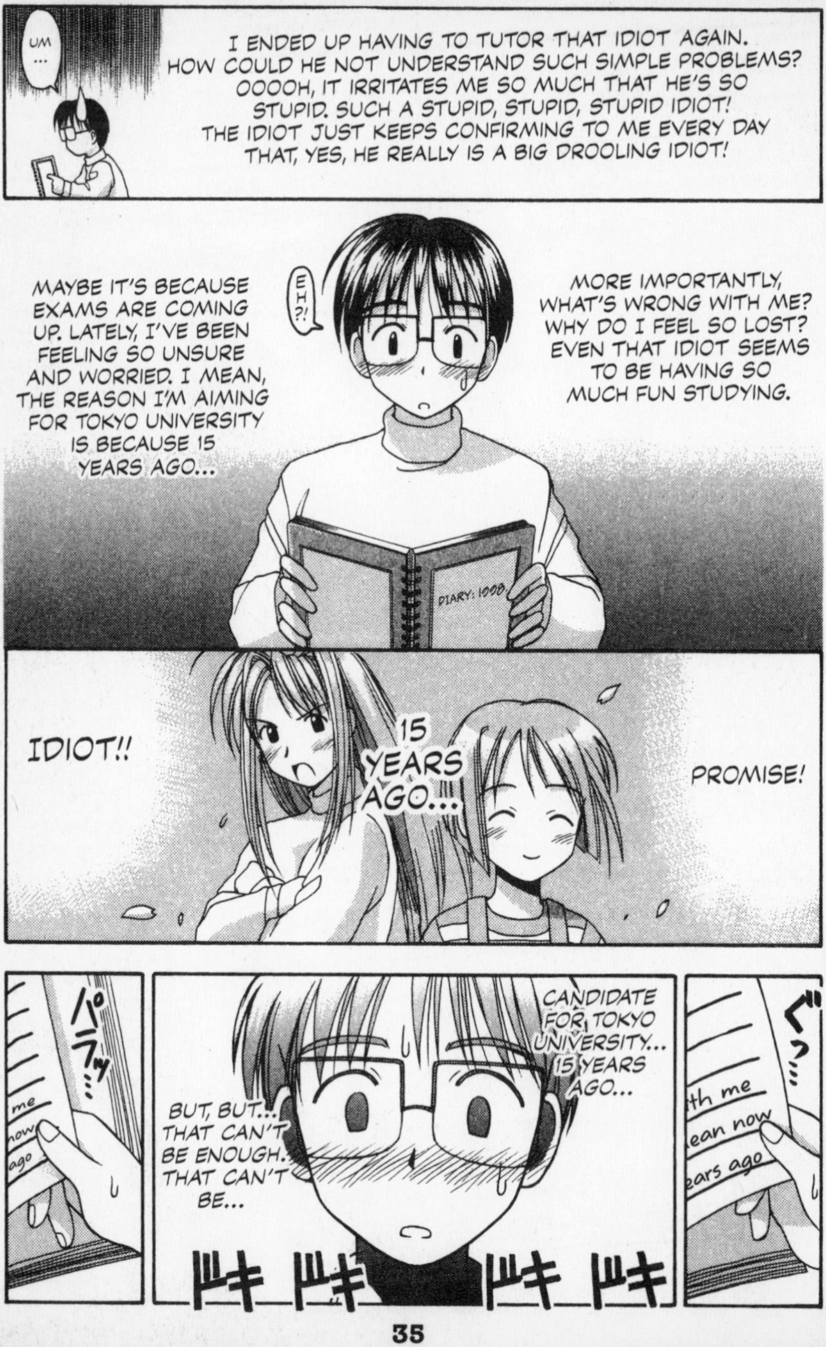

I ENDED UP HAVING TO TUTOR THAT IDIOT AGAIN. HOW COULD HE NOT UNDERSTAND SUCH SIMPLE PROBLEMS? OOOOH, IT IRRITATES ME SO MUCH THAT HE'S SO STUPID. SUCH A STUPID, STUPID, STUPID IDIOT! THE IDIOT JUST KEEPS CONFIRMING TO ME EVERY DAY THAT, YES, HE REALLY IS A BIG DROOLING IDIOT!
UM ...
MORE IMPORTANTLY, WHAT'S WRONG WITH ME? WHY DO I FEEL SO LOST? EVEN THAT IDIOT SEEMS TO BE HAVING SO MUCH FUN STUDYING.
EH?!
MAYBE IT'S BECAUSE EXAMS ARE COMING UP. LATELY, I'VE BEEN FEELING SO UNSURE AND WORRIED. I MEAN, THE REASON I'M AIMING FOR TOKYO UNIVERSITY IS BECAUSE 15 YEARS AGO...
DIARY: 1998
PROMISE!
15 YEARS AGO...
IDIOT!!
ぐっ…
th me
ean now
ears ago
CANDIDATE FOR TOKYO UNIVERSITY... 15 YEARS AGO...
BUT, BUT... THAT CAN'T BE ENOUGH... THAT CAN'T BE...
ドキ ドキ ドキ ドキ
パラッ…
me
now
ago

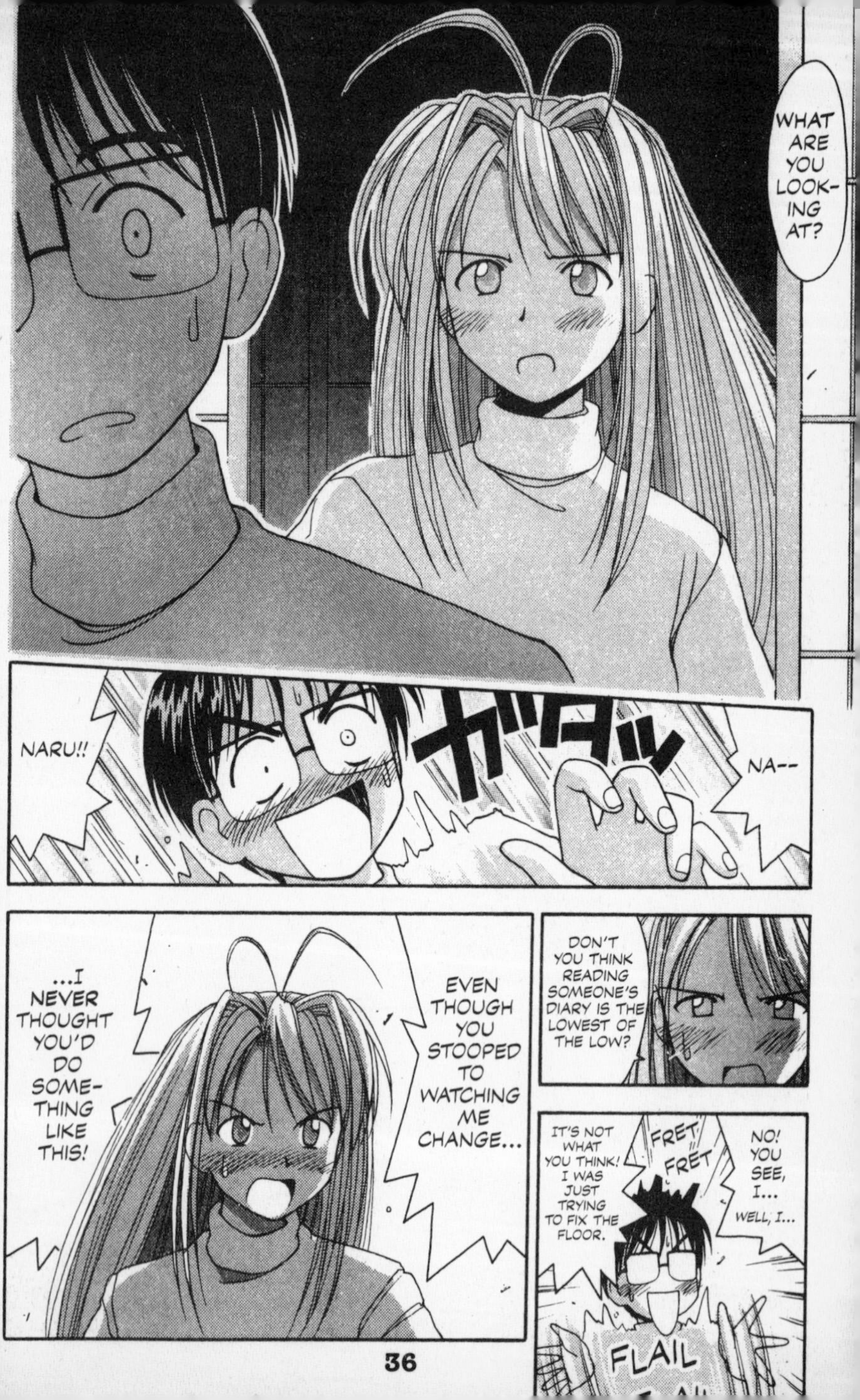
WHAT ARE YOU LOOKING AT?
NA--
NARU!!
DON'T YOU THINK READING SOMEONE'S DIARY IS THE LOWEST OF THE LOW?
NO! YOU SEE, I... WELL, I...
FRET FRET
IT'S NOT WHAT YOU THINK! I WAS JUST TRYING TO FIX THE FLOOR.
FLAIL
EVEN THOUGH YOU STOOPED TO WATCHING ME CHANGE...
...I NEVER THOUGHT YOU'D DO SOMETHING LIKE THIS!

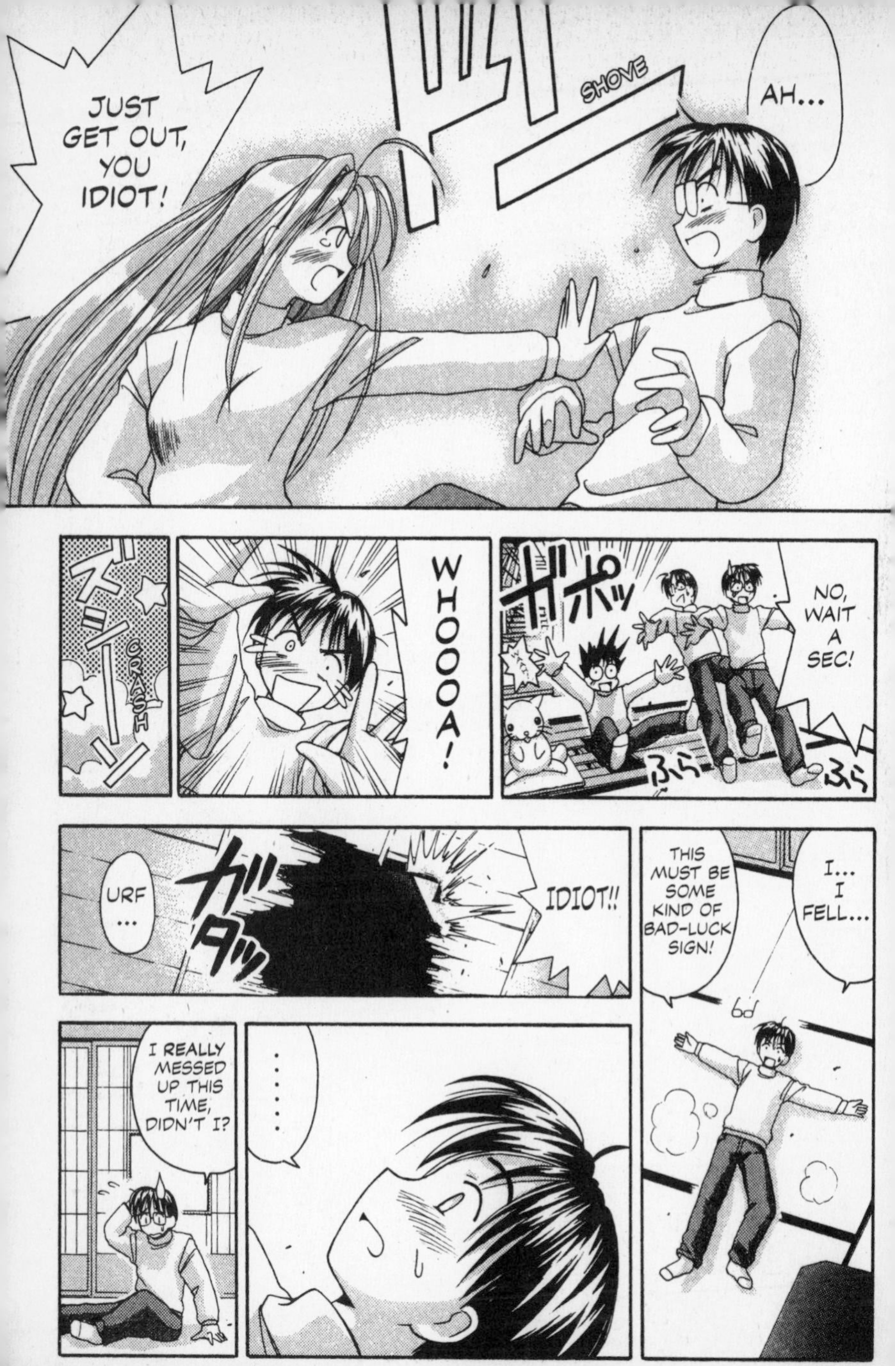
AH...
SHOVE
JUST GET OUT, YOU IDIOT!
NO, WAIT A SEC!
ガポッ
ふら
ふら
WHOOOOA!
CRASH
I... I FELL...
THIS MUST BE SOME KIND OF BAD-LUCK SIGN!
IDIOT!!
URF ...
......
I REALLY MESSED UP THIS TIME, DIDN'T I?

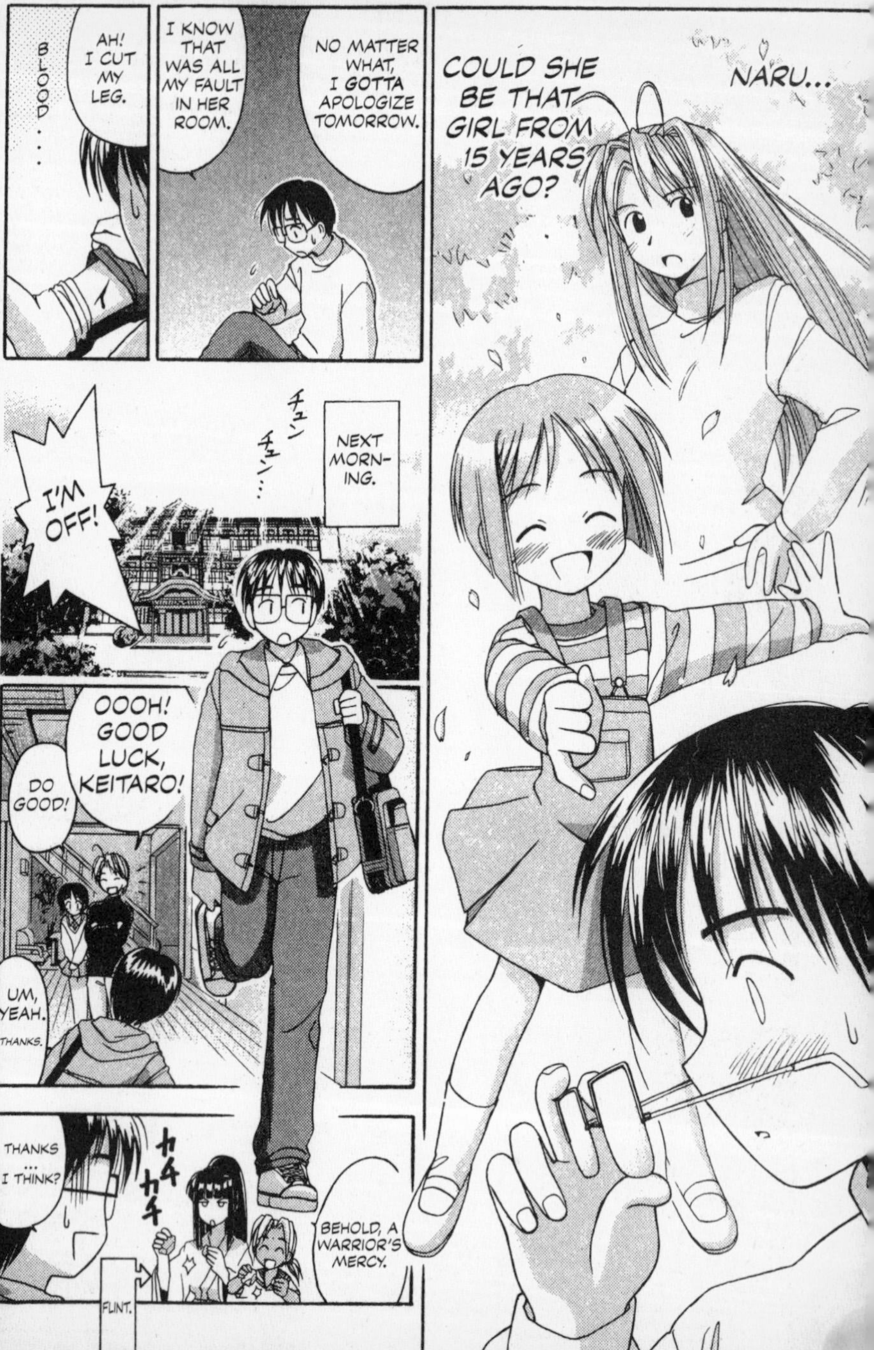
NARU...
COULD SHE BE THAT GIRL FROM 15 YEARS AGO?
NO MATTER WHAT, I GOTTA APOLOGIZE TOMORROW.
I KNOW THAT WAS ALL MY FAULT IN HER ROOM.
AH! I CUT MY LEG.
BLOOD...
NEXT MORNING.
チュン チュン...
I'M OFF!
OOOH! GOOD LUCK, KEITARO!
DO GOOD!
UM, YEAH.
THANKS.
BEHOLD, A WARRIOR'S MERCY.
カチ カチ
THANKS... I THINK?
FLINT.

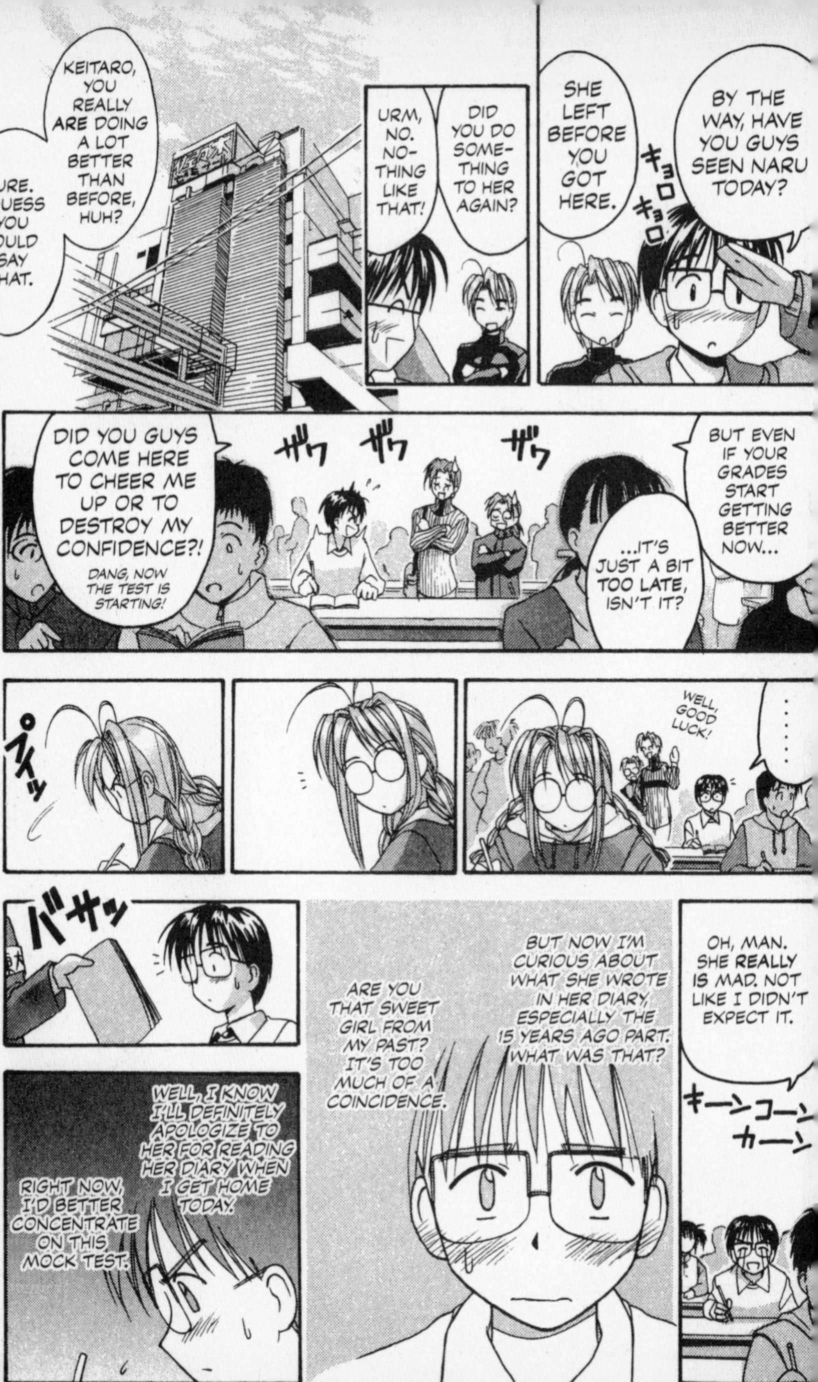
BY THE WAY, HAVE YOU GUYS SEEN NARU TODAY?
キョロキョロ
SHE LEFT BEFORE YOU GOT HERE.
DID YOU DO SOMETHING TO HER AGAIN?
URM, NO. NOTHING LIKE THAT!
KEITARO, YOU REALLY ARE DOING A LOT BETTER THAN BEFORE, HUH?
SURE. I GUESS YOU COULD SAY THAT.
BUT EVEN IF YOUR GRADES START GETTING BETTER NOW...
...IT'S JUST A BIT TOO LATE, ISN'T IT?
ザワ ザワ ザワ
DID YOU GUYS COME HERE TO CHEER ME UP OR TO DESTROY MY CONFIDENCE?!
DANG, NOW THE TEST IS STARTING!
......
WELL, GOOD LUCK!
プイッ
OH, MAN. SHE REALLY IS MAD. NOT LIKE I DIDN'T EXPECT IT.
キーンコーンカーン
BUT NOW I'M CURIOUS ABOUT WHAT SHE WROTE IN HER DIARY, ESPECIALLY THE 15 YEARS AGO PART. WHAT WAS THAT?
ARE YOU THAT SWEET GIRL FROM MY PAST? IT'S TOO MUCH OF A COINCIDENCE.
バサッ
WELL, I KNOW I'LL DEFINITELY APOLOGIZE TO HER FOR READING HER DIARY WHEN I GET HOME TODAY.
RIGHT NOW, I'D BETTER CONCENTRATE ON THIS MOCK TEST.

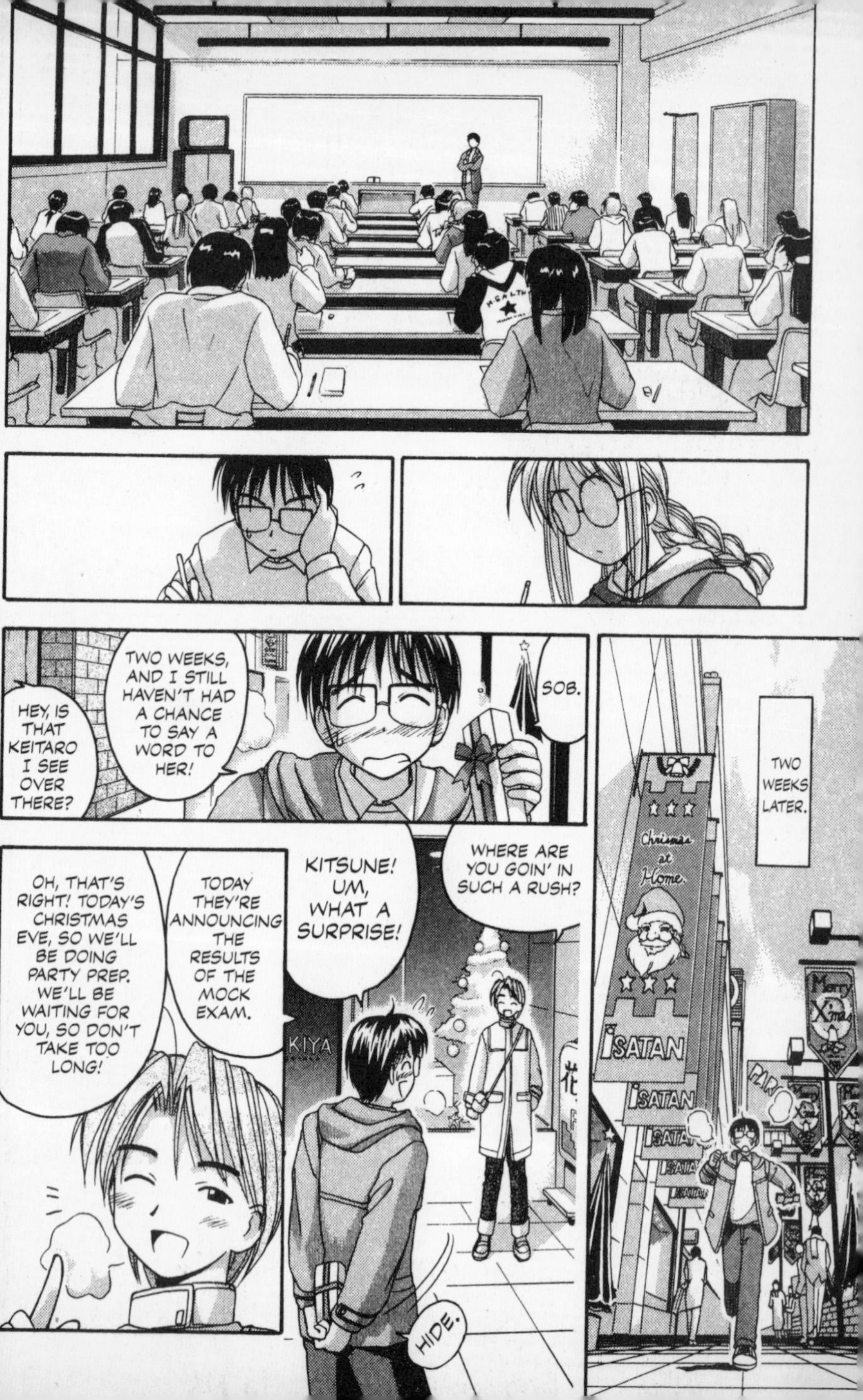
TWO WEEKS LATER.
Christmas at Home
ISATAN
SOB.
TWO WEEKS, AND I STILL HAVEN'T HAD A CHANCE TO SAY A WORD TO HER!
HEY, IS THAT KEITARO I SEE OVER THERE?
WHERE ARE YOU GOIN' IN SUCH A RUSH?
KITSUNE! UM, WHAT A SURPRISE!
TODAY THEY'RE ANNOUNCING THE RESULTS OF THE MOCK EXAM.
OH, THAT'S RIGHT! TODAY'S CHRISTMAS EVE, SO WE'LL BE DOING PARTY PREP. WE'LL BE WAITING FOR YOU, SO DON'T TAKE TOO LONG!
HIDE.

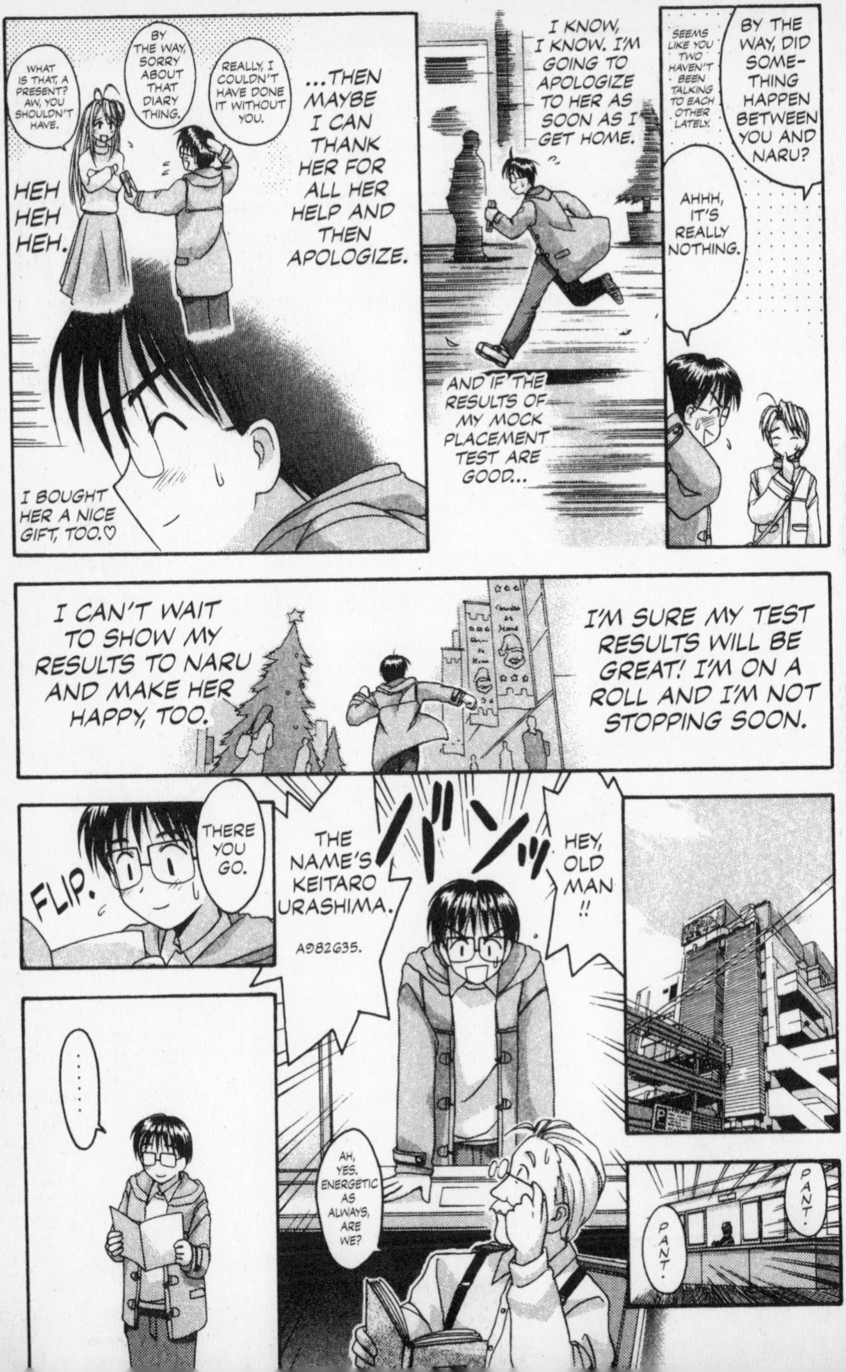
BY THE WAY, DID SOMETHING HAPPEN BETWEEN YOU AND NARU?
SEEMS LIKE YOU TWO HAVEN'T BEEN TALKING TO EACH OTHER LATELY.
AHHH, IT'S REALLY NOTHING.
I KNOW, I KNOW. I'M GOING TO APOLOGIZE TO HER AS SOON AS I GET HOME.
AND IF THE RESULTS OF MY MOCK PLACEMENT TEST ARE GOOD...
...THEN MAYBE I CAN THANK HER FOR ALL HER HELP AND THEN APOLOGIZE.
REALLY, I COULDN'T HAVE DONE IT WITHOUT YOU.
BY THE WAY, SORRY ABOUT THAT DIARY THING.
WHAT IS THAT, A PRESENT? AW, YOU SHOULDN'T HAVE.
HEH HEH HEH.
I BOUGHT HER A NICE GIFT, TOO.♡
I'M SURE MY TEST RESULTS WILL BE GREAT! I'M ON A ROLL AND I'M NOT STOPPING SOON.
I CAN'T WAIT TO SHOW MY RESULTS TO NARU AND MAKE HER HAPPY, TOO.
PANT.
PANT.
HEY, OLD MAN!!
THE NAME'S KEITARO URASHIMA.
A982635.
AH, YES. ENERGETIC AS ALWAYS, ARE WE?
THERE YOU GO.
FLIP.
......

School Name	Evaluation	Chance of Passing
Tokyo University Lib I.	D	0%

National Average	Overall Evaluation
4 9	You may wish to change your desired school. You did not pass. Your efforts are futile.

HEY, KEITARO!

WHAT'S HE DOING JUST STANDING THERE?

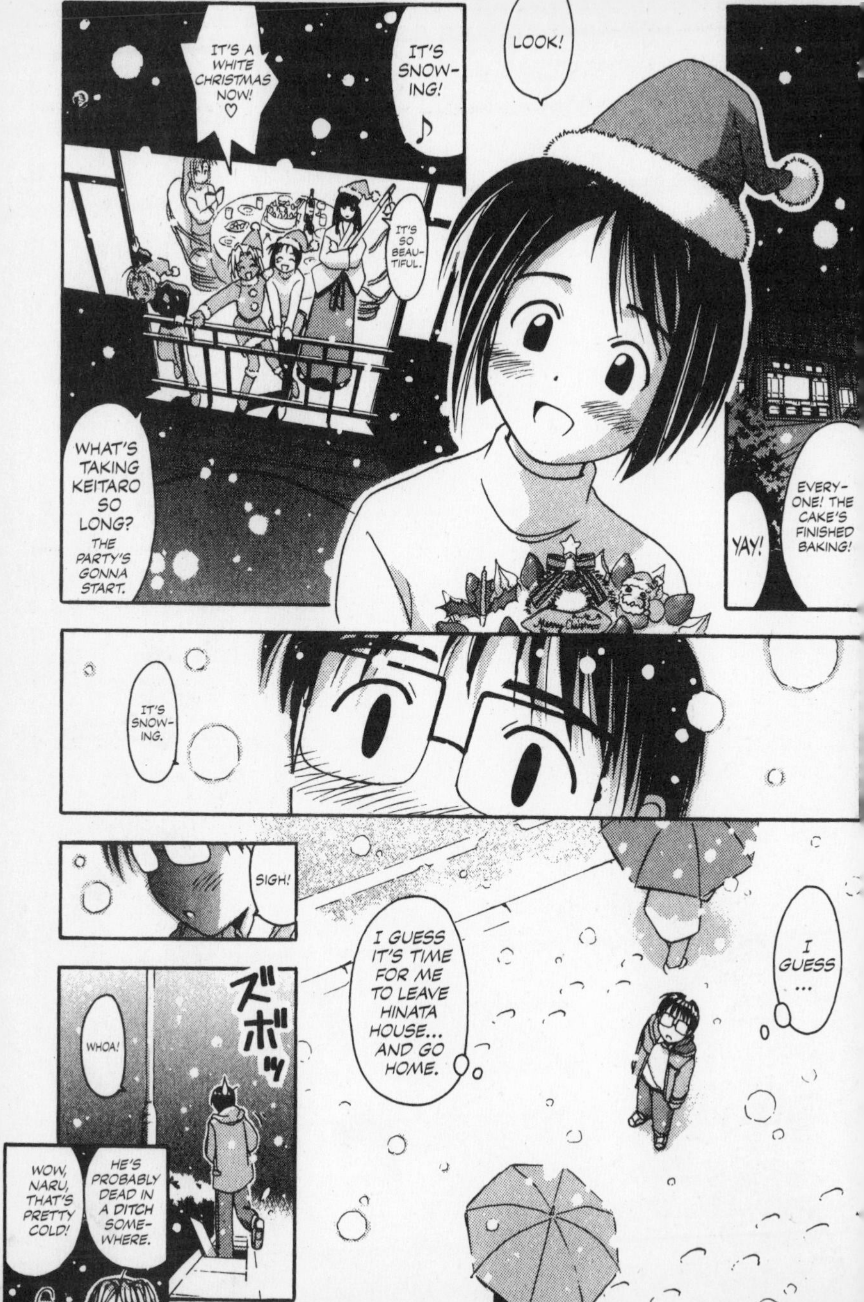
EVERY-ONE! THE CAKE'S FINISHED BAKING!
YAY!
LOOK!
IT'S SNOWING! ♪
IT'S A WHITE CHRISTMAS NOW! ♡
IT'S SO BEAUTIFUL.
WHAT'S TAKING KEITARO SO LONG? THE PARTY'S GONNA START.
IT'S SNOWING.
I GUESS...
I GUESS IT'S TIME FOR ME TO LEAVE HINATA HOUSE... AND GO HOME.
SIGH!
ズボッ
WHOA!
HE'S PROBABLY DEAD IN A DITCH SOMEWHERE.
WOW, NARU, THAT'S PRETTY COLD!

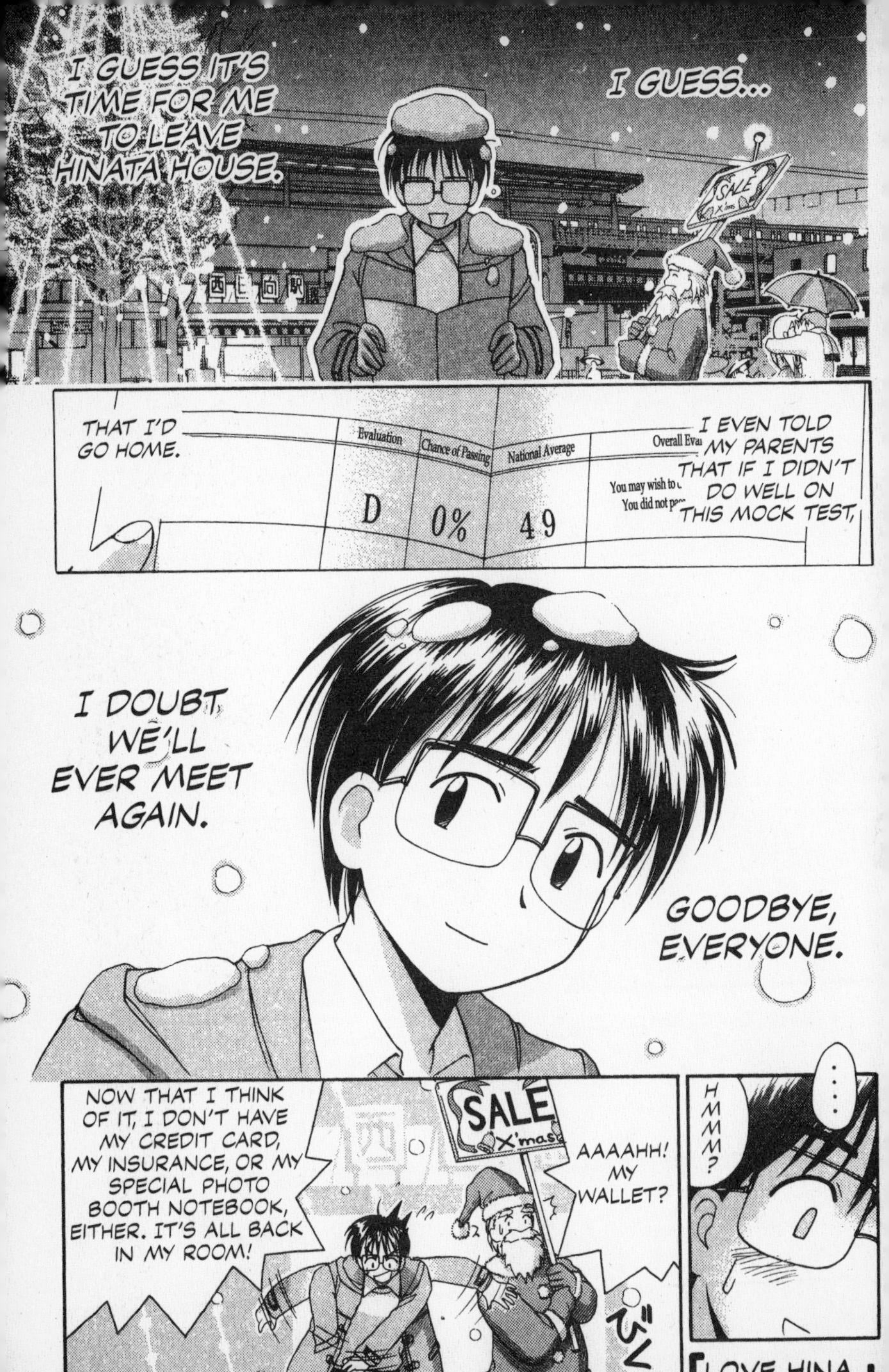
I GUESS...
I GUESS IT'S TIME FOR ME TO LEAVE HINATA HOUSE.
SALE X'mas
I EVEN TOLD MY PARENTS THAT IF I DIDN'T DO WELL ON THIS MOCK TEST,
THAT I'D GO HOME.
Evaluation
Chance of Passing
National Average
D
0%
49
I DOUBT WE'LL EVER MEET AGAIN.
GOODBYE, EVERYONE.
...
HMMM?
SALE X'mas
AAAAHH! MY WALLET?
NOW THAT I THINK OF IT, I DON'T HAVE MY CREDIT CARD, MY INSURANCE, OR MY SPECIAL PHOTO BOOTH NOTEBOOK, EITHER. IT'S ALL BACK IN MY ROOM!
びくっ

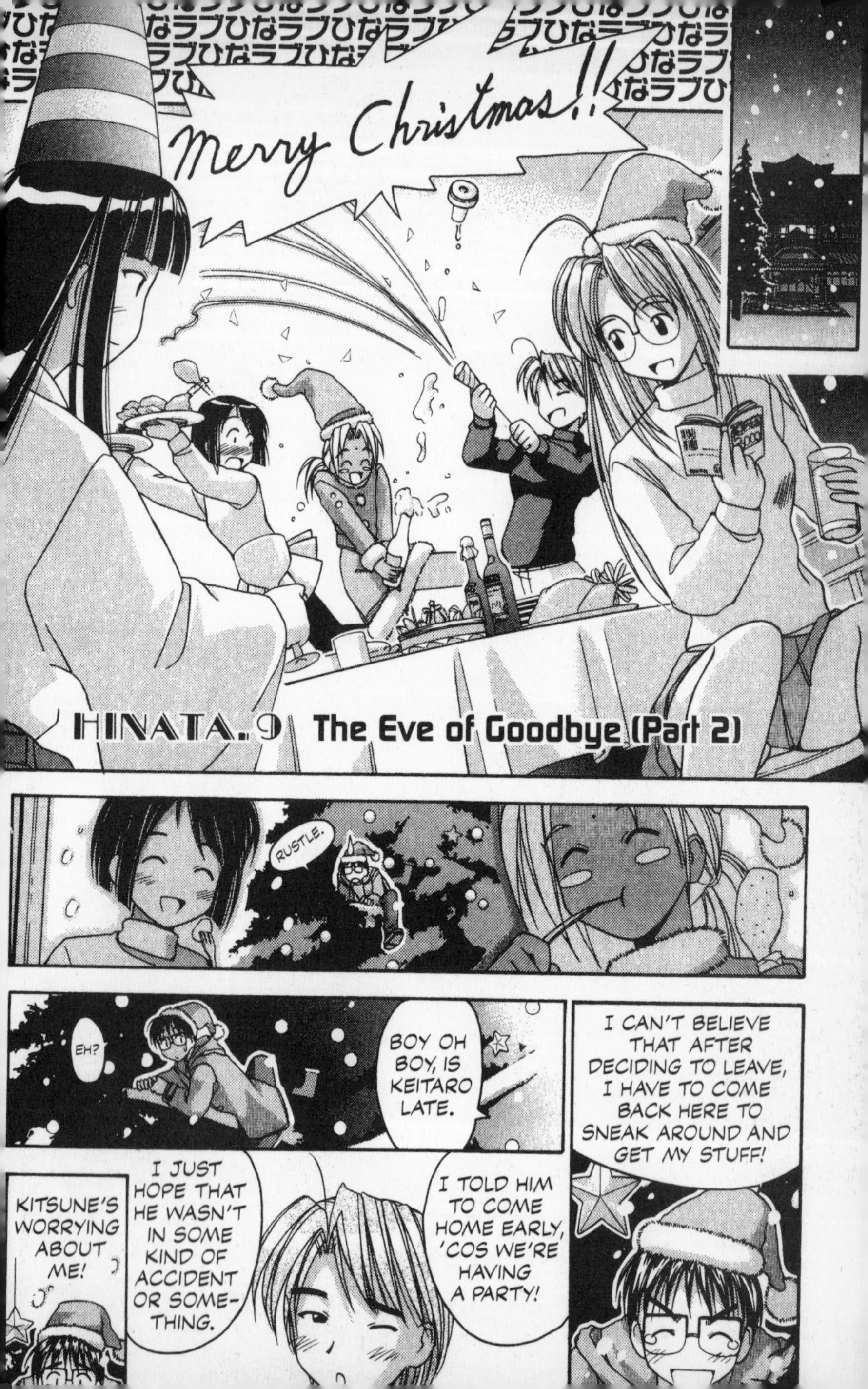
Merry Christmas!!
HINATA. 9 The Eve of Goodbye (Part 2)
RUSTLE.
I CAN'T BELIEVE THAT AFTER DECIDING TO LEAVE, I HAVE TO COME BACK HERE TO SNEAK AROUND AND GET MY STUFF!
BOY OH BOY, IS KEITARO LATE.
EH?
I TOLD HIM TO COME HOME EARLY, 'COS WE'RE HAVING A PARTY!
I JUST HOPE THAT HE WASN'T IN SOME KIND OF ACCIDENT OR SOME-THING.
KITSUNE'S WORRYING ABOUT ME!

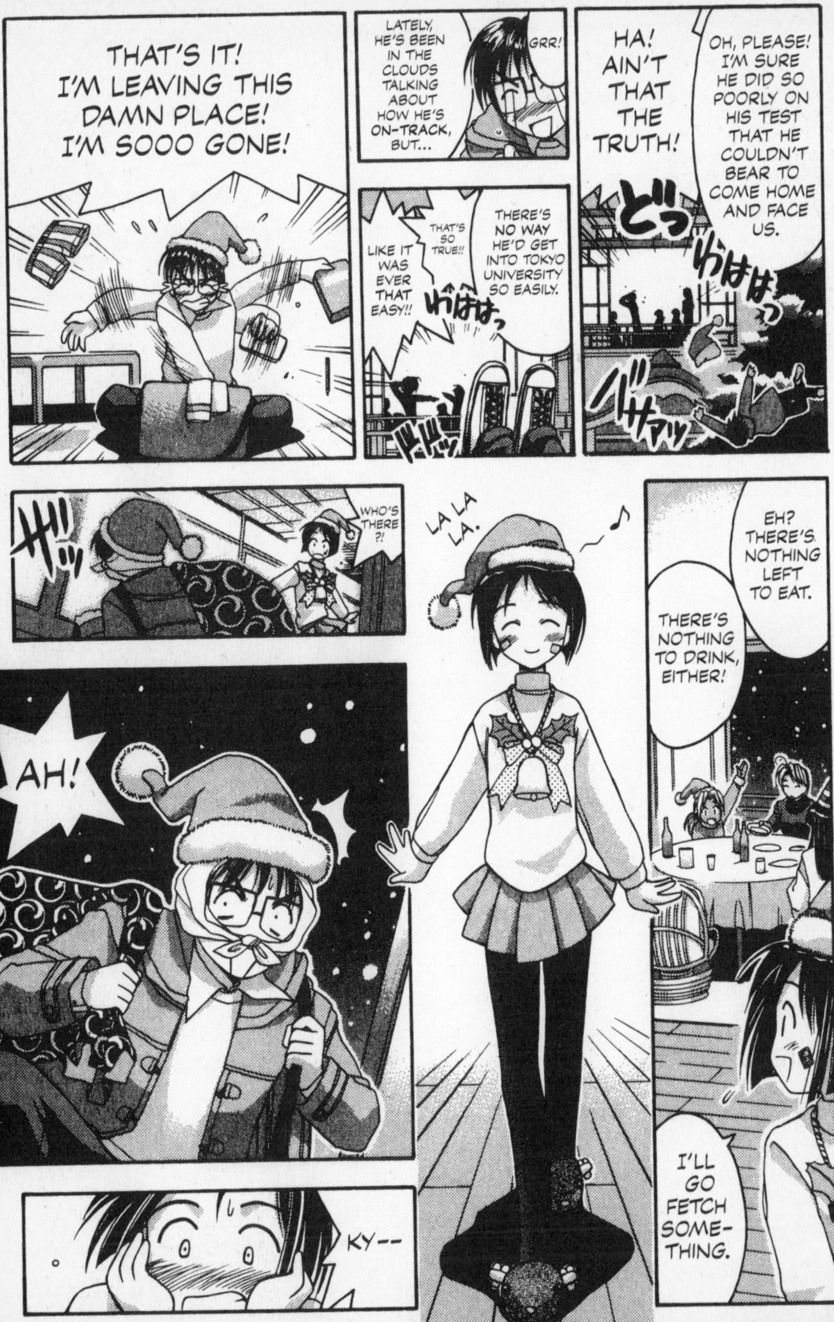
HA! AIN'T THAT THE TRUTH!
OH, PLEASE! I'M SURE HE DID SO POORLY ON HIS TEST THAT HE COULDN'T BEAR TO COME HOME AND FACE US.
どっ
わははっ
LATELY, HE'S BEEN IN THE CLOUDS TALKING ABOUT HOW HE'S ON-TRACK, BUT...
GRR!
THERE'S NO WAY HE'D GET INTO TOKYO UNIVERSITY SO EASILY.
THAT'S SO TRUE!!
LIKE IT WAS EVER THAT EASY!!
わははっ
THAT'S IT! I'M LEAVING THIS DAMN PLACE! I'M SOOO GONE!
EH? THERE'S. NOTHING LEFT TO EAT.
THERE'S NOTHING TO DRINK, EITHER!
I'LL GO FETCH SOME-THING.
LA LA LA.
♪
WHO'S THERE?!
AH!
KY--

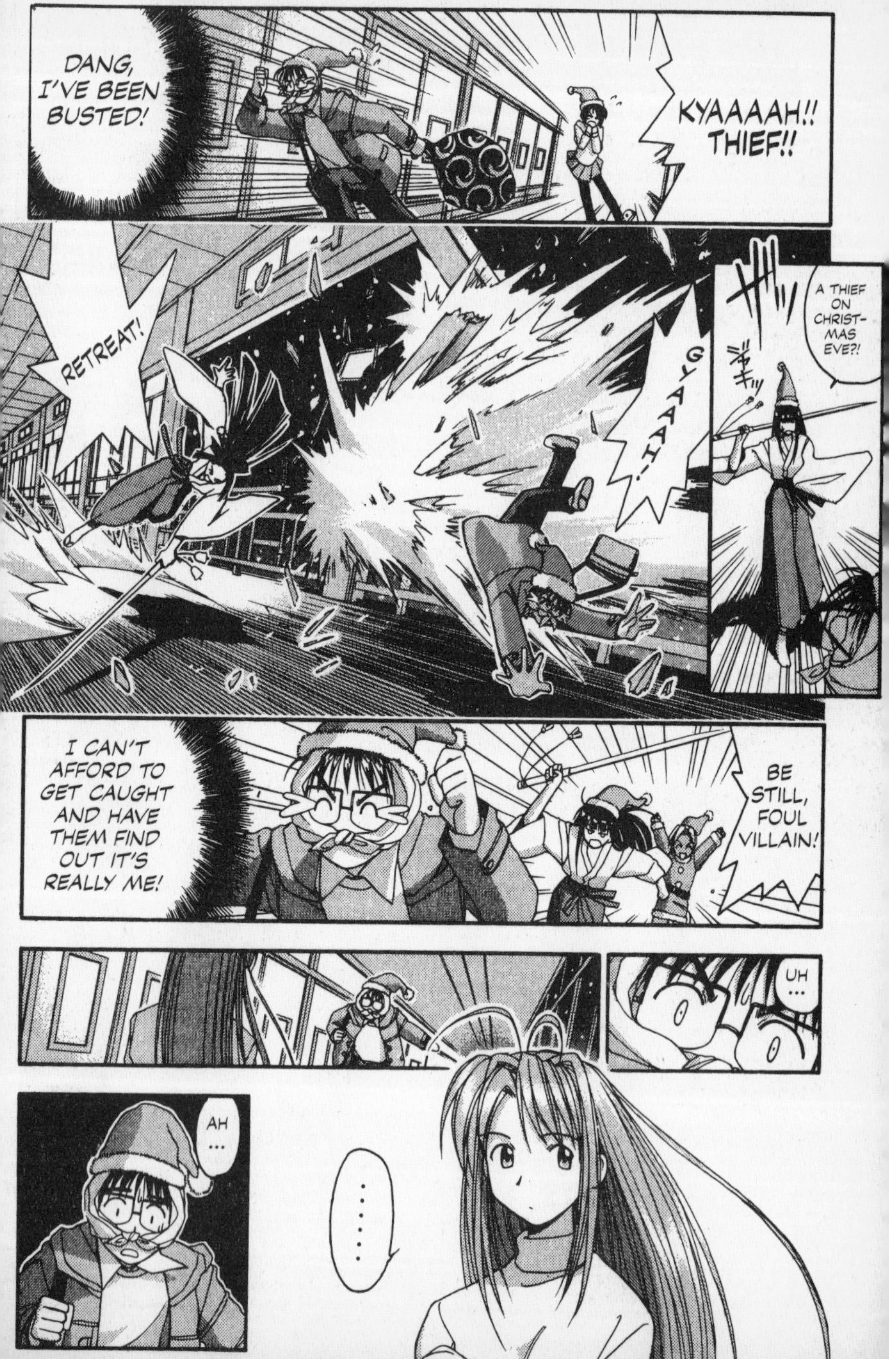
KYAAAAH!! THIEF!!
DANG, I'VE BEEN BUSTED!
A THIEF ON CHRIST-MAS EVE?!
GYAAAAH!!
RETREAT!
BE STILL, FOUL VILLAIN!
I CAN'T AFFORD TO GET CAUGHT AND HAVE THEM FIND OUT IT'S REALLY ME!
UH ...
......
AH ...

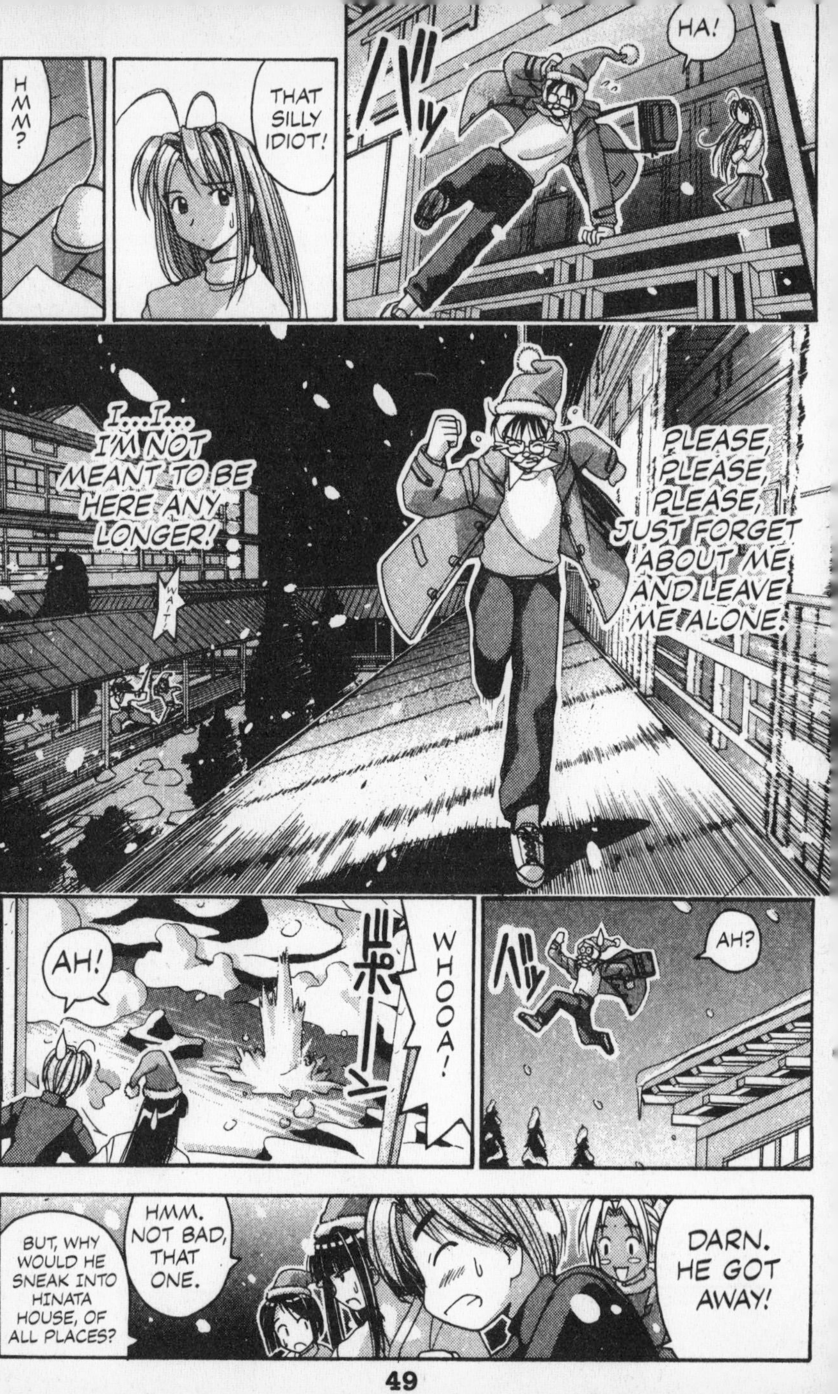

HA!
バッ
THAT SILLY IDIOT!
HMM?
PLEASE, PLEASE, PLEASE, JUST FORGET ABOUT ME AND LEAVE ME ALONE.
I...I... I'M NOT MEANT TO BE HERE ANY LONGER!
WAIT!
AH?
バッ
WHOOA!
ボーン
AH!
DARN. HE GOT AWAY!
HMM. NOT BAD, THAT ONE.
BUT, WHY WOULD HE SNEAK INTO HINATA HOUSE, OF ALL PLACES?

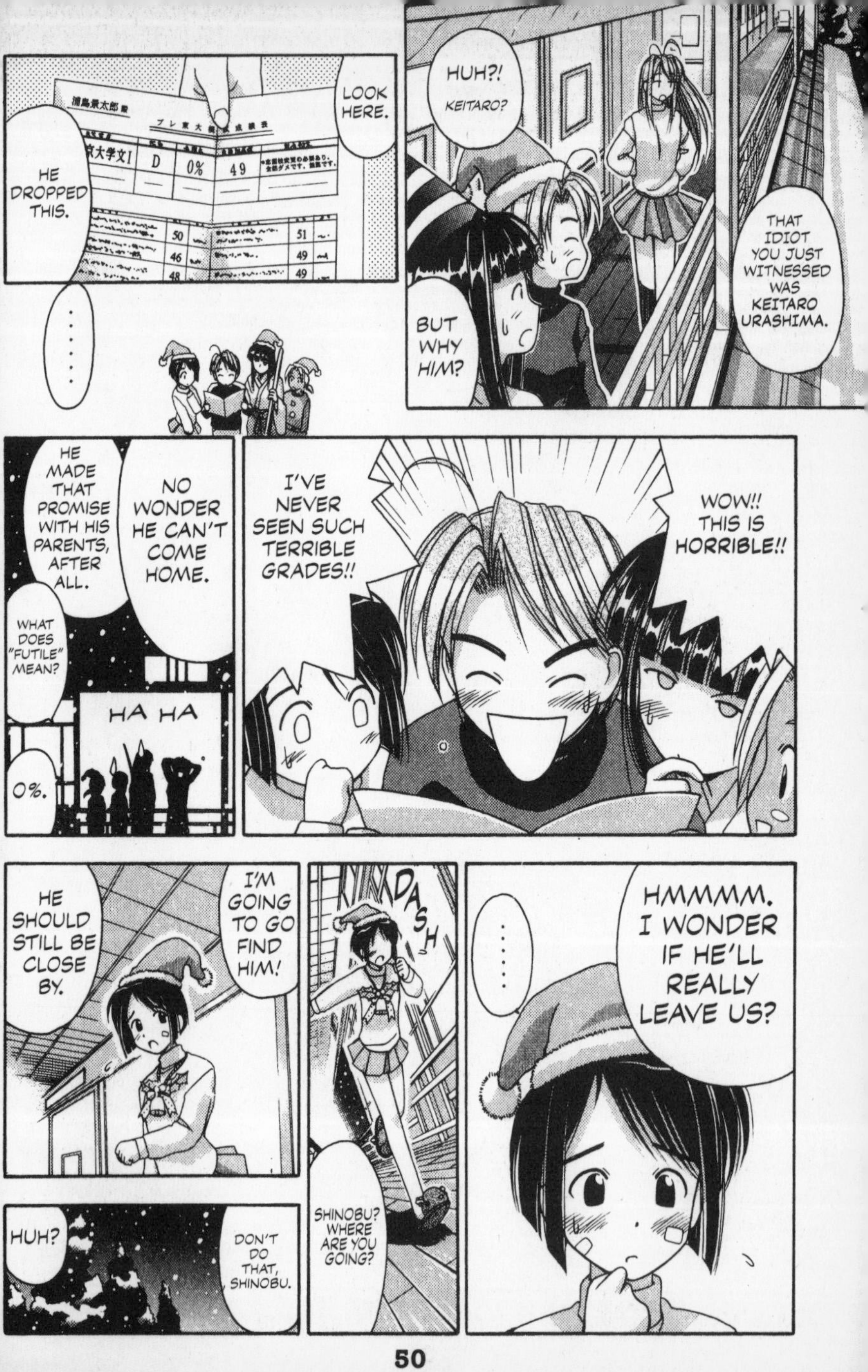
HUH?! KEITARO?
THAT IDIOT YOU JUST WITNESSED WAS KEITARO URASHIMA.
BUT WHY HIM?
LOOK HERE.
HE DROPPED THIS.
......
WOW!! THIS IS HORRIBLE!!
I'VE NEVER SEEN SUCH TERRIBLE GRADES!!
NO WONDER HE CAN'T COME HOME.
HE MADE THAT PROMISE WITH HIS PARENTS, AFTER ALL.
WHAT DOES "FUTILE" MEAN?
HA HA
0%.
HMMMM. I WONDER IF HE'LL REALLY LEAVE US?
......
DASH
I'M GOING TO GO FIND HIM!
SHINOBU? WHERE ARE YOU GOING?
HE SHOULD STILL BE CLOSE BY.
DON'T DO THAT, SHINOBU.
HUH?

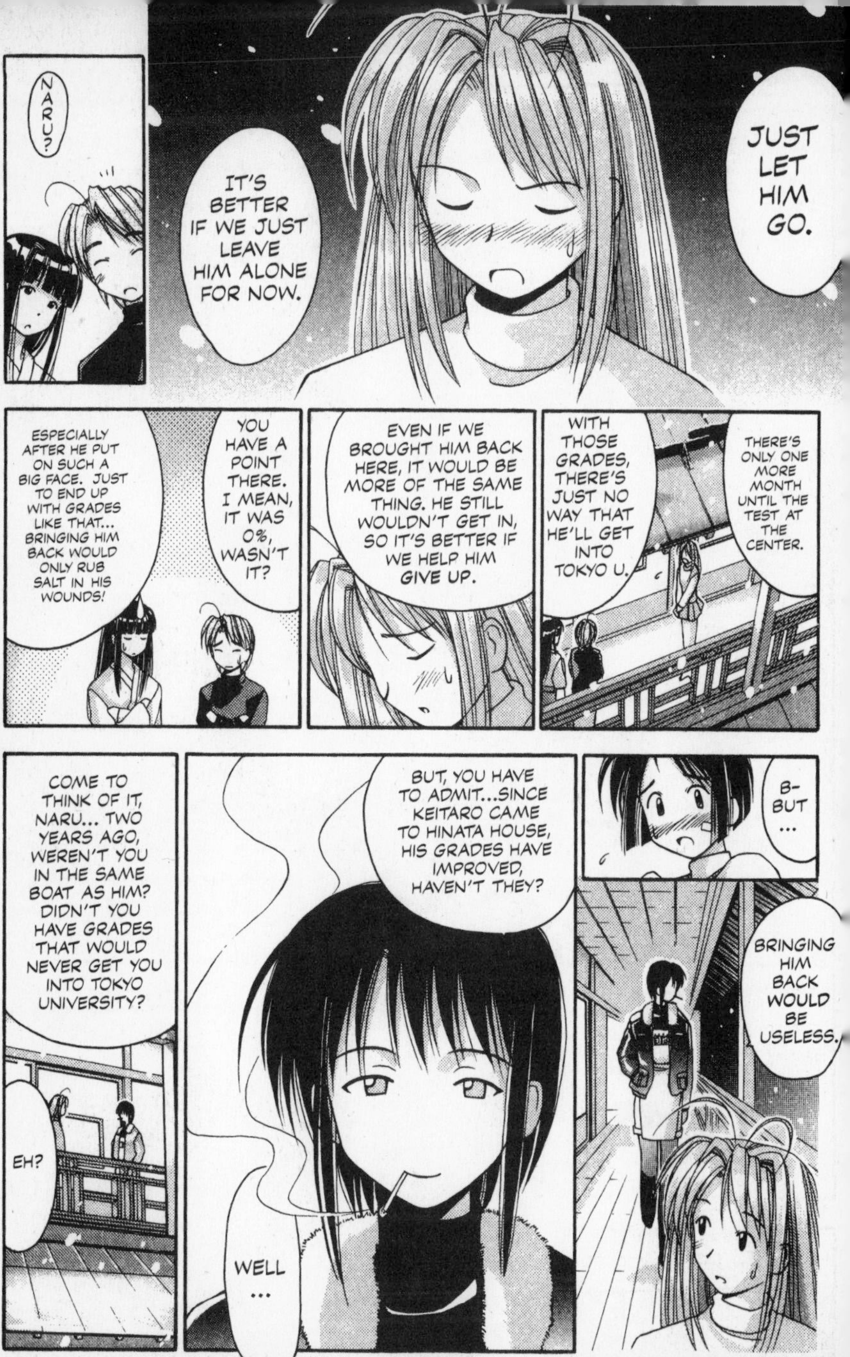
JUST LET HIM GO.
IT'S BETTER IF WE JUST LEAVE HIM ALONE FOR NOW.
NARU?
THERE'S ONLY ONE MORE MONTH UNTIL THE TEST AT THE CENTER.
WITH THOSE GRADES, THERE'S JUST NO WAY THAT HE'LL GET INTO TOKYO U.
EVEN IF WE BROUGHT HIM BACK HERE, IT WOULD BE MORE OF THE SAME THING. HE STILL WOULDN'T GET IN, SO IT'S BETTER IF WE HELP HIM GIVE UP.
YOU HAVE A POINT THERE. I MEAN, IT WAS 0%, WASN'T IT?
ESPECIALLY AFTER HE PUT ON SUCH A BIG FACE. JUST TO END UP WITH GRADES LIKE THAT... BRINGING HIM BACK WOULD ONLY RUB SALT IN HIS WOUNDS!
B-BUT ...
BRINGING HIM BACK WOULD BE USELESS.
BUT, YOU HAVE TO ADMIT...SINCE KEITARO CAME TO HINATA HOUSE, HIS GRADES HAVE IMPROVED, HAVEN'T THEY?
WELL ...
COME TO THINK OF IT, NARU... TWO YEARS AGO, WEREN'T YOU IN THE SAME BOAT AS HIM? DIDN'T YOU HAVE GRADES THAT WOULD NEVER GET YOU INTO TOKYO UNIVERSITY?
EH?

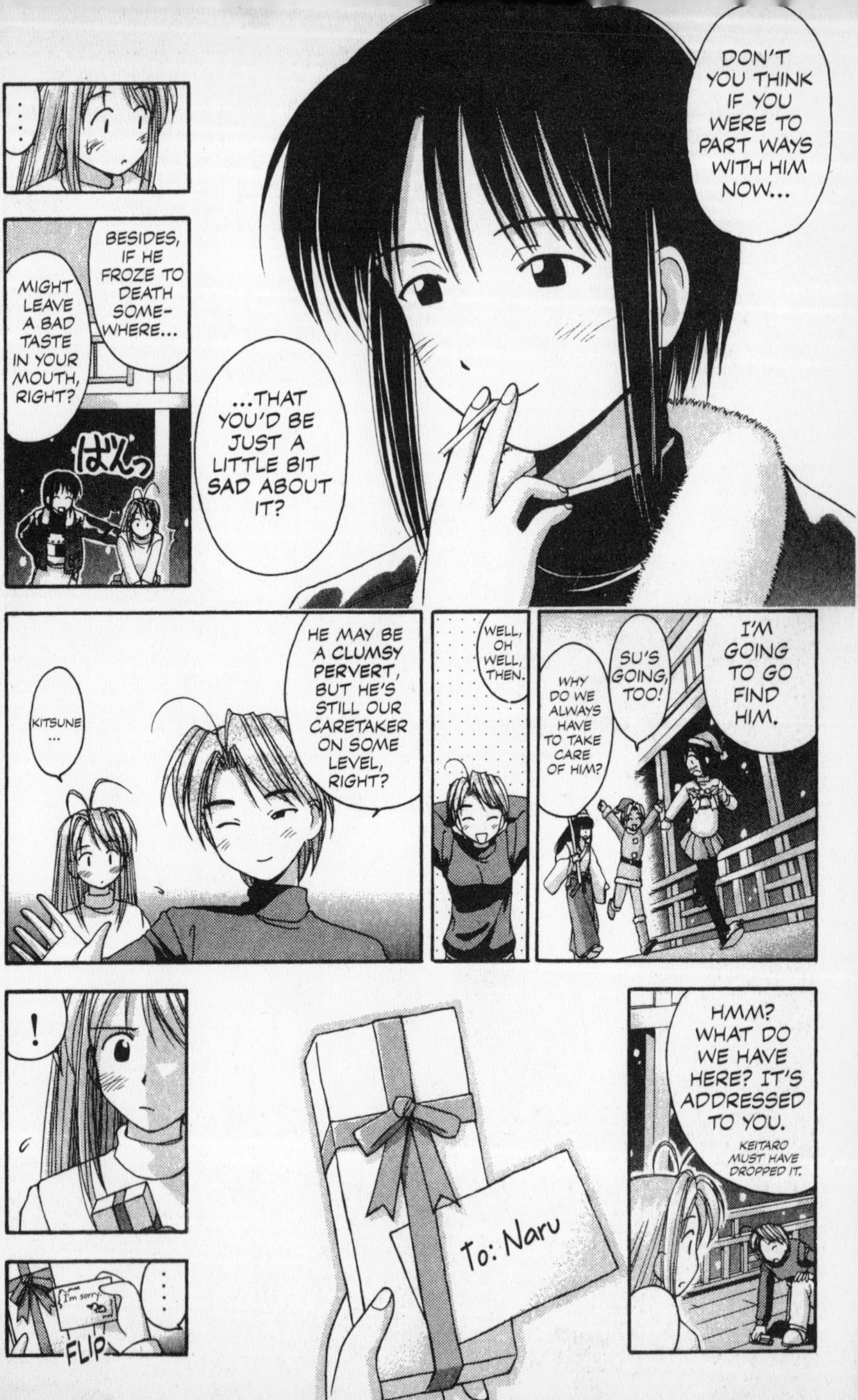
DON'T YOU THINK IF YOU WERE TO PART WAYS WITH HIM NOW...
...THAT YOU'D BE JUST A LITTLE BIT SAD ABOUT IT?
....
BESIDES, IF HE FROZE TO DEATH SOME-WHERE...
MIGHT LEAVE A BAD TASTE IN YOUR MOUTH, RIGHT?
ぱんっ
I'M GOING TO GO FIND HIM.
SU'S GOING, TOO!
WHY DO WE ALWAYS HAVE TO TAKE CARE OF HIM?
WELL, OH WELL, THEN.
HE MAY BE A CLUMSY PERVERT, BUT HE'S STILL OUR CARETAKER ON SOME LEVEL, RIGHT?
KITSUNE ...
HMM? WHAT DO WE HAVE HERE? IT'S ADDRESSED TO YOU.
KEITARO MUST HAVE DROPPED IT.
To: Naru
!
I'm sorry
....
FLIP

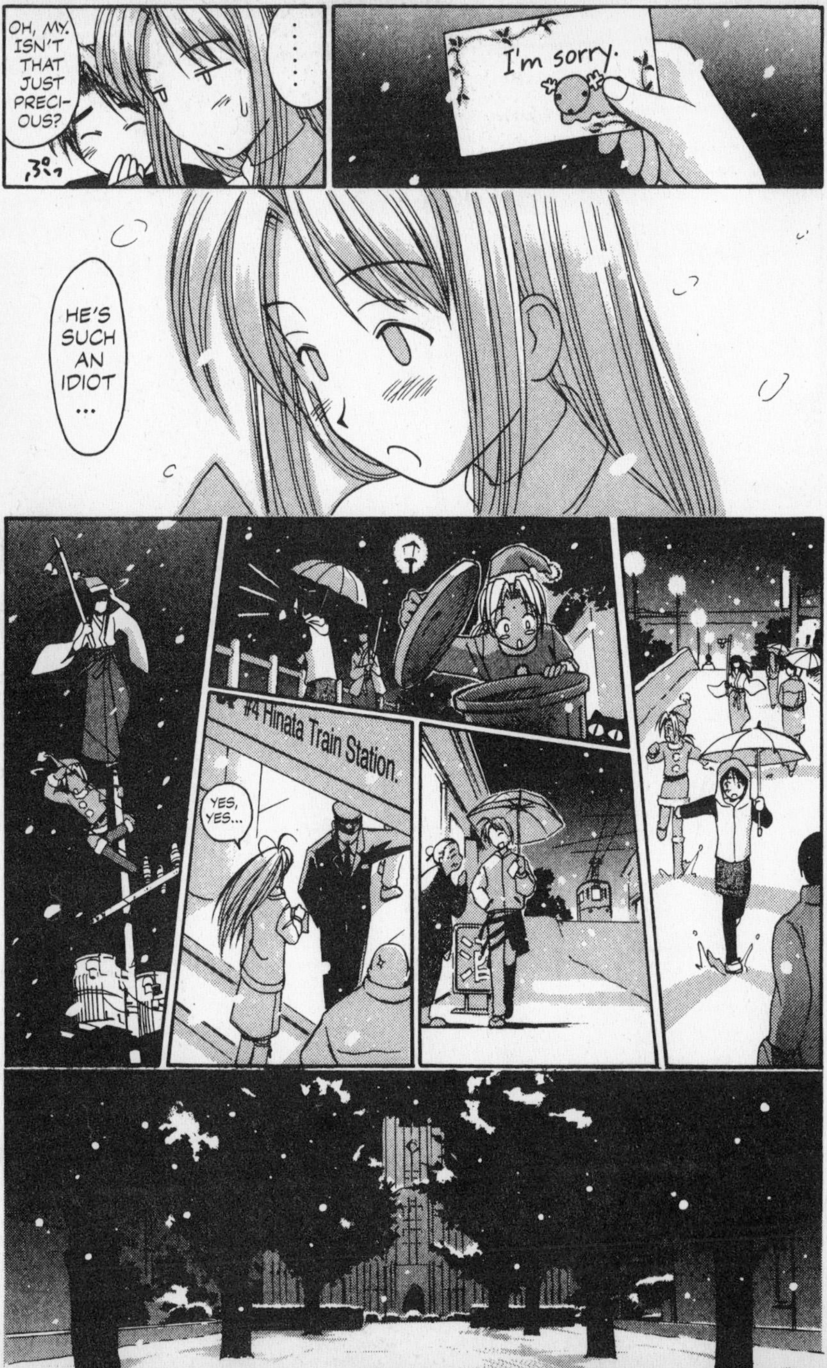
I'm sorry.
......
OH, MY. ISN'T THAT JUST PRECIOUS?
ぷっ
HE'S SUCH AN IDIOT...
#4 Hinata Train Station.
YES, YES...

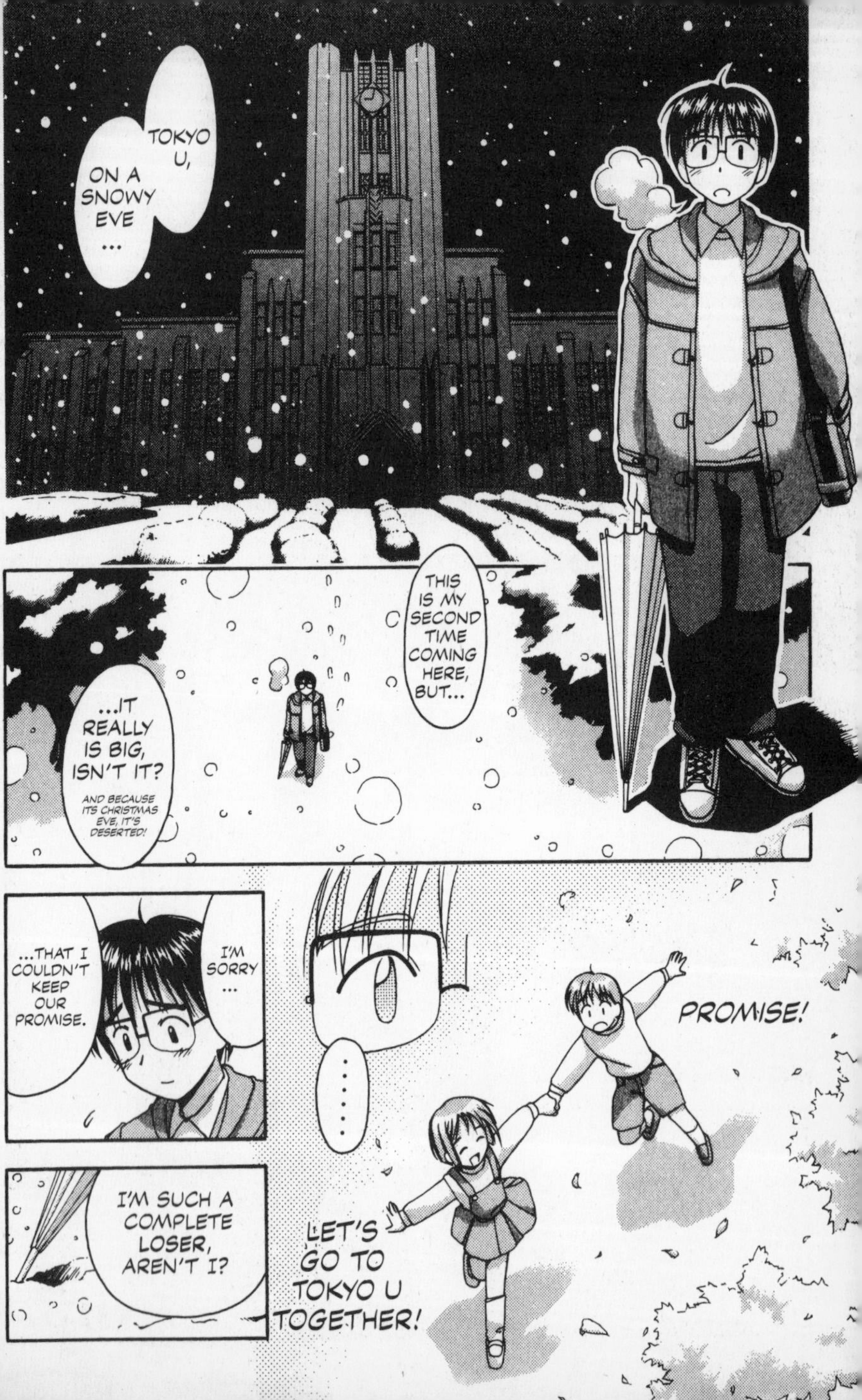

TOKYO U, ON A SNOWY EVE ...
THIS IS MY SECOND TIME COMING HERE, BUT...
...IT REALLY IS BIG, ISN'T IT?
AND BECAUSE ITS CHRISTMAS EVE, IT'S DESERTED!
PROMISE!
......
LET'S GO TO TOKYO U TOGETHER!
I'M SORRY ...
...THAT I COULDN'T KEEP OUR PROMISE.
I'M SUCH A COMPLETE LOSER, AREN'T I?

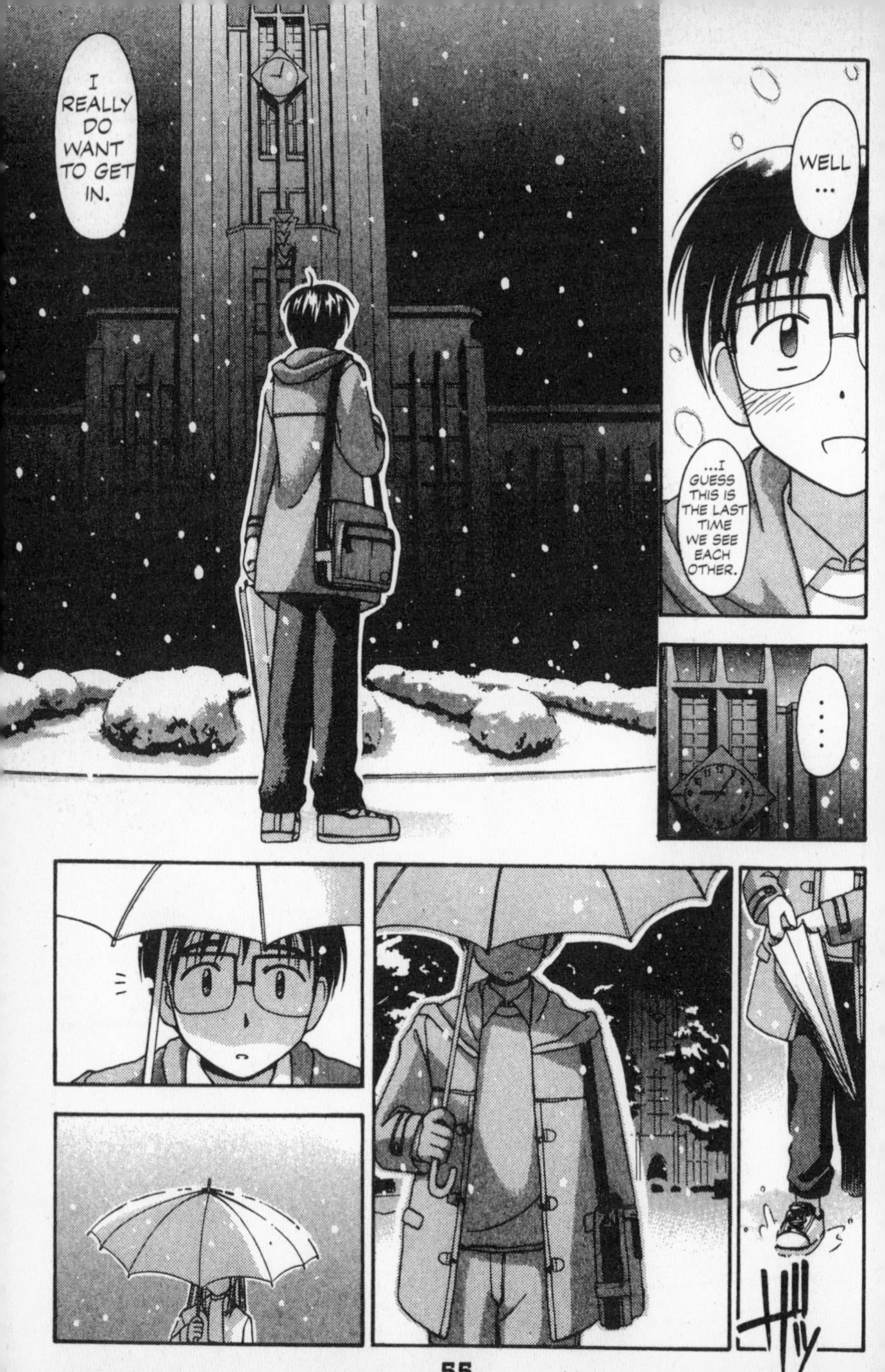
WELL ...
...I GUESS THIS IS THE LAST TIME WE SEE EACH OTHER.
....
I REALLY DO WANT TO GET IN.

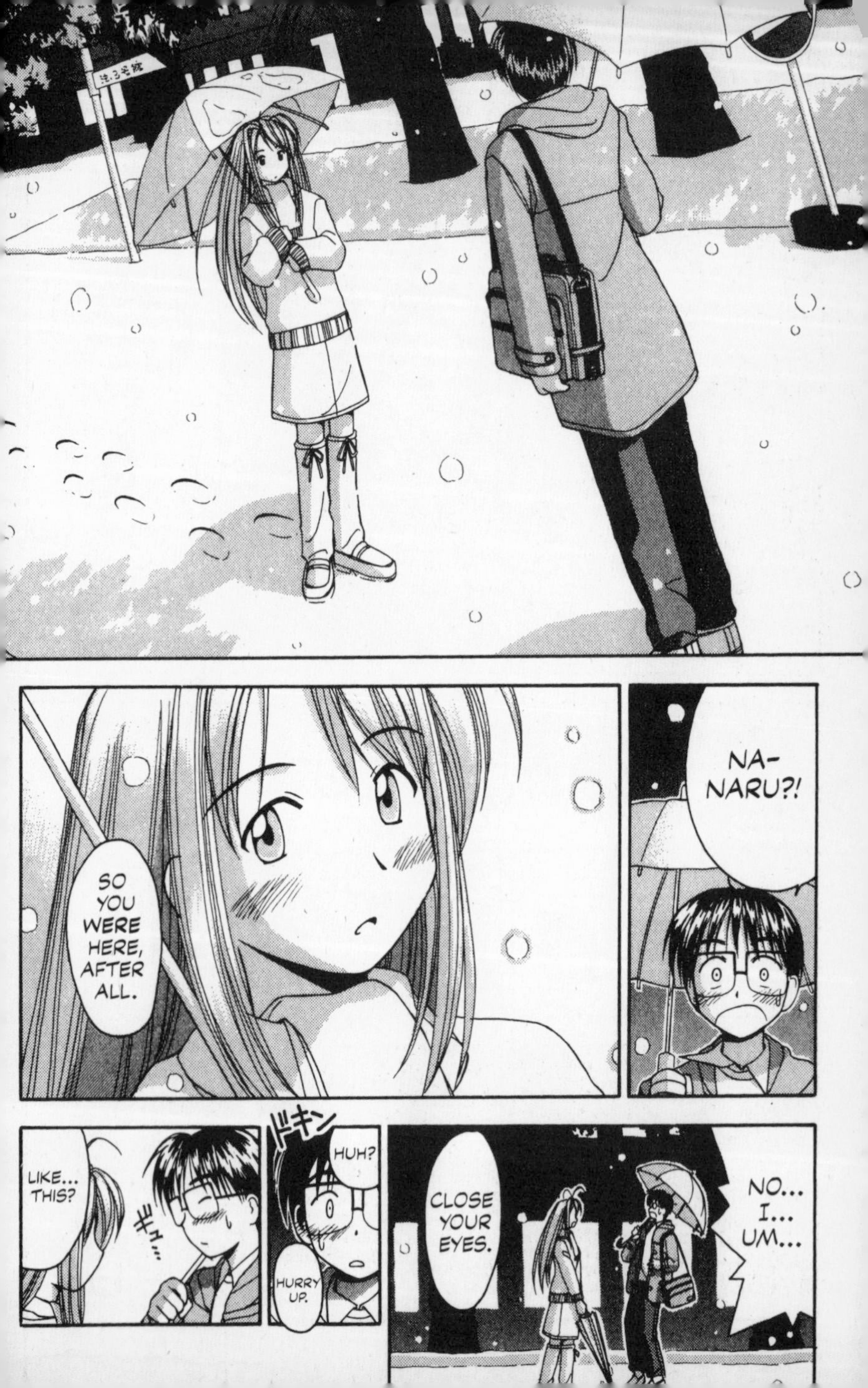
NA-NARU?!
SO YOU WERE HERE, AFTER ALL.
NO... I... UM...
CLOSE YOUR EYES.
HUH?
ドキン
HURRY UP.
LIKE... THIS?

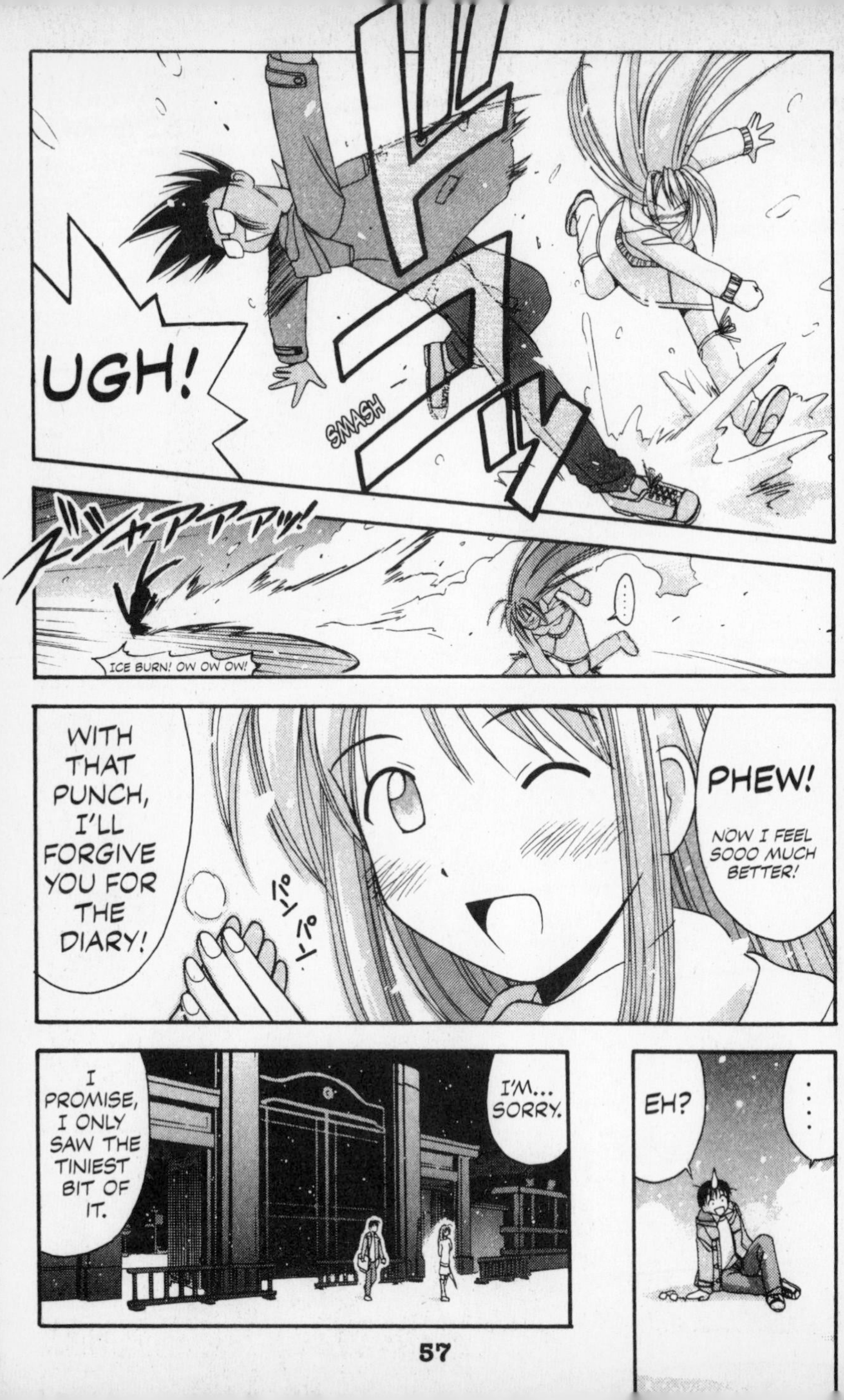
UGH!
SMASH
ICE BURN! OW OW OW!
...
PHEW!
NOW I FEEL SOOO MUCH BETTER!
WITH THAT PUNCH, I'LL FORGIVE YOU FOR THE DIARY!
...
EH?
I'M... SORRY.
I PROMISE, I ONLY SAW THE TINIEST BIT OF IT.

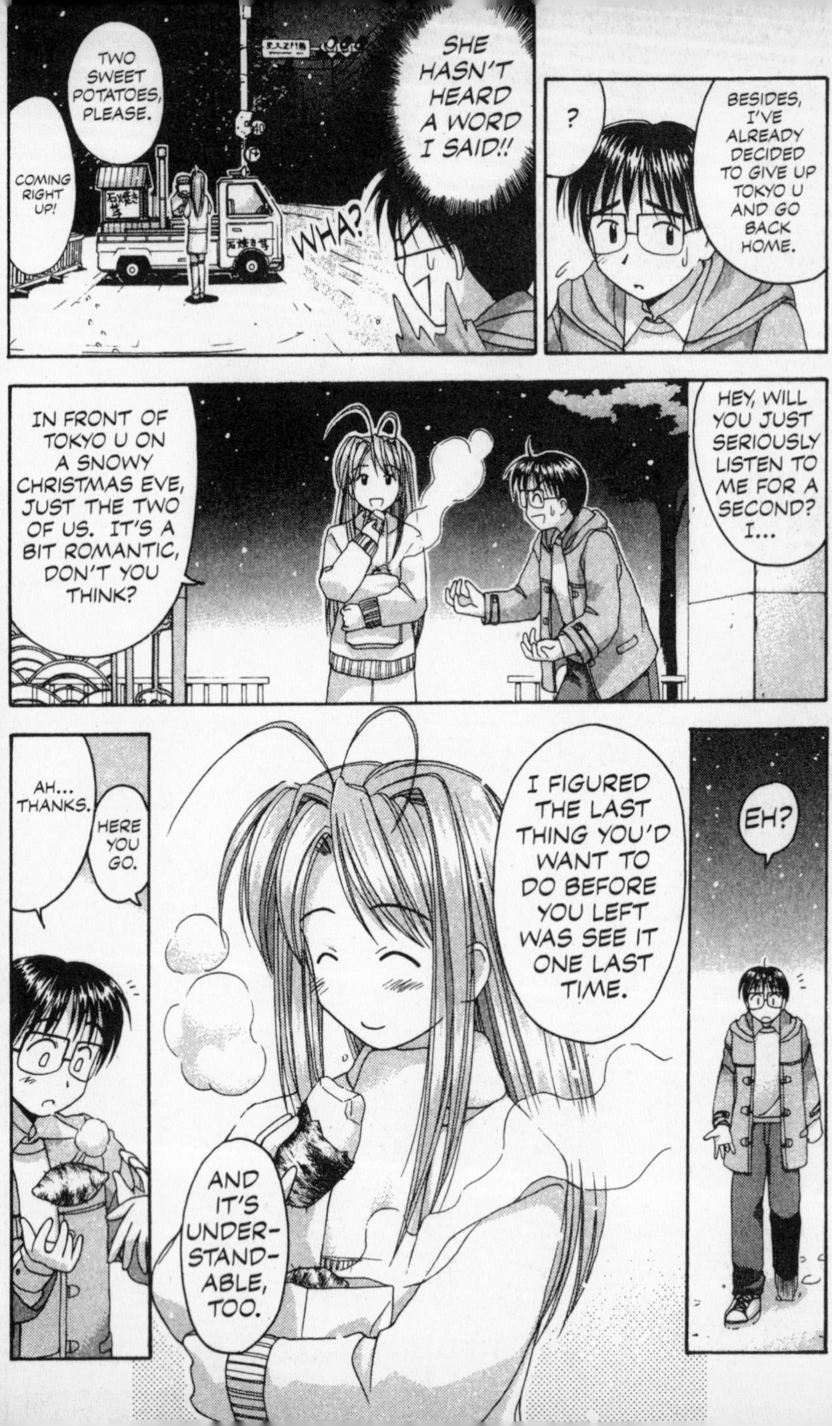
BESIDES, I'VE ALREADY DECIDED TO GIVE UP TOKYO U AND GO BACK HOME.
?
SHE HASN'T HEARD A WORD I SAID!!
WHA?
TWO SWEET POTATOES, PLEASE.
COMING RIGHT UP!
HEY, WILL YOU JUST SERIOUSLY LISTEN TO ME FOR A SECOND? I...
IN FRONT OF TOKYO U ON A SNOWY CHRISTMAS EVE, JUST THE TWO OF US. IT'S A BIT ROMANTIC, DON'T YOU THINK?
EH?
I FIGURED THE LAST THING YOU'D WANT TO DO BEFORE YOU LEFT WAS SEE IT ONE LAST TIME.
AND IT'S UNDER-STAND-ABLE, TOO.
HERE YOU GO.
AH... THANKS.

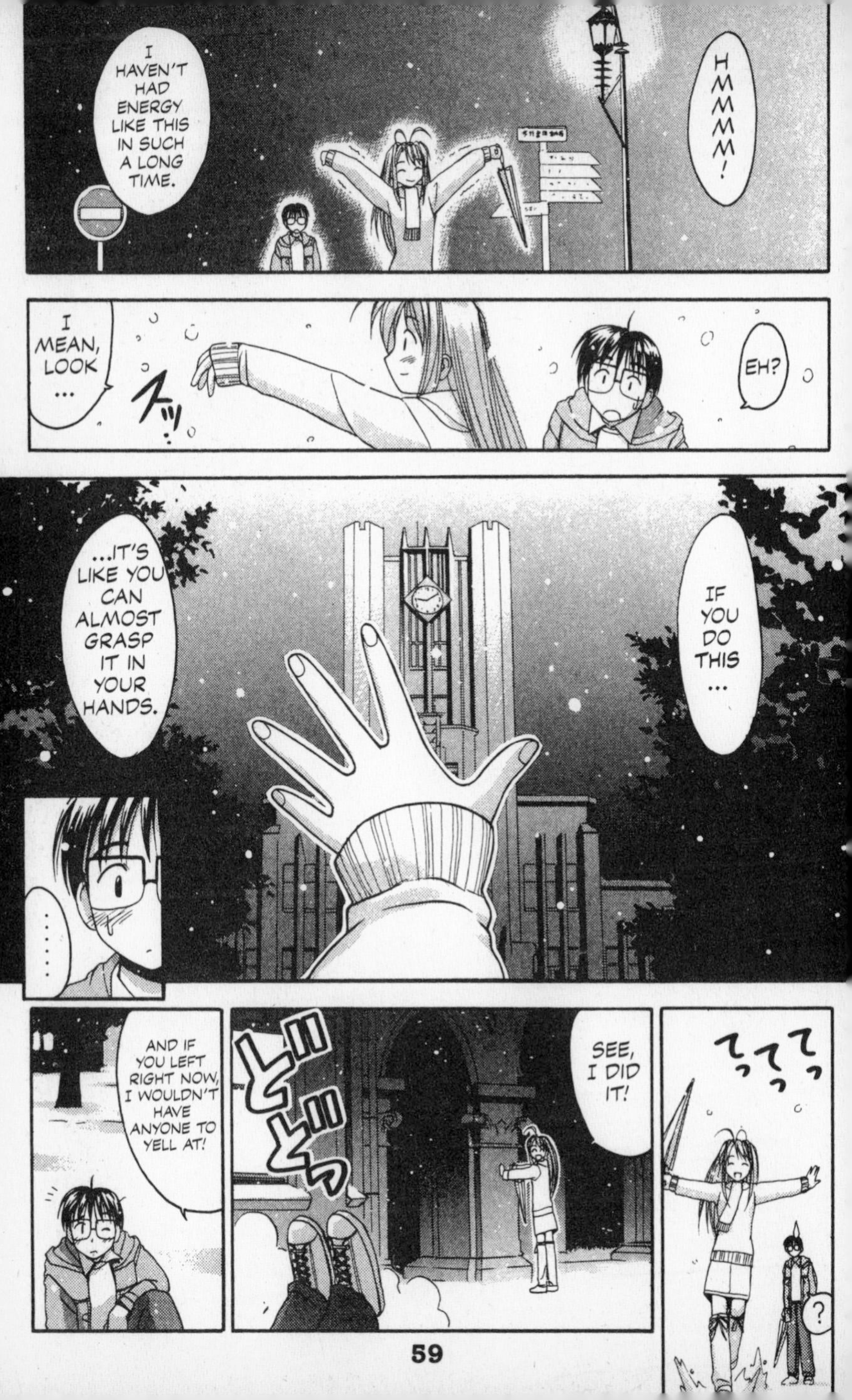
HMMMM!
I HAVEN'T HAD ENERGY LIKE THIS IN SUCH A LONG TIME.
EH?
I MEAN, LOOK ...
スッ
IF YOU DO THIS ...
...IT'S LIKE YOU CAN ALMOST GRASP IT IN YOUR HANDS.
......
?
SEE, I DID IT!
どどっ
AND IF YOU LEFT RIGHT NOW, I WOULDN'T HAVE ANYONE TO YELL AT!

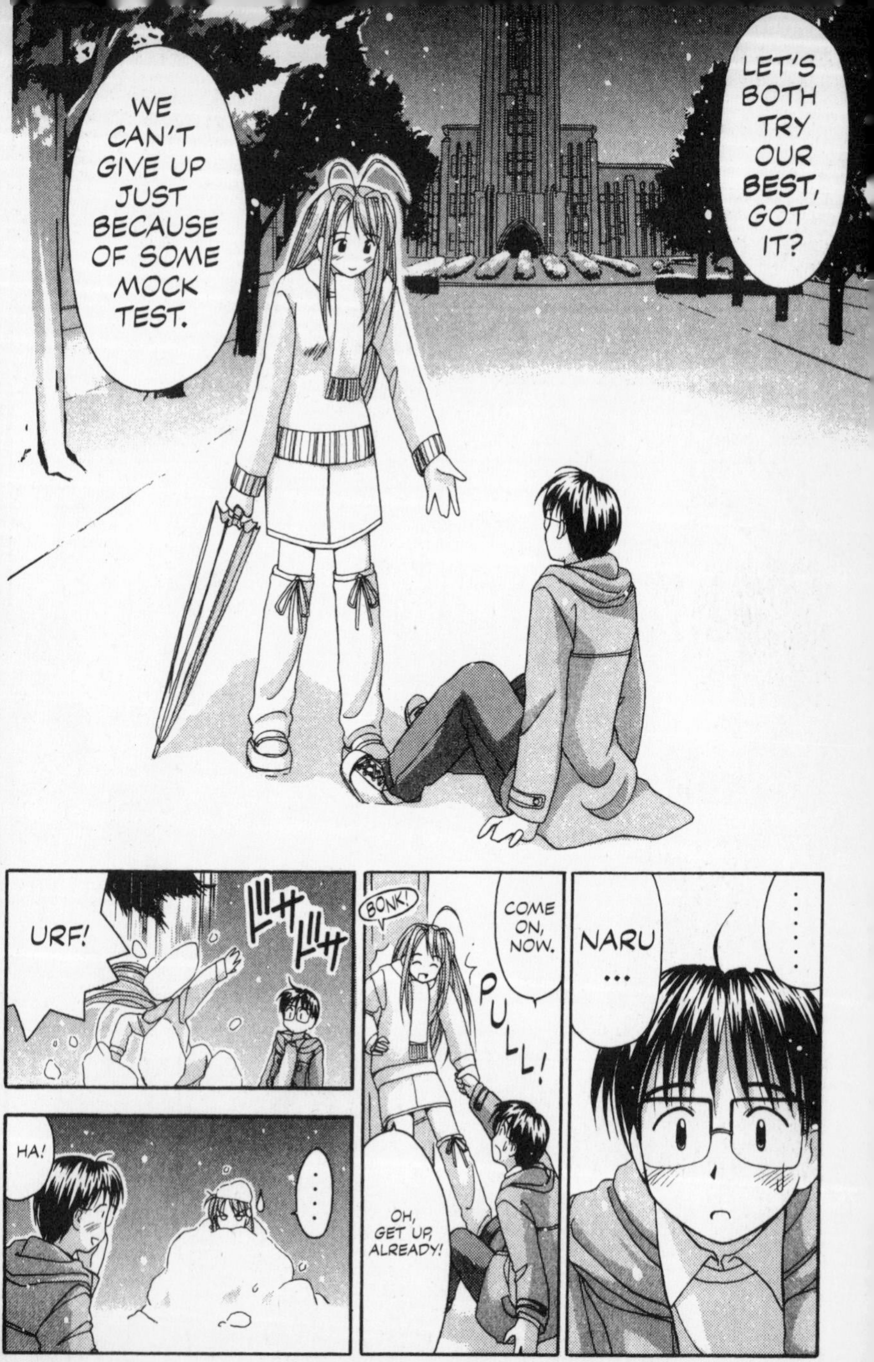
LET'S BOTH TRY OUR BEST, GOT IT?
WE CAN'T GIVE UP JUST BECAUSE OF SOME MOCK TEST.
......
NARU ...
COME ON, NOW.
BONK!
PULL!
OH, GET UP, ALREADY!
ドサドサ
URF!
....
HA!

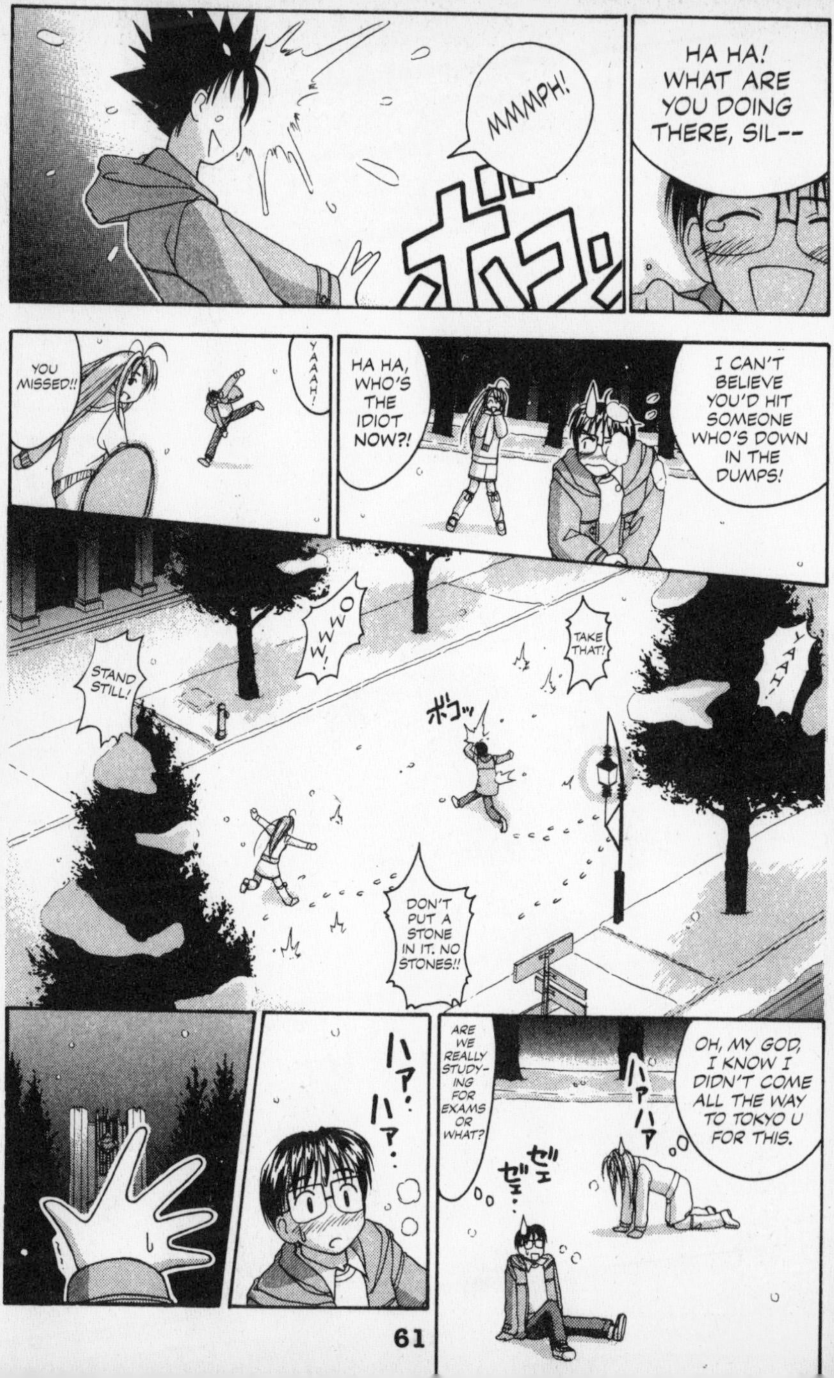
HA HA! WHAT ARE YOU DOING THERE, SIL--
MMMPH!
I CAN'T BELIEVE YOU'D HIT SOMEONE WHO'S DOWN IN THE DUMPS!
HA HA, WHO'S THE IDIOT NOW?!
YAAAH!
YOU MISSED!!
YAAAH!
TAKE THAT!
ボコッ
OWWW!
STAND STILL!
DON'T PUT A STONE IN IT. NO STONES!!
OH, MY GOD, I KNOW I DIDN'T COME ALL THE WAY TO TOKYO U FOR THIS.
ハァハァ
ゼェゼェ・・
ARE WE REALLY STUDYING FOR EXAMS OR WHAT?
ハァ・・ハァ・・

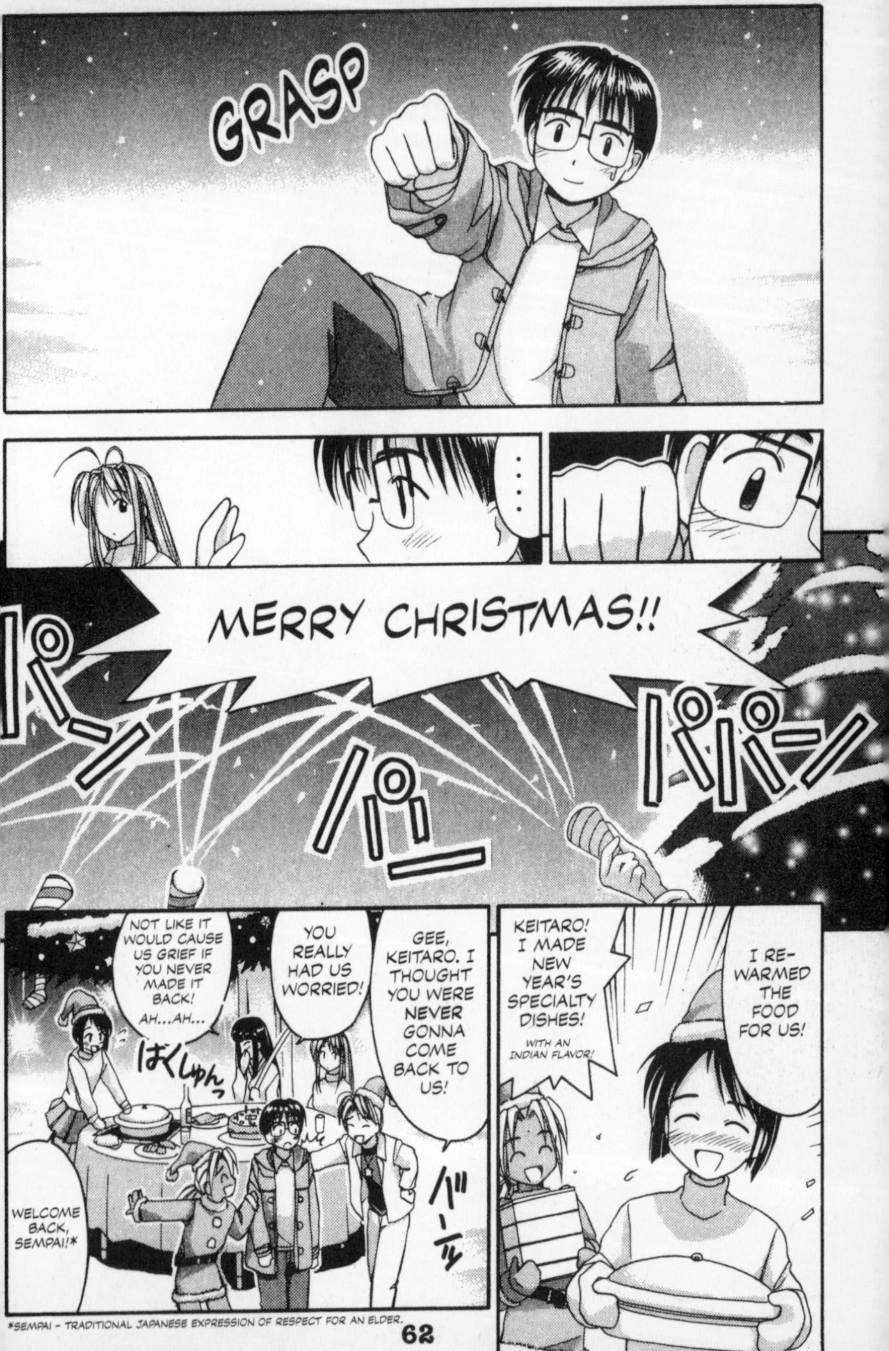
GRASP
...
MERRY CHRISTMAS!!
パパーン
パー
パーン
I RE-WARMED THE FOOD FOR US!
KEITARO! I MADE NEW YEAR'S SPECIALTY DISHES!
WITH AN INDIAN FLAVOR!
GEE, KEITARO. I THOUGHT YOU WERE NEVER GONNA COME BACK TO US!
YOU REALLY HAD US WORRIED!
NOT LIKE IT WOULD CAUSE US GRIEF IF YOU NEVER MADE IT BACK!
AH...AH...
ばくしゅんっ
WELCOME BACK, SEMPAI!*

*SEMPAI - TRADITIONAL JAPANESE EXPRESSION OF RESPECT FOR AN ELDER.

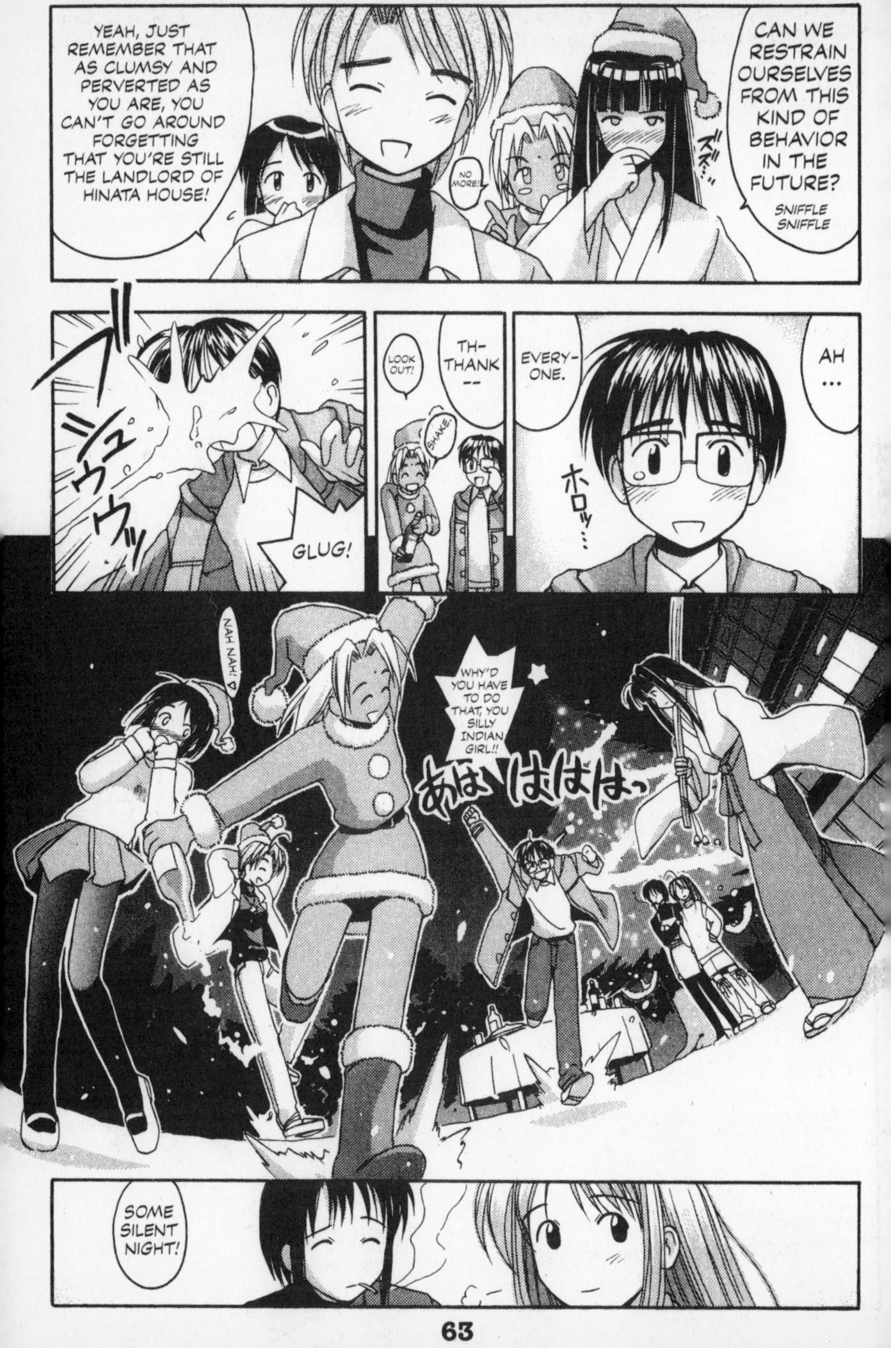
CAN WE RESTRAIN OURSELVES FROM THIS KIND OF BEHAVIOR IN THE FUTURE?
SNIFFLE SNIFFLE
ズズ…
NO MORE!
YEAH, JUST REMEMBER THAT AS CLUMSY AND PERVERTED AS YOU ARE, YOU CAN'T GO AROUND FORGETTING THAT YOU'RE STILL THE LANDLORD OF HINATA HOUSE!
AH ...
EVERY- ONE.
ホロッ…
TH- THANK --
SHAKE.
LOOK OUT!
ブ
シュウウウッ
GLUG!
WHY'D YOU HAVE TO DO THAT, YOU SILLY INDIAN GIRL!!
あは はははっ
NAH NAH! ♡
SOME SILENT NIGHT!

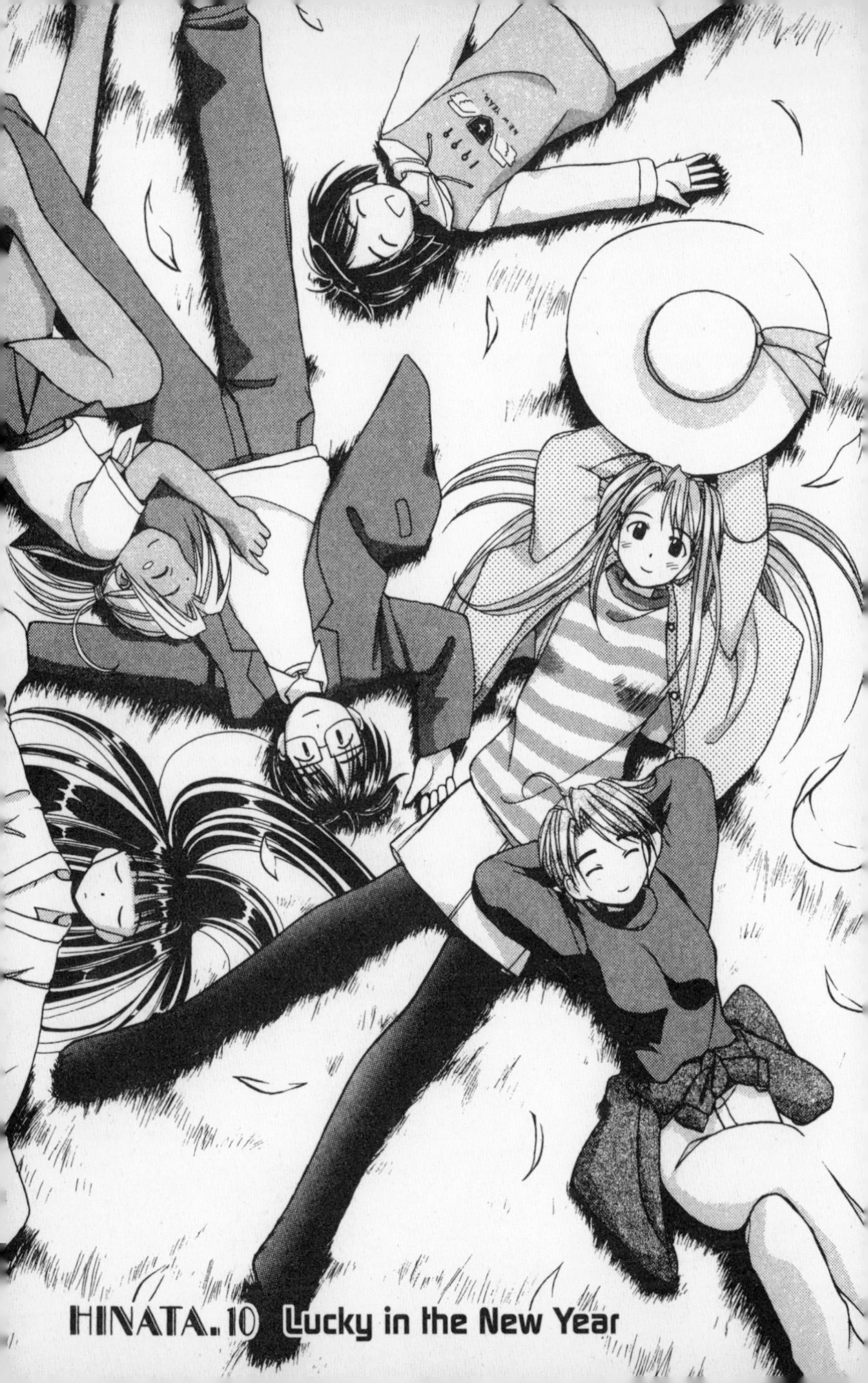

HINATA. 10 Lucky in the New Year

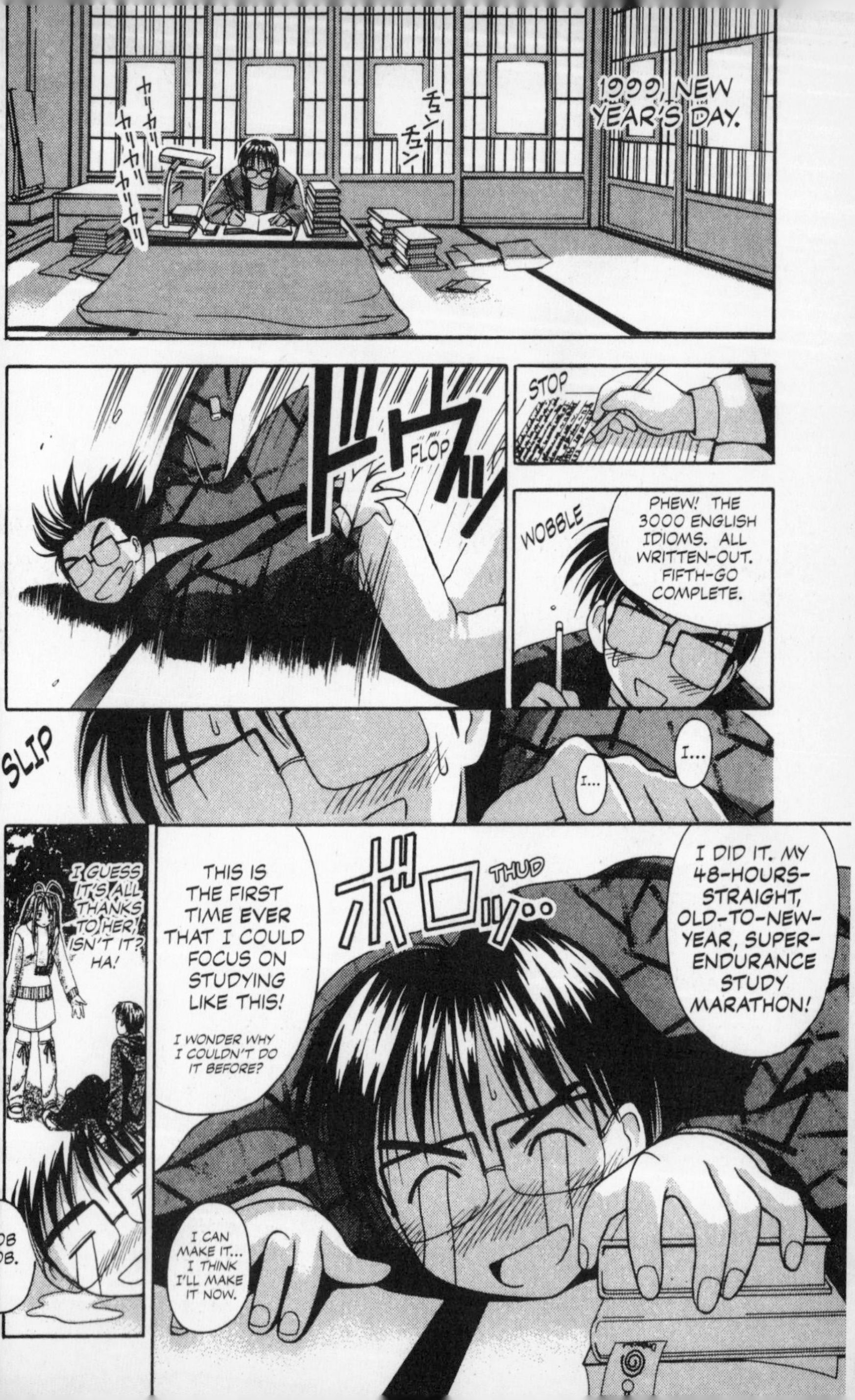

1999, NEW YEAR'S DAY.
チュン
チュン
STOP
WOBBLE
PHEW! THE 3000 ENGLISH IDIOMS. ALL WRITTEN-OUT. FIFTH-GO COMPLETE.
FLOP
I...
I...
SLIP
I DID IT. MY 48-HOURS-STRAIGHT, OLD-TO-NEW-YEAR, SUPER-ENDURANCE STUDY MARATHON!
THUD
THIS IS THE FIRST TIME EVER THAT I COULD FOCUS ON STUDYING LIKE THIS!
I WONDER WHY I COULDN'T DO IT BEFORE?
I CAN MAKE IT... I THINK I'LL MAKE IT NOW.
I GUESS IT'S ALL THANKS TO HER, ISN'T IT? HA!
OB
OB.

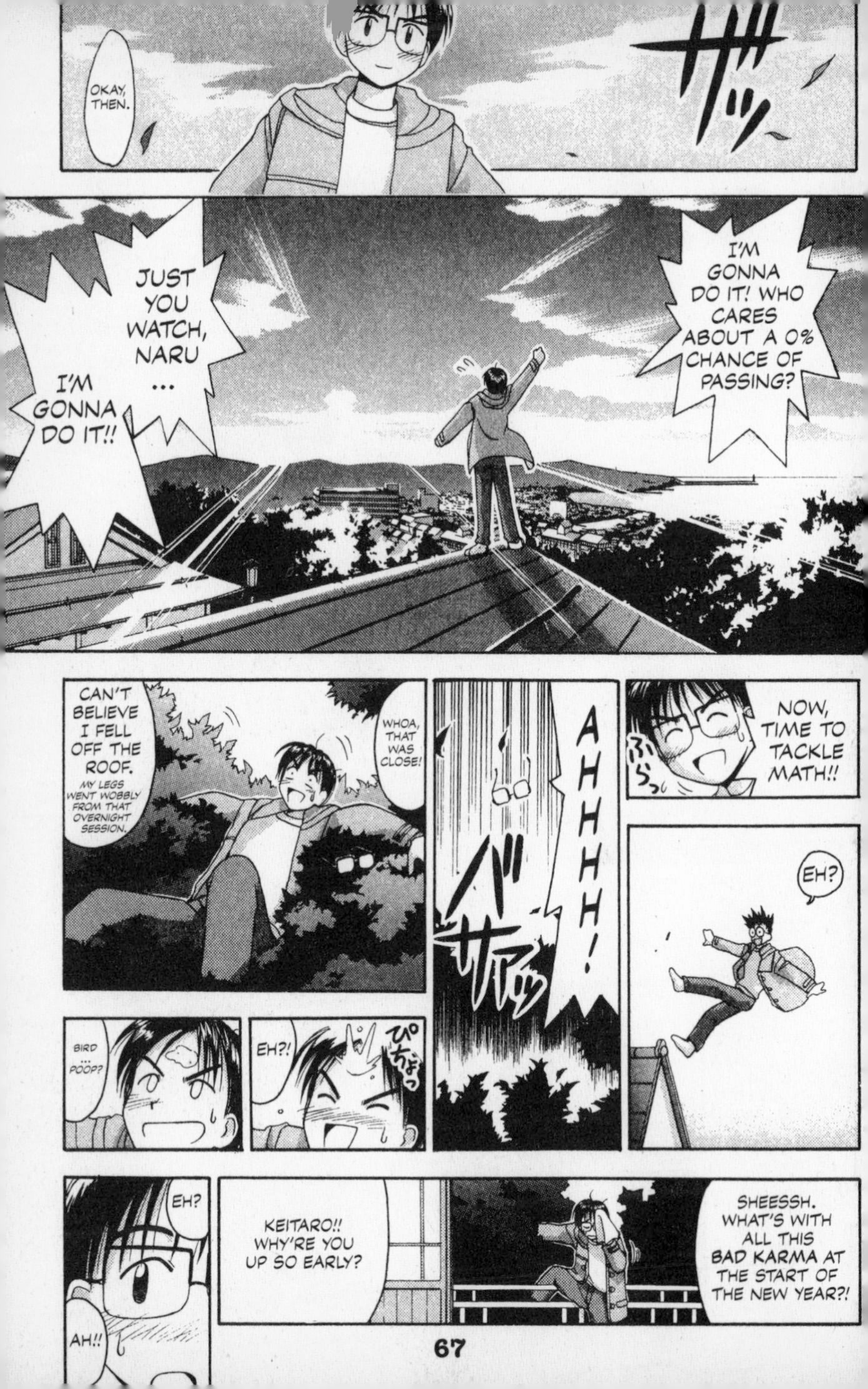
ザッ
OKAY, THEN.
I'M GONNA DO IT! WHO CARES ABOUT A 0% CHANCE OF PASSING?
JUST YOU WATCH, NARU ...
I'M GONNA DO IT!!
ふらっ
NOW, TIME TO TACKLE MATH!!
EH?
AHHHHH!
バサァッ
WHOA, THAT WAS CLOSE!
CAN'T BELIEVE I FELL OFF THE ROOF.
MY LEGS WENT WOBBLY FROM THAT OVERNIGHT SESSION.
ぴちょっ
EH?!
BIRD ... POOP?
SHEESSH. WHAT'S WITH ALL THIS BAD KARMA AT THE START OF THE NEW YEAR?!
KEITARO!! WHY'RE YOU UP SO EARLY?
EH?
AH!!

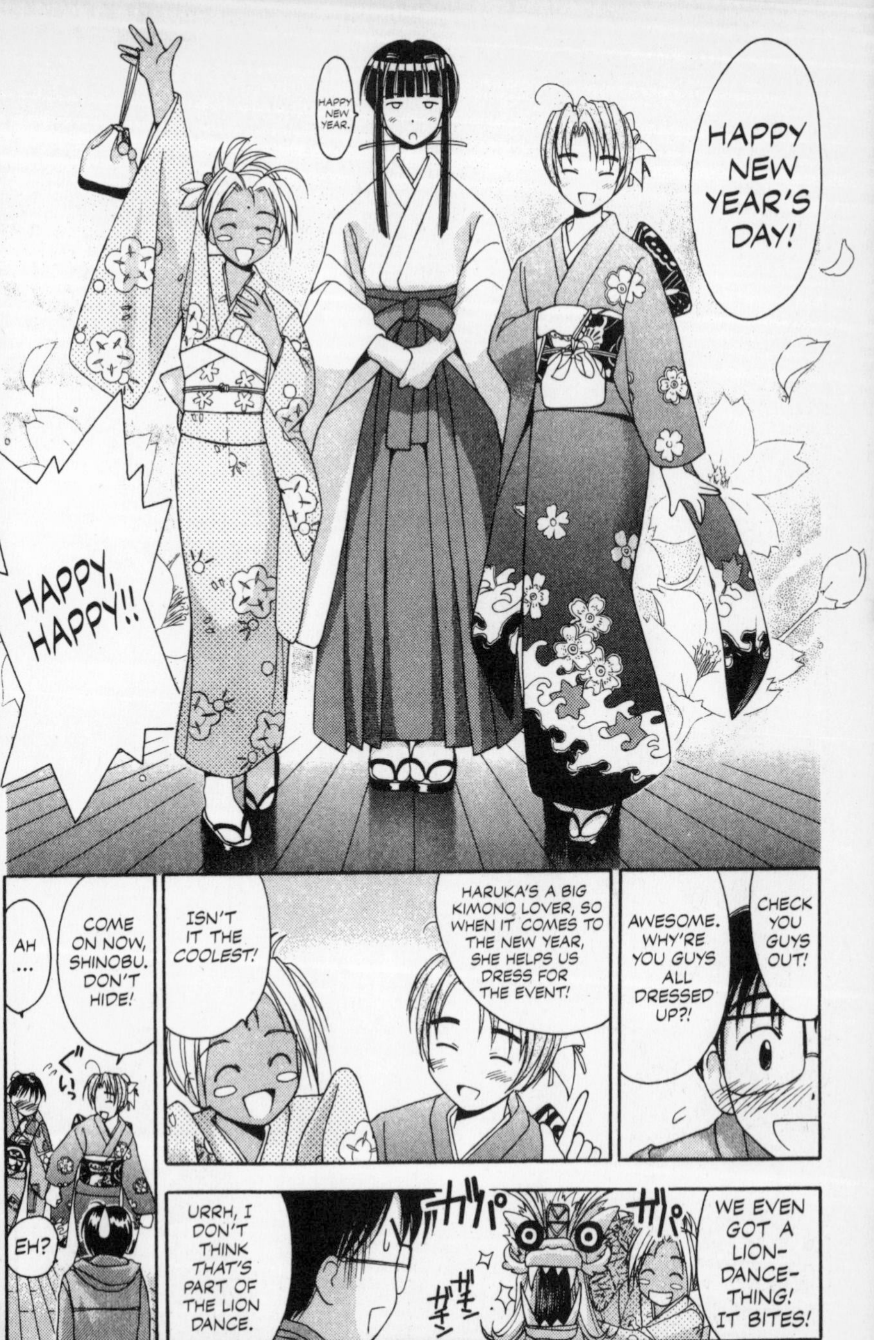
HAPPY NEW YEAR'S DAY!
HAPPY NEW YEAR.
HAPPY, HAPPY!!
CHECK YOU GUYS OUT!
AWESOME. WHY'RE YOU GUYS ALL DRESSED UP?!
HARUKA'S A BIG KIMONO LOVER, SO WHEN IT COMES TO THE NEW YEAR, SHE HELPS US DRESS FOR THE EVENT!
ISN'T IT THE COOLEST!
WE EVEN GOT A LION-DANCE-THING! IT BITES!
ガパ
ガパ
URRH, I DON'T THINK THAT'S PART OF THE LION DANCE.
COME ON NOW, SHINOBU. DON'T HIDE!
AH ...
ぐいっ
EH?

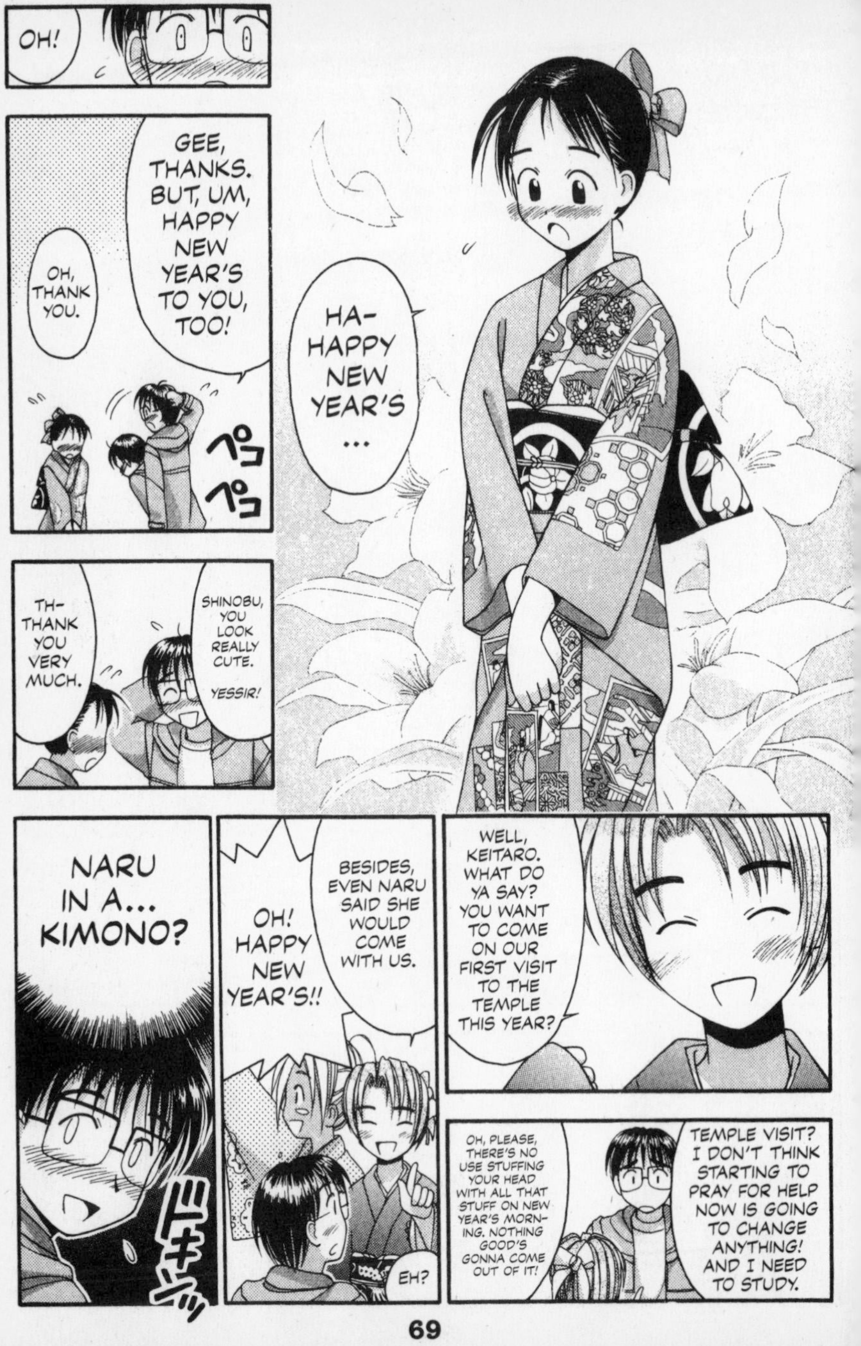
HA-HAPPY NEW YEAR'S ...
OH!
GEE, THANKS. BUT, UM, HAPPY NEW YEAR'S TO YOU, TOO!
OH, THANK YOU.
ペコ ペコ
SHINOBU, YOU LOOK REALLY CUTE.
YESSIR!
TH-THANK YOU VERY MUCH.
WELL, KEITARO. WHAT DO YA SAY? YOU WANT TO COME ON OUR FIRST VISIT TO THE TEMPLE THIS YEAR?
TEMPLE VISIT? I DON'T THINK STARTING TO PRAY FOR HELP NOW IS GOING TO CHANGE ANYTHING! AND I NEED TO STUDY.
OH, PLEASE, THERE'S NO USE STUFFING YOUR HEAD WITH ALL THAT STUFF ON NEW YEAR'S MORNING. NOTHING GOOD'S GONNA COME OUT OF IT!
BESIDES, EVEN NARU SAID SHE WOULD COME WITH US.
OH! HAPPY NEW YEAR'S!!
EH?
NARU IN A... KIMONO?
ドキッ

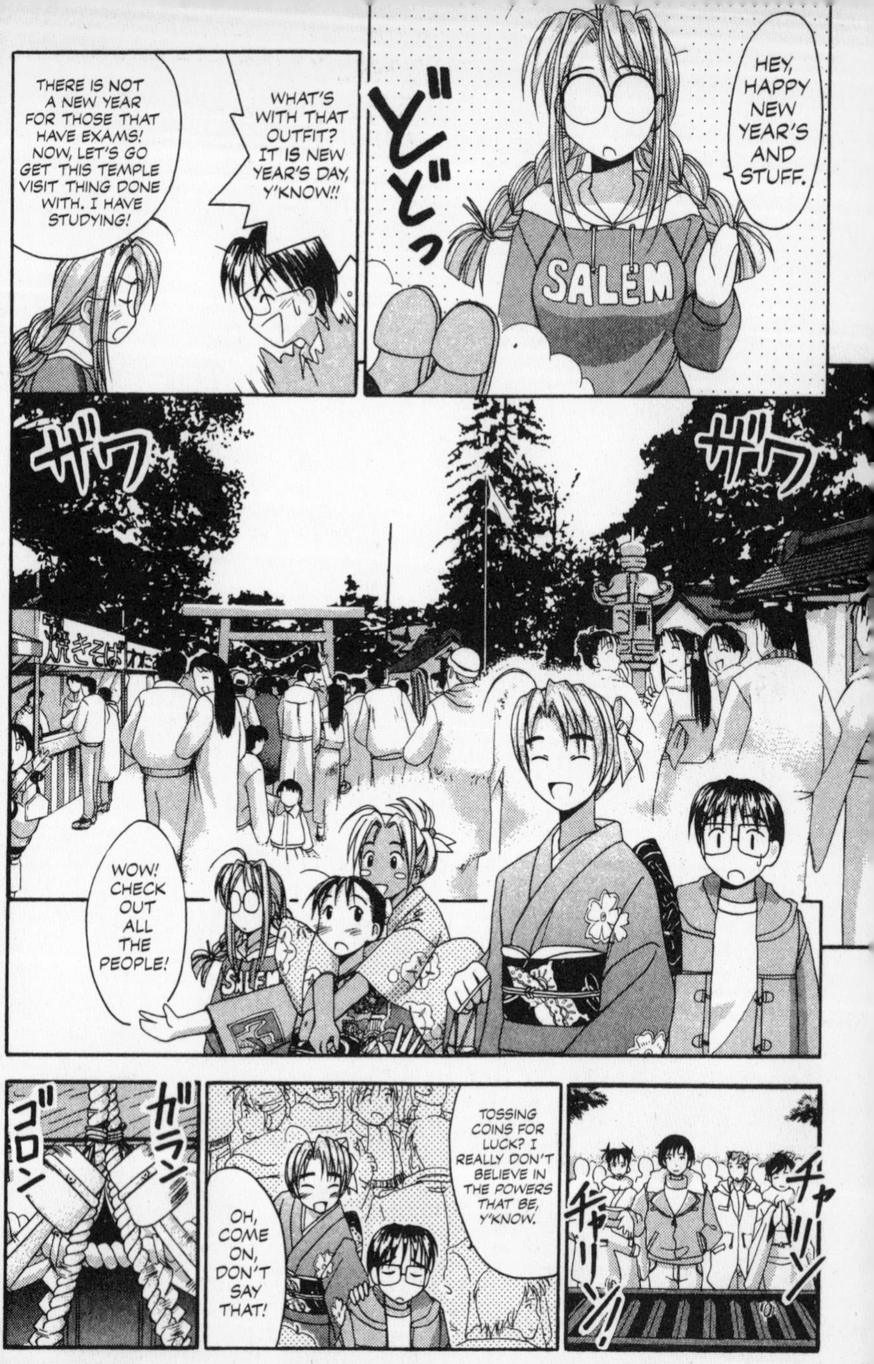
どどっ
HEY, HAPPY NEW YEAR'S AND STUFF.
WHAT'S WITH THAT OUTFIT? IT IS NEW YEAR'S DAY, Y'KNOW!!
THERE IS NOT A NEW YEAR FOR THOSE THAT HAVE EXAMS! NOW, LET'S GO GET THIS TEMPLE VISIT THING DONE WITH. I HAVE STUDYING!
ザワ
ザワ
焼きそば
WOW! CHECK OUT ALL THE PEOPLE!
チャリーン
チャリーン
TOSSING COINS FOR LUCK? I REALLY DON'T BELIEVE IN THE POWERS THAT BE, Y'KNOW.
OH, COME ON, DON'T SAY THAT!
ガラン
ゴロン

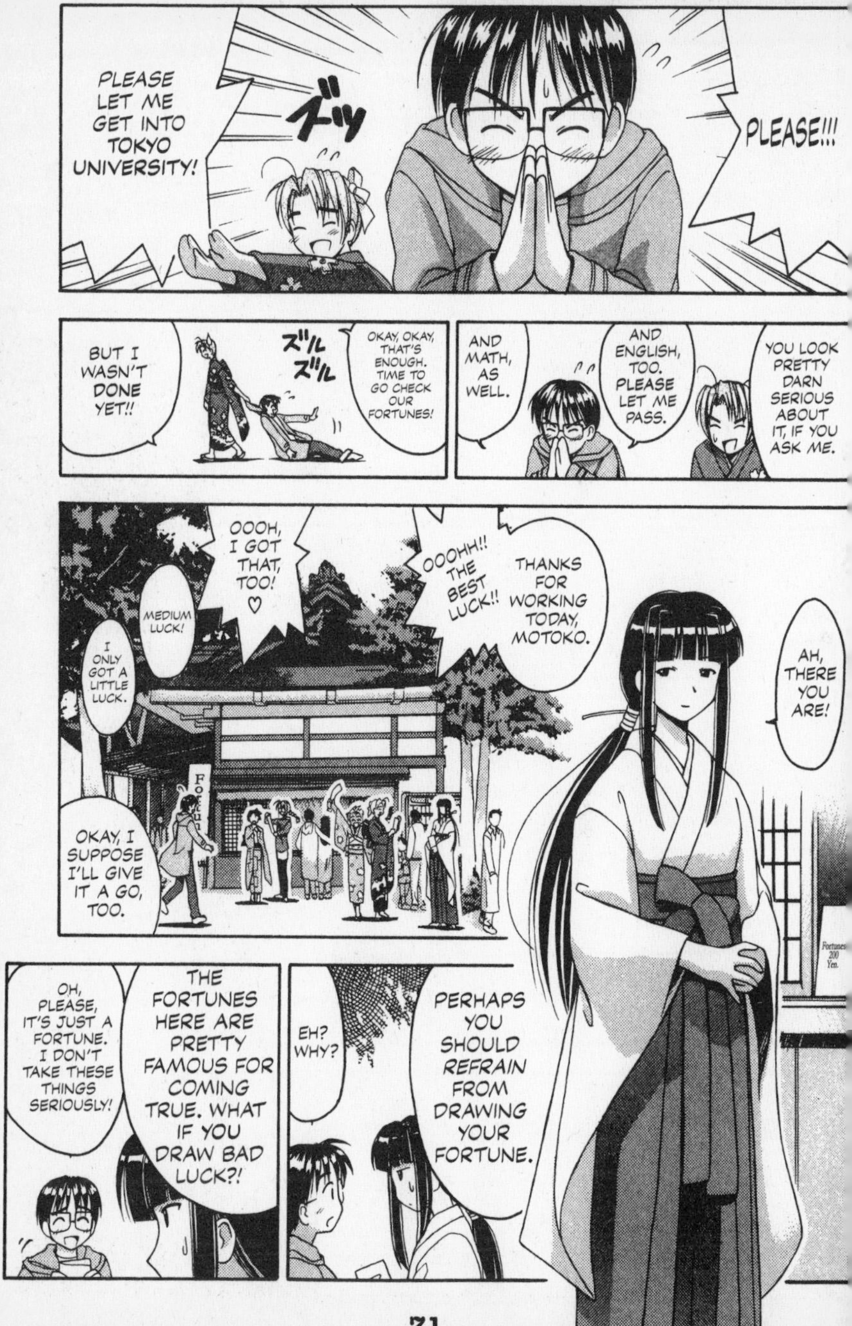
PLEASE!!!
ズッ
PLEASE LET ME GET INTO TOKYO UNIVERSITY!
YOU LOOK PRETTY DARN SERIOUS ABOUT IT, IF YOU ASK ME.
AND ENGLISH, TOO. PLEASE LET ME PASS.
AND MATH, AS WELL.
OKAY, OKAY, THAT'S ENOUGH. TIME TO GO CHECK OUR FORTUNES!
ズル ズル
BUT I WASN'T DONE YET!!
AH, THERE YOU ARE!
THANKS FOR WORKING TODAY, MOTOKO.
OOOHH!! THE BEST LUCK!!
OOOH, I GOT THAT, TOO! ♡
MEDIUM LUCK!
I ONLY GOT A LITTLE LUCK.
OKAY, I SUPPOSE I'LL GIVE IT A GO, TOO.
Fortunes 200 Yen.
PERHAPS YOU SHOULD REFRAIN FROM DRAWING YOUR FORTUNE.
EH? WHY?
THE FORTUNES HERE ARE PRETTY FAMOUS FOR COMING TRUE. WHAT IF YOU DRAW BAD LUCK?!
OH, PLEASE, IT'S JUST A FORTUNE. I DON'T TAKE THESE THINGS SERIOUSLY!

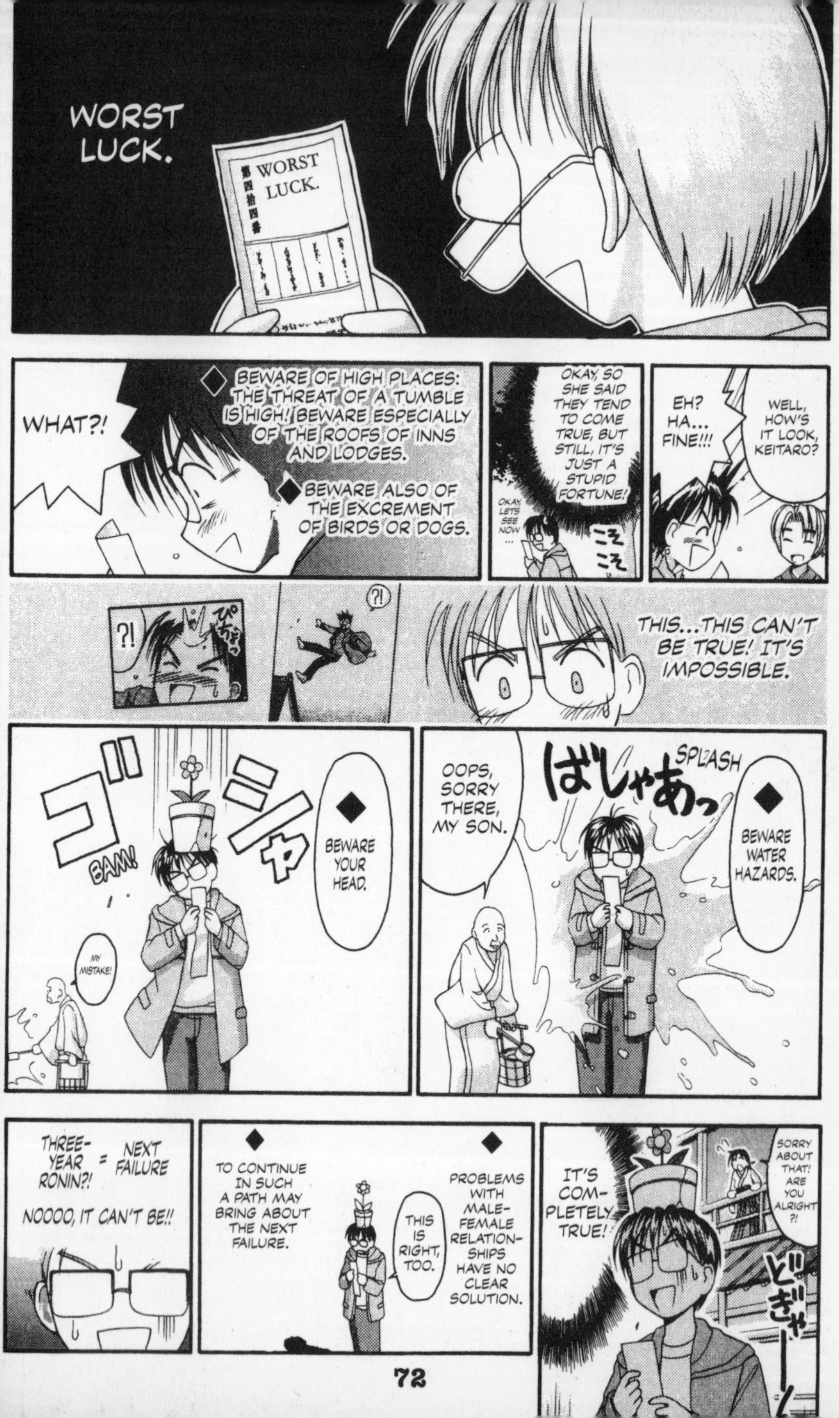
WORST LUCK.
第四拾四番
WORST LUCK.
WELL, HOW'S IT LOOK, KEITARO?
EH? HA... FINE!!!
OKAY, SO SHE SAID THEY TEND TO COME TRUE, BUT STILL, IT'S JUST A STUPID FORTUNE!
こそこそ
OKAY, LETS SEE NOW ...
BEWARE OF HIGH PLACES: THE THREAT OF A TUMBLE IS HIGH! BEWARE ESPECIALLY OF THE ROOFS OF INNS AND LODGES.
BEWARE ALSO OF THE EXCREMENT OF BIRDS OR DOGS.
WHAT?!
THIS...THIS CAN'T BE TRUE! IT'S IMPOSSIBLE.
?!
?!
BEWARE WATER HAZARDS.
ばしゃあっ
SPLASH
OOPS, SORRY THERE, MY SON.
BEWARE YOUR HEAD.
ゴシャ
BAM!
MY MISTAKE!
SORRY ABOUT THAT! ARE YOU ALRIGHT ?!
IT'S COM-PLETELY TRUE!
どぎゃー!
PROBLEMS WITH MALE-FEMALE RELATION-SHIPS HAVE NO CLEAR SOLUTION.
TO CONTINUE IN SUCH A PATH MAY BRING ABOUT THE NEXT FAILURE.
THIS IS RIGHT, TOO.
THREE-YEAR RONIN?! = NEXT FAILURE
NOOOO, IT CAN'T BE!!

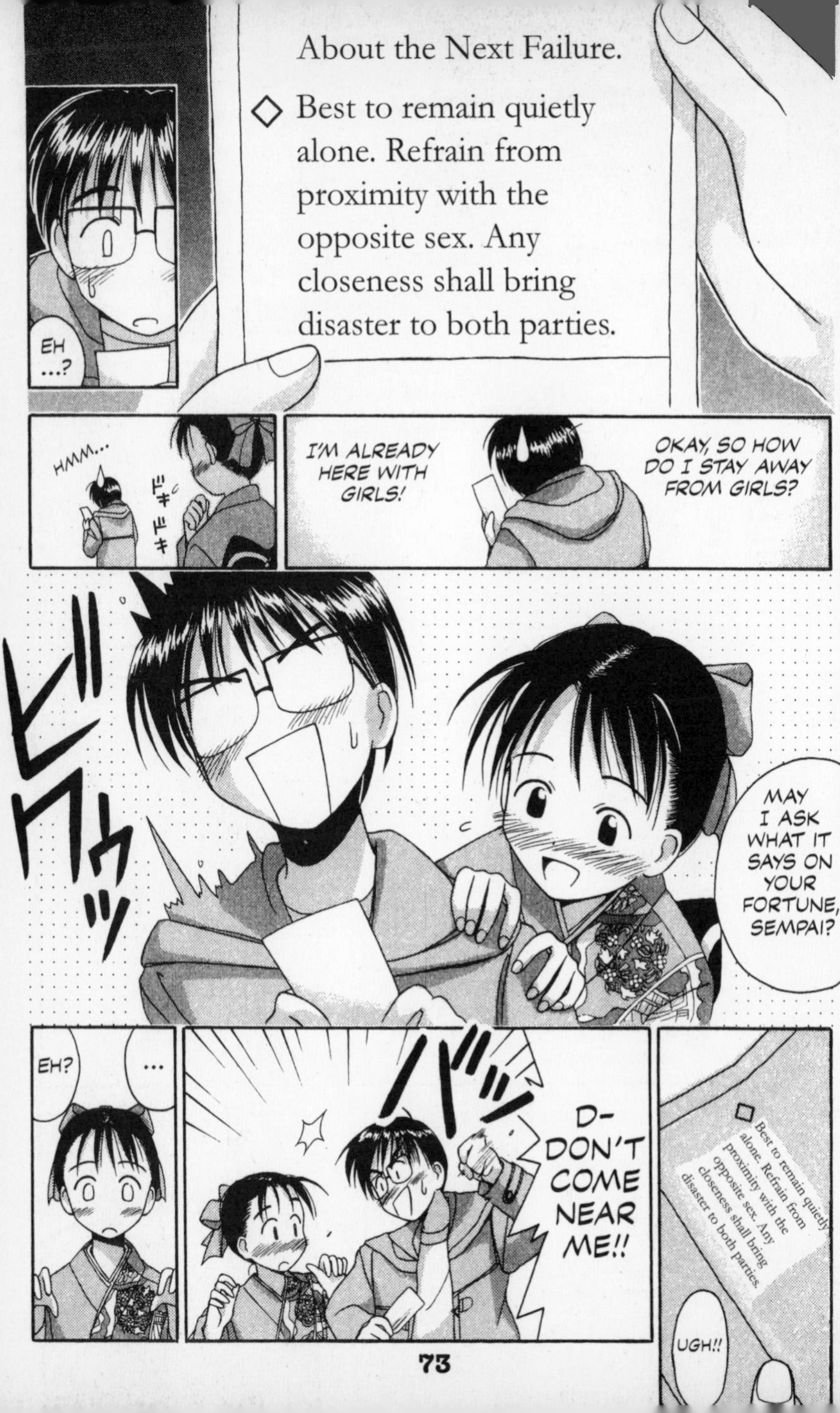
About the Next Failure.
◇ Best to remain quietly alone. Refrain from proximity with the opposite sex. Any closeness shall bring disaster to both parties.
EH ...?
OKAY, SO HOW DO I STAY AWAY FROM GIRLS?
I'M ALREADY HERE WITH GIRLS!
HMM...
ドキ ドキ
MAY I ASK WHAT IT SAYS ON YOUR FORTUNE, SEMPAI?
ビクゥッ
◇ Best to remain quietly alone. Refrain from proximity with the opposite sex. Any closeness shall bring disaster to both parties.
UGH!!
バッ
D- DON'T COME NEAR ME!!
...
EH?

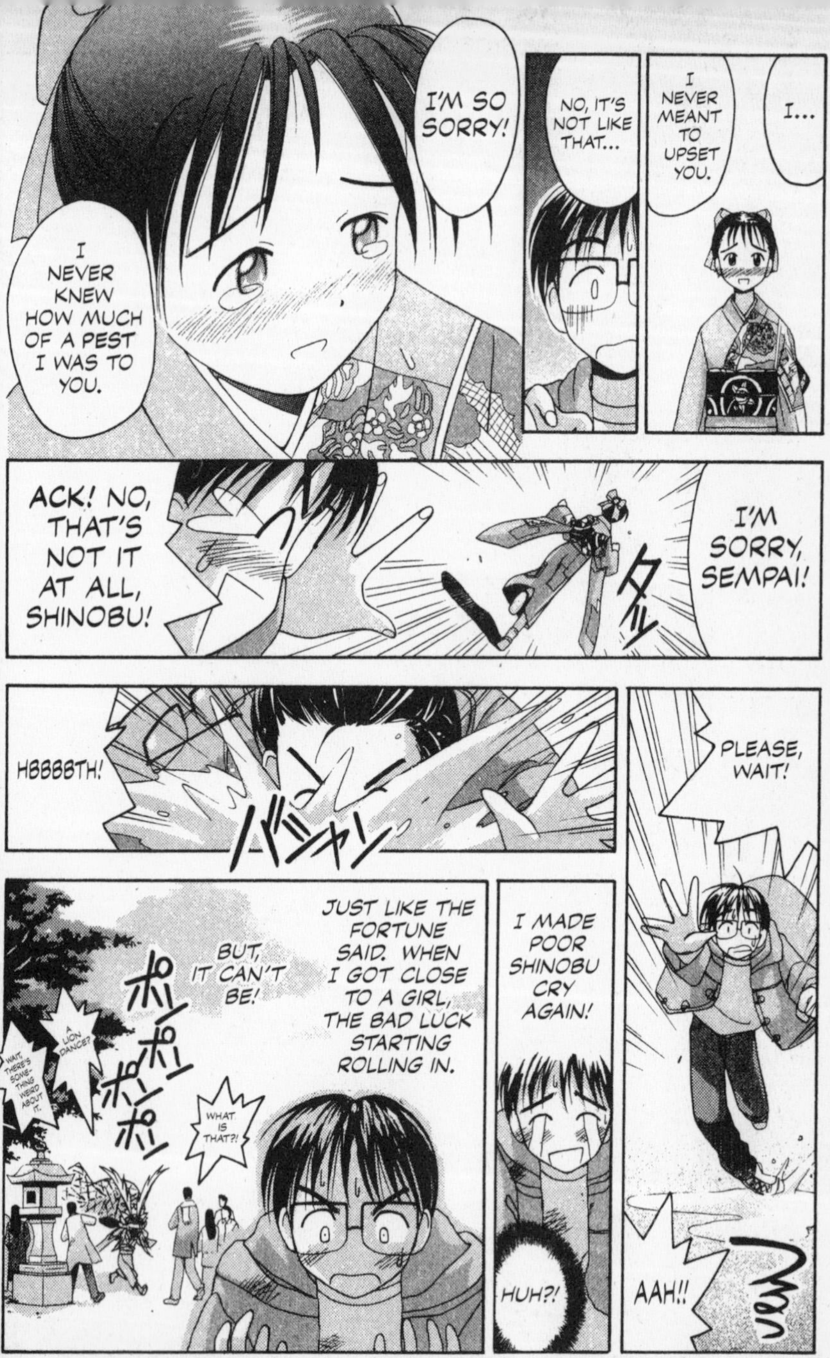
I...
I NEVER MEANT TO UPSET YOU.
NO, IT'S NOT LIKE THAT...
I'M SO SORRY!
I NEVER KNEW HOW MUCH OF A PEST I WAS TO YOU.
I'M SORRY, SEMPAI!
ACK! NO, THAT'S NOT IT AT ALL, SHINOBU!
PLEASE, WAIT!
AAH!!
HBBBBTH!
I MADE POOR SHINOBU CRY AGAIN!
HUH?!
JUST LIKE THE FORTUNE SAID. WHEN I GOT CLOSE TO A GIRL, THE BAD LUCK STARTING ROLLING IN.
BUT, IT CAN'T BE!
A LION DANCE?
WAIT, THERE'S SOME-THING WEIRD ABOUT IT.
WHAT IS THAT?!

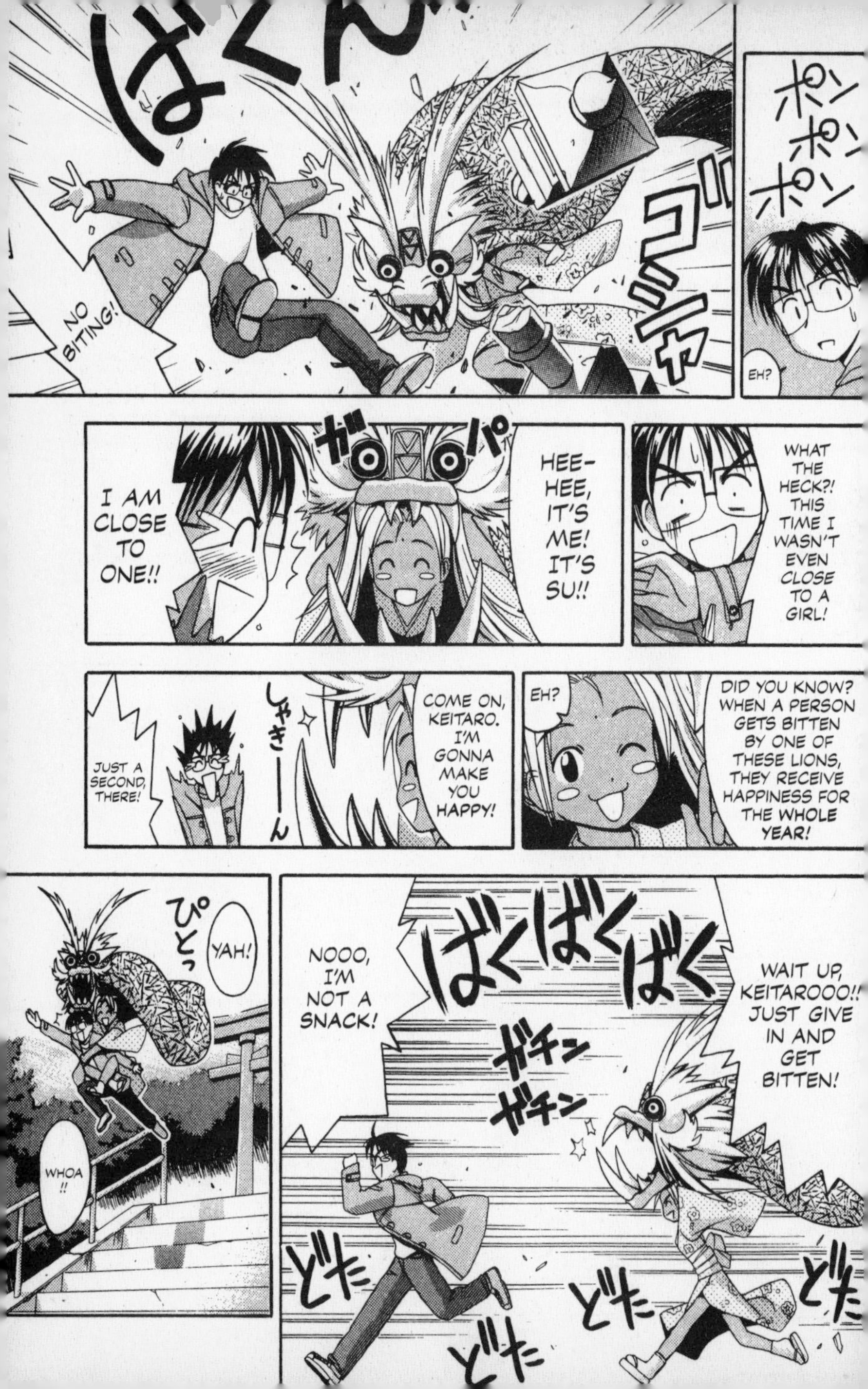
ポンポンポン
EH?
ばくん
ゴシャ
NO BITING!
WHAT THE HECK?! THIS TIME I WASN'T EVEN CLOSE TO A GIRL!
がパ
HEE-HEE, IT'S ME! IT'S SU!!
I AM CLOSE TO ONE!!
DID YOU KNOW? WHEN A PERSON GETS BITTEN BY ONE OF THESE LIONS, THEY RECEIVE HAPPINESS FOR THE WHOLE YEAR!
EH?
COME ON, KEITARO. I'M GONNA MAKE YOU HAPPY!
しゃきーーん
JUST A SECOND, THERE!
WAIT UP, KEITAROOO!! JUST GIVE IN AND GET BITTEN!
ばくばくばく
NOOO, I'M NOT A SNACK!
ガチン
ガチン
どた
どた
どた
どた
ぴとっ
YAH!
WHOA!!

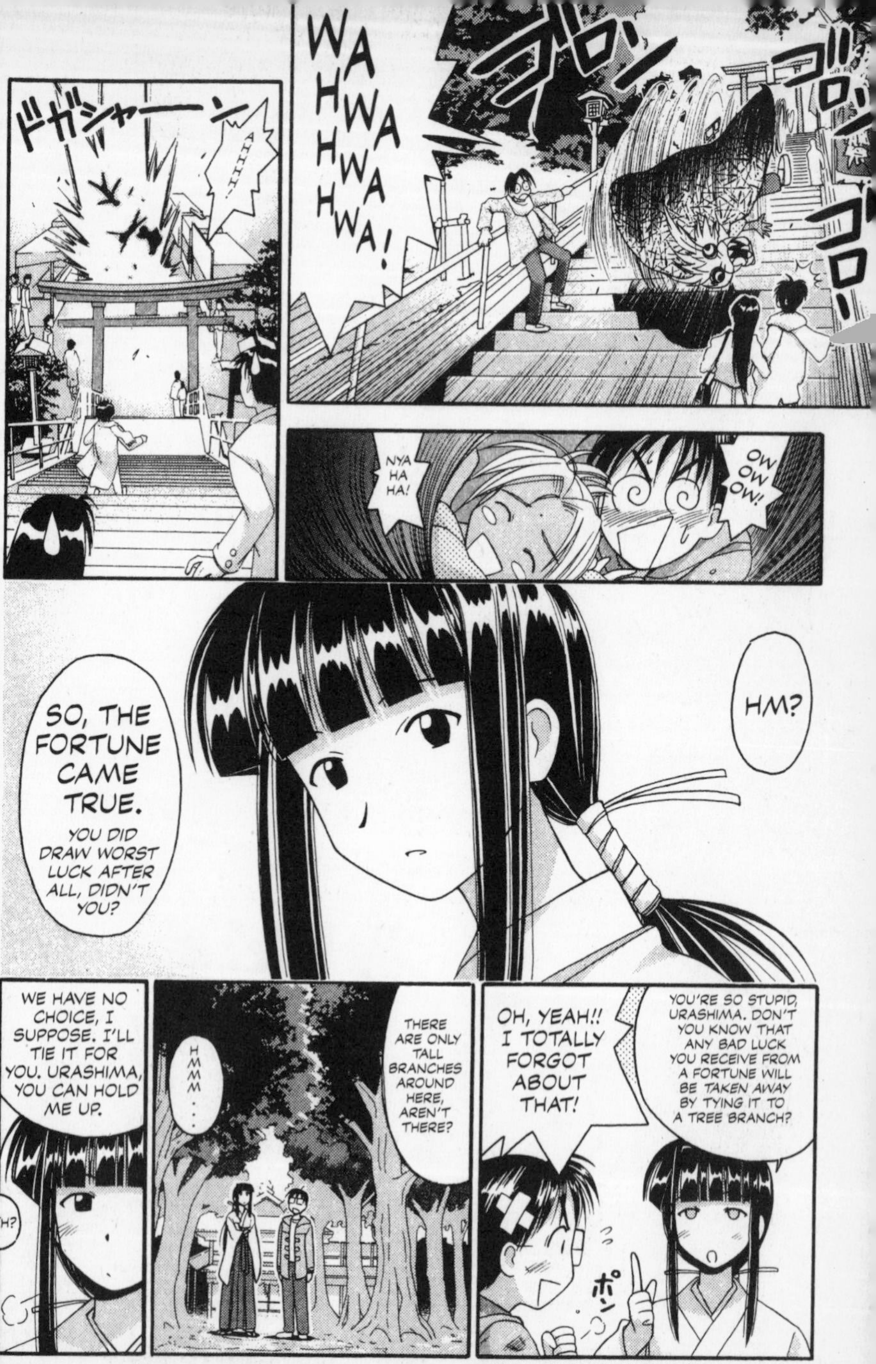
ゴロン
WAHWAHWAHWAHWA!
ゴロゴロ
NYA HA HA!
OW OW OW!
ドガシャーーン
AHHH!
HM?
SO, THE FORTUNE CAME TRUE.
YOU DID DRAW WORST LUCK AFTER ALL, DIDN'T YOU?
YOU'RE SO STUPID, URASHIMA. DON'T YOU KNOW THAT ANY BAD LUCK YOU RECEIVE FROM A FORTUNE WILL BE TAKEN AWAY BY TYING IT TO A TREE BRANCH?
OH, YEAH!! I TOTALLY FORGOT ABOUT THAT!
ポン
THERE ARE ONLY TALL BRANCHES AROUND HERE, AREN'T THERE?
HMMM...
WE HAVE NO CHOICE, I SUPPOSE. I'LL TIE IT FOR YOU. URASHIMA, YOU CAN HOLD ME UP.
EH?

DON'T REALLY DO THIS. THE TEMPLE KEEPERS WILL GET MAD!

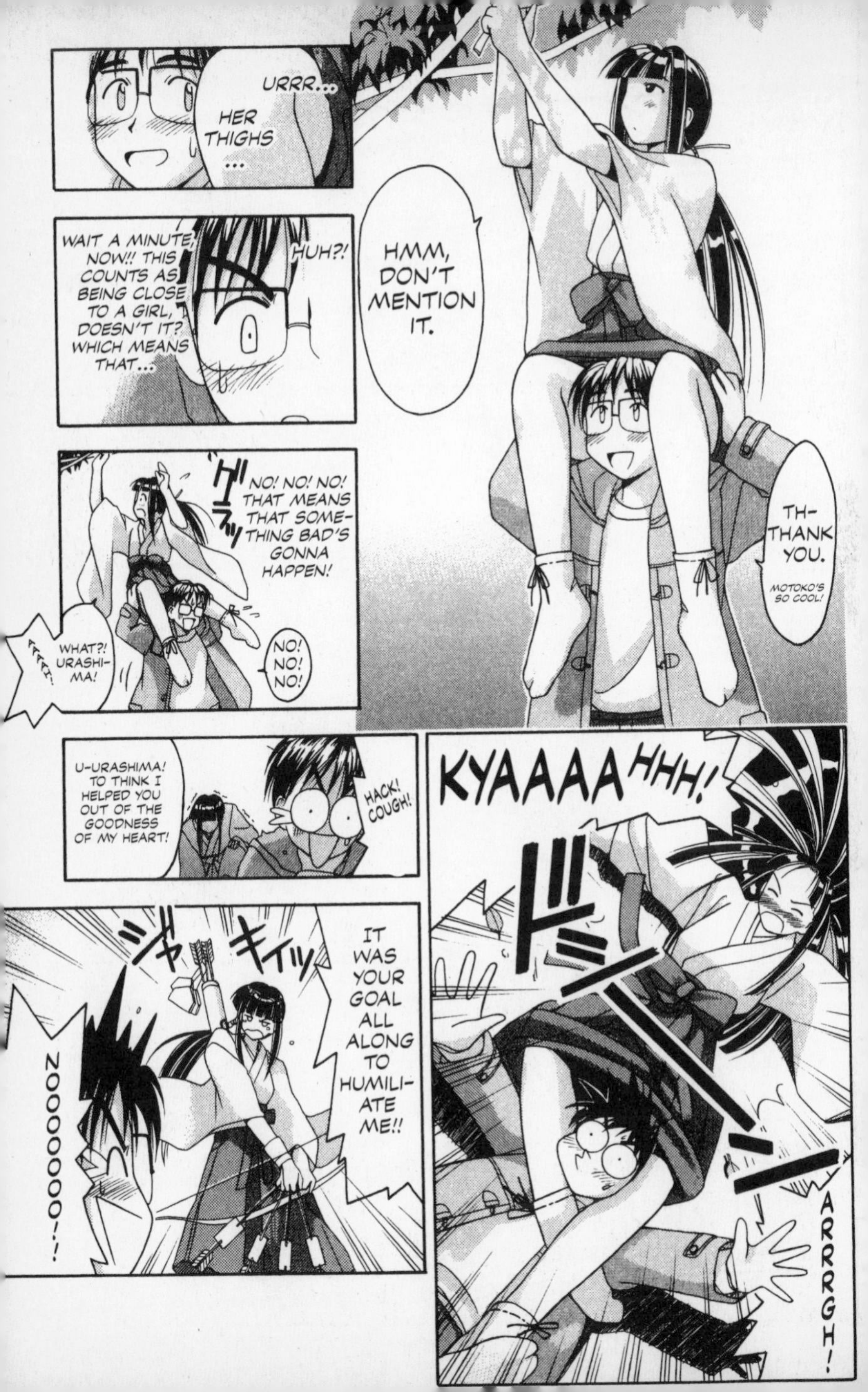

TH-THANK YOU.
MOTOKO'S SO COOL!
HMM, DON'T MENTION IT.
URRR...
HER THIGHS ...
HUH?!
WAIT A MINUTE, NOW!! THIS COUNTS AS BEING CLOSE TO A GIRL, DOESN'T IT? WHICH MEANS THAT...
NO! NO! NO! THAT MEANS THAT SOMETHING BAD'S GONNA HAPPEN!
NO! NO! NO!
WHAT?! URASHIMA!
KYAAAAHHH!
ARRRGH!
HACK! COUGH!
U-URASHIMA! TO THINK I HELPED YOU OUT OF THE GOODNESS OF MY HEART!
IT WAS YOUR GOAL ALL ALONG TO HUMILIATE ME!!
NOOOOOOO!!

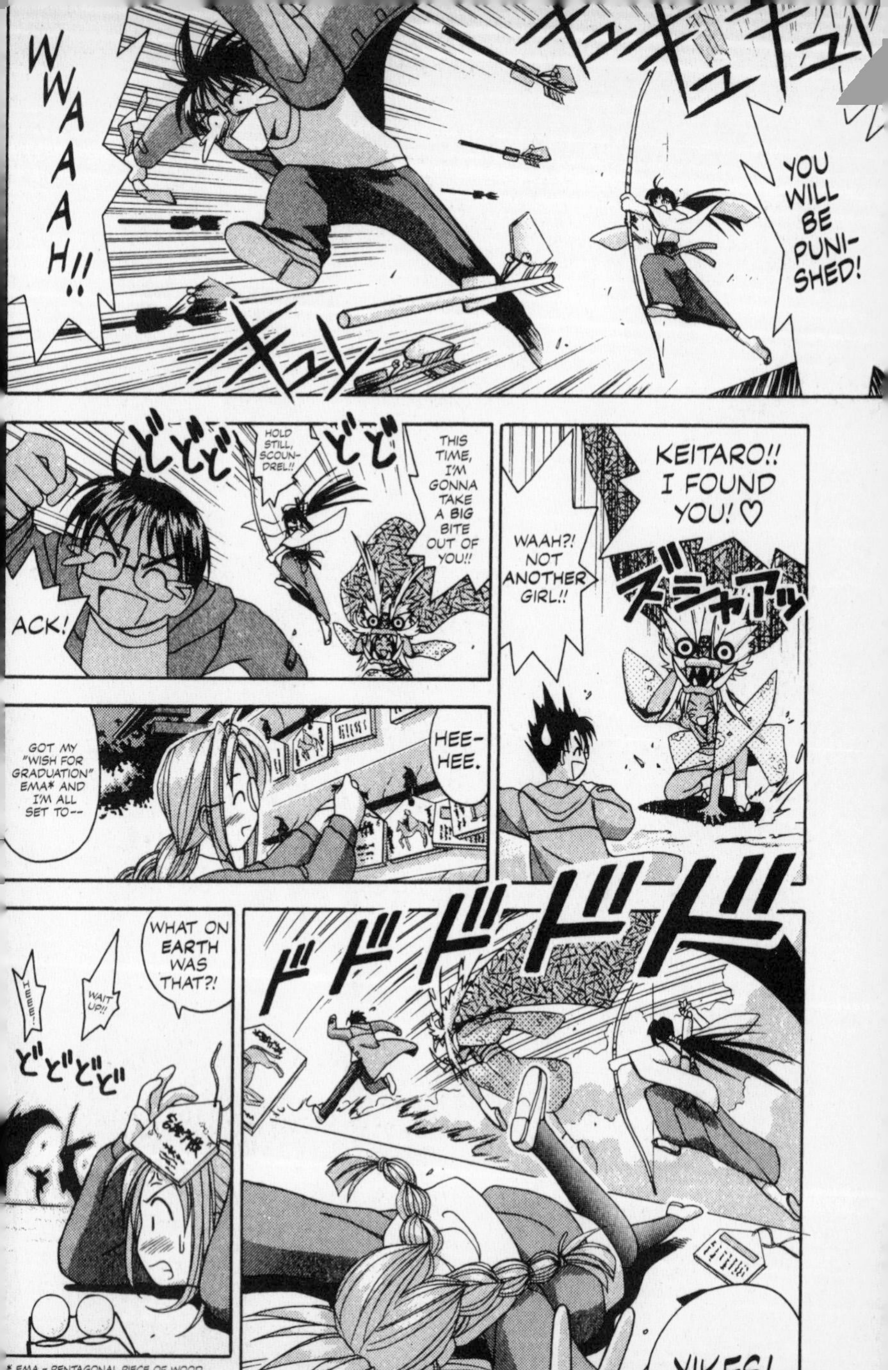
キュ
YOU WILL BE PUNI-SHED!
WWAAAAH!!
キュッ
KEITARO!! I FOUND YOU! ♡
WAAH?! NOT ANOTHER GIRL!!
ズシャアッ
THIS TIME, I'M GONNA TAKE A BIG BITE OUT OF YOU!!
どど
HOLD STILL, SCOUN-DREL!!
どどど
ACK!
HEE-HEE.
GOT MY "WISH FOR GRADUATION" EMA* AND I'M ALL SET TO--
ドドドド
YIKES!
WHAT ON EARTH WAS THAT?!
WAIT UP!!
HEEE!!
どどどど

* EMA - PENTAGONAL PIECE OF WOOD IMBUED WITH A PERSON'S STRONGEST WISH. JAPANESE NEW YEAR'S CUSTOM.

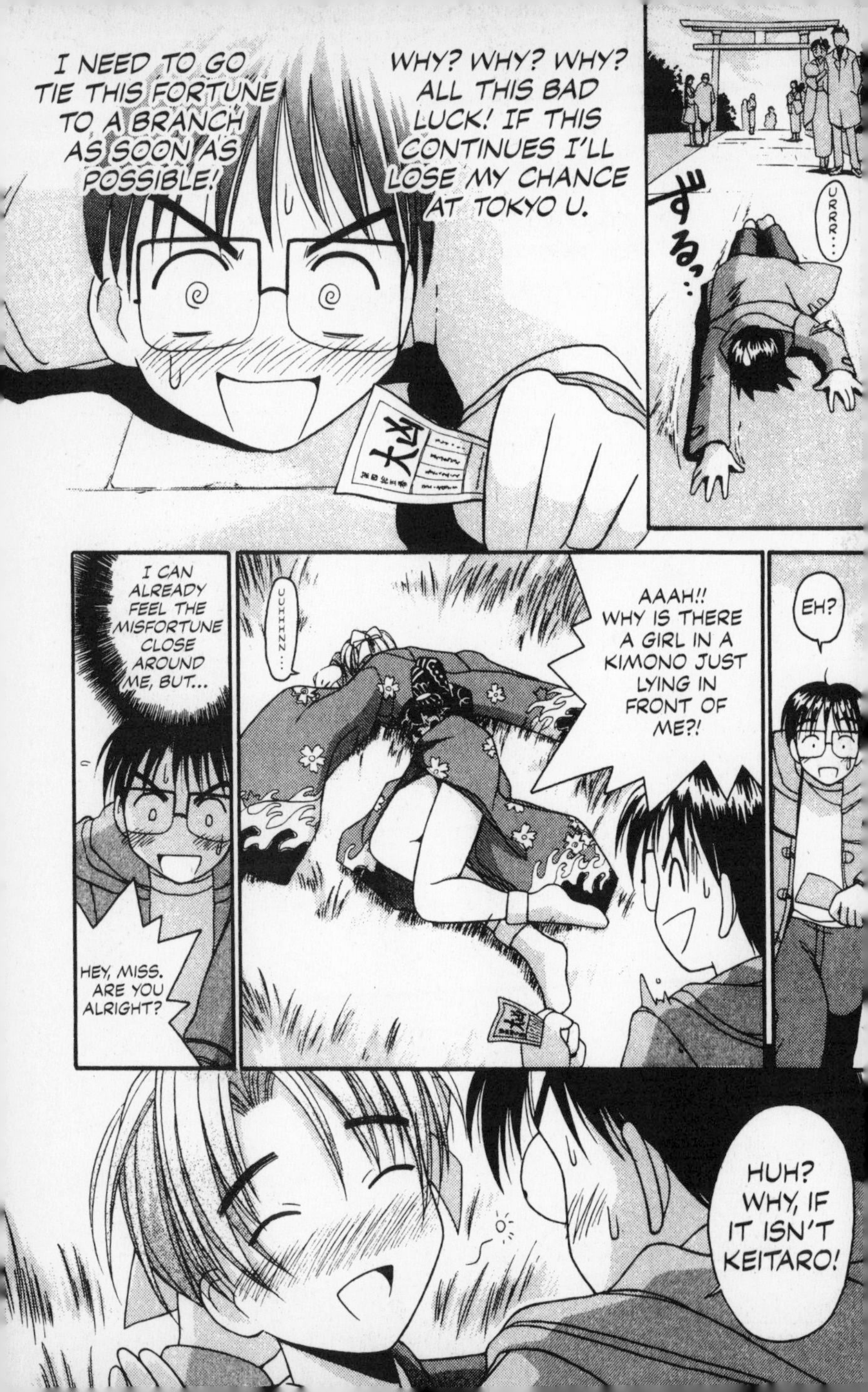
URRR...
ずるっ
WHY? WHY? WHY? ALL THIS BAD LUCK! IF THIS CONTINUES I'LL LOSE MY CHANCE AT TOKYO U.
I NEED TO GO TIE THIS FORTUNE TO A BRANCH AS SOON AS POSSIBLE!
EH?
AAAH!! WHY IS THERE A GIRL IN A KIMONO JUST LYING IN FRONT OF ME?!
UUHHHNN...
I CAN ALREADY FEEL THE MISFORTUNE CLOSE AROUND ME, BUT...
HEY, MISS. ARE YOU ALRIGHT?
HUH? WHY, IF IT ISN'T KEITARO!

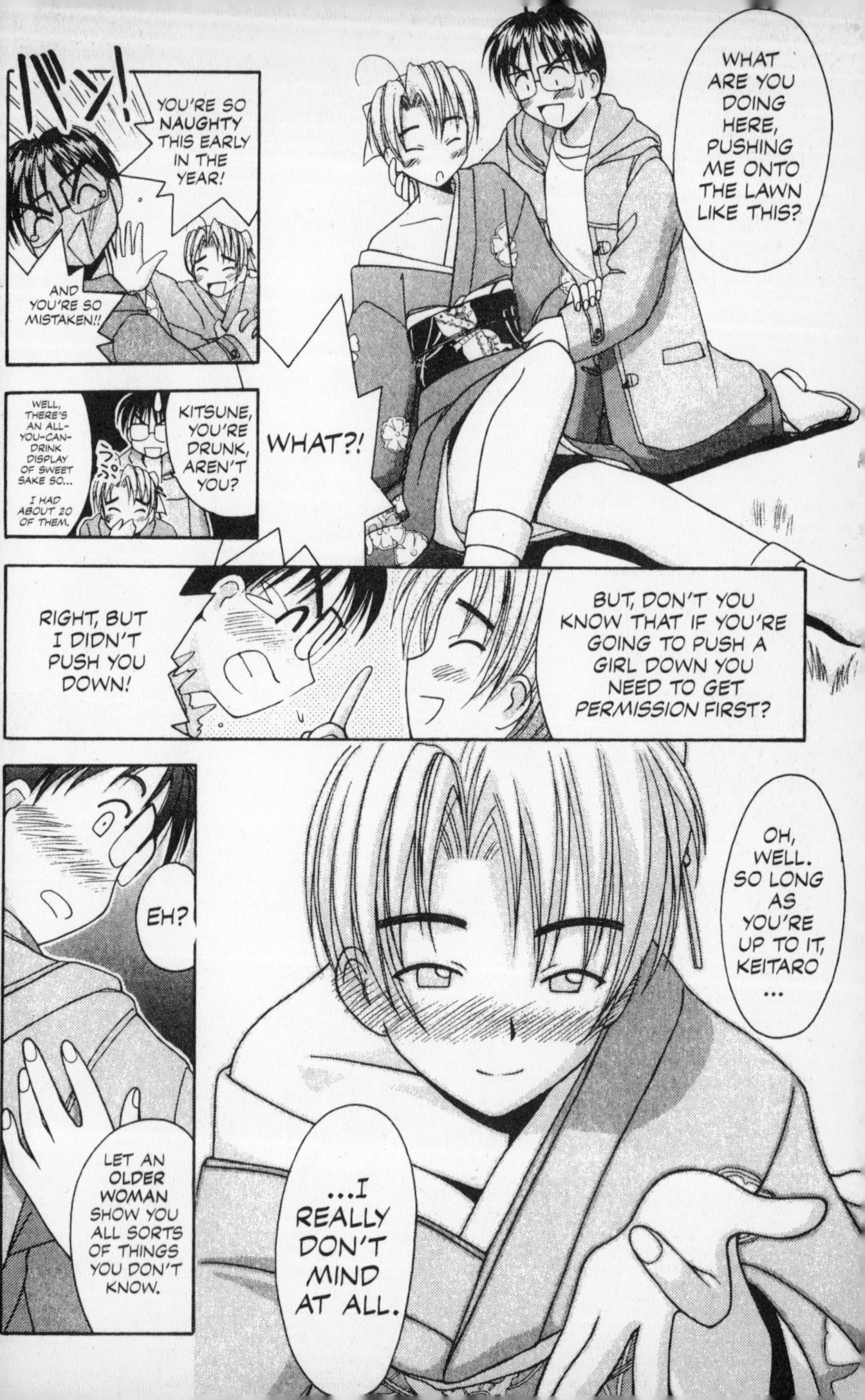
WHAT ARE YOU DOING HERE, PUSHING ME ONTO THE LAWN LIKE THIS?
WHAT?!
YOU'RE SO NAUGHTY THIS EARLY IN THE YEAR!
AND YOU'RE SO MISTAKEN!!
KITSUNE, YOU'RE DRUNK, AREN'T YOU?
WELL, THERE'S AN ALL-YOU-CAN-DRINK DISPLAY OF SWEET SAKE SO...
I HAD ABOUT 20 OF THEM.
BUT, DON'T YOU KNOW THAT IF YOU'RE GOING TO PUSH A GIRL DOWN YOU NEED TO GET PERMISSION FIRST?
RIGHT, BUT I DIDN'T PUSH YOU DOWN!
OH, WELL. SO LONG AS YOU'RE UP TO IT, KEITARO ...
...I REALLY DON'T MIND AT ALL.
LET AN OLDER WOMAN SHOW YOU ALL SORTS OF THINGS YOU DON'T KNOW.
EH?

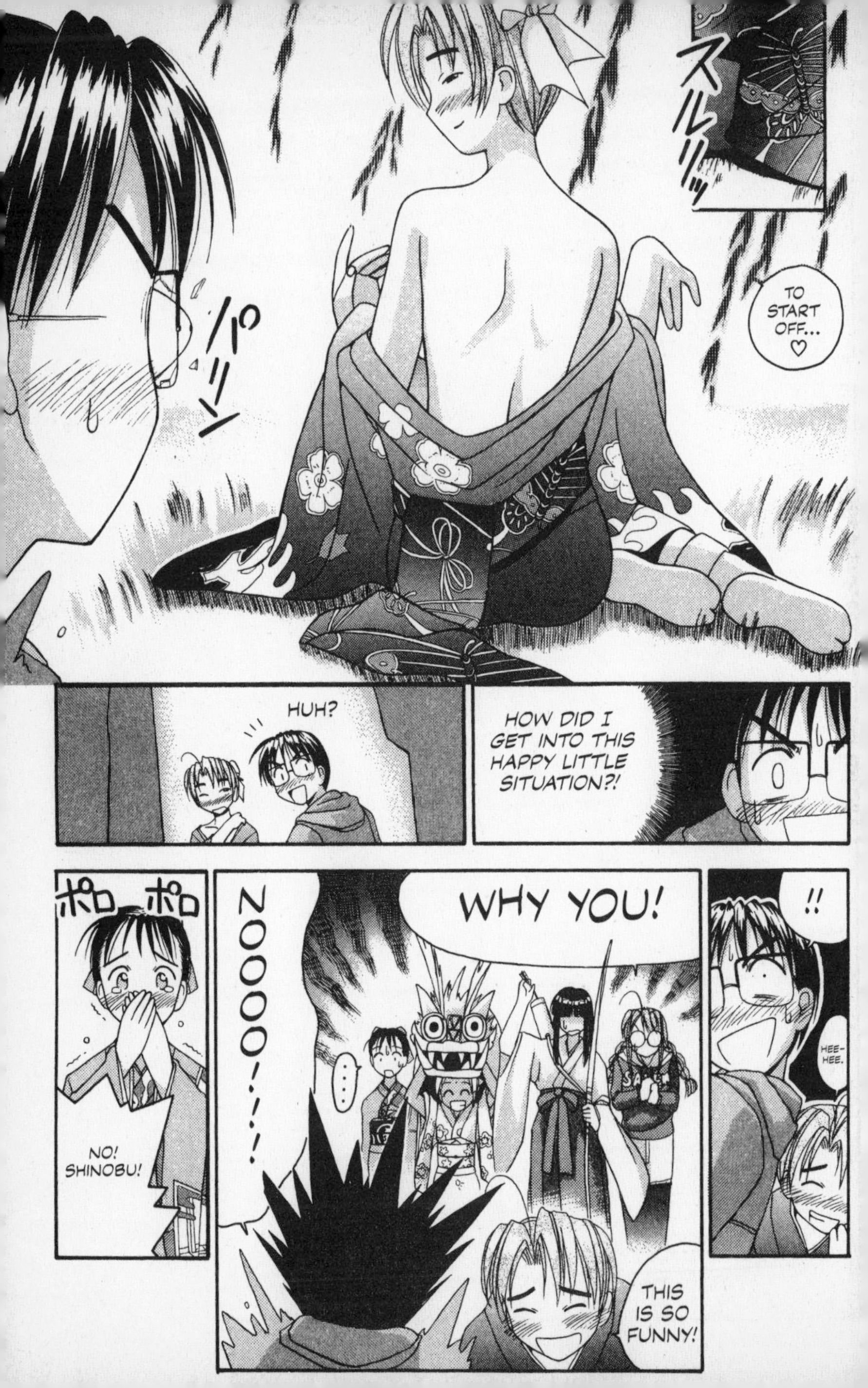

スルリッ
TO START OFF... ♡
パリーン
HOW DID I GET INTO THIS HAPPY LITTLE SITUATION?!
HUH?
!!
HEE-HEE.
WHY YOU!
NOOOOO!!!!
...
THIS IS SO FUNNY!
ポロ ポロ
NO! SHINOBU!

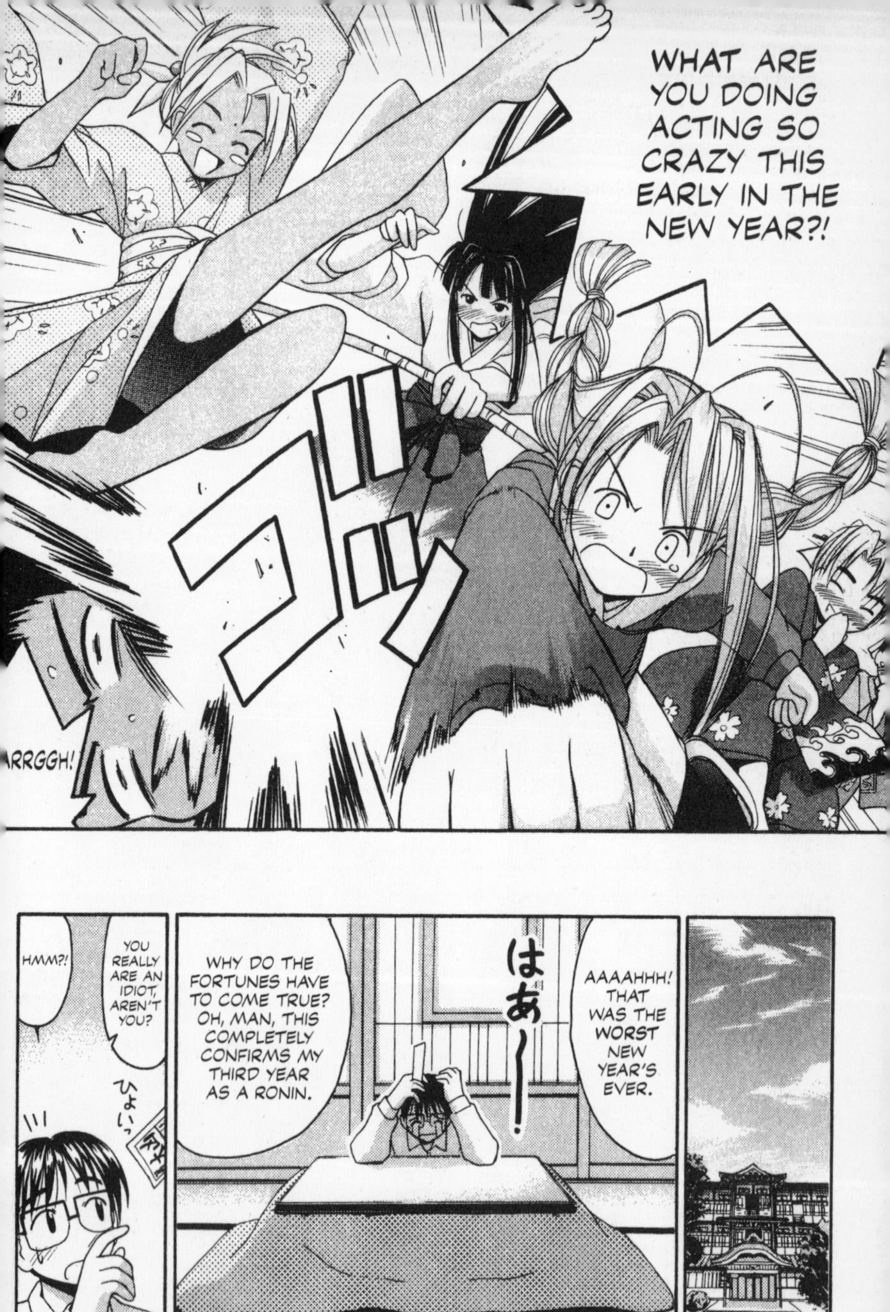
WHAT ARE YOU DOING ACTING SO CRAZY THIS EARLY IN THE NEW YEAR?!
ゴッ
ARRGGH!
AAAAHHH! THAT WAS THE WORST NEW YEAR'S EVER.
はあ〜!
WHY DO THE FORTUNES HAVE TO COME TRUE? OH, MAN, THIS COMPLETELY CONFIRMS MY THIRD YEAR AS A RONIN.
YOU REALLY ARE AN IDIOT, AREN'T YOU?
ひょいっ
HMM?!

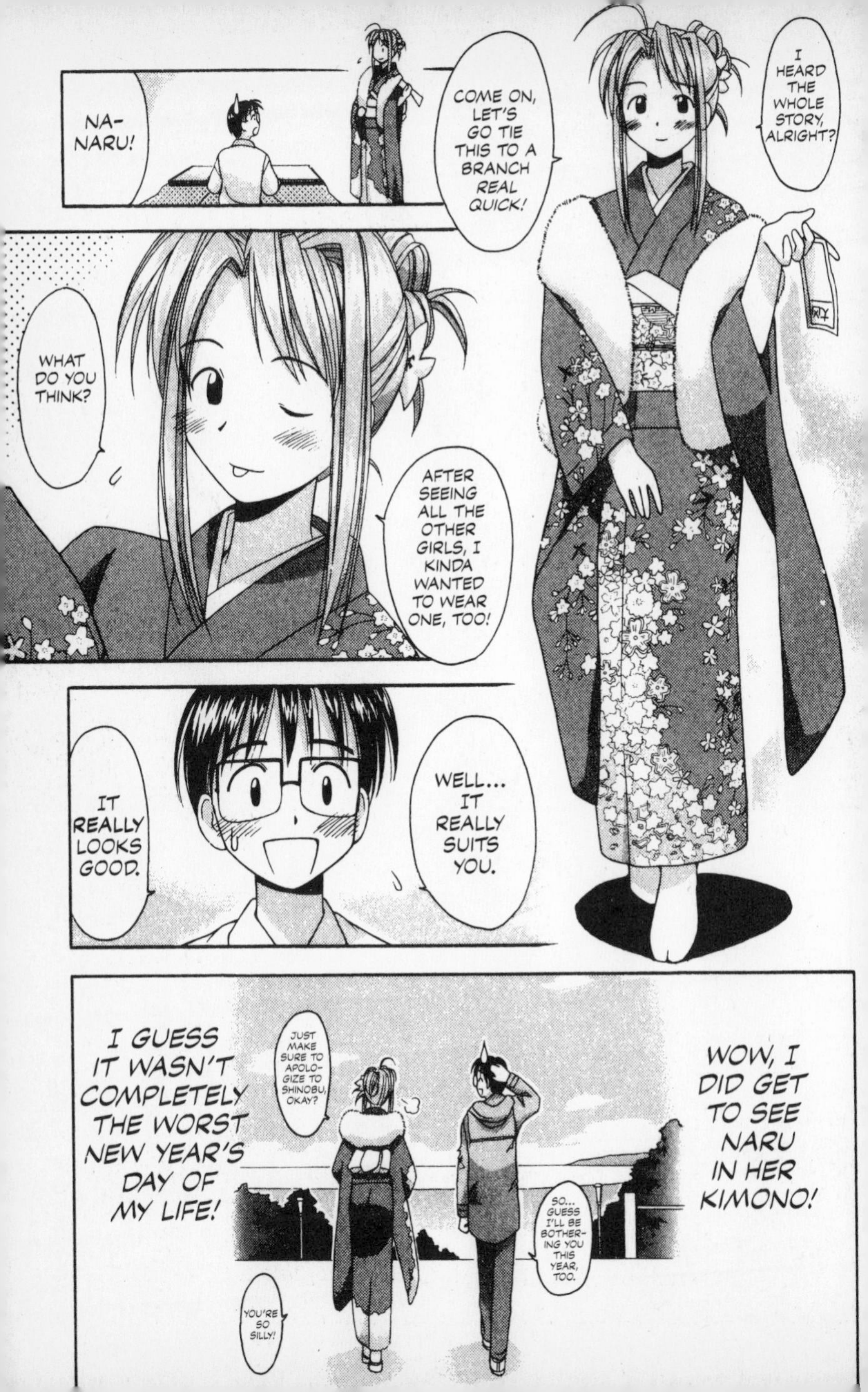
I HEARD THE WHOLE STORY, ALRIGHT?
COME ON, LET'S GO TIE THIS TO A BRANCH REAL QUICK!
NA-NARU!
AFTER SEEING ALL THE OTHER GIRLS, I KINDA WANTED TO WEAR ONE, TOO!
WHAT DO YOU THINK?
WELL... IT REALLY SUITS YOU.
IT REALLY LOOKS GOOD.
WOW, I DID GET TO SEE NARU IN HER KIMONO!
JUST MAKE SURE TO APOLOGIZE TO SHINOBU, OKAY?
SO... GUESS I'LL BE BOTHERING YOU THIS YEAR, TOO.
YOU'RE SO SILLY!
I GUESS IT WASN'T COMPLETELY THE WORST NEW YEAR'S DAY OF MY LIFE!

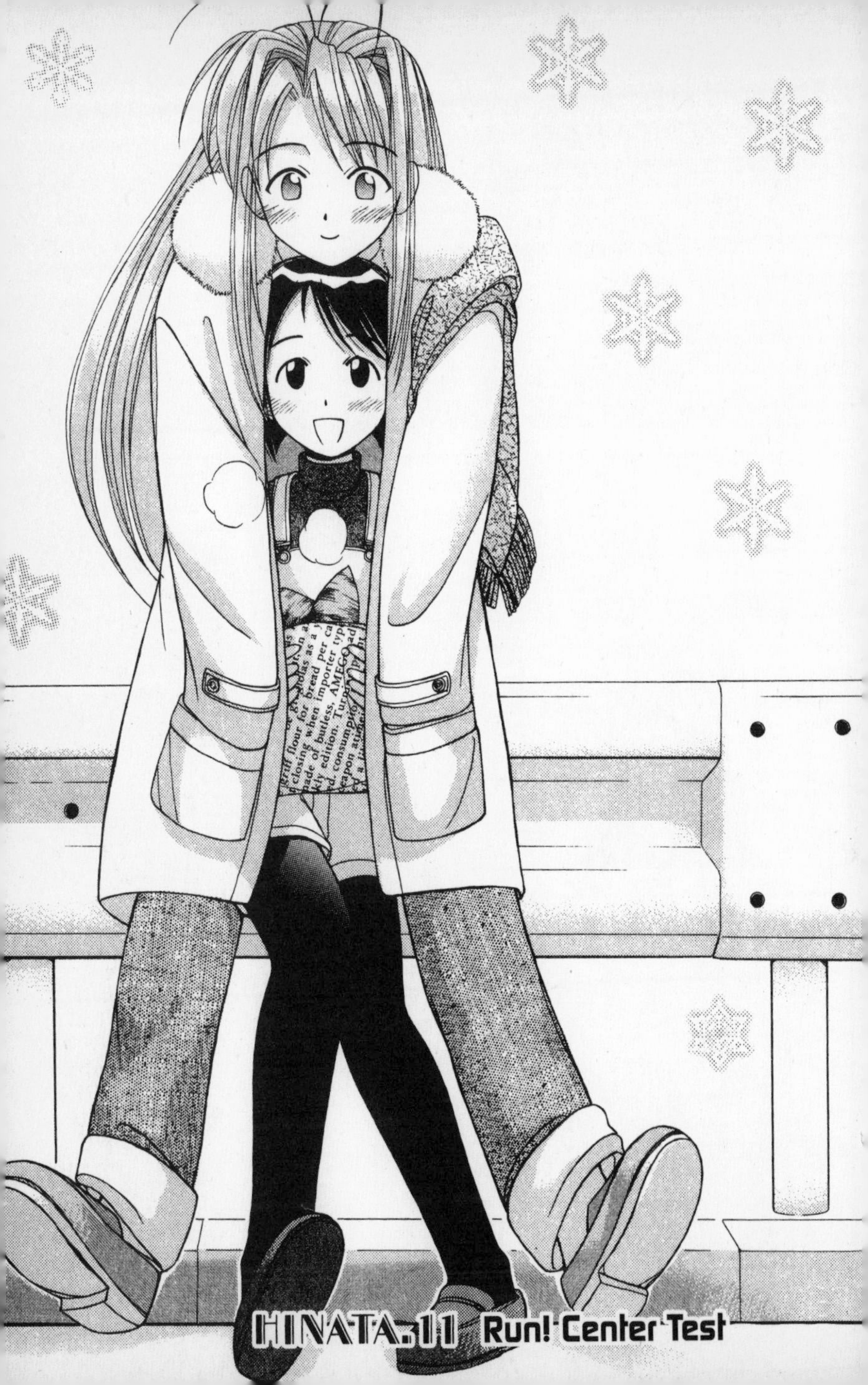

HINATA. 11 Run! Center Test

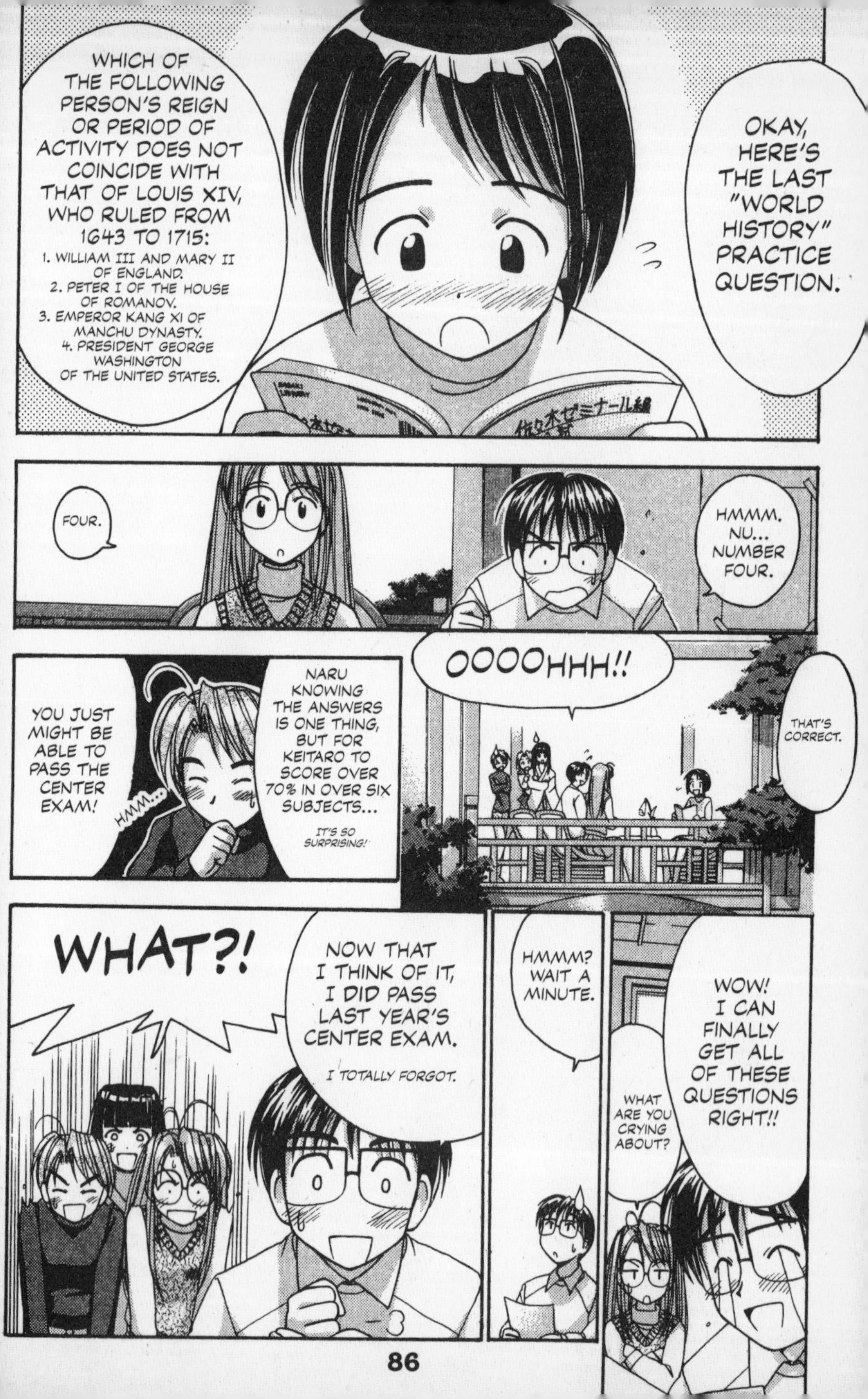

OKAY, HERE'S THE LAST "WORLD HISTORY" PRACTICE QUESTION.
WHICH OF THE FOLLOWING PERSON'S REIGN OR PERIOD OF ACTIVITY DOES NOT COINCIDE WITH THAT OF LOUIS XIV, WHO RULED FROM 1643 TO 1715:
1. WILLIAM III AND MARY II OF ENGLAND.
2. PETER I OF THE HOUSE OF ROMANOV.
3. EMPEROR KANG XI OF MANCHU DYNASTY.
4. PRESIDENT GEORGE WASHINGTON OF THE UNITED STATES.
HMMM. NU... NUMBER FOUR.
FOUR.
THAT'S CORRECT.
OOOOHHH!!
NARU KNOWING THE ANSWERS IS ONE THING, BUT FOR KEITARO TO SCORE OVER 70% IN OVER SIX SUBJECTS...
IT'S SO SURPRISING!
HMM...
YOU JUST MIGHT BE ABLE TO PASS THE CENTER EXAM!
WOW! I CAN FINALLY GET ALL OF THESE QUESTIONS RIGHT!!
WHAT ARE YOU CRYING ABOUT?
HMMM? WAIT A MINUTE.
NOW THAT I THINK OF IT, I DID PASS LAST YEAR'S CENTER EXAM.
I TOTALLY FORGOT.
WHAT?!

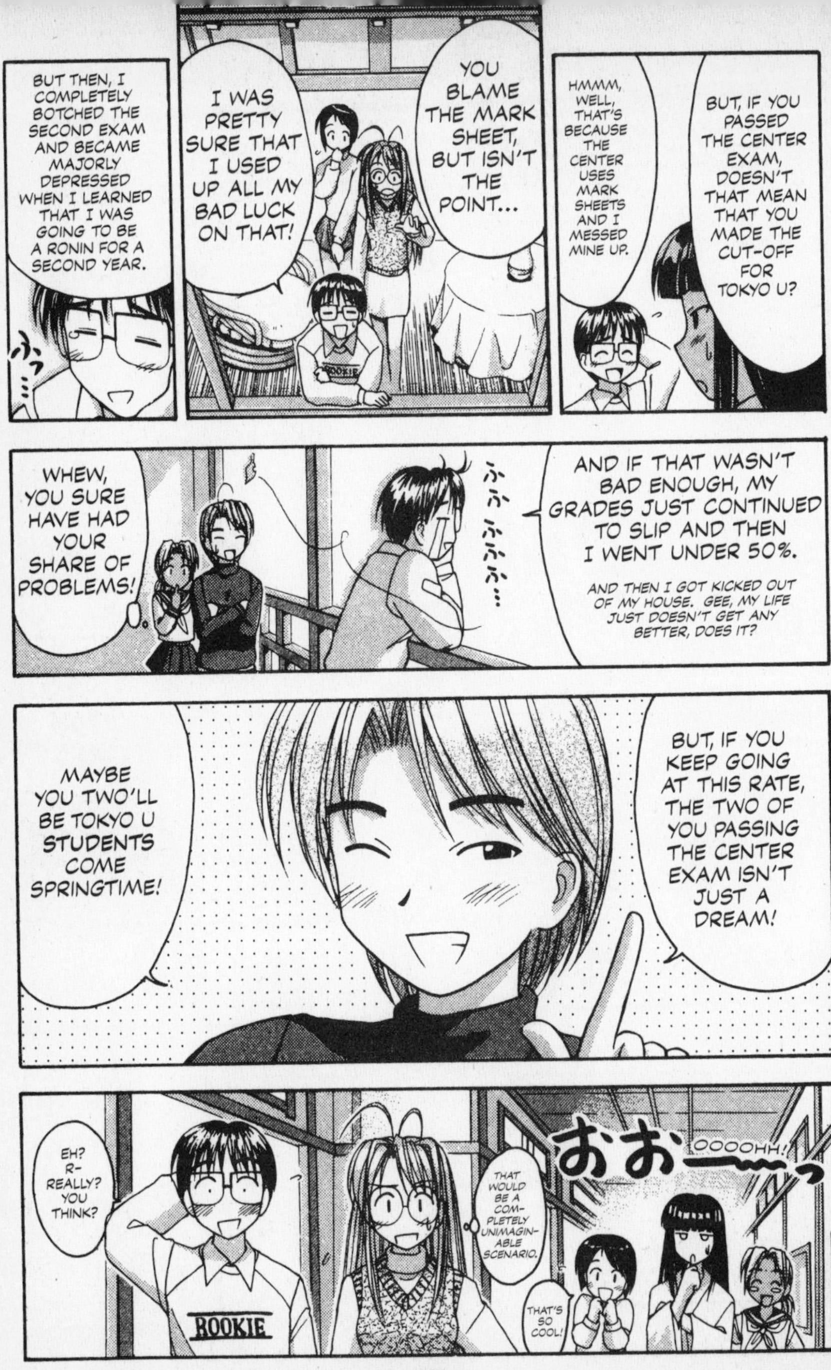
BUT, IF YOU PASSED THE CENTER EXAM, DOESN'T THAT MEAN THAT YOU MADE THE CUT-OFF FOR TOKYO U?
HMMM, WELL, THAT'S BECAUSE THE CENTER USES MARK SHEETS AND I MESSED MINE UP.
YOU BLAME THE MARK SHEET, BUT ISN'T THE POINT...
I WAS PRETTY SURE THAT I USED UP ALL MY BAD LUCK ON THAT!
BUT THEN, I COMPLETELY BOTCHED THE SECOND EXAM AND BECAME MAJORLY DEPRESSED WHEN I LEARNED THAT I WAS GOING TO BE A RONIN FOR A SECOND YEAR.
ふぅ…
AND IF THAT WASN'T BAD ENOUGH, MY GRADES JUST CONTINUED TO SLIP AND THEN I WENT UNDER 50%.
AND THEN I GOT KICKED OUT OF MY HOUSE. GEE, MY LIFE JUST DOESN'T GET ANY BETTER, DOES IT?
ふふ ふふふ…
WHEW, YOU SURE HAVE HAD YOUR SHARE OF PROBLEMS!
BUT, IF YOU KEEP GOING AT THIS RATE, THE TWO OF YOU PASSING THE CENTER EXAM ISN'T JUST A DREAM!
MAYBE YOU TWO'LL BE TOKYO U STUDENTS COME SPRINGTIME!
おおーーっ OOOOHH!
THAT'S SO COOL!
THAT WOULD BE A COMPLETELY UNIMAGINABLE SCENARIO.
EH? R-REALLY? YOU THINK?
ROOKIE

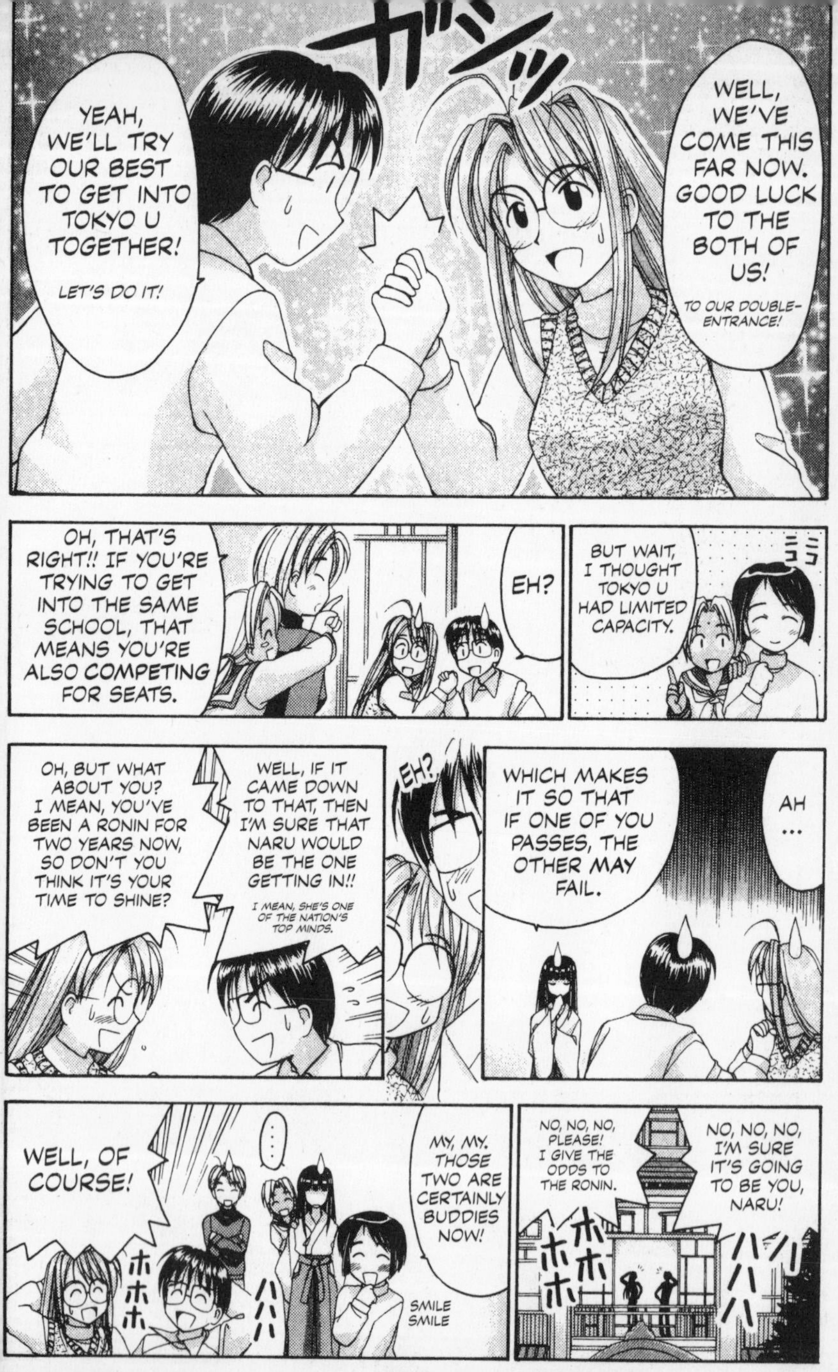
ガシッ
WELL, WE'VE COME THIS FAR NOW. GOOD LUCK TO THE BOTH OF US!
TO OUR DOUBLE-ENTRANCE!
YEAH, WE'LL TRY OUR BEST TO GET INTO TOKYO U TOGETHER!
LET'S DO IT!
ニコ
BUT WAIT, I THOUGHT TOKYO U HAD LIMITED CAPACITY.
EH?
OH, THAT'S RIGHT!! IF YOU'RE TRYING TO GET INTO THE SAME SCHOOL, THAT MEANS YOU'RE ALSO COMPETING FOR SEATS.
AH ...
WHICH MAKES IT SO THAT IF ONE OF YOU PASSES, THE OTHER MAY FAIL.
EH?
WELL, IF IT CAME DOWN TO THAT, THEN I'M SURE THAT NARU WOULD BE THE ONE GETTING IN!!
I MEAN, SHE'S ONE OF THE NATION'S TOP MINDS.
OH, BUT WHAT ABOUT YOU? I MEAN, YOU'VE BEEN A RONIN FOR TWO YEARS NOW, SO DON'T YOU THINK IT'S YOUR TIME TO SHINE?
NO, NO, NO, I'M SURE IT'S GOING TO BE YOU, NARU!
ハハハ
NO, NO, NO, PLEASE! I GIVE THE ODDS TO THE RONIN.
ホホホ
MY, MY. THOSE TWO ARE CERTAINLY BUDDIES NOW!
...
WELL, OF COURSE!
ハハハ
ホホホ
SMILE SMILE

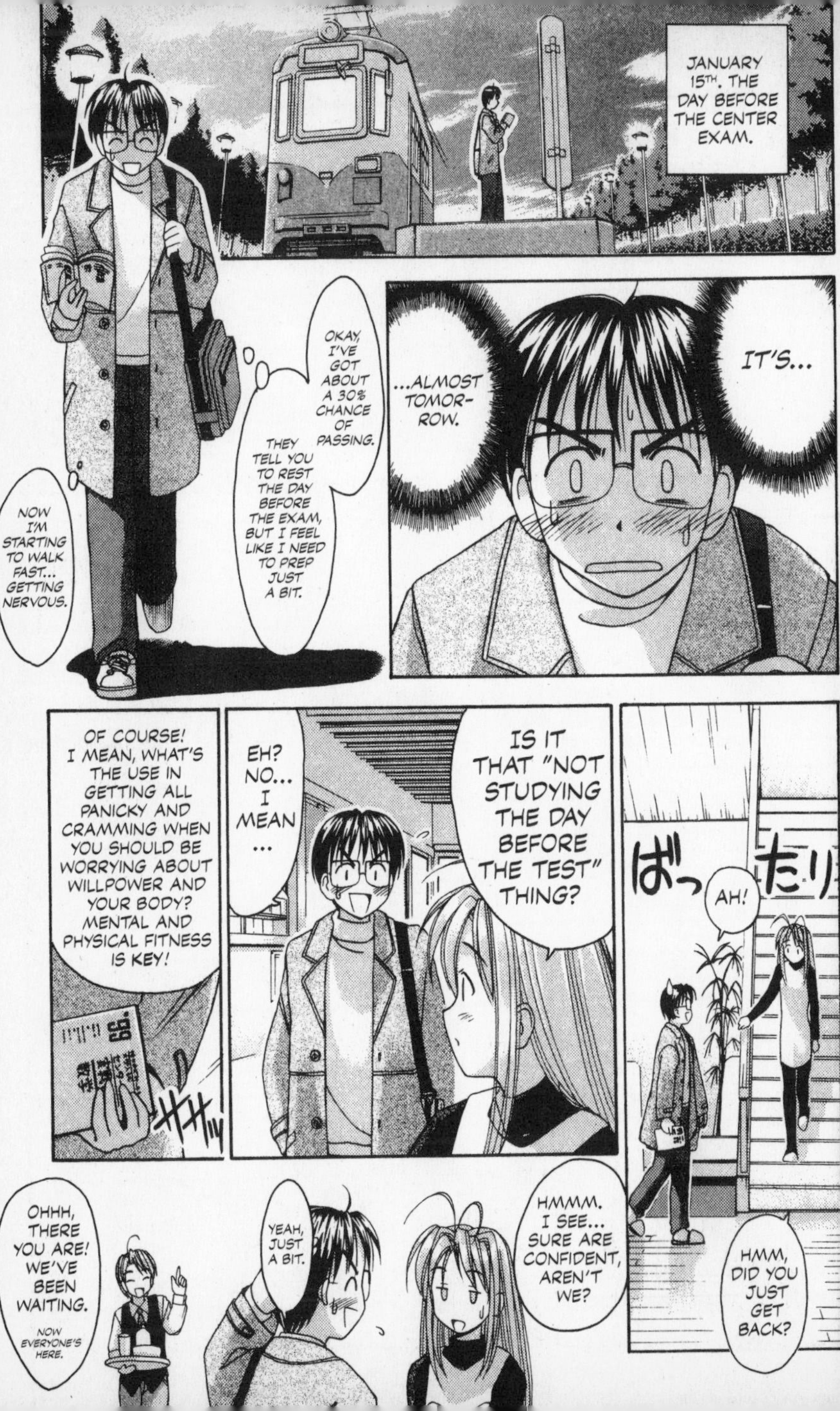
JANUARY 15TH. THE DAY BEFORE THE CENTER EXAM.
IT'S...
...ALMOST TOMORROW.
OKAY, I'VE GOT ABOUT A 30% CHANCE OF PASSING.
THEY TELL YOU TO REST THE DAY BEFORE THE EXAM, BUT I FEEL LIKE I NEED TO PREP JUST A BIT.
NOW I'M STARTING TO WALK FAST... GETTING NERVOUS.
ぱったり
AH!
HMM, DID YOU JUST GET BACK?
IS IT THAT "NOT STUDYING THE DAY BEFORE THE TEST" THING?
EH? NO... I MEAN ...
OF COURSE! I MEAN, WHAT'S THE USE IN GETTING ALL PANICKY AND CRAMMING WHEN YOU SHOULD BE WORRYING ABOUT WILLPOWER AND YOUR BODY? MENTAL AND PHYSICAL FITNESS IS KEY!
HMMM. I SEE... SURE ARE CONFIDENT, AREN'T WE?
YEAH, JUST A BIT.
OHHH, THERE YOU ARE! WE'VE BEEN WAITING.
NOW EVERYONE'S HERE.

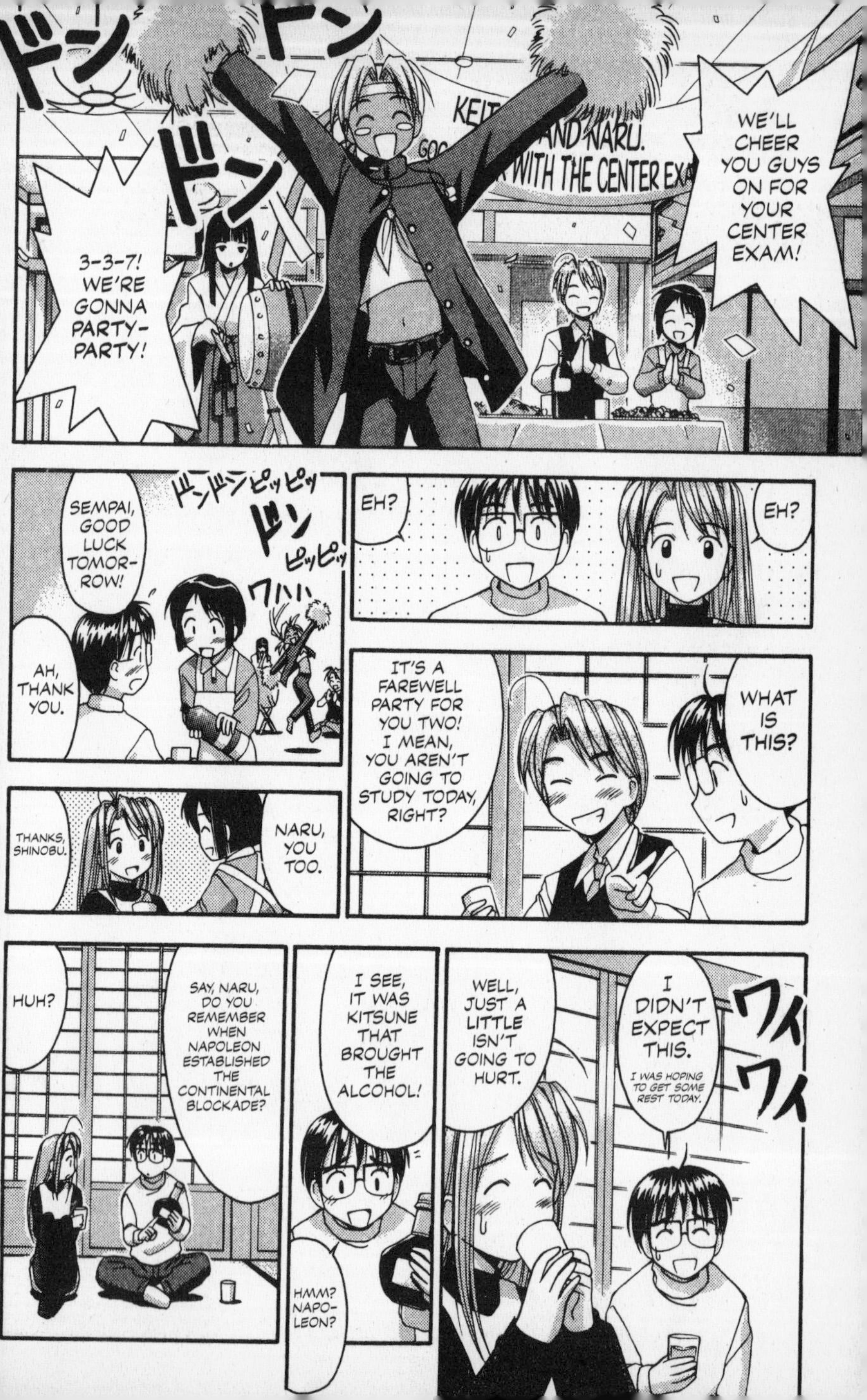
WE'LL CHEER YOU GUYS ON FOR YOUR CENTER EXAM!
AND NARU.
WITH THE CENTER
ドーン
ドーン
ドン
3-3-7! WE'RE GONNA PARTY-PARTY!
EH?
EH?
ドンドンピッピッ
ドン
ピッピッ
ワハハ
SEMPAI, GOOD LUCK TOMORROW!
AH, THANK YOU.
WHAT IS THIS?
IT'S A FAREWELL PARTY FOR YOU TWO! I MEAN, YOU AREN'T GOING TO STUDY TODAY, RIGHT?
NARU, YOU TOO.
THANKS, SHINOBU.
ワイワイ
I DIDN'T EXPECT THIS.
I WAS HOPING TO GET SOME REST TODAY.
WELL, JUST A LITTLE ISN'T GOING TO HURT.
I SEE, IT WAS KITSUNE THAT BROUGHT THE ALCOHOL!
HMM? NAPOLEON?
SAY, NARU, DO YOU REMEMBER WHEN NAPOLEON ESTABLISHED THE CONTINENTAL BLOCKADE?
HUH?

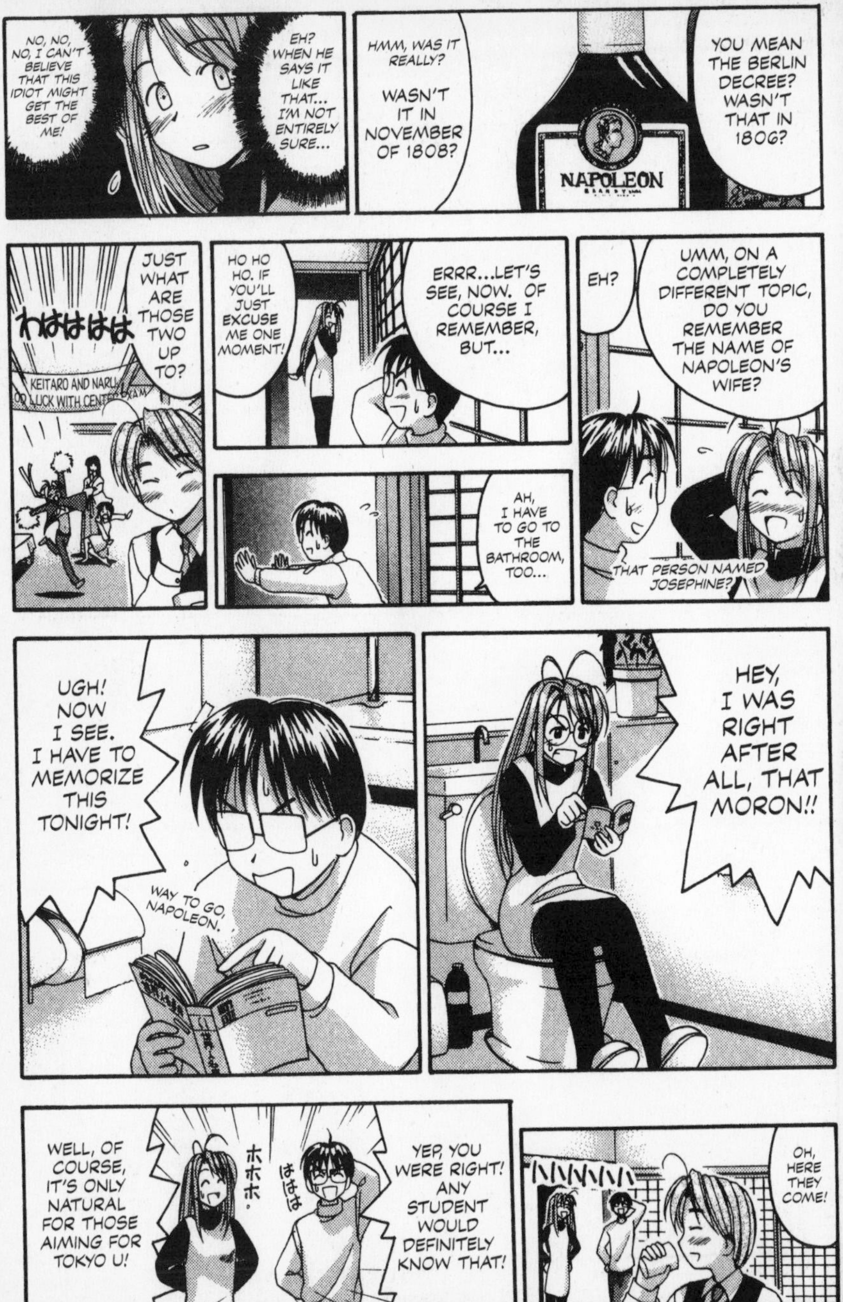
YOU MEAN THE BERLIN DECREE? WASN'T THAT IN 1806?
NAPOLEON
HMM, WAS IT REALLY?
WASN'T IT IN NOVEMBER OF 1808?
EH? WHEN HE SAYS IT LIKE THAT... I'M NOT ENTIRELY SURE...
NO, NO, NO, I CAN'T BELIEVE THAT THIS IDIOT MIGHT GET THE BEST OF ME!
UMM, ON A COMPLETELY DIFFERENT TOPIC, DO YOU REMEMBER THE NAME OF NAPOLEON'S WIFE?
EH?
THAT PERSON NAMED JOSEPHINE?
ERRR...LET'S SEE, NOW. OF COURSE I REMEMBER, BUT...
HO HO HO. IF YOU'LL JUST EXCUSE ME ONE MOMENT!
AH, I HAVE TO GO TO THE BATHROOM, TOO...
JUST WHAT ARE THOSE TWO UP TO?
わはははは
KEITARO AND NARU
OD LUCK WITH CENTER EXAM
HEY, I WAS RIGHT AFTER ALL, THAT MORON!!
UGH! NOW I SEE. I HAVE TO MEMORIZE THIS TONIGHT!
WAY TO GO, NAPOLEON.
OH, HERE THEY COME!
ハハハハハハ
YEP, YOU WERE RIGHT! ANY STUDENT WOULD DEFINITELY KNOW THAT!
ははは
ホホホ。
WELL, OF COURSE, IT'S ONLY NATURAL FOR THOSE AIMING FOR TOKYO U!

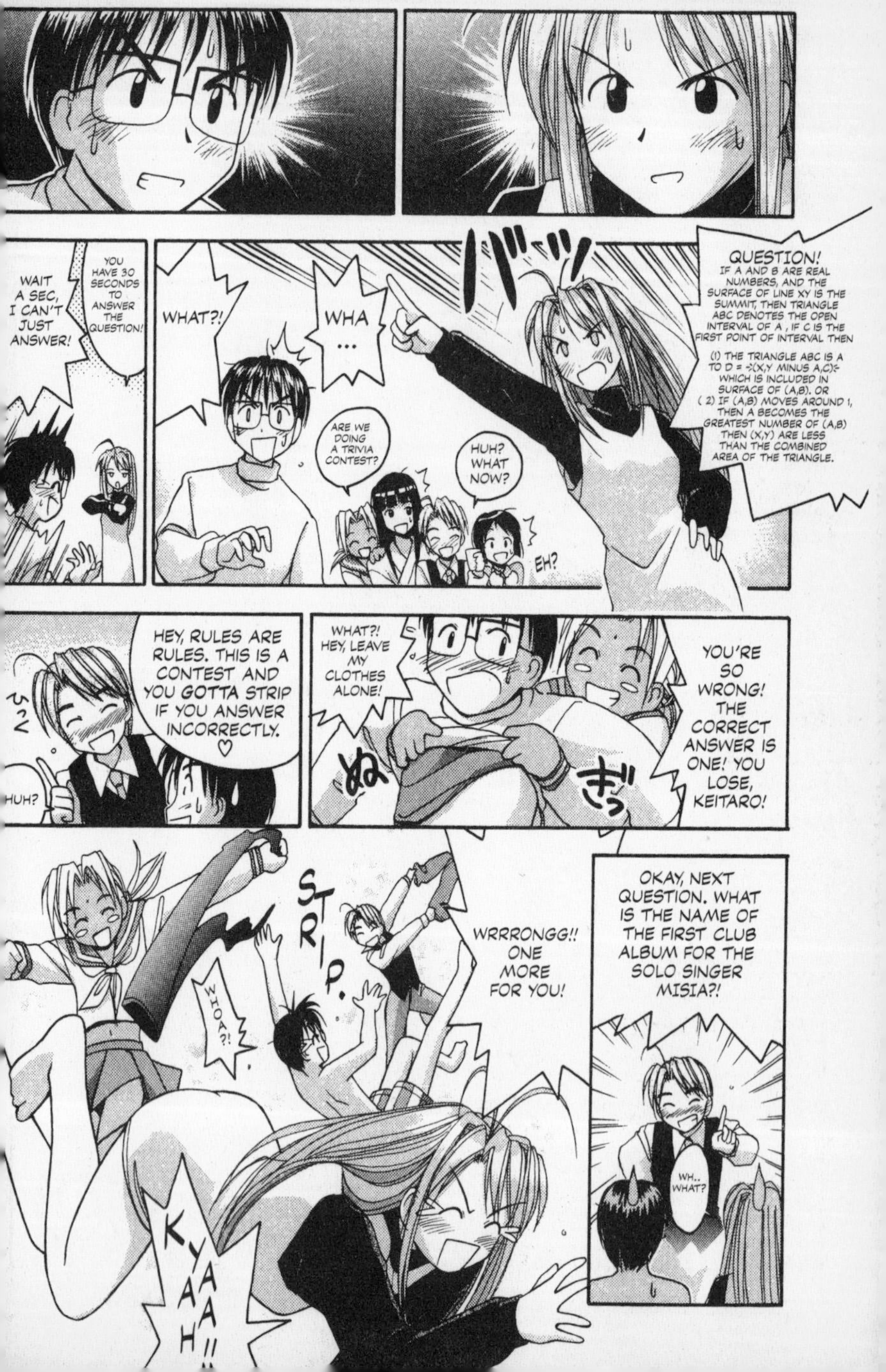
QUESTION! IF A AND B ARE REAL NUMBERS, AND THE SURFACE OF LINE XY IS THE SUMMIT, THEN TRIANGLE ABC DENOTES THE OPEN INTERVAL OF A , IF C IS THE FIRST POINT OF INTERVAL THEN
(1) THE TRIANGLE ABC IS A TO D = ->(X,Y MINUS A,C)<- WHICH IS INCLUDED IN SURFACE OF (A,B). OR (2) IF (A,B) MOVES AROUND 1, THEN A BECOMES THE GREATEST NUMBER OF (A,B) THEN (X,Y) ARE LESS THAN THE COMBINED AREA OF THE TRIANGLE.
WHA ...
WHAT?!
ARE WE DOING A TRIVIA CONTEST?
HUH? WHAT NOW?
EH?
YOU HAVE 30 SECONDS TO ANSWER THE QUESTION!
WAIT A SEC, I CAN'T JUST ANSWER!
YOU'RE SO WRONG! THE CORRECT ANSWER IS ONE! YOU LOSE, KEITARO!
WHAT?! HEY, LEAVE MY CLOTHES ALONE!
ぎっ
ぬ
HEY, RULES ARE RULES. THIS IS A CONTEST AND YOU GOTTA STRIP IF YOU ANSWER INCORRECTLY. ♡
HUH?
OKAY, NEXT QUESTION. WHAT IS THE NAME OF THE FIRST CLUB ALBUM FOR THE SOLO SINGER MISIA?!
WH.. WHAT?
WRRRONGG!! ONE MORE FOR YOU!
STRIP.
WHOA?!
KYAAAH!!

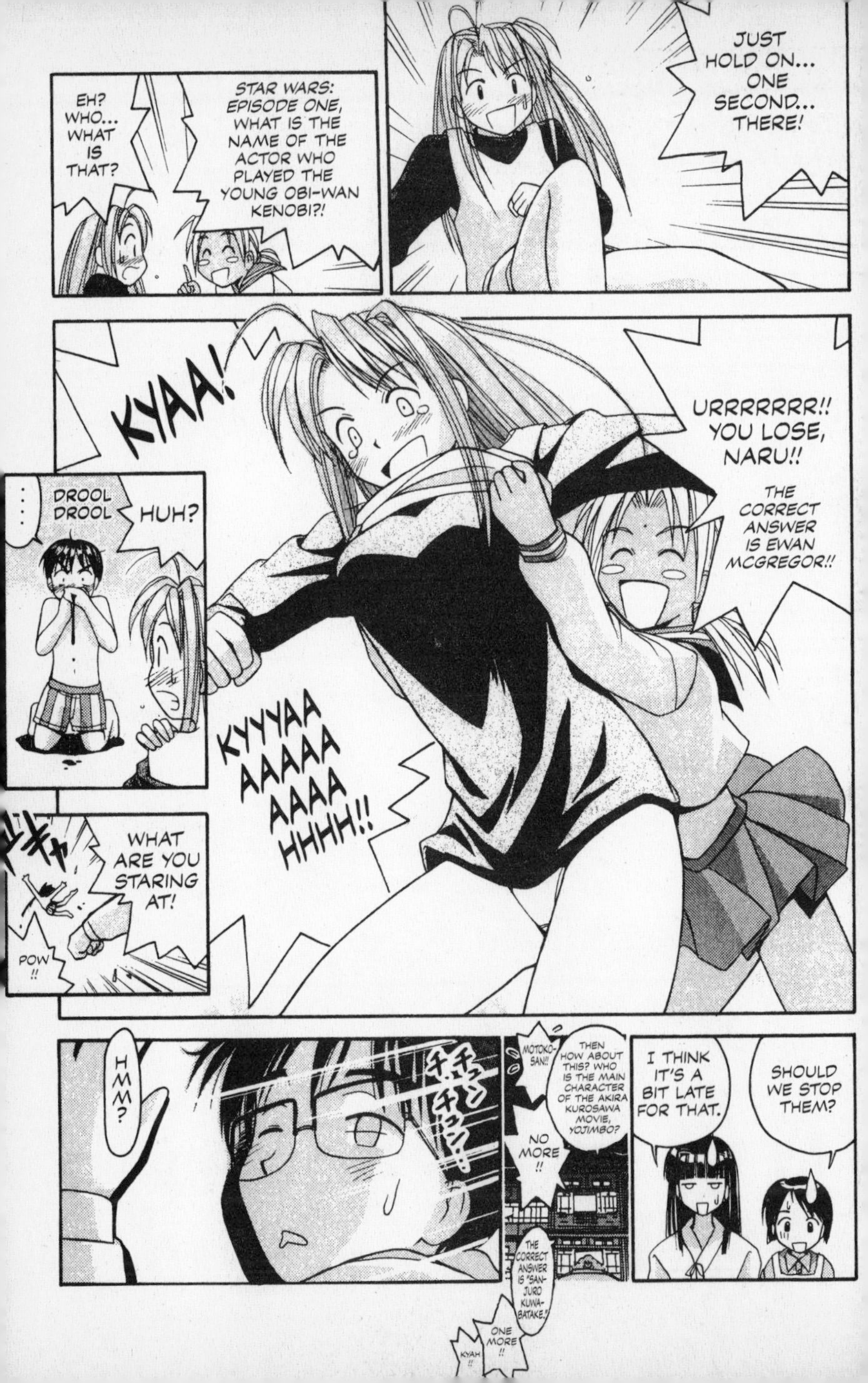
JUST HOLD ON... ONE SECOND... THERE!
STAR WARS: EPISODE ONE, WHAT IS THE NAME OF THE ACTOR WHO PLAYED THE YOUNG OBI-WAN KENOBI?!
EH? WHO... WHAT IS THAT?
URRRRRRR!! YOU LOSE, NARU!!
THE CORRECT ANSWER IS EWAN MCGREGOR!!
KYAA!
KYYYAA AAAAA AAAA HHHH!!
HUH?
DROOL DROOL
......
WHAT ARE YOU STARING AT!
POW!!
SHOULD WE STOP THEM?
I THINK IT'S A BIT LATE FOR THAT.
THEN HOW ABOUT THIS? WHO IS THE MAIN CHARACTER OF THE AKIRA KUROSAWA MOVIE, YOJIMBO?
MOTOKO-SAN!!
NO MORE!!
THE CORRECT ANSWER IS "SANJURO KUWABATAKE."
ONE MORE!!
KYAH!!
HMM?

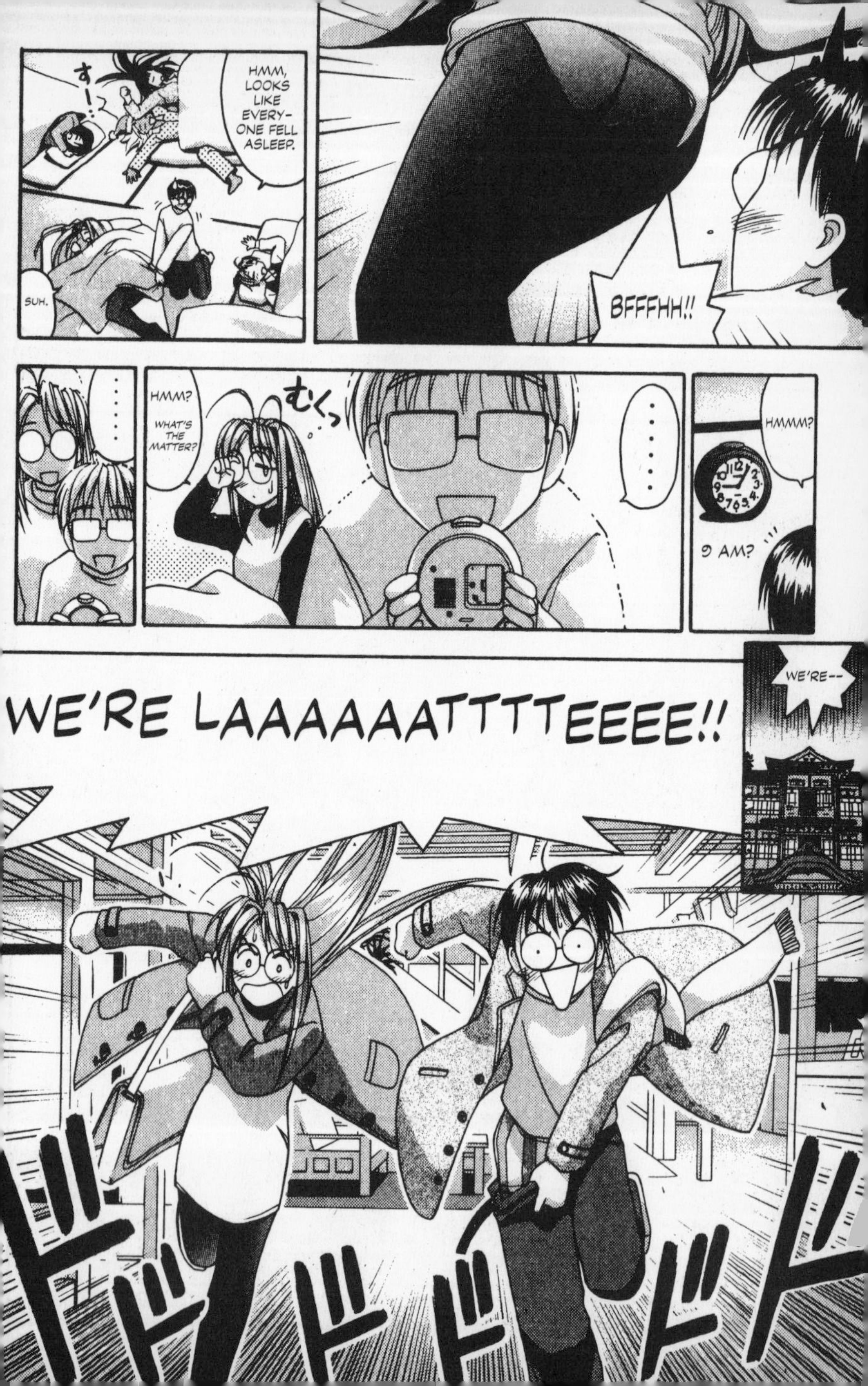
BFFFHH!!
HMM, LOOKS LIKE EVERY-ONE FELL ASLEEP.
すー…
SUH.
HMMM?
9 AM?
……
むくっ
HMM? WHAT'S THE MATTER?
……
WE'RE--
WE'RE LAAAAAATTTTEEEE!!
ドドドドドド

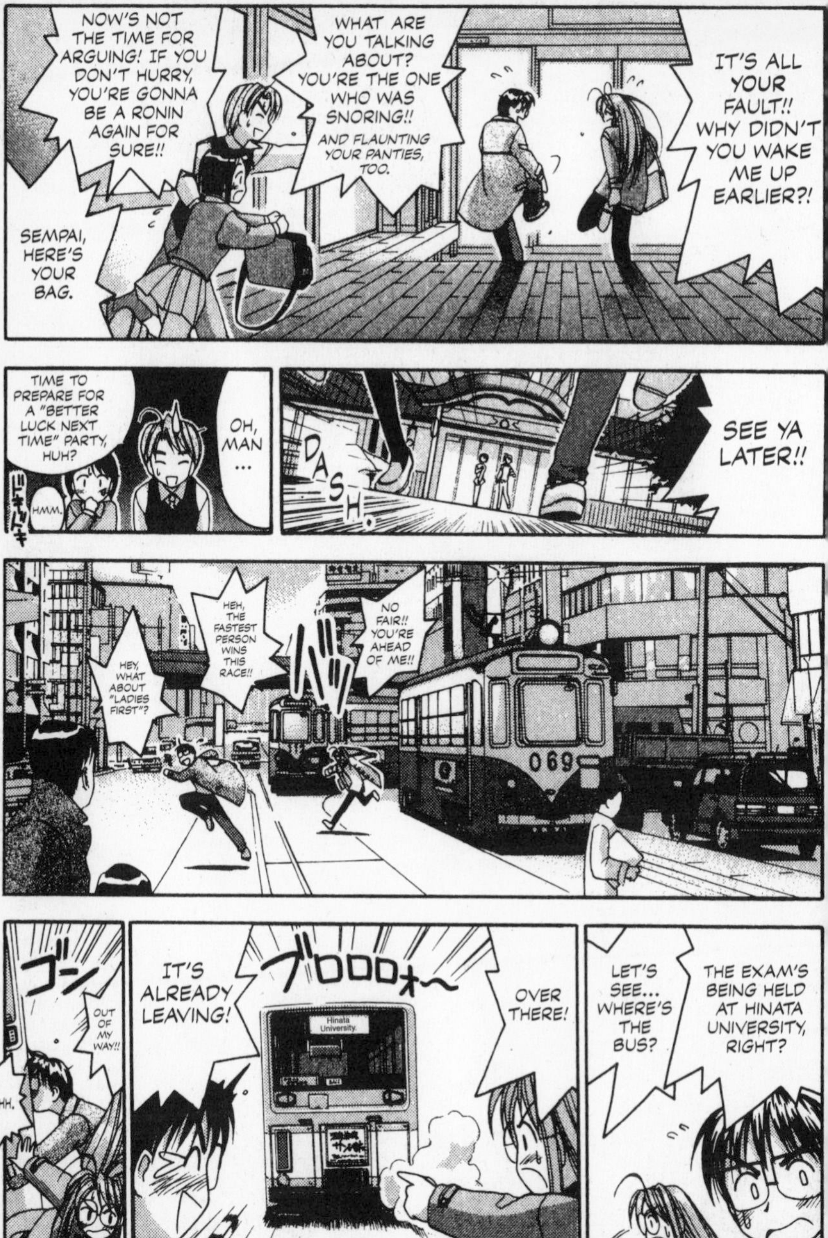
IT'S ALL YOUR FAULT!! WHY DIDN'T YOU WAKE ME UP EARLIER?!
WHAT ARE YOU TALKING ABOUT? YOU'RE THE ONE WHO WAS SNORING!!
AND FLAUNTING YOUR PANTIES, TOO.
NOW'S NOT THE TIME FOR ARGUING! IF YOU DON'T HURRY, YOU'RE GONNA BE A RONIN AGAIN FOR SURE!!
SEMPAI, HERE'S YOUR BAG.
SEE YA LATER!!
DASH.
OH, MAN ...
TIME TO PREPARE FOR A "BETTER LUCK NEXT TIME" PARTY, HUH?
HMM.
NO FAIR!! YOU'RE AHEAD OF ME!!
HEH, THE FASTEST PERSON WINS THIS RACE!!
HEY, WHAT ABOUT "LADIES FIRST"?
069
THE EXAM'S BEING HELD AT HINATA UNIVERSITY, RIGHT?
LET'S SEE... WHERE'S THE BUS?
OVER THERE!
ブロロロォ～
IT'S ALREADY LEAVING!
Hinata University.
ゴーン
OUT OF MY WAY!!
BUUHH.

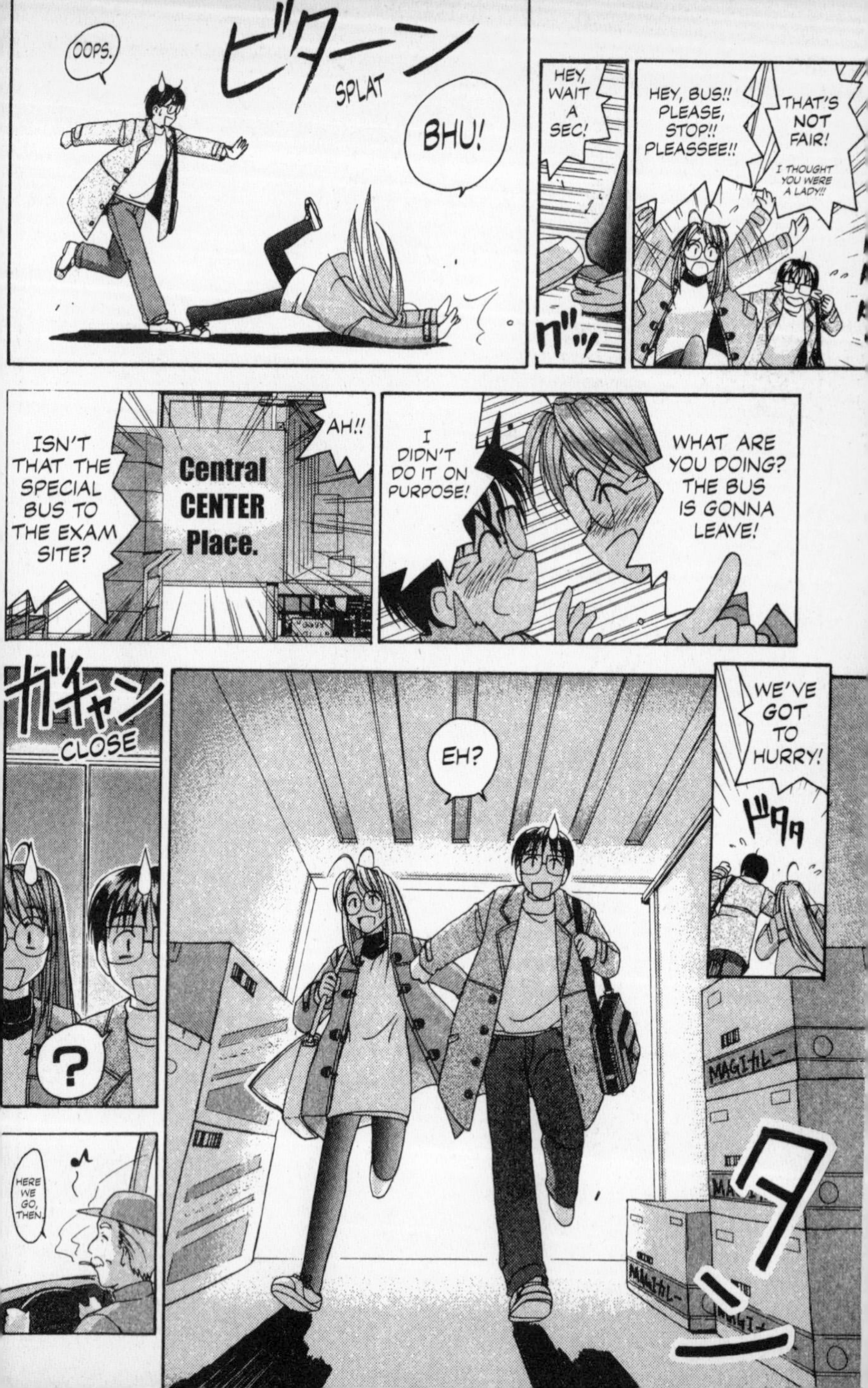
THAT'S NOT FAIR!
I THOUGHT YOU WERE A LADY!!
HEY, BUS!! PLEASE, STOP!! PLEASSEE!!
HEY, WAIT A SEC!
ガッ
ビターン
SPLAT
BHU!
OOPS.
WHAT ARE YOU DOING? THE BUS IS GONNA LEAVE!
I DIDN'T DO IT ON PURPOSE!
AH!!
Central CENTER Place.
ISN'T THAT THE SPECIAL BUS TO THE EXAM SITE?
WE'VE GOT TO HURRY!
ドタタ
EH?
ター
MAGIカレー
ガチャン
CLOSE
?
HERE WE GO, THEN.

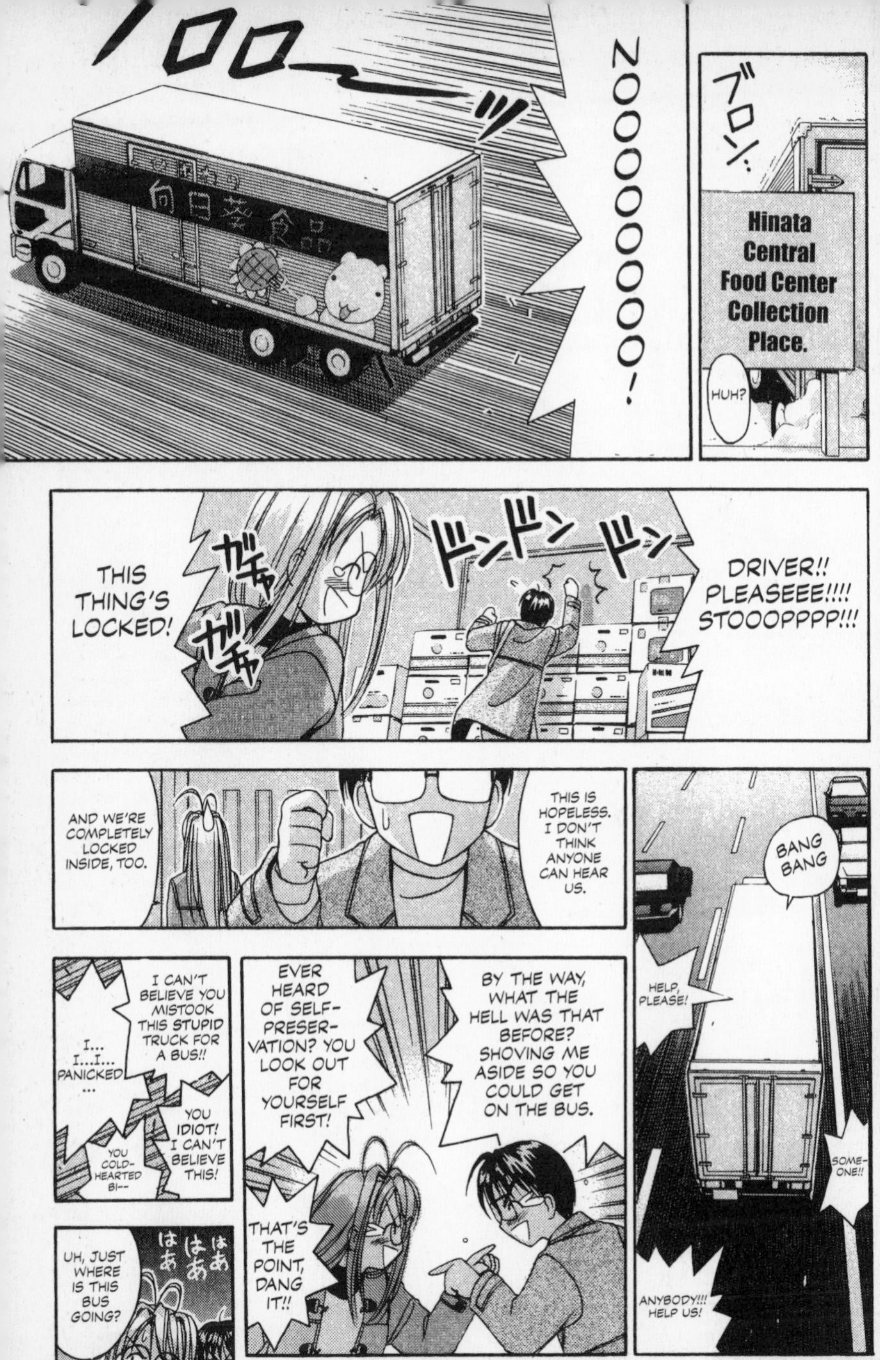
ブロン
Hinata Central Food Center Collection Place.
HUH?
ノロロ〜ッ
NOOOOOOOOO!
向日葵食品
DRIVER!! PLEASEEE!!!! STOOOPPPP!!!
ドンドン
ドン
ガチャ
ガチャ
THIS THING'S LOCKED!
BANG BANG
HELP, PLEASE!
SOME-ONE!!
ANYBODY!!! HELP US!
THIS IS HOPELESS. I DON'T THINK ANYONE CAN HEAR US.
AND WE'RE COMPLETELY LOCKED INSIDE, TOO.
BY THE WAY, WHAT THE HELL WAS THAT BEFORE? SHOVING ME ASIDE SO YOU COULD GET ON THE BUS.
EVER HEARD OF SELF-PRESER-VATION? YOU LOOK OUT FOR YOURSELF FIRST!
THAT'S THE POINT, DANG IT!!
I CAN'T BELIEVE YOU MISTOOK THIS STUPID TRUCK FOR A BUS!!
I... I...I... PANICKED...
YOU IDIOT! I CAN'T BELIEVE THIS!
YOU COLD-HEARTED BI--
はあ はあ はあ
UH, JUST WHERE IS THIS BUS GOING?

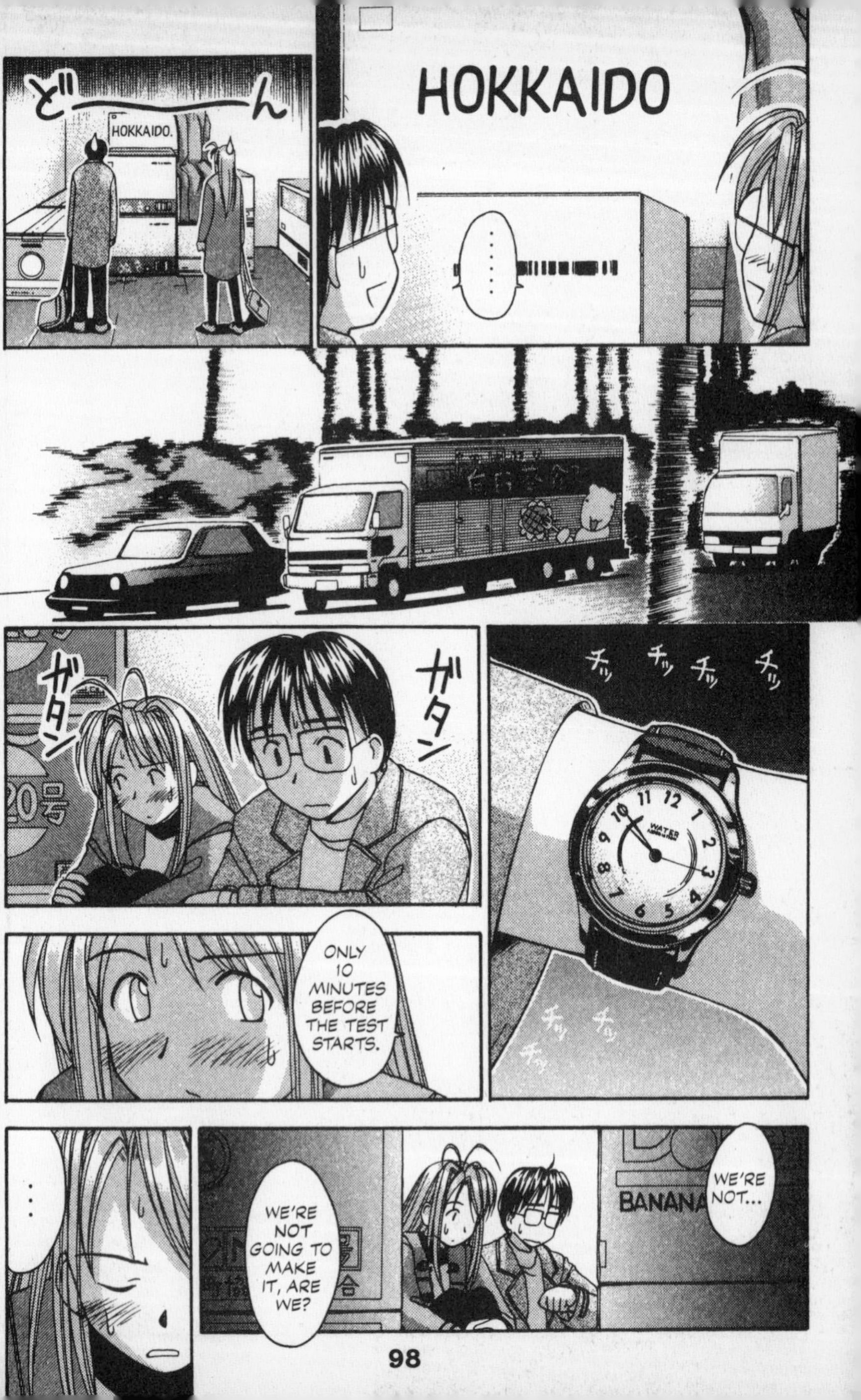

HOKKAIDO
……
どーーーん
HOKKAIDO.
チッ チッ チッ チッ
チッ チッ チッ
ガタン
ガタン
20号
ONLY 10 MINUTES BEFORE THE TEST STARTS.
BANANA
WE'RE NOT...
WE'RE NOT GOING TO MAKE IT, ARE WE?
...

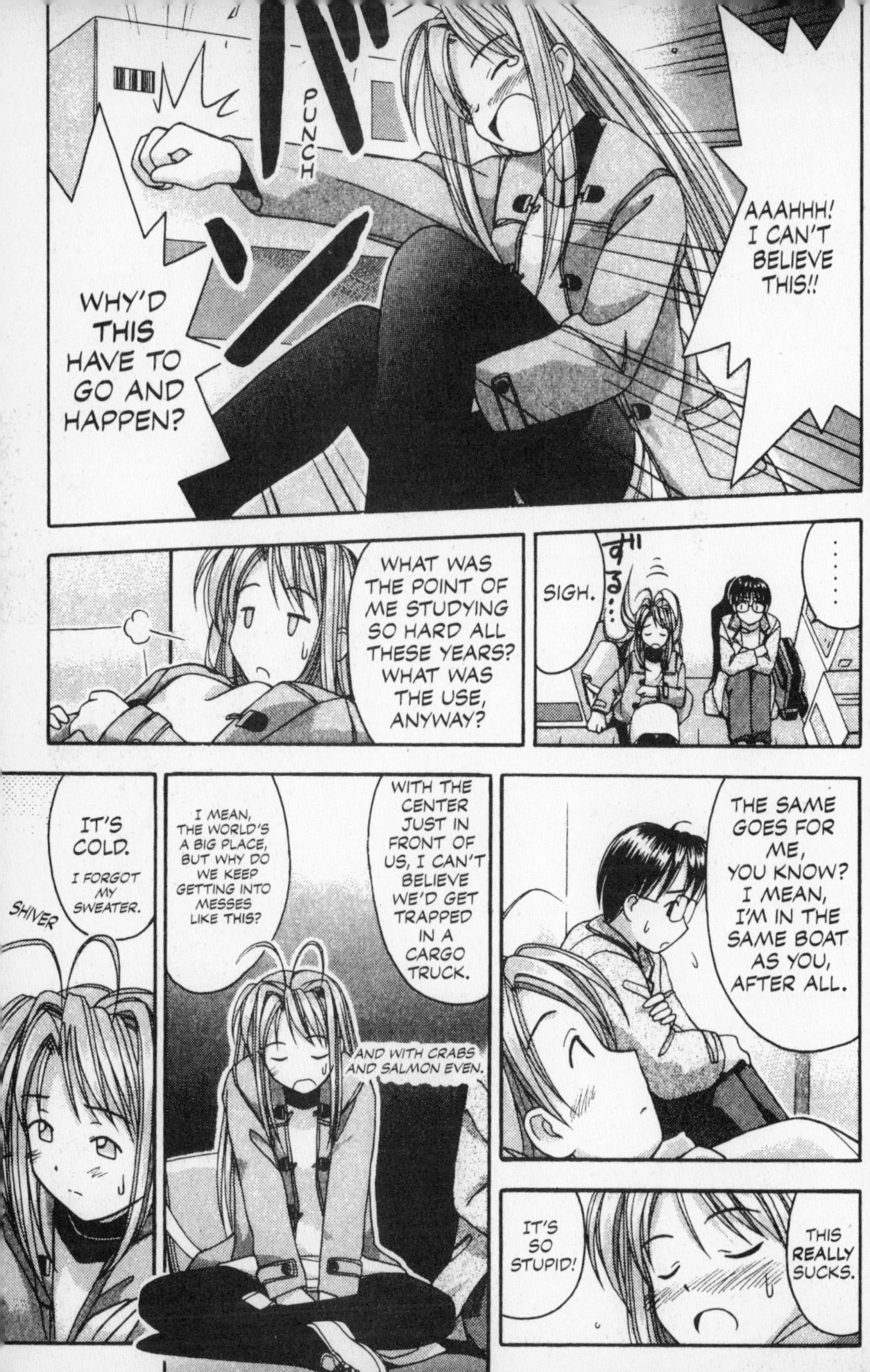
PUNCH
AAAHHH! I CAN'T BELIEVE THIS!!
WHY'D THIS HAVE TO GO AND HAPPEN?
......
ずる…
SIGH.
WHAT WAS THE POINT OF ME STUDYING SO HARD ALL THESE YEARS? WHAT WAS THE USE, ANYWAY?
THE SAME GOES FOR ME, YOU KNOW? I MEAN, I'M IN THE SAME BOAT AS YOU, AFTER ALL.
THIS REALLY SUCKS.
IT'S SO STUPID!
WITH THE CENTER JUST IN FRONT OF US, I CAN'T BELIEVE WE'D GET TRAPPED IN A CARGO TRUCK.
I MEAN, THE WORLD'S A BIG PLACE, BUT WHY DO WE KEEP GETTING INTO MESSES LIKE THIS?
AND WITH CRABS AND SALMON EVEN.
IT'S COLD.
I FORGOT MY SWEATER.
SHIVER

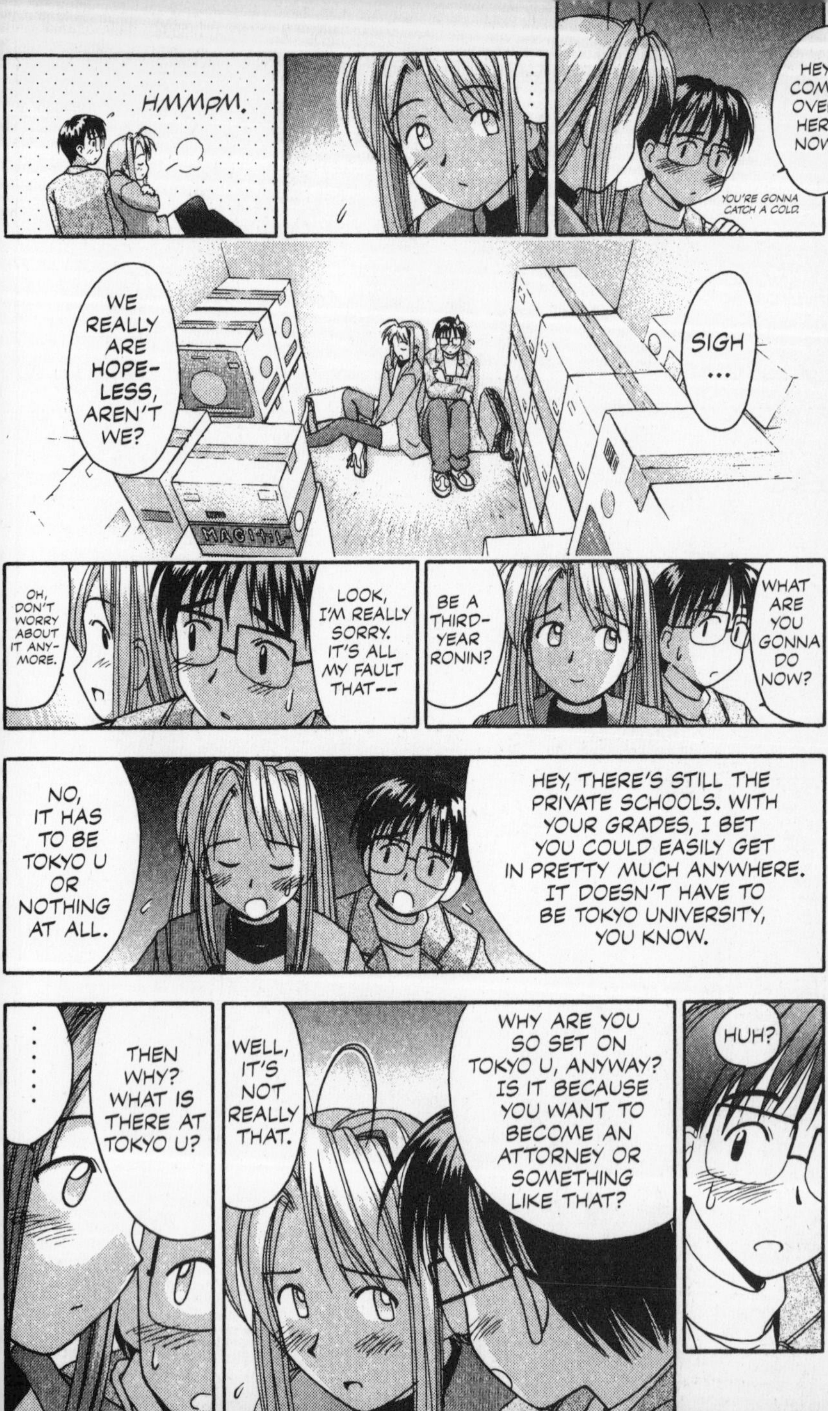
HEY, COME OVER HERE NOW.
YOU'RE GONNA CATCH A COLD.
...
HMMPM.
SIGH...
WE REALLY ARE HOPELESS, AREN'T WE?
WHAT ARE YOU GONNA DO NOW?
BE A THIRD-YEAR RONIN?
LOOK, I'M REALLY SORRY. IT'S ALL MY FAULT THAT--
OH, DON'T WORRY ABOUT IT ANYMORE.
HEY, THERE'S STILL THE PRIVATE SCHOOLS. WITH YOUR GRADES, I BET YOU COULD EASILY GET IN PRETTY MUCH ANYWHERE. IT DOESN'T HAVE TO BE TOKYO UNIVERSITY, YOU KNOW.
NO, IT HAS TO BE TOKYO U OR NOTHING AT ALL.
HUH?
WHY ARE YOU SO SET ON TOKYO U, ANYWAY? IS IT BECAUSE YOU WANT TO BECOME AN ATTORNEY OR SOMETHING LIKE THAT?
WELL, IT'S NOT REALLY THAT.
THEN WHY? WHAT IS THERE AT TOKYO U?
......

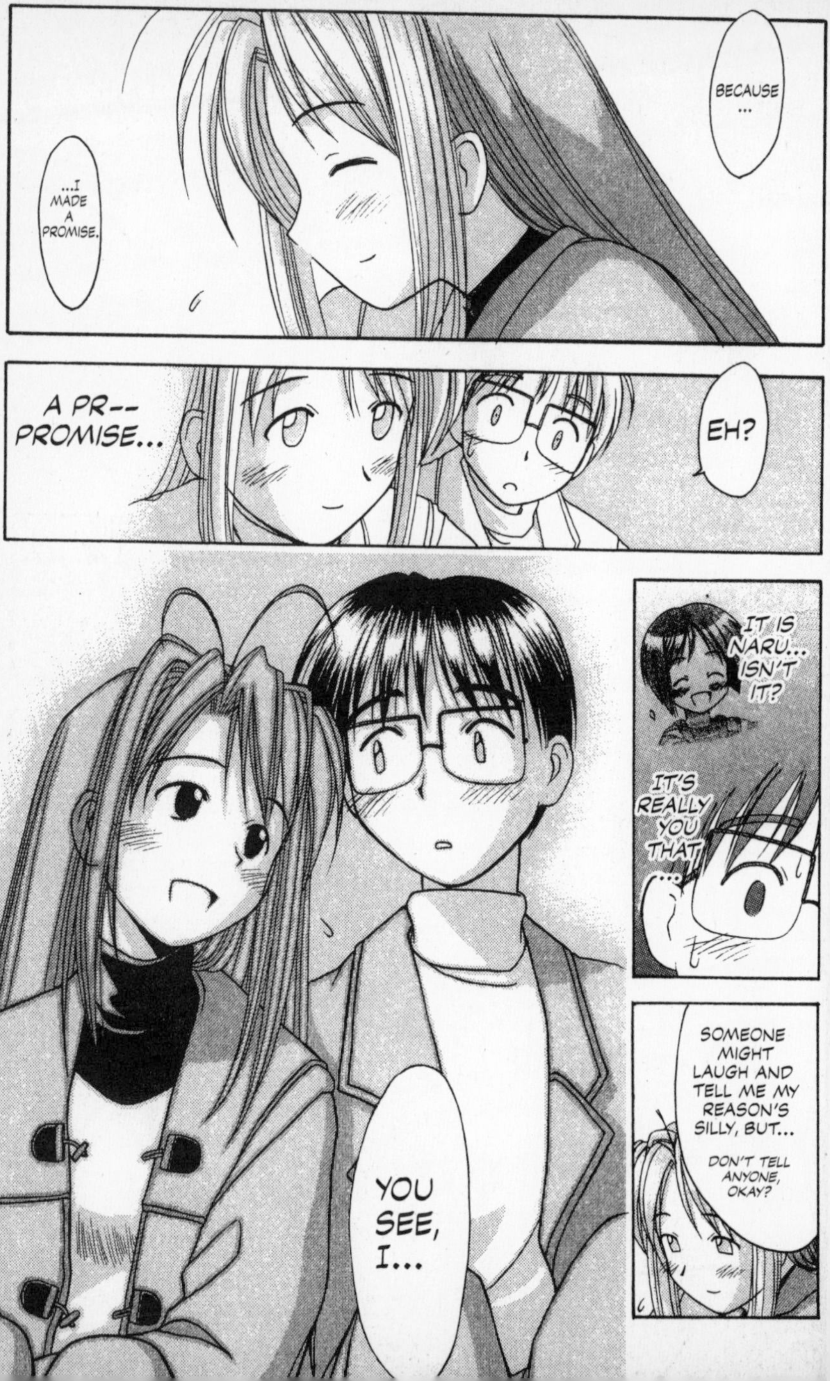
BECAUSE ...
...I MADE A PROMISE.
EH?
A PR-- PROMISE...
IT IS NARU... ISN'T IT?
IT'S REALLY YOU THAT ...
SOMEONE MIGHT LAUGH AND TELL ME MY REASON'S SILLY, BUT...
DON'T TELL ANYONE, OKAY?
YOU SEE, I...

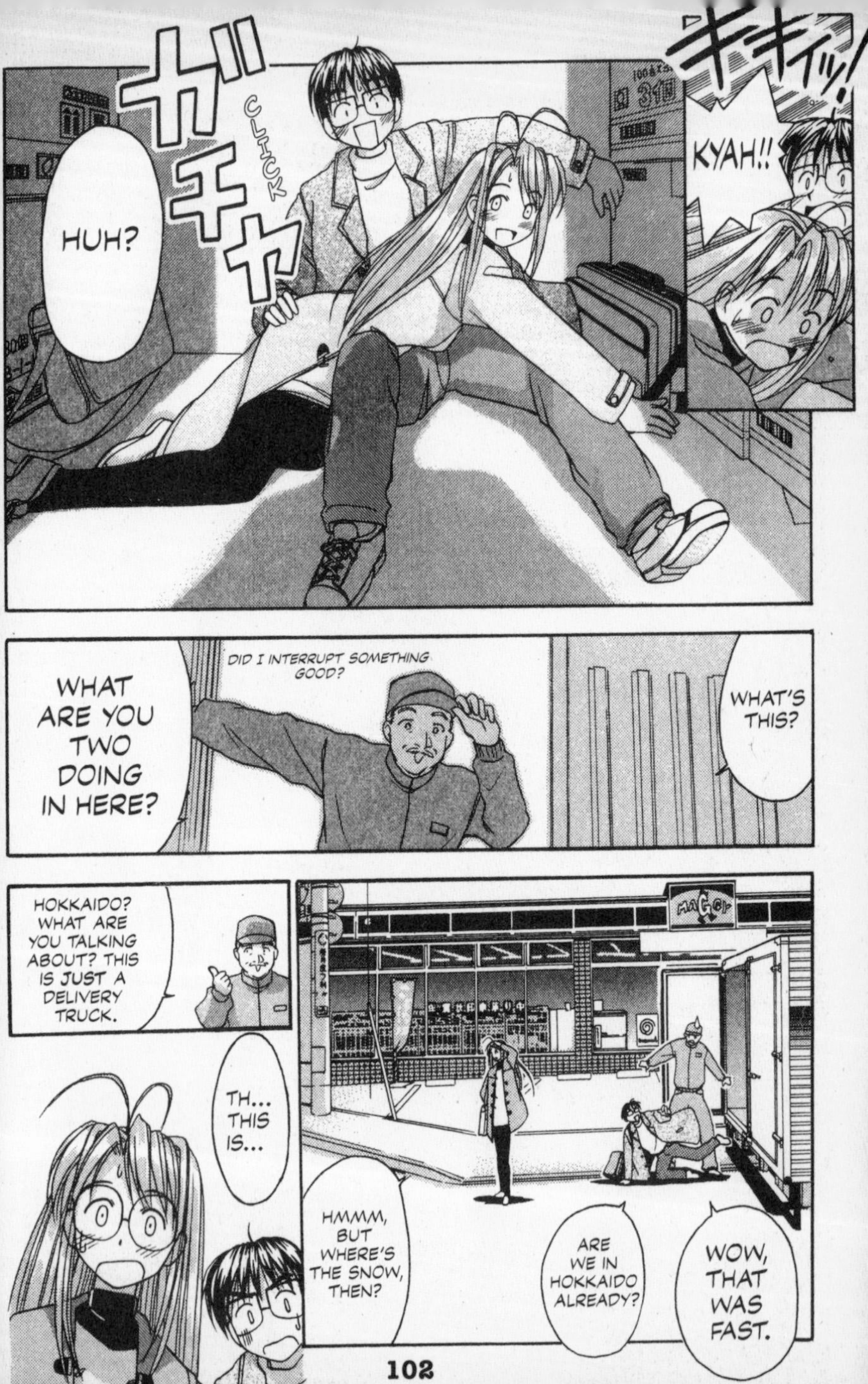
キキィッ!
KYAH!!
ガチャ
CLICK
HUH?
WHAT'S THIS?
DID I INTERRUPT SOMETHING GOOD?
WHAT ARE YOU TWO DOING IN HERE?
WOW, THAT WAS FAST.
ARE WE IN HOKKAIDO ALREADY?
HMMM, BUT WHERE'S THE SNOW, THEN?
HOKKAIDO? WHAT ARE YOU TALKING ABOUT? THIS IS JUST A DELIVERY TRUCK.
TH... THIS IS...

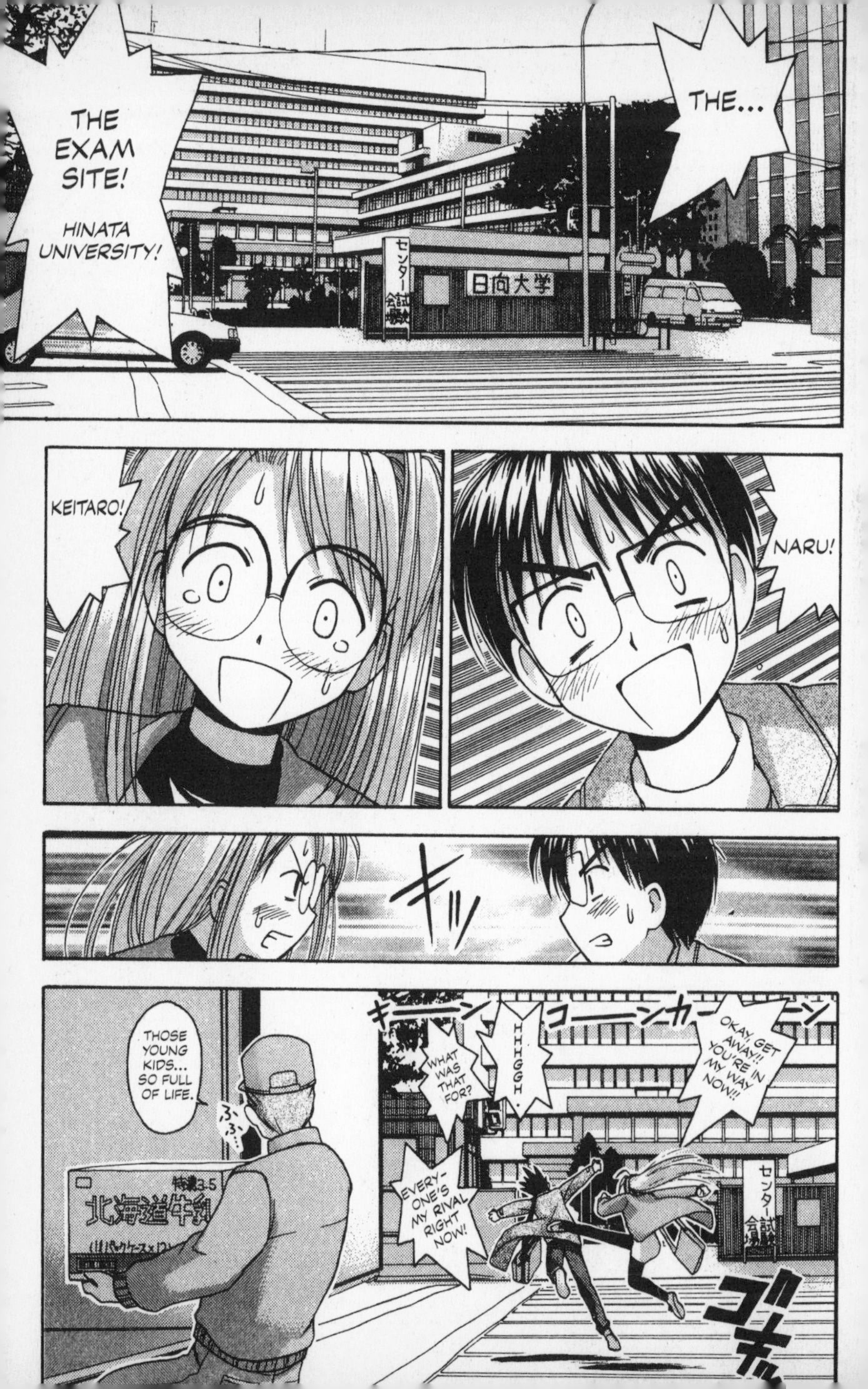
THE...
THE EXAM SITE!
HINATA UNIVERSITY!
日向大学
センター試験会場
NARU!
KEITARO!
キッ
キーンコーンカーンコーン
OKAY, GET AWAY!! YOU'RE IN MY WAY NOW!!
HHHGGH.
WHAT WAS THAT FOR?
EVERY-ONE'S MY RIVAL RIGHT NOW!
センター試験会場
ゴギッ
THOSE YOUNG KIDS... SO FULL OF LIFE.
ふふ…
特選3.5
北海道牛乳

ビターン
SPLAT

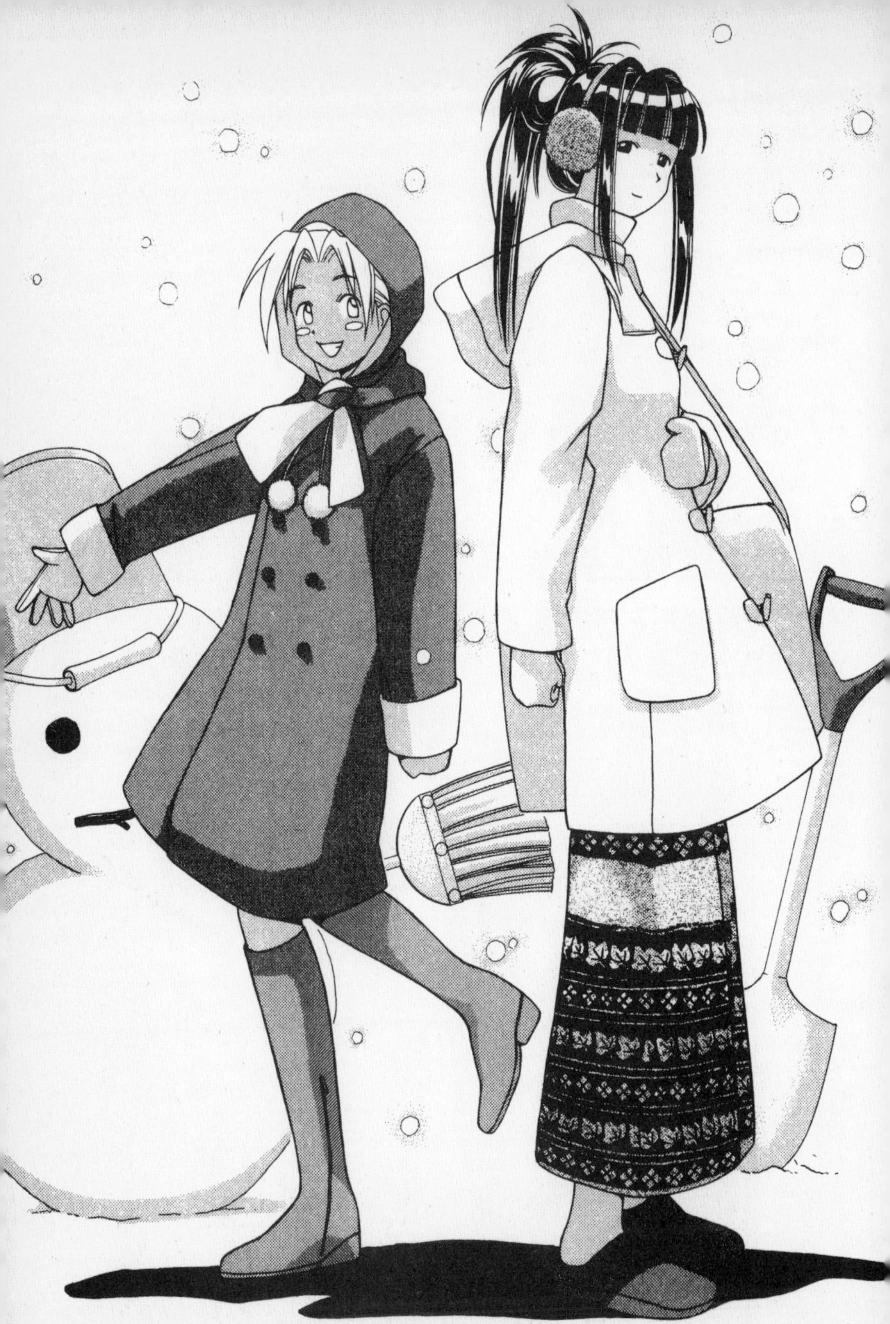

HINATA. 12 Happy or Unhappy?

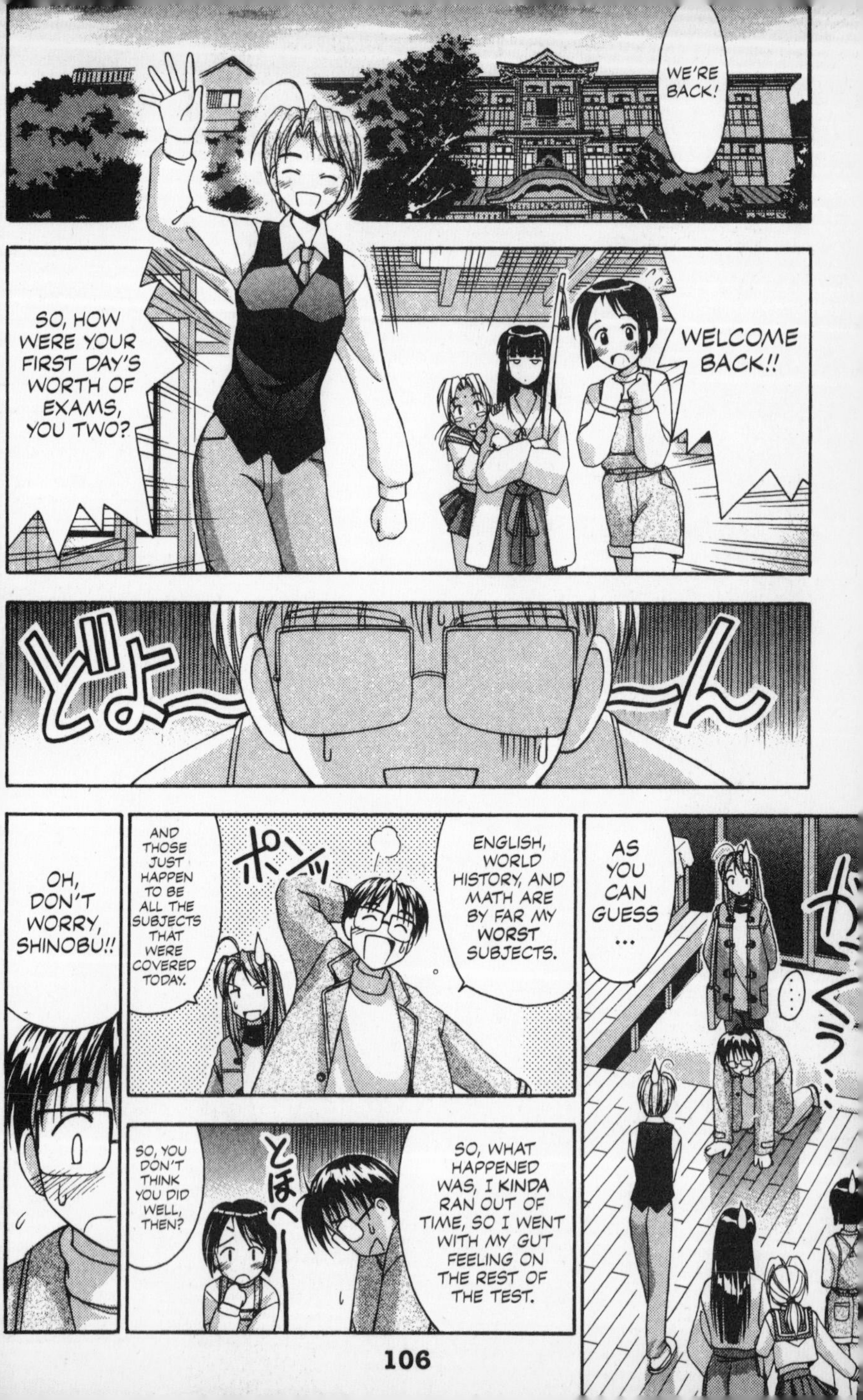
WE'RE BACK!
WELCOME BACK!!
SO, HOW WERE YOUR FIRST DAY'S WORTH OF EXAMS, YOU TWO?
どよ～～ん
AS YOU CAN GUESS ...
...
ENGLISH, WORLD HISTORY, AND MATH ARE BY FAR MY WORST SUBJECTS.
ポンッ
AND THOSE JUST HAPPEN TO BE ALL THE SUBJECTS THAT WERE COVERED TODAY.
SO, WHAT HAPPENED WAS, I KINDA RAN OUT OF TIME, SO I WENT WITH MY GUT FEELING ON THE REST OF THE TEST.
とほへ
SO, YOU DON'T THINK YOU DID WELL, THEN?
OH, DON'T WORRY, SHINOBU!!

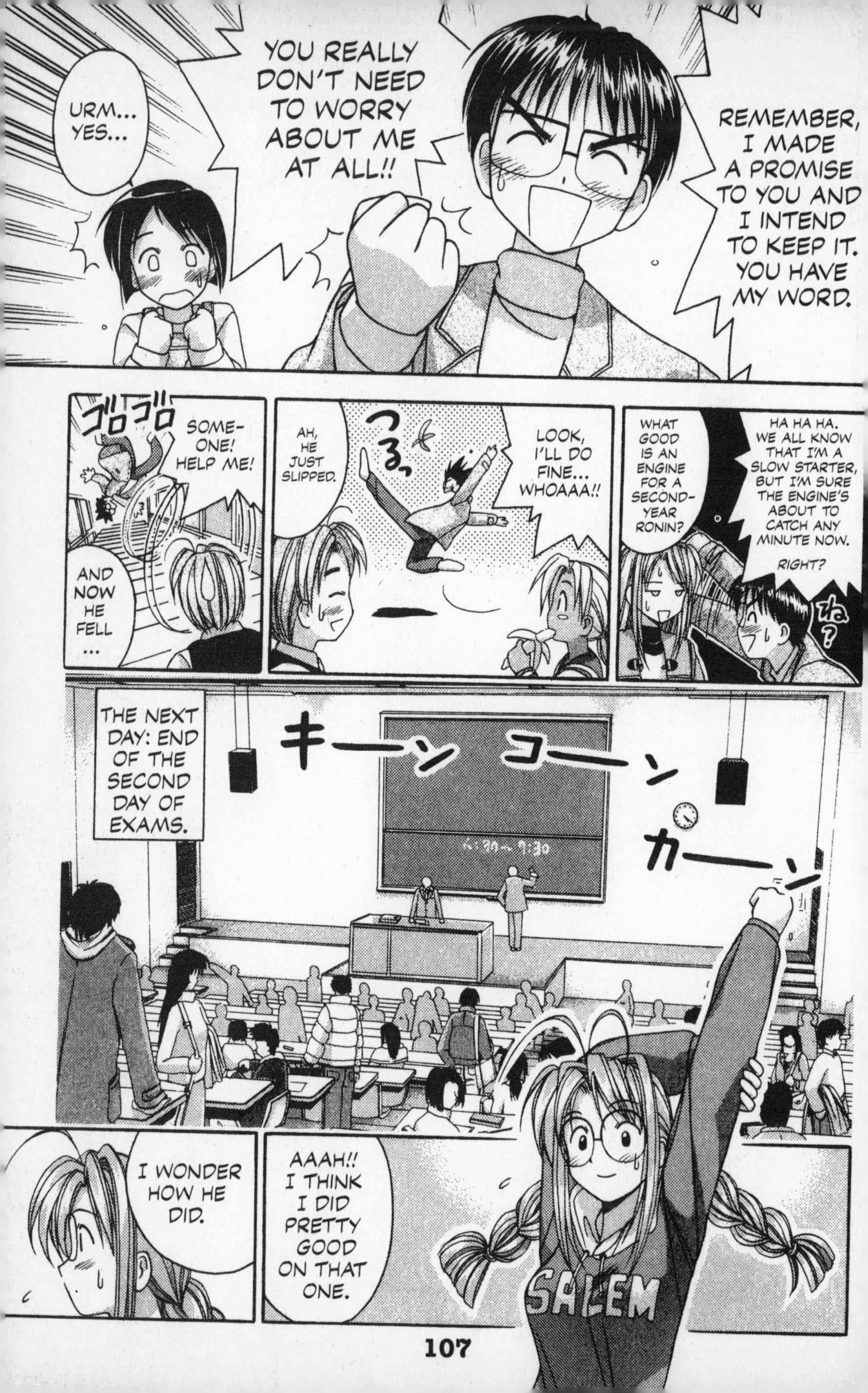
REMEMBER, I MADE A PROMISE TO YOU AND I INTEND TO KEEP IT. YOU HAVE MY WORD.
YOU REALLY DON'T NEED TO WORRY ABOUT ME AT ALL!!
URM... YES...
HA HA HA. WE ALL KNOW THAT I'M A SLOW STARTER, BUT I'M SURE THE ENGINE'S ABOUT TO CATCH ANY MINUTE NOW.
RIGHT?
ね？
WHAT GOOD IS AN ENGINE FOR A SECOND-YEAR RONIN?
LOOK, I'LL DO FINE... WHOAAA!!
つるっ
AH, HE JUST SLIPPED.
ゴロゴロ
SOME-ONE! HELP ME!
AND NOW HE FELL ...
THE NEXT DAY: END OF THE SECOND DAY OF EXAMS.
キーン コーン
カーン
AAAH!! I THINK I DID PRETTY GOOD ON THAT ONE.
SALEM
I WONDER HOW HE DID.

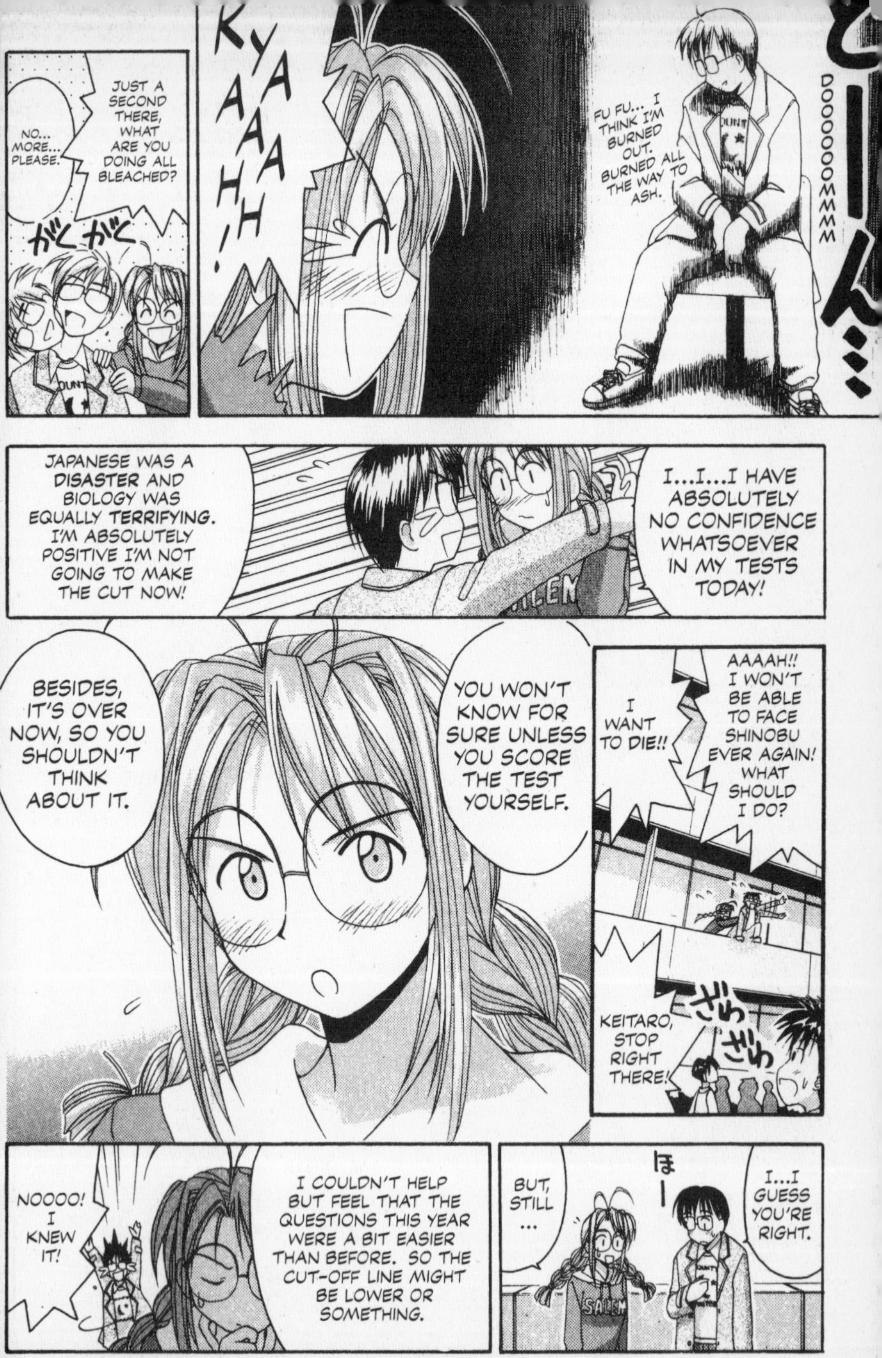
どーん…
DOOOOOOMMMM
FU FU... I THINK I'M BURNED OUT. BURNED ALL THE WAY TO ASH.
KYAAAAHH!
JUST A SECOND THERE, WHAT ARE YOU DOING ALL BLEACHED?
NO... MORE... PLEASE.
がくがく
I...I...I HAVE ABSOLUTELY NO CONFIDENCE WHATSOEVER IN MY TESTS TODAY!
JAPANESE WAS A DISASTER AND BIOLOGY WAS EQUALLY TERRIFYING. I'M ABSOLUTELY POSITIVE I'M NOT GOING TO MAKE THE CUT NOW!
AAAAH!! I WON'T BE ABLE TO FACE SHINOBU EVER AGAIN! WHAT SHOULD I DO?
I WANT TO DIE!!
ざわざわ
KEITARO, STOP RIGHT THERE!
YOU WON'T KNOW FOR SURE UNLESS YOU SCORE THE TEST YOURSELF.
BESIDES, IT'S OVER NOW, SO YOU SHOULDN'T THINK ABOUT IT.
I...I GUESS YOU'RE RIGHT.
ほー
BUT, STILL ...
I COULDN'T HELP BUT FEEL THAT THE QUESTIONS THIS YEAR WERE A BIT EASIER THAN BEFORE. SO THE CUT-OFF LINE MIGHT BE LOWER OR SOMETHING.
NOOOO! I KNEW IT!

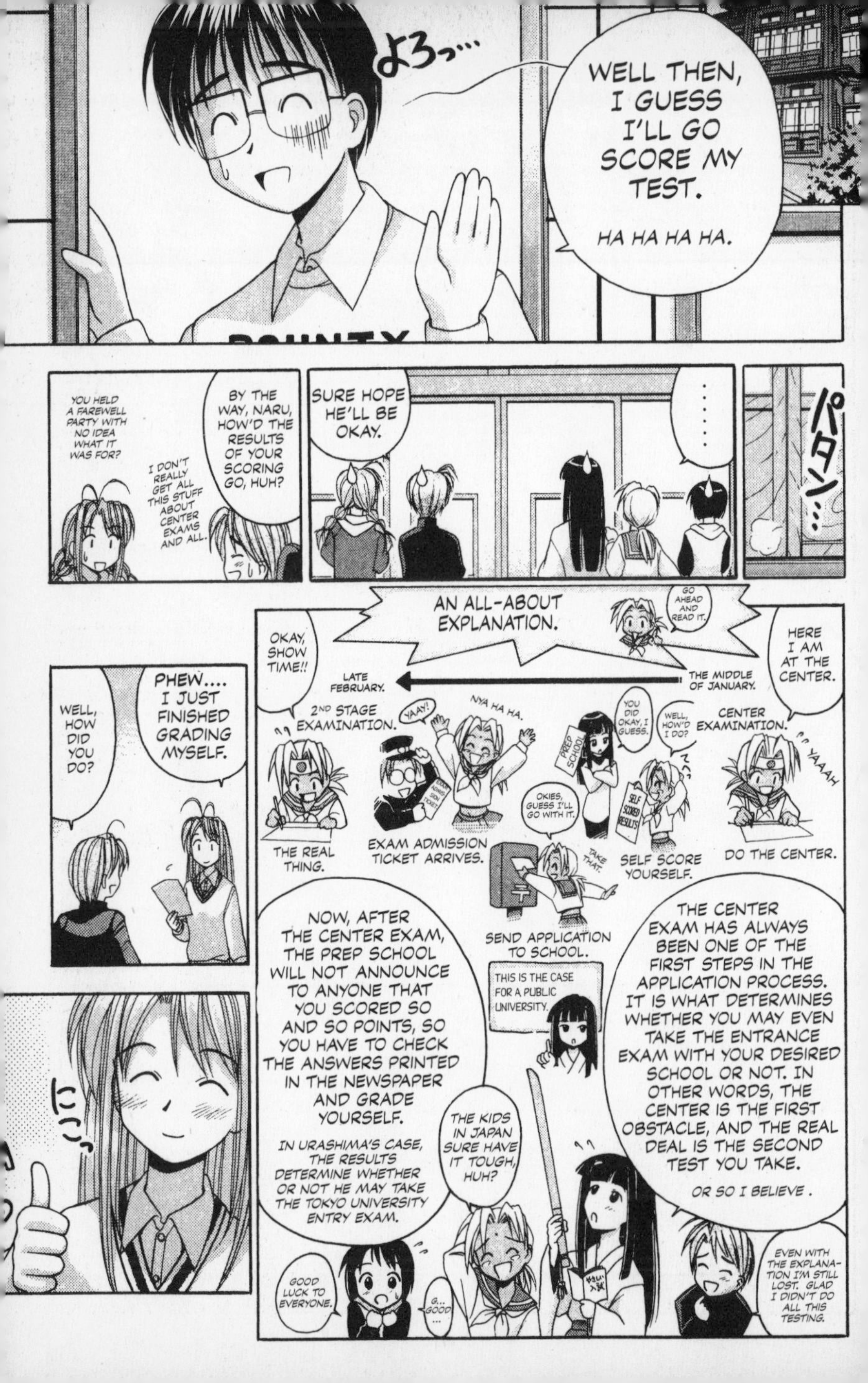
WELL THEN, I GUESS I'LL GO SCORE MY TEST.
HA HA HA HA.
よろっ…
POINT X
パタン…
......
SURE HOPE HE'LL BE OKAY.
BY THE WAY, NARU, HOW'D THE RESULTS OF YOUR SCORING GO, HUH?
YOU HELD A FAREWELL PARTY WITH NO IDEA WHAT IT WAS FOR?
I DON'T REALLY GET ALL THIS STUFF ABOUT CENTER EXAMS AND ALL.
AN ALL-ABOUT EXPLANATION.
GO AHEAD AND READ IT.
HERE I AM AT THE CENTER.
THE MIDDLE OF JANUARY.
LATE FEBRUARY.
OKAY, SHOW TIME!!
CENTER EXAMINATION.
YAAAH
DO THE CENTER.
WELL, HOW'D I DO?
YOU DID OKAY, I GUESS.
PREP SCHOOL
SELF SCORED RESULTS
SELF SCORE YOURSELF.
OKIES, GUESS I'LL GO WITH IT.
TAKE THAT.
SEND APPLICATION TO SCHOOL.
NYA HA HA.
YAAY!
EXAM ADMISSION TICKET ARRIVES.
2ND STAGE EXAMINATION.
THE REAL THING.
THIS IS THE CASE FOR A PUBLIC UNIVERSITY.
THE CENTER EXAM HAS ALWAYS BEEN ONE OF THE FIRST STEPS IN THE APPLICATION PROCESS. IT IS WHAT DETERMINES WHETHER YOU MAY EVEN TAKE THE ENTRANCE EXAM WITH YOUR DESIRED SCHOOL OR NOT. IN OTHER WORDS, THE CENTER IS THE FIRST OBSTACLE, AND THE REAL DEAL IS THE SECOND TEST YOU TAKE.
OR SO I BELIEVE .
NOW, AFTER THE CENTER EXAM, THE PREP SCHOOL WILL NOT ANNOUNCE TO ANYONE THAT YOU SCORED SO AND SO POINTS, SO YOU HAVE TO CHECK THE ANSWERS PRINTED IN THE NEWSPAPER AND GRADE YOURSELF.
IN URASHIMA'S CASE, THE RESULTS DETERMINE WHETHER OR NOT HE MAY TAKE THE TOKYO UNIVERSITY ENTRY EXAM.
THE KIDS IN JAPAN SURE HAVE IT TOUGH, HUH?
EVEN WITH THE EXPLANATION I'M STILL LOST. GLAD I DIDN'T DO ALL THIS TESTING.
G... GOOD ...
GOOD LUCK TO EVERYONE.
PHEW.... I JUST FINISHED GRADING MYSELF.
WELL, HOW DID YOU DO?
にこっ

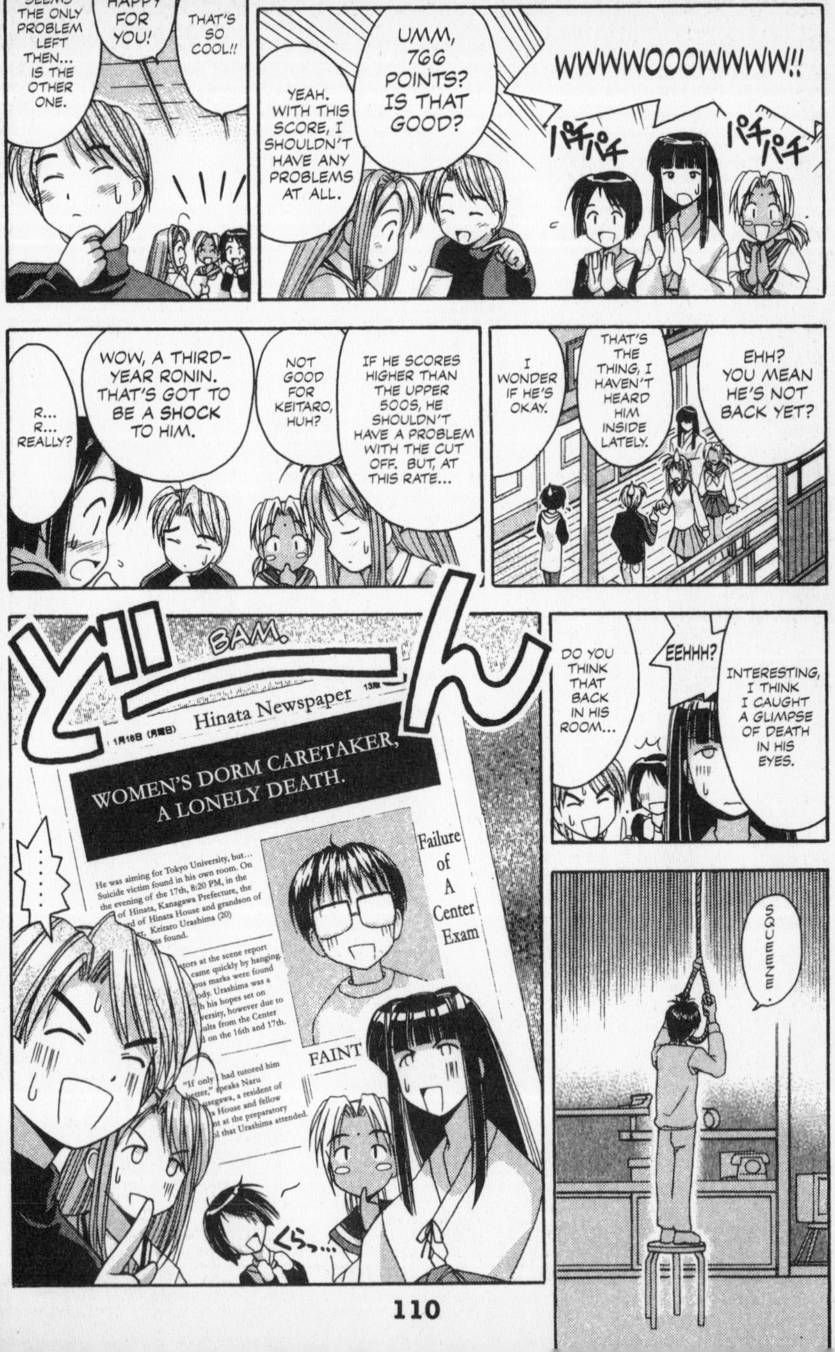
WWWWOOOWWWW!!
パチパチ
パチパチ
UMM, 766 POINTS? IS THAT GOOD?
YEAH. WITH THIS SCORE, I SHOULDN'T HAVE ANY PROBLEMS AT ALL.
THAT'S SO COOL!!
I'M SOOO HAPPY FOR YOU!
IT SEEMS THE ONLY PROBLEM LEFT THEN... IS THE OTHER ONE.
EHH? YOU MEAN HE'S NOT BACK YET?
THAT'S THE THING, I HAVEN'T HEARD HIM INSIDE LATELY.
I WONDER IF HE'S OKAY.
IF HE SCORES HIGHER THAN THE UPPER 500S, HE SHOULDN'T HAVE A PROBLEM WITH THE CUT OFF. BUT, AT THIS RATE...
NOT GOOD FOR KEITARO, HUH?
WOW, A THIRD-YEAR RONIN. THAT'S GOT TO BE A SHOCK TO HIM.
R... R... REALLY?
INTERESTING, I THINK I CAUGHT A GLIMPSE OF DEATH IN HIS EYES.
EEHHH?
DO YOU THINK THAT BACK IN HIS ROOM...
SQUEEZE.
どーーん
BAM.
13版
Hinata Newspaper
1月16日 (月曜日)
WOMEN'S DORM CARETAKER, A LONELY DEATH.
Failure of A Center Exam
He was aiming for Tokyo University, but... Suicide victim found in his own room. On the evening of the 17th, 8:20 PM, in the
of Hinata, Kanagawa Prefecture, the
of Hinata House and grandson of
Keitaro Urashima (20)
found.
tors at the scene report
came quickly by hanging.
ous marks were found
ody. Urashima was a
h his hopes set on
versity, however due to
ults from the Center
on the 16th and 17th.
"If only I had tutored him better," speaks Naru
segawa, a resident of
House and fellow
at the preparatory
that Urashima attended.
FAINT
......
くらっ...

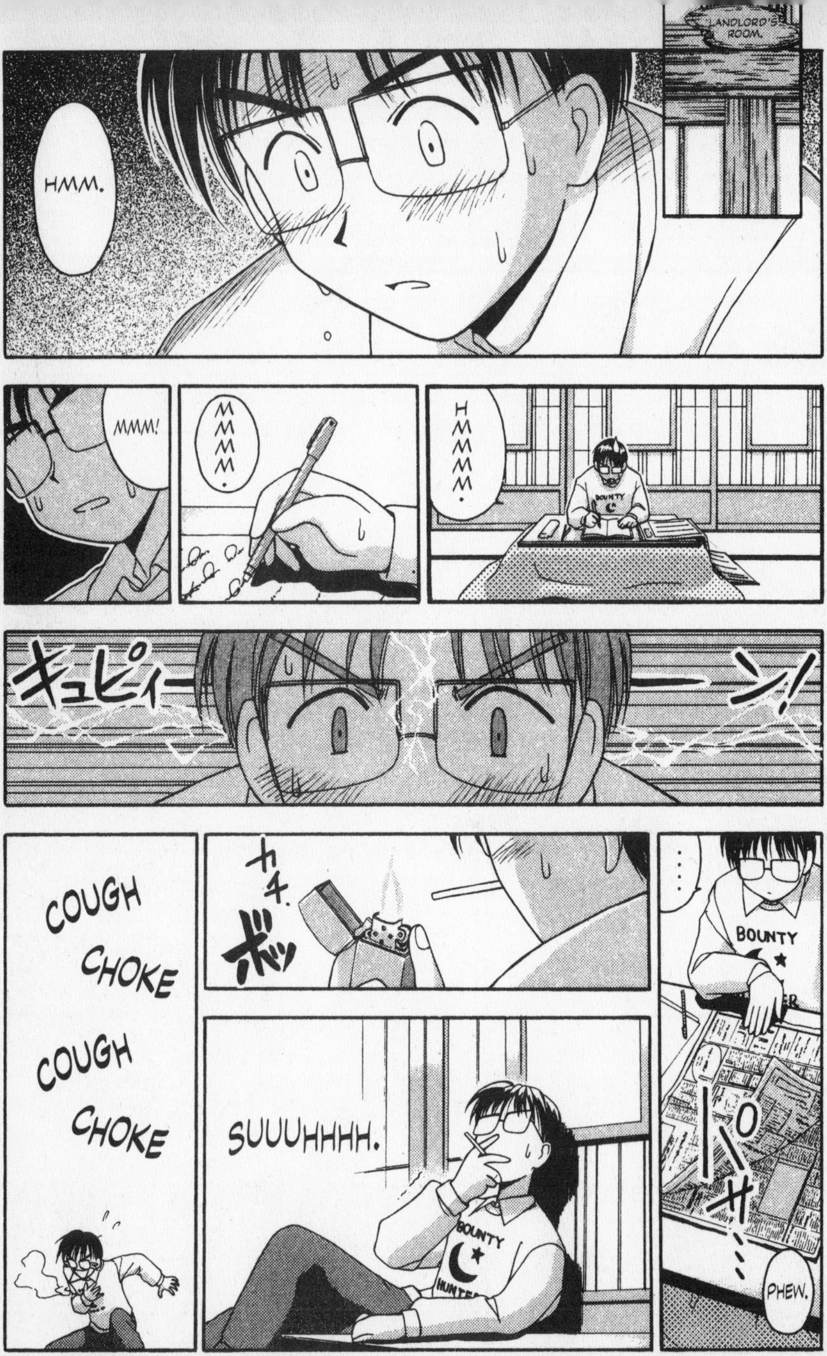
LANDLORD'S ROOM.
HMM.
HMMMM.
MMMM.
MMM!
キュピィーーン!
....
PHEW.
カチ.
ボッ
SUUUHHHH.
COUGH
CHOKE
COUGH
CHOKE

HE CAN'T SMOKE.

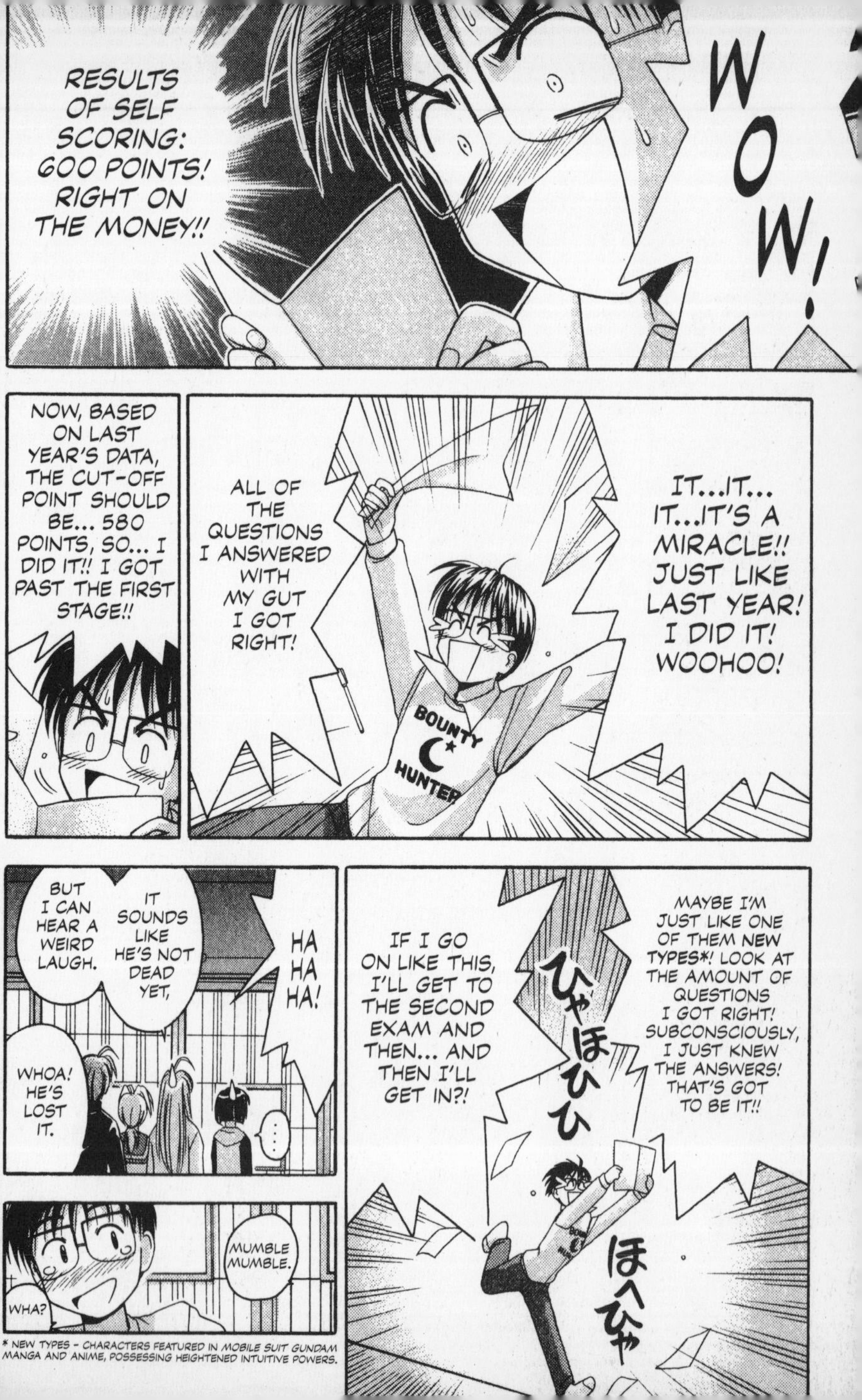
WOW!
RESULTS OF SELF SCORING: 600 POINTS! RIGHT ON THE MONEY!!
IT...IT... IT...IT'S A MIRACLE!! JUST LIKE LAST YEAR! I DID IT! WOOHOO!
ALL OF THE QUESTIONS I ANSWERED WITH MY GUT I GOT RIGHT!
BOUNTY HUNTER
NOW, BASED ON LAST YEAR'S DATA, THE CUT-OFF POINT SHOULD BE... 580 POINTS, SO... I DID IT!! I GOT PAST THE FIRST STAGE!!
MAYBE I'M JUST LIKE ONE OF THEM NEW TYPES*! LOOK AT THE AMOUNT OF QUESTIONS I GOT RIGHT! SUBCONSCIOUSLY, I JUST KNEW THE ANSWERS! THAT'S GOT TO BE IT!!
ひゃほひひ
IF I GO ON LIKE THIS, I'LL GET TO THE SECOND EXAM AND THEN... AND THEN I'LL GET IN?!
ほへひゃ
HA HA HA!
IT SOUNDS LIKE HE'S NOT DEAD YET,
BUT I CAN HEAR A WEIRD LAUGH.
WHOA! HE'S LOST IT.
...
MUMBLE MUMBLE.
WHA?

* NEW TYPES – CHARACTERS FEATURED IN MOBILE SUIT GUNDAM MANGA AND ANIME, POSSESSING HEIGHTENED INTUITIVE POWERS.

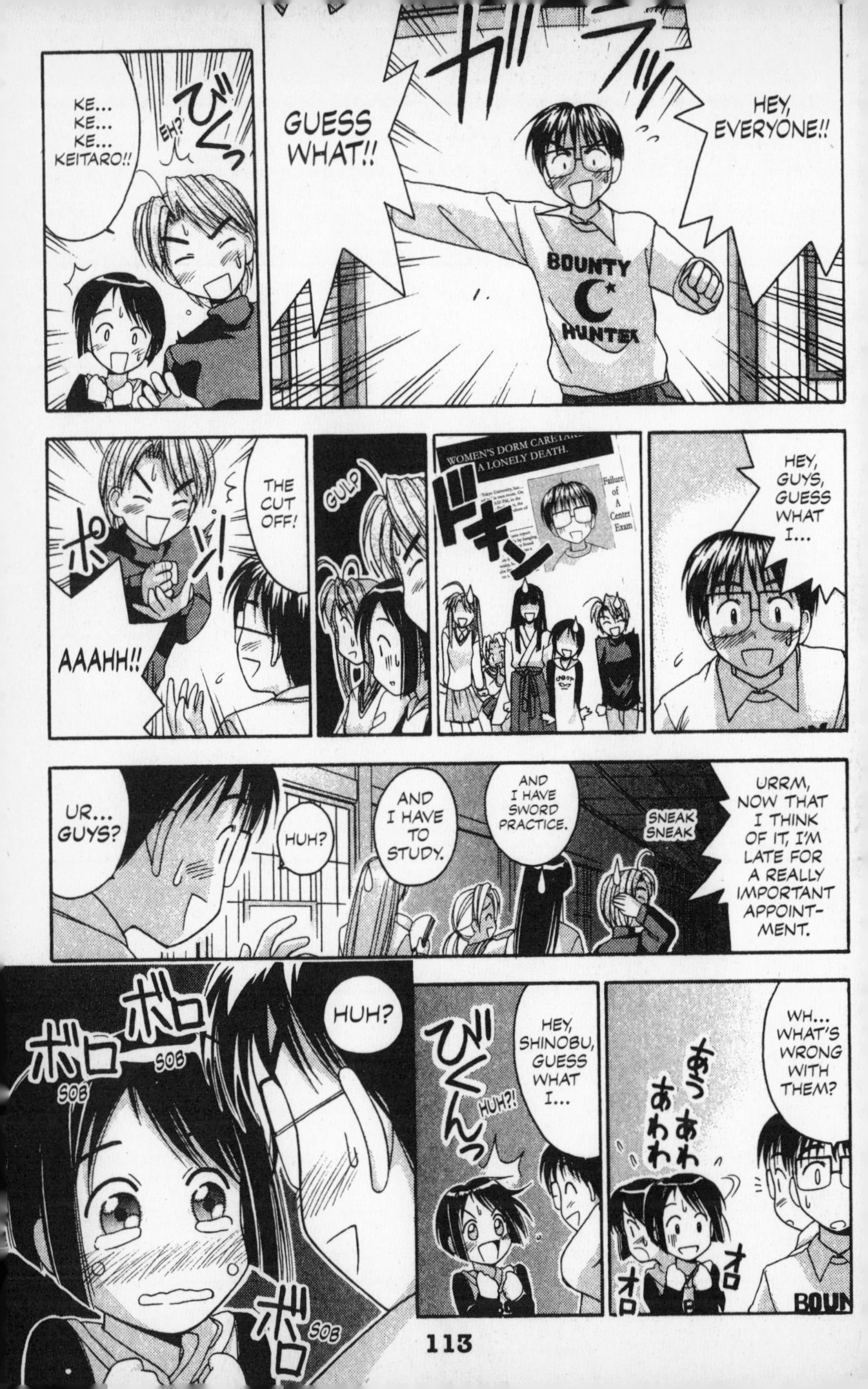
GUESS WHAT!!
HEY, EVERYONE!!
BOUNTY
KE... KE... KE... KEITARO!!
EH?
HEY, GUYS, GUESS WHAT I...
WOMEN'S DORM CARETAK
A LONELY DEATH.
Failure of A Center Exam
GULP
THE CUT OFF!
AAAHH!!
URRM, NOW THAT I THINK OF IT, I'M LATE FOR A REALLY IMPORTANT APPOINT-MENT.
SNEAK SNEAK
AND I HAVE SWORD PRACTICE.
AND I HAVE TO STUDY.
HUH?
UR... GUYS?
WH... WHAT'S WRONG WITH THEM?
HEY, SHINOBU, GUESS WHAT I...
HUH?!
HUH?
SOB
SOB
SOB

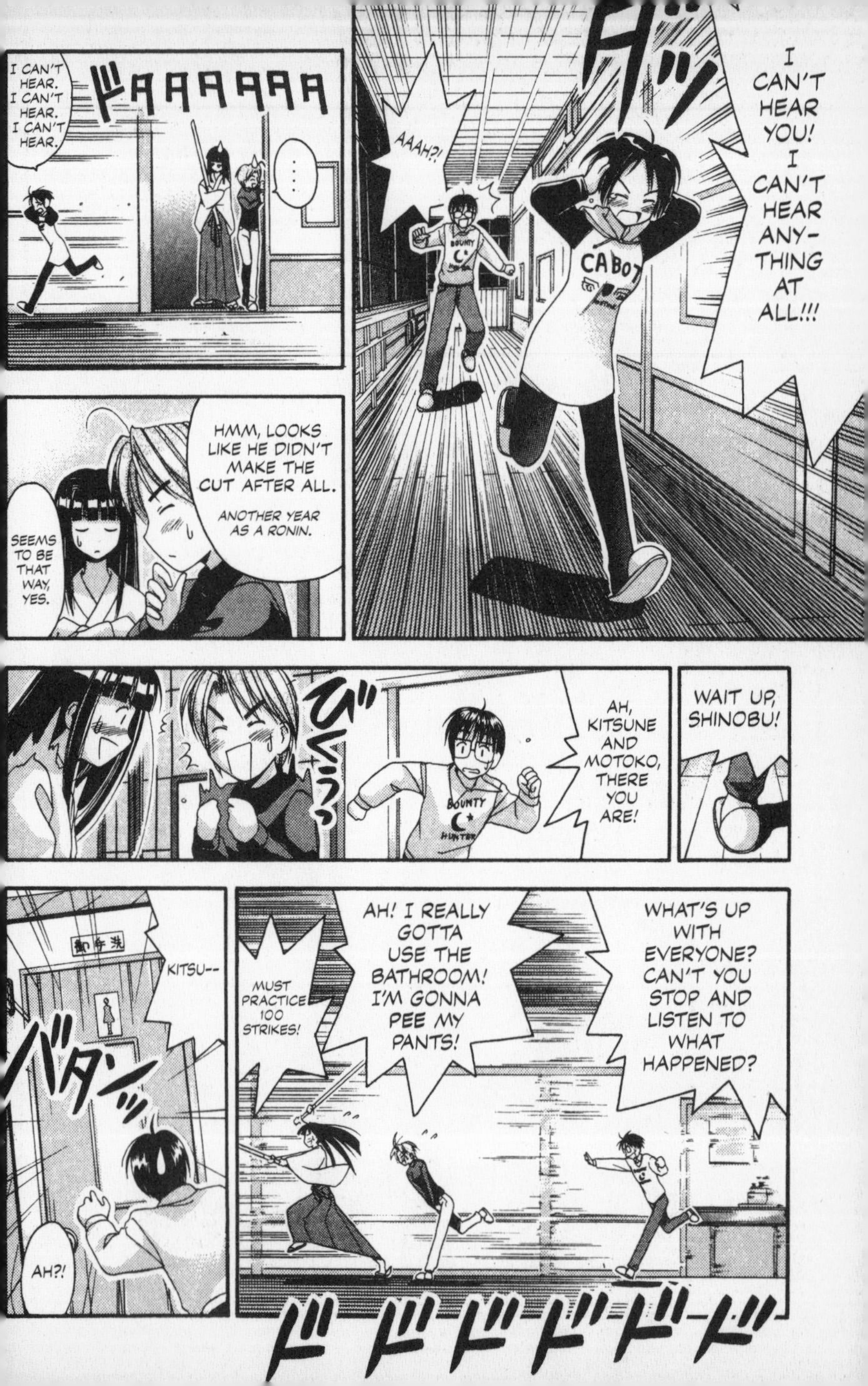
I CAN'T HEAR YOU! I CAN'T HEAR ANYTHING AT ALL!!!
AAAH?!
I CAN'T HEAR. I CAN'T HEAR. I CAN'T HEAR.
. . . .
HMM, LOOKS LIKE HE DIDN'T MAKE THE CUT AFTER ALL.
ANOTHER YEAR AS A RONIN.
SEEMS TO BE THAT WAY, YES.
WAIT UP, SHINOBU!
AH, KITSUNE AND MOTOKO, THERE YOU ARE!
WHAT'S UP WITH EVERYONE? CAN'T YOU STOP AND LISTEN TO WHAT HAPPENED?
AH! I REALLY GOTTA USE THE BATHROOM! I'M GONNA PEE MY PANTS!
MUST PRACTICE 100 STRIKES!
KITSU--
AH?!

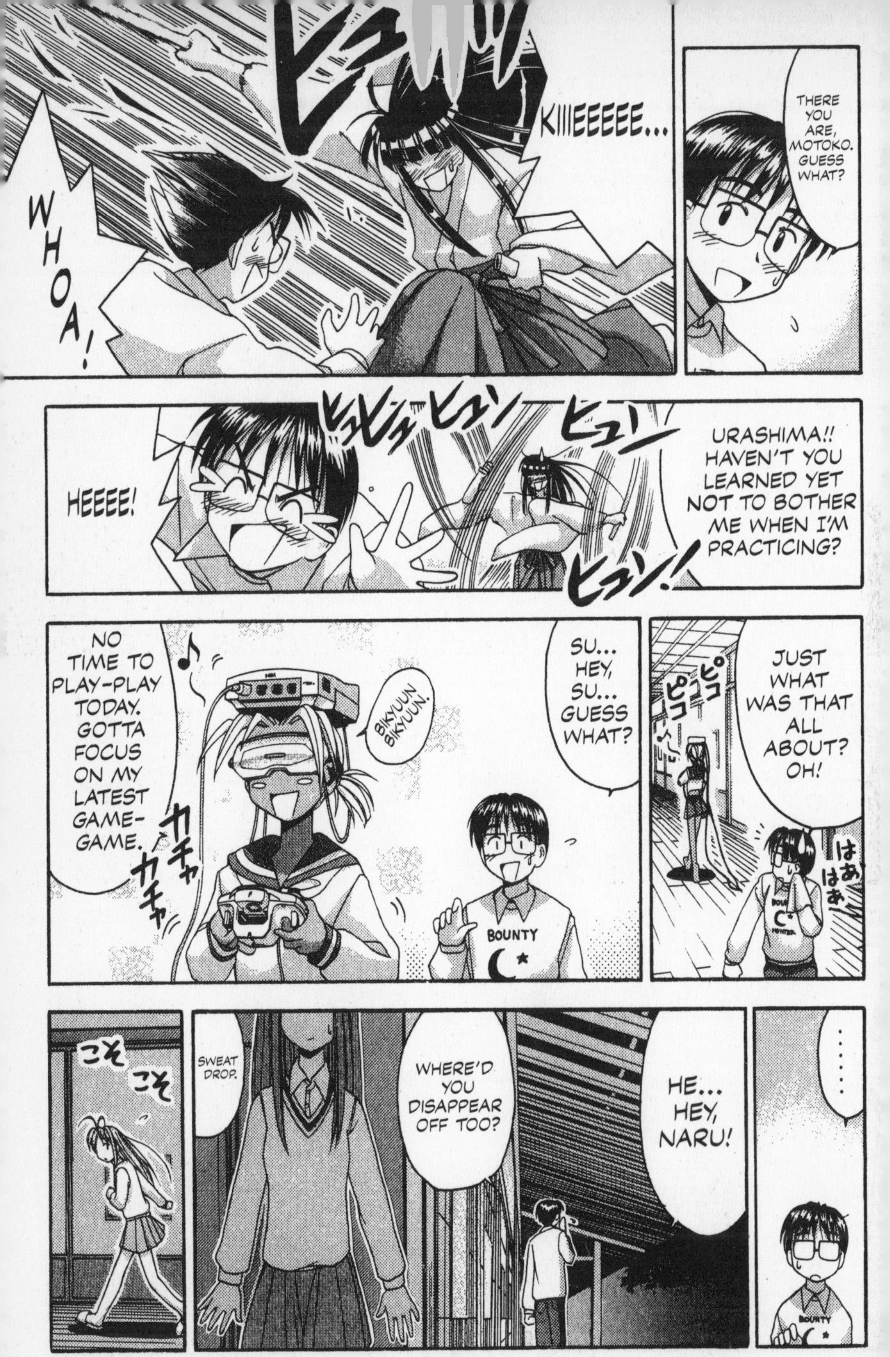
THERE YOU ARE, MOTOKO. GUESS WHAT?
KIIIEEEEE...
WHOA!
URASHIMA!! HAVEN'T YOU LEARNED YET NOT TO BOTHER ME WHEN I'M PRACTICING?
HEEEE!
JUST WHAT WAS THAT ALL ABOUT? OH!
ピコ ピコ
はあ はあ
SU... HEY, SU... GUESS WHAT?
BOUNTY
BIKYUUN BIKYUUN.
NO TIME TO PLAY-PLAY TODAY. GOTTA FOCUS ON MY LATEST GAME-GAME.
カチャ カチャ
......
BOUNTY
HE... HEY, NARU!
WHERE'D YOU DISAPPEAR OFF TOO?
SWEAT DROP.
こそ こそ

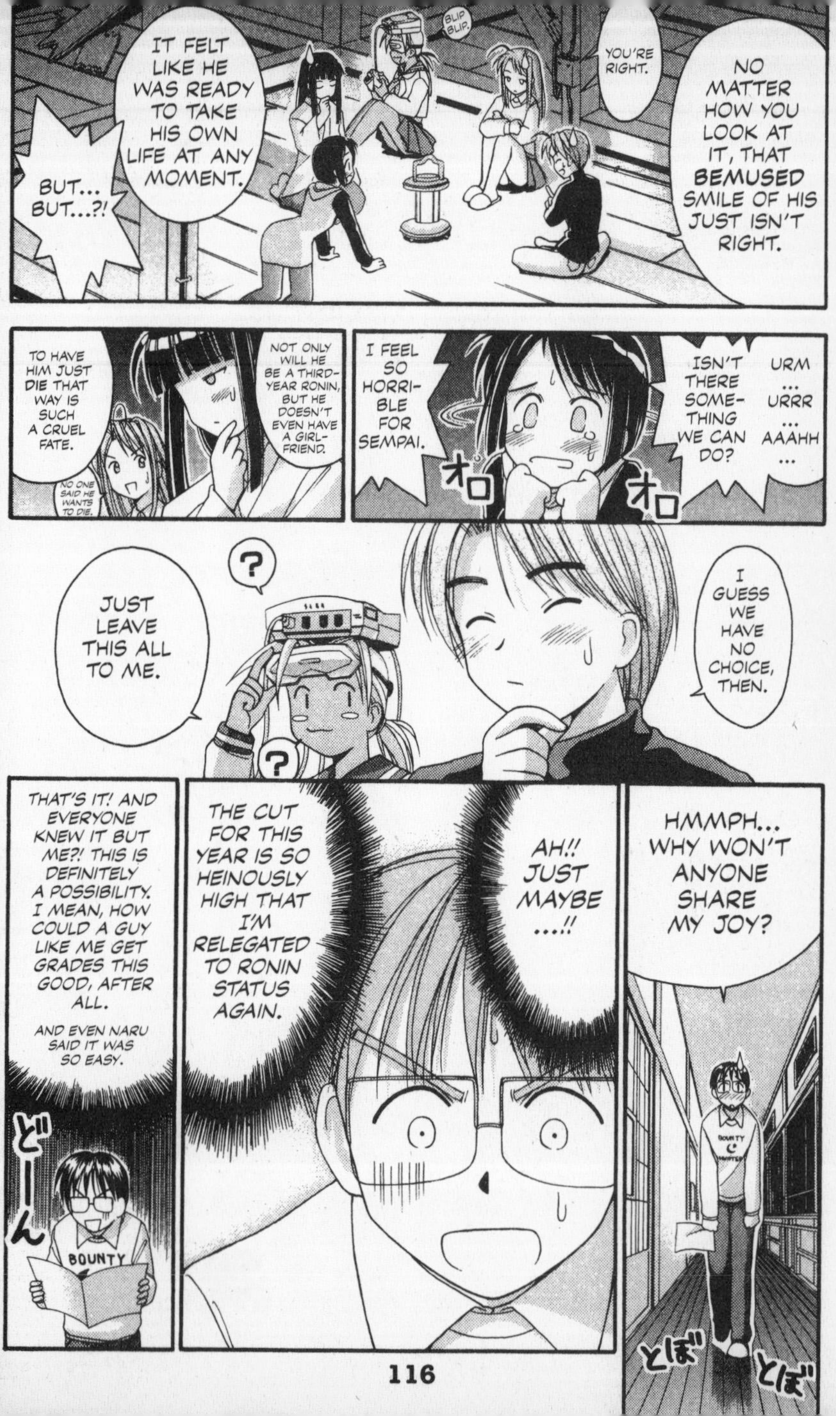
NO MATTER HOW YOU LOOK AT IT, THAT BEMUSED SMILE OF HIS JUST ISN'T RIGHT.
YOU'RE RIGHT.
BLIP BLIP.
IT FELT LIKE HE WAS READY TO TAKE HIS OWN LIFE AT ANY MOMENT.
BUT... BUT...?!
URM ... URRR ... AAAHH ...
ISN'T THERE SOMETHING WE CAN DO?
I FEEL SO HORRIBLE FOR SEMPAI.
オロ
オロ
NOT ONLY WILL HE BE A THIRD-YEAR RONIN, BUT HE DOESN'T EVEN HAVE A GIRLFRIEND.
TO HAVE HIM JUST DIE THAT WAY IS SUCH A CRUEL FATE.
NO ONE SAID HE WANTS TO DIE.
I GUESS WE HAVE NO CHOICE, THEN.
?
JUST LEAVE THIS ALL TO ME.
?
HMMPH... WHY WON'T ANYONE SHARE MY JOY?
とぼ
とぼ
AH!! JUST MAYBE ...!!
THE CUT FOR THIS YEAR IS SO HEINOUSLY HIGH THAT I'M RELEGATED TO RONIN STATUS AGAIN.
THAT'S IT! AND EVERYONE KNEW IT BUT ME?! THIS IS DEFINITELY A POSSIBILITY. I MEAN, HOW COULD A GUY LIKE ME GET GRADES THIS GOOD, AFTER ALL.
AND EVEN NARU SAID IT WAS SO EASY.
どーん
BOUNTY

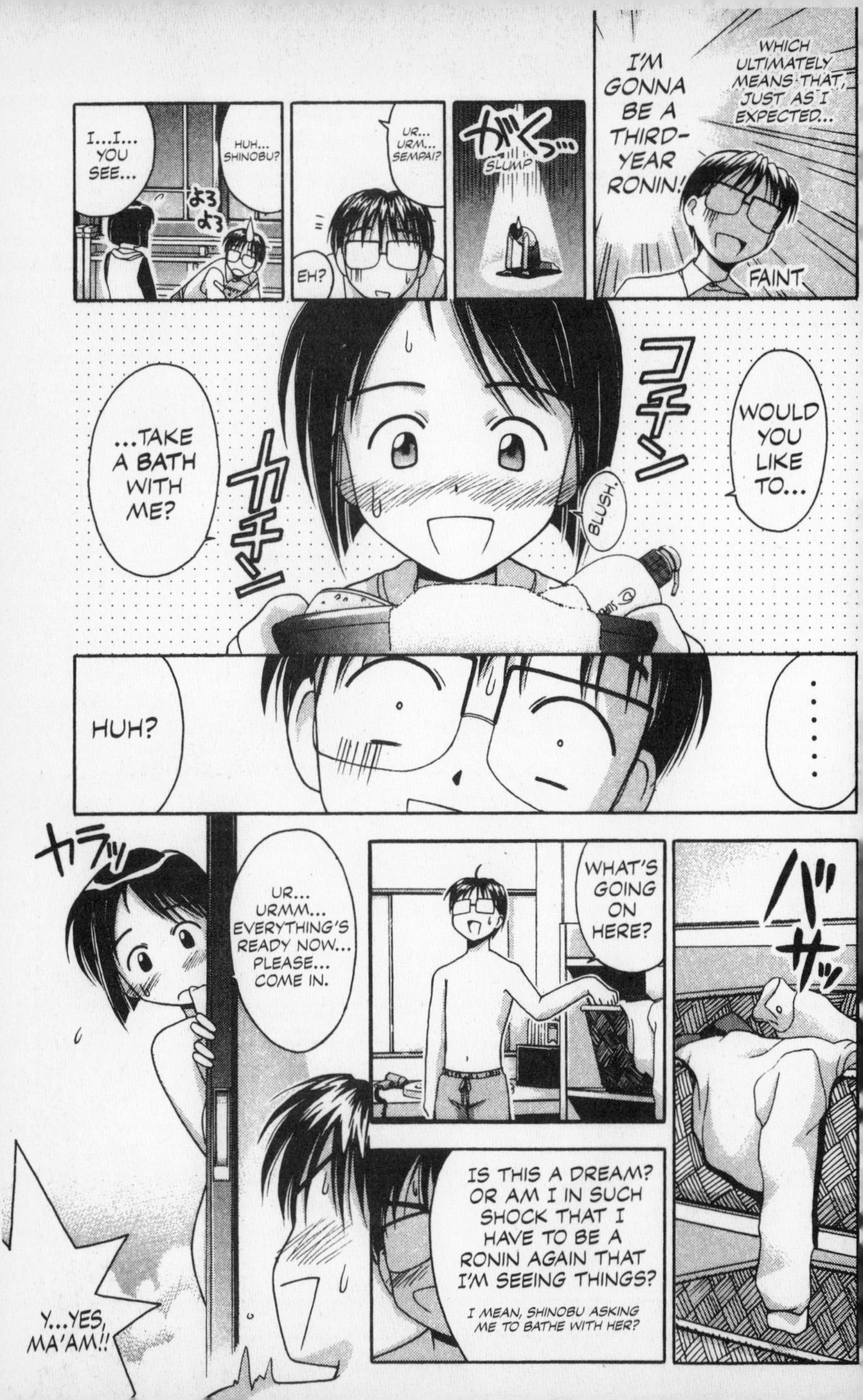
WHICH ULTIMATELY MEANS THAT, JUST AS I EXPECTED...
I'M GONNA BE A THIRD-YEAR RONIN!
FAINT
SLUMP
UR... URM... SEMPAI?
EH?
HUH... SHINOBU?
I...I... YOU SEE...
WOULD YOU LIKE TO...
BLUSH.
...TAKE A BATH WITH ME?
......
HUH?
WHAT'S GOING ON HERE?
IS THIS A DREAM? OR AM I IN SUCH SHOCK THAT I HAVE TO BE A RONIN AGAIN THAT I'M SEEING THINGS?
I MEAN, SHINOBU ASKING ME TO BATHE WITH HER?
UR... URMM... EVERYTHING'S READY NOW... PLEASE... COME IN.
Y...YES, MA'AM!!

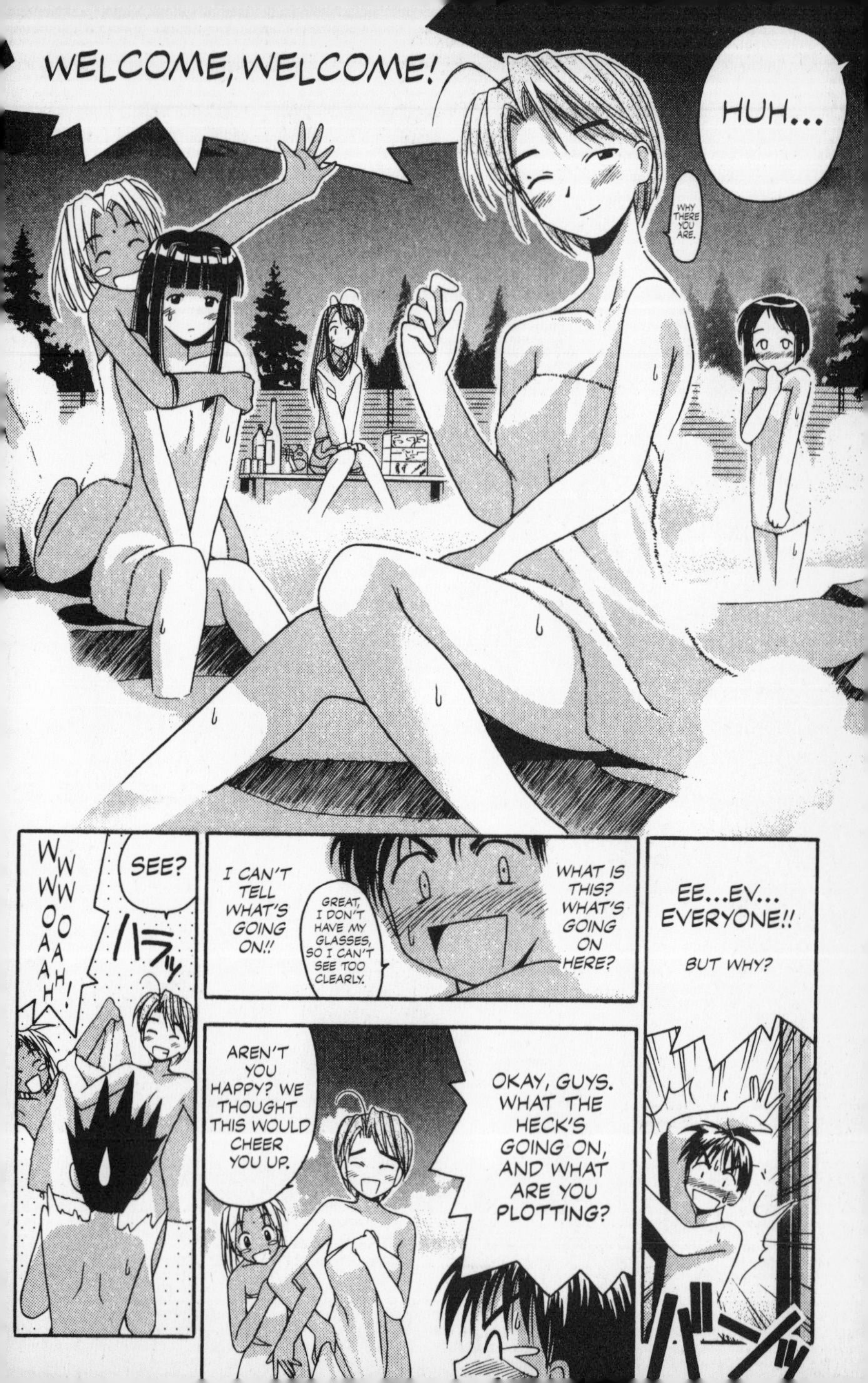
HUH...
WHY THERE YOU ARE.
WELCOME, WELCOME!
EE...EV... EVERYONE!!
BUT WHY?
WHAT IS THIS? WHAT'S GOING ON HERE?
GREAT, I DON'T HAVE MY GLASSES, SO I CAN'T SEE TOO CLEARLY.
I CAN'T TELL WHAT'S GOING ON!!
OKAY, GUYS. WHAT THE HECK'S GOING ON, AND WHAT ARE YOU PLOTTING?
AREN'T YOU HAPPY? WE THOUGHT THIS WOULD CHEER YOU UP.
SEE?
ハラッ
WWWWOOAAAH!

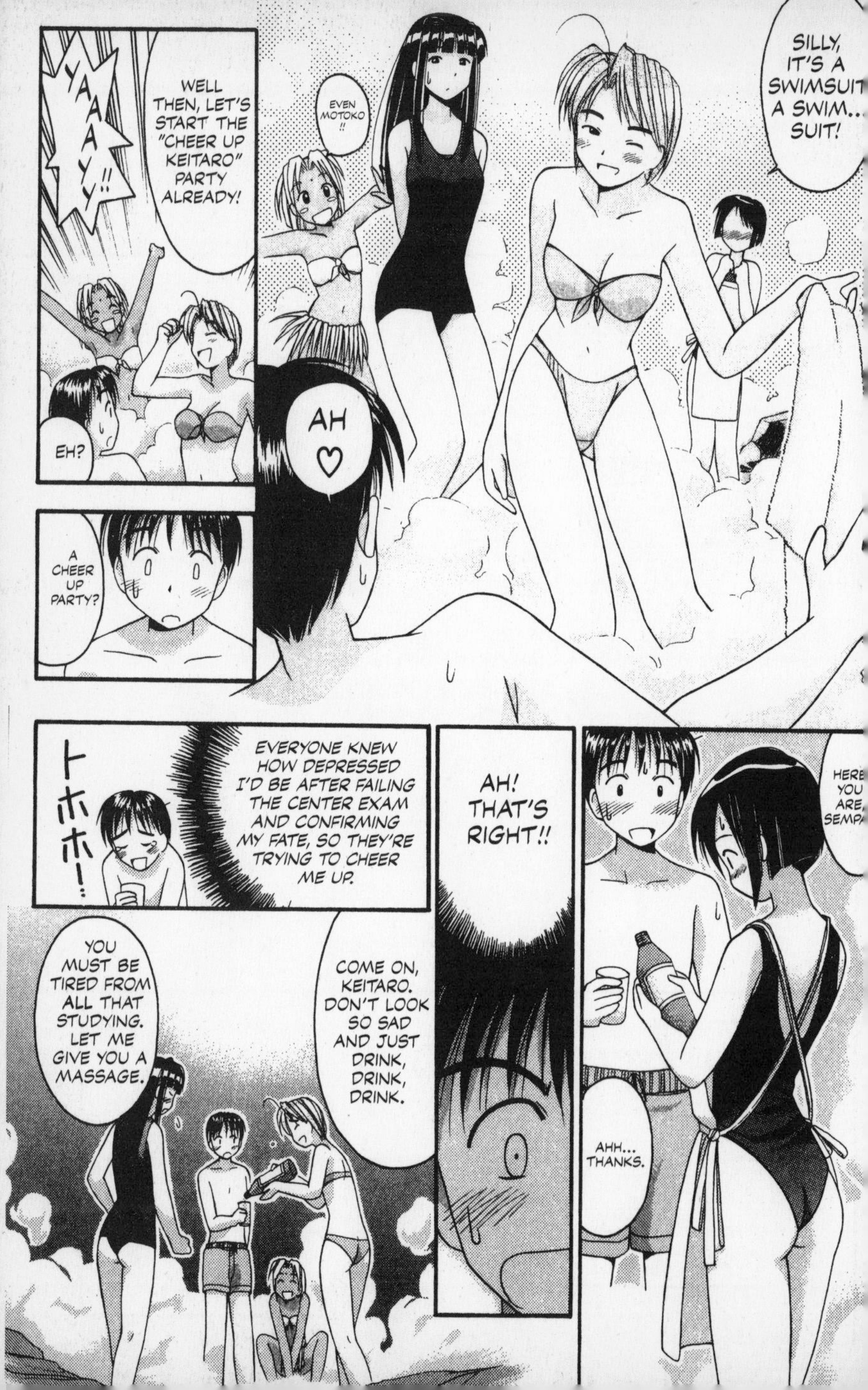
SILLY, IT'S A SWIMSUIT A SWIM... SUIT!
EVEN MOTOKO!!
AH ♡
YAAAYY!!
WELL THEN, LET'S START THE "CHEER UP KEITARO" PARTY ALREADY!
EH?
A CHEER UP PARTY?
HERE YOU ARE, SEMPA
AHH... THANKS.
AH! THAT'S RIGHT!!
トホホー!!
EVERYONE KNEW HOW DEPRESSED I'D BE AFTER FAILING THE CENTER EXAM AND CONFIRMING MY FATE, SO THEY'RE TRYING TO CHEER ME UP.
COME ON, KEITARO. DON'T LOOK SO SAD AND JUST DRINK, DRINK, DRINK.
YOU MUST BE TIRED FROM ALL THAT STUDYING. LET ME GIVE YOU A MASSAGE.

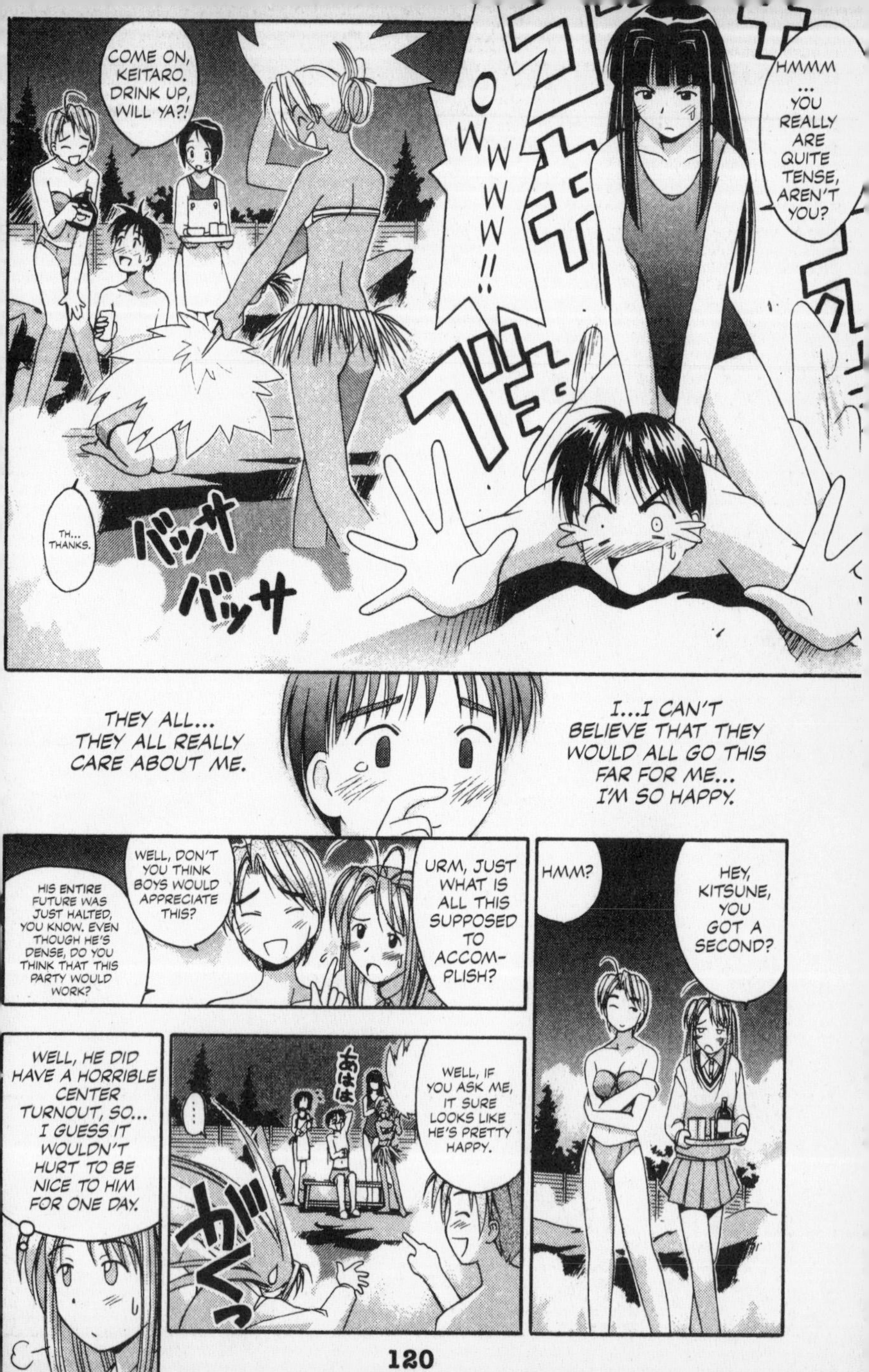
HMMM ... YOU REALLY ARE QUITE TENSE, AREN'T YOU?
OWWWWWWW!!
COME ON, KEITARO. DRINK UP, WILL YA?!
TH... THANKS.
バッサ
バッサ
I...I CAN'T BELIEVE THAT THEY WOULD ALL GO THIS FAR FOR ME... I'M SO HAPPY.
THEY ALL... THEY ALL REALLY CARE ABOUT ME.
HEY, KITSUNE, YOU GOT A SECOND?
HMM?
URM, JUST WHAT IS ALL THIS SUPPOSED TO ACCOM-PLISH?
WELL, DON'T YOU THINK BOYS WOULD APPRECIATE THIS?
HIS ENTIRE FUTURE WAS JUST HALTED, YOU KNOW. EVEN THOUGH HE'S DENSE, DO YOU THINK THAT THIS PARTY WOULD WORK?
WELL, IF YOU ASK ME, IT SURE LOOKS LIKE HE'S PRETTY HAPPY.
あはは
....
がくっ
WELL, HE DID HAVE A HORRIBLE CENTER TURNOUT, SO... I GUESS IT WOULDN'T HURT TO BE NICE TO HIM FOR ONE DAY.

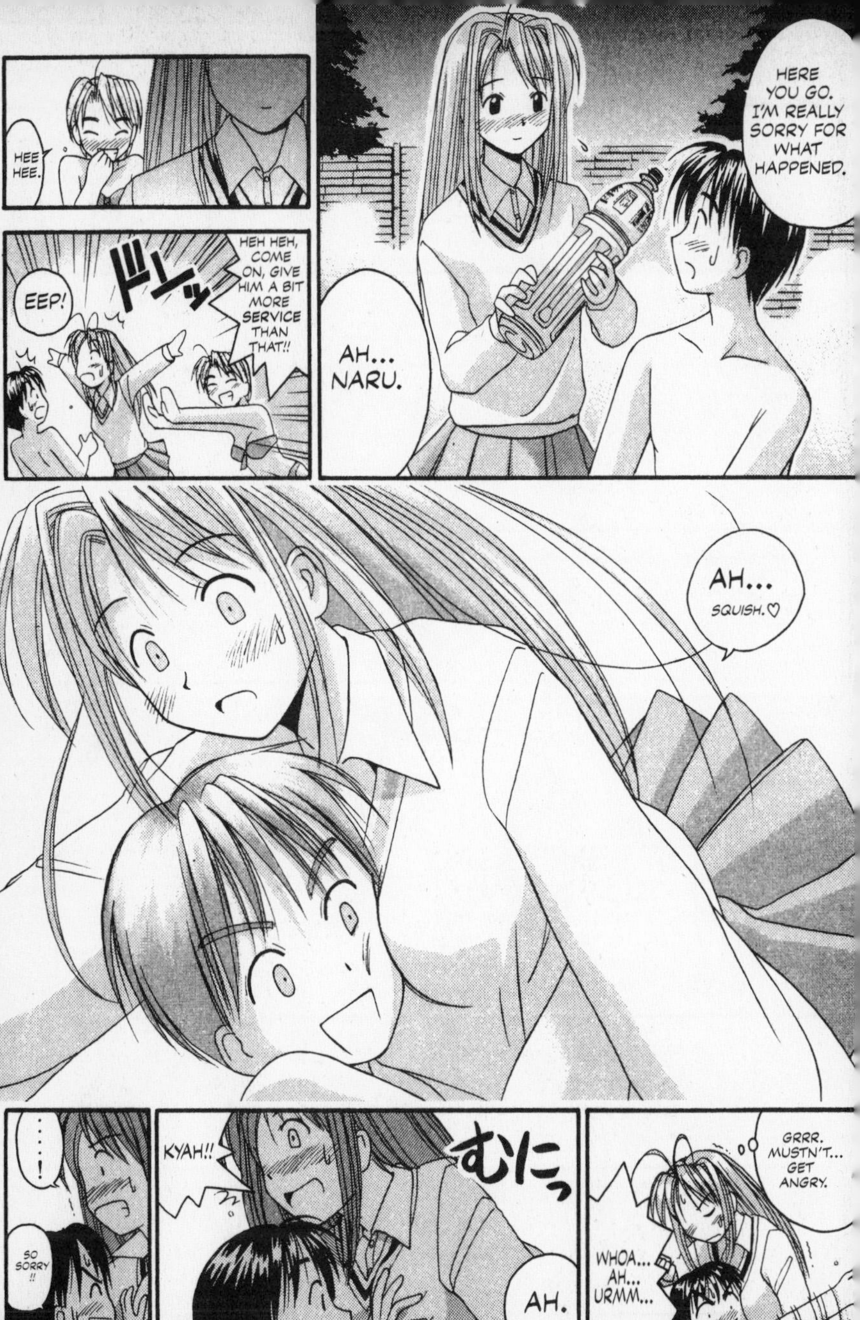
HERE YOU GO. I'M REALLY SORRY FOR WHAT HAPPENED.
AH... NARU.
HEE HEE.
HEH HEH, COME ON, GIVE HIM A BIT MORE SERVICE THAN THAT!!
ドンッ
EEP!
AH...
SQUISH.♡
GRRR. MUSTN'T... GET ANGRY.
WHOA... AH... URMM...
むにっ
KYAH!!
AH.
...!
SO SORRY!!

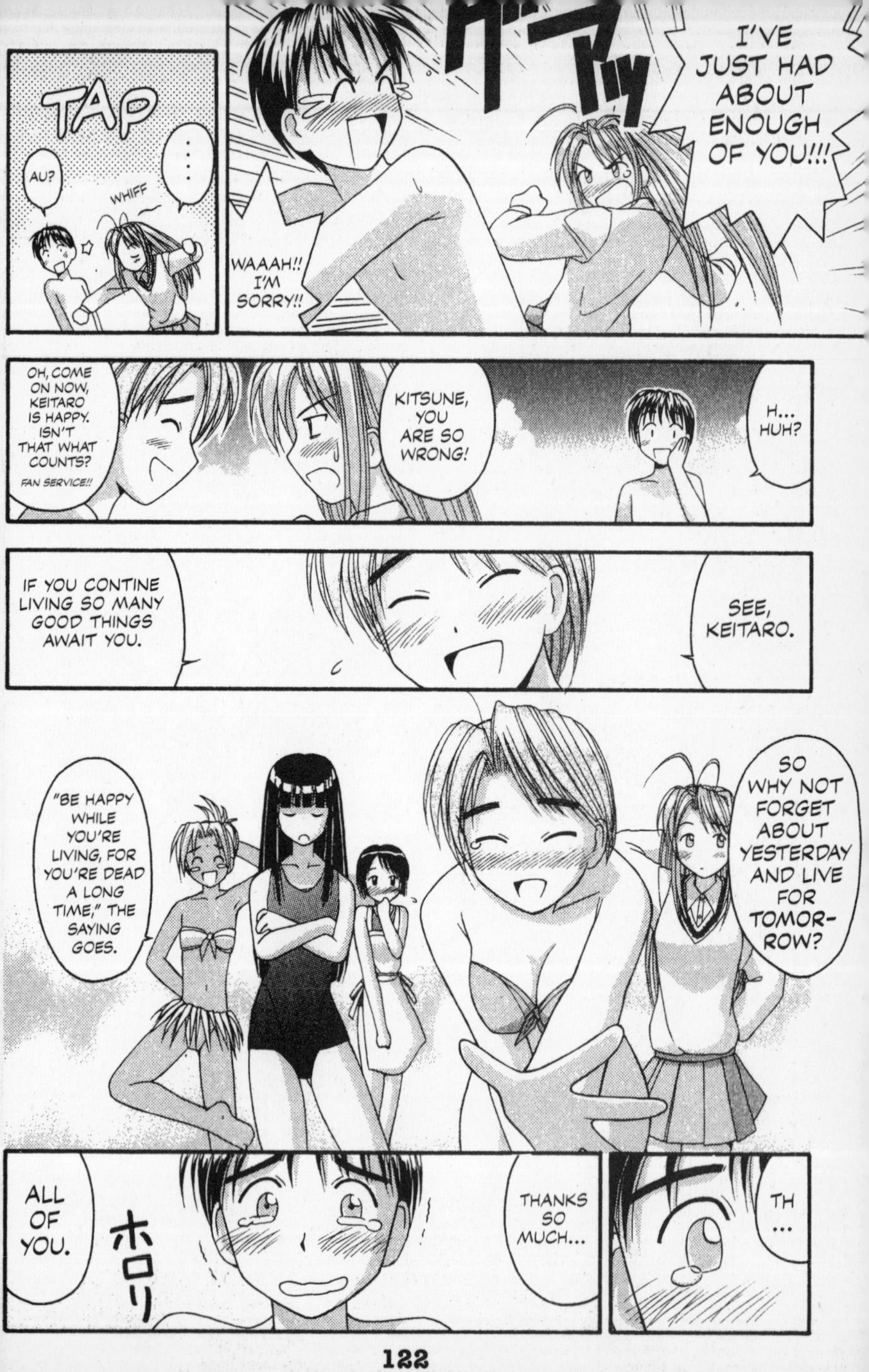
グアッ
I'VE JUST HAD ABOUT ENOUGH OF YOU!!!
WAAAH!! I'M SORRY!!
....
TAP
AU?
WHIFF
H... HUH?
KITSUNE, YOU ARE SO WRONG!
OH, COME ON NOW, KEITARO IS HAPPY. ISN'T THAT WHAT COUNTS?
FAN SERVICE!!
SEE, KEITARO.
IF YOU CONTINE LIVING SO MANY GOOD THINGS AWAIT YOU.
SO WHY NOT FORGET ABOUT YESTERDAY AND LIVE FOR TOMOR-ROW?
"BE HAPPY WHILE YOU'RE LIVING, FOR YOU'RE DEAD A LONG TIME," THE SAYING GOES.
TH ...
THANKS SO MUCH...
ホロリ
ALL OF YOU.

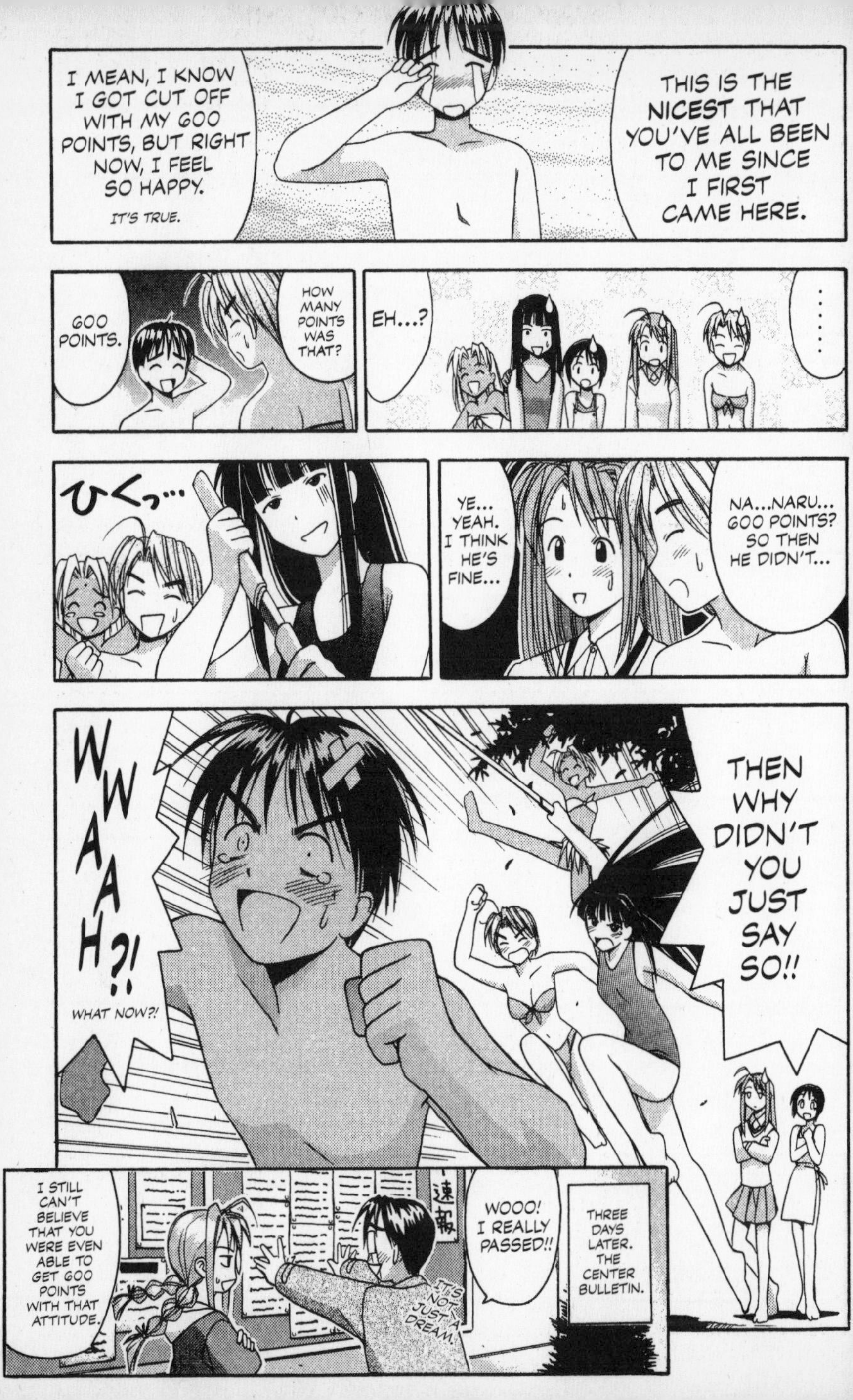
THIS IS THE NICEST THAT YOU'VE ALL BEEN TO ME SINCE I FIRST CAME HERE.
I MEAN, I KNOW I GOT CUT OFF WITH MY 600 POINTS, BUT RIGHT NOW, I FEEL SO HAPPY.
IT'S TRUE.
......
EH...?
HOW MANY POINTS WAS THAT?
600 POINTS.
NA...NARU... 600 POINTS? SO THEN HE DIDN'T...
YE... YEAH. I THINK HE'S FINE...
ひくっ…
THEN WHY DIDN'T YOU JUST SAY SO!!
WWAAH?!
WHAT NOW?!
THREE DAYS LATER. THE CENTER BULLETIN.
速報
WOOO! I REALLY PASSED!!
IT'S NOT JUST A DREAM.
I STILL CAN'T BELIEVE THAT YOU WERE EVEN ABLE TO GET 600 POINTS WITH THAT ATTITUDE.

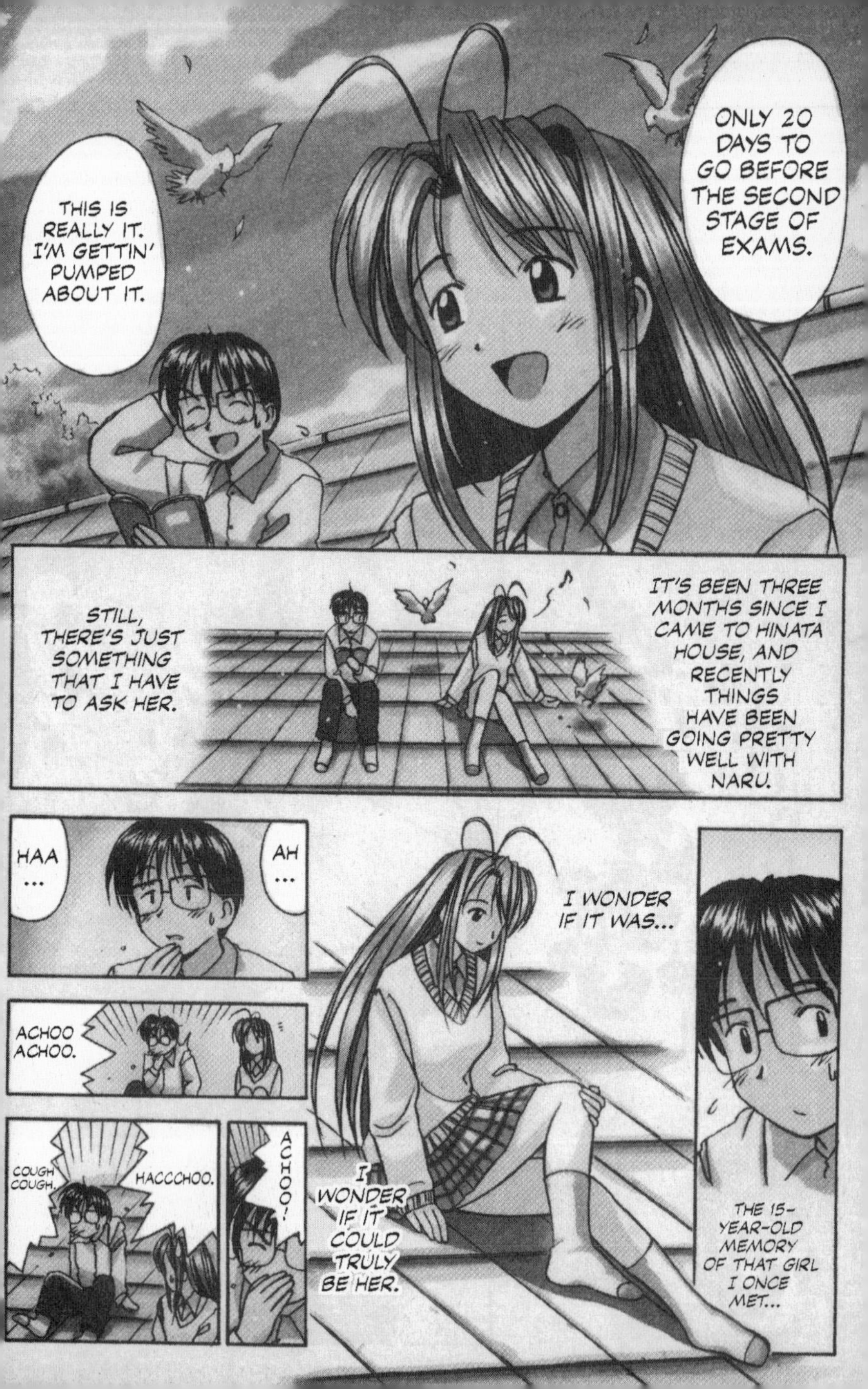
ONLY 20 DAYS TO GO BEFORE THE SECOND STAGE OF EXAMS.
THIS IS REALLY IT. I'M GETTIN' PUMPED ABOUT IT.
IT'S BEEN THREE MONTHS SINCE I CAME TO HINATA HOUSE, AND RECENTLY THINGS HAVE BEEN GOING PRETTY WELL WITH NARU.
STILL, THERE'S JUST SOMETHING THAT I HAVE TO ASK HER.
THE 15-YEAR-OLD MEMORY OF THAT GIRL I ONCE MET...
I WONDER IF IT WAS...
I WONDER IF IT COULD TRULY BE HER.
AH ...
HAA ...
ACHOO ACHOO.
ACHOO!
HACCCHOO.
COUGH COUGH.

HINATA. 13

In Dreams.

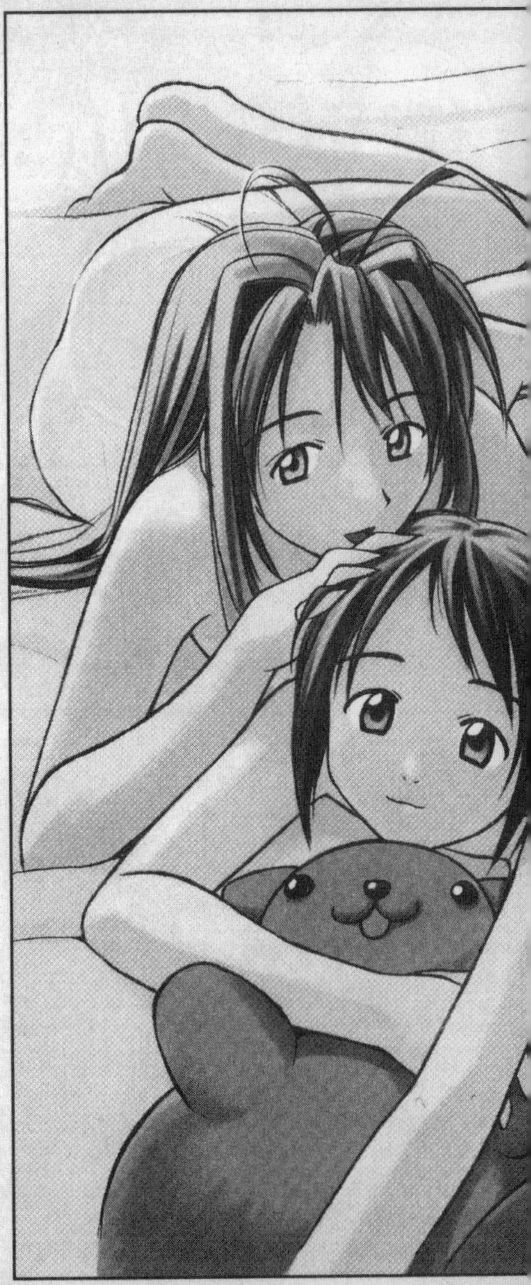

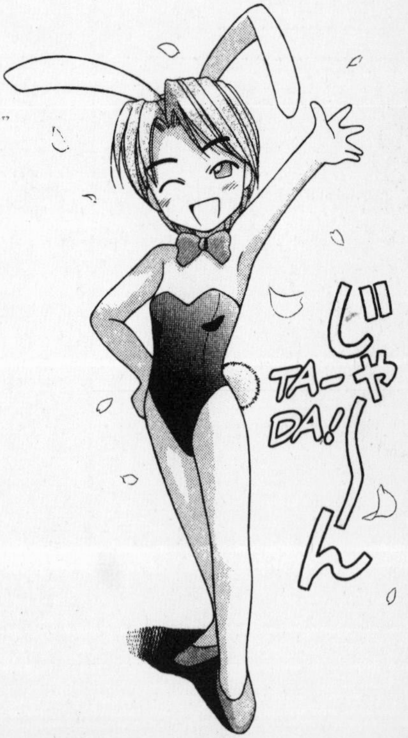
じゃーーん
TA-DA!

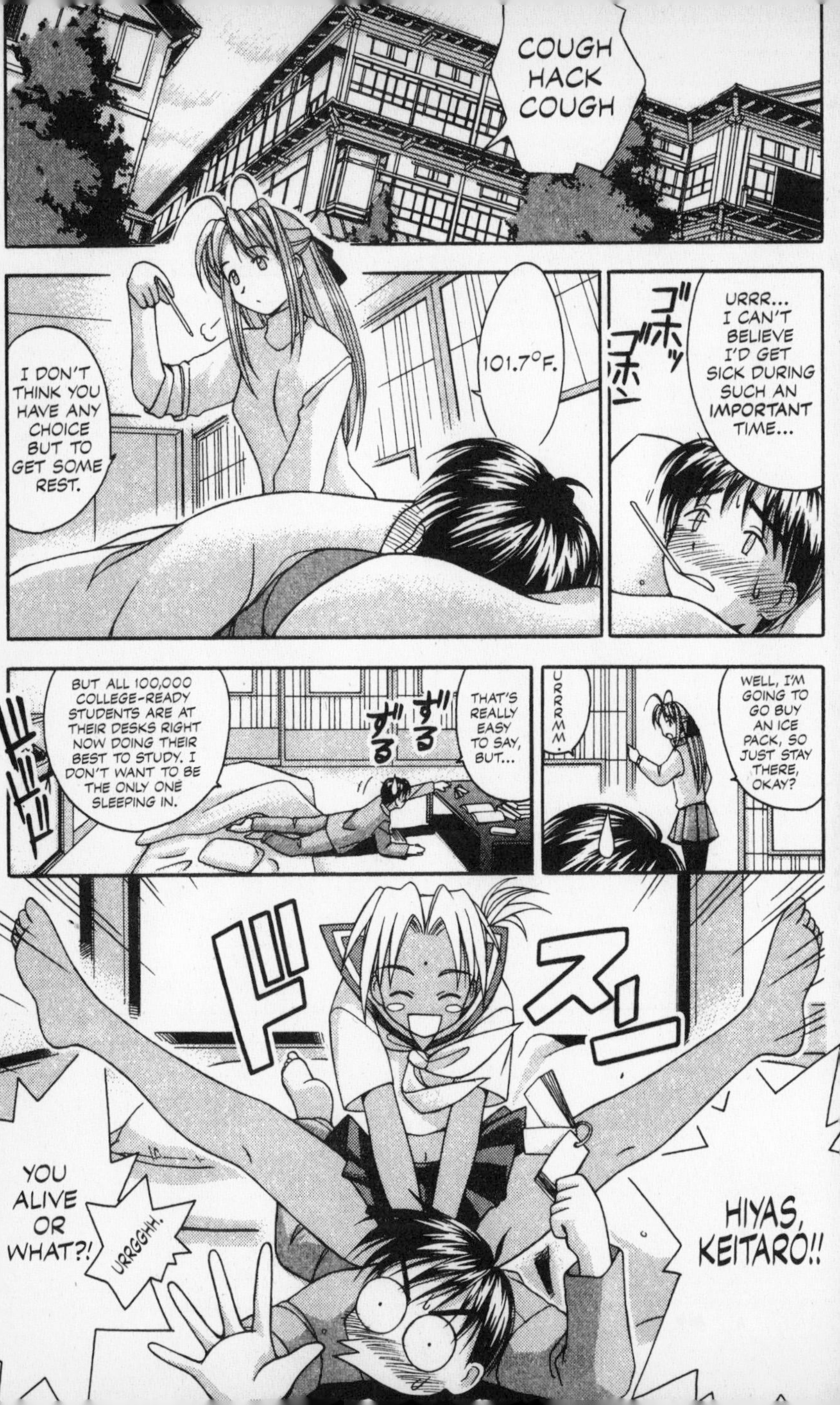
COUGH HACK COUGH
ゴホッ ゴホン
URRR... I CAN'T BELIEVE I'D GET SICK DURING SUCH AN IMPORTANT TIME...
101.7°F.
I DON'T THINK YOU HAVE ANY CHOICE BUT TO GET SOME REST.
WELL, I'M GOING TO GO BUY AN ICE PACK, SO JUST STAY THERE, OKAY?
URRRMM.
THAT'S REALLY EASY TO SAY, BUT...
ずる ずる
BUT ALL 100,000 COLLEGE-READY STUDENTS ARE AT THEIR DESKS RIGHT NOW DOING THEIR BEST TO STUDY. I DON'T WANT TO BE THE ONLY ONE SLEEPING IN.
ドスン
HIYAS, KEITARO!!
YOU ALIVE OR WHAT?!
URRGGHH.

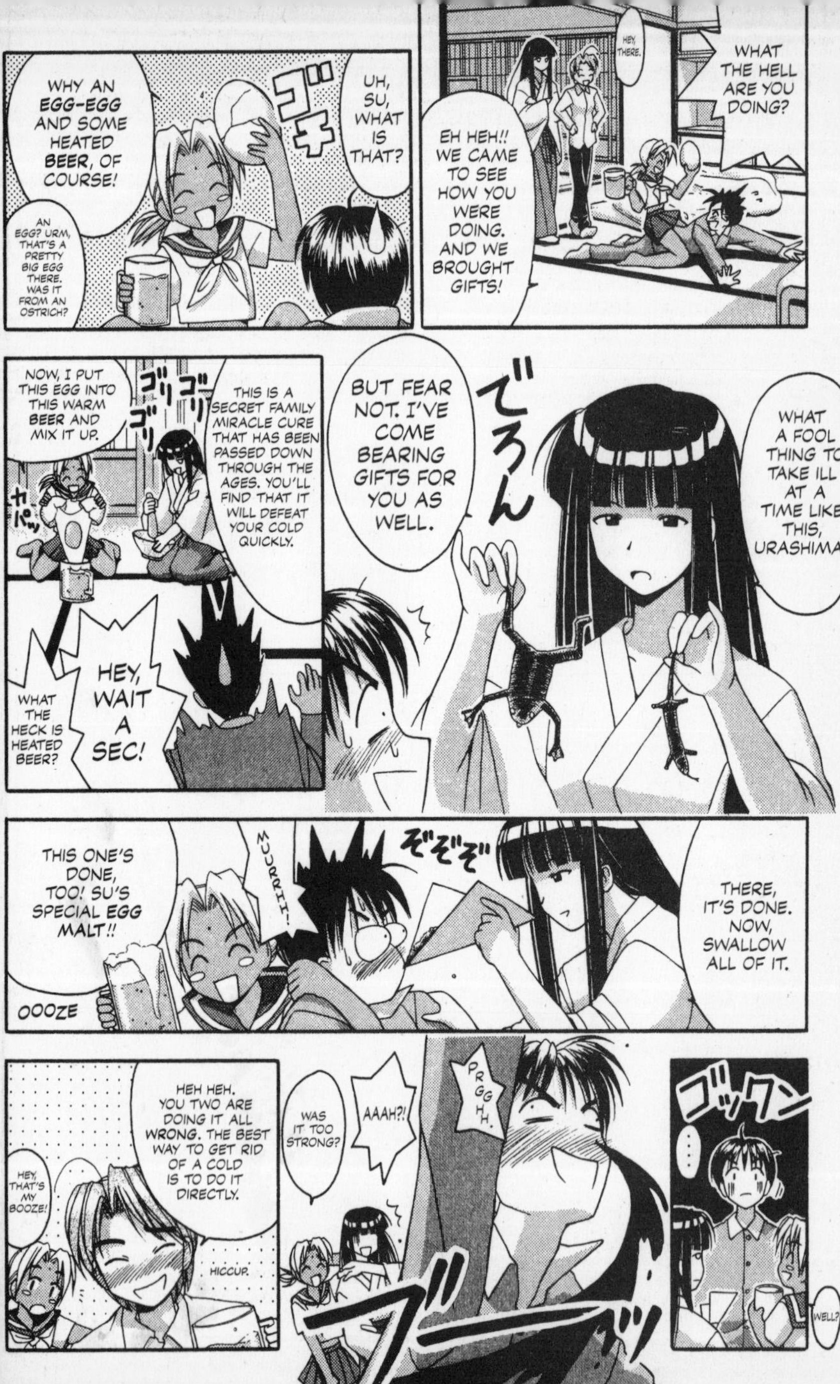
HEY, THERE.
WHAT THE HELL ARE YOU DOING?
EH HEH!! WE CAME TO SEE HOW YOU WERE DOING. AND WE BROUGHT GIFTS!
UH, SU, WHAT IS THAT?
ゴチ
WHY AN EGG-EGG AND SOME HEATED BEER, OF COURSE!
AN EGG? URM, THAT'S A PRETTY BIG EGG THERE. WAS IT FROM AN OSTRICH?
WHAT A FOOL THING TO TAKE ILL AT A TIME LIKE THIS, URASHIMA.
でろん
BUT FEAR NOT. I'VE COME BEARING GIFTS FOR YOU AS WELL.
THIS IS A SECRET FAMILY MIRACLE CURE THAT HAS BEEN PASSED DOWN THROUGH THE AGES. YOU'LL FIND THAT IT WILL DEFEAT YOUR COLD QUICKLY.
ゴリゴリ
ゴリ
NOW, I PUT THIS EGG INTO THIS WARM BEER AND MIX IT UP.
カパッ
HEY, WAIT A SEC!
WHAT THE HECK IS HEATED BEER?
THERE, IT'S DONE. NOW, SWALLOW ALL OF IT.
ぞぞぞ
MUURRHH!
THIS ONE'S DONE, TOO! SU'S SPECIAL EGG MALT!!
OOOZE
ゴックン
...
WELL?
PRGGHH.
AAAH?!
WAS IT TOO STRONG?
ブーッ
HEH HEH. YOU TWO ARE DOING IT ALL WRONG. THE BEST WAY TO GET RID OF A COLD IS TO DO IT DIRECTLY.
HICCUP.
HEY, THAT'S MY BOOZE!

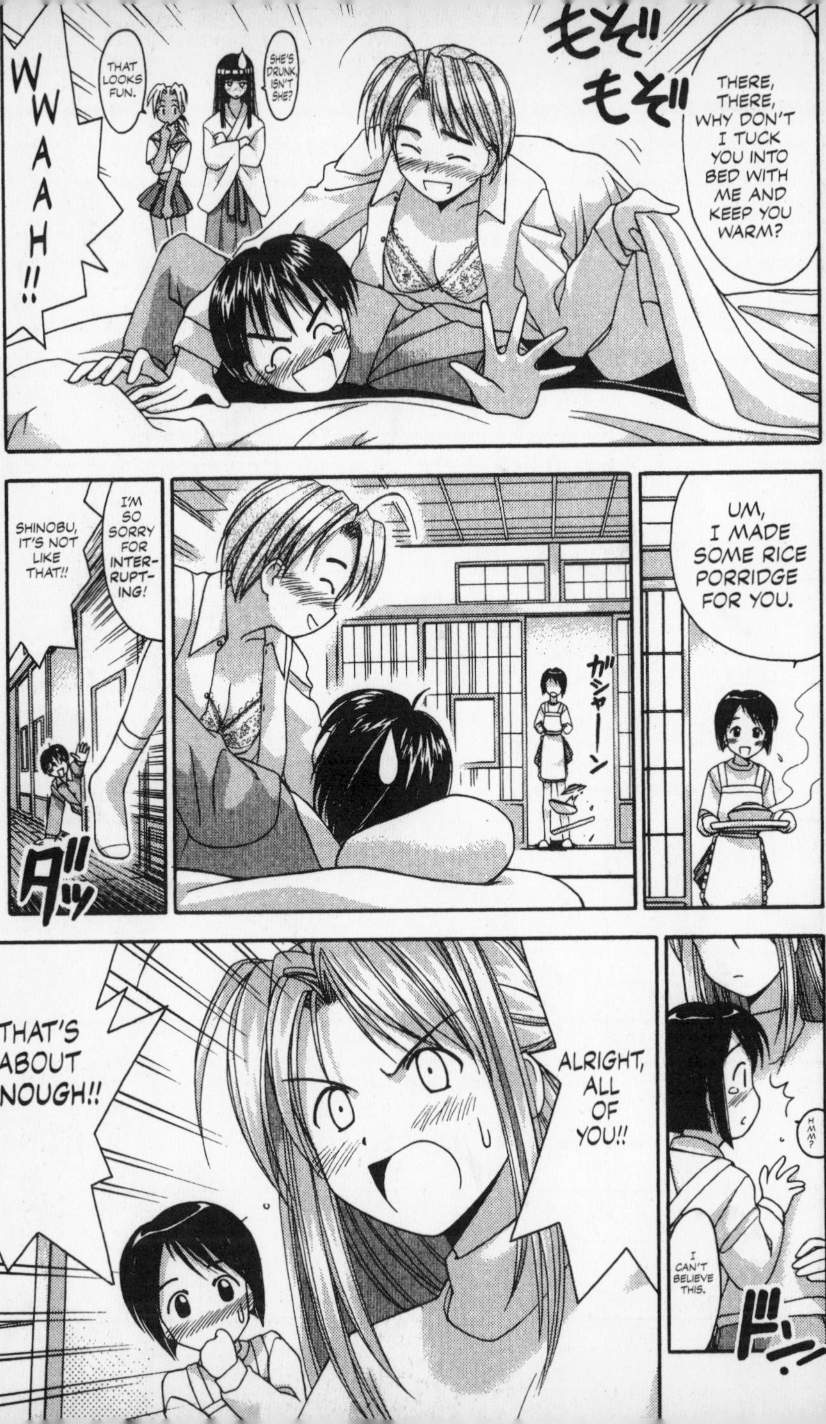
もぞもぞ
THERE, THERE, WHY DON'T I TUCK YOU INTO BED WITH ME AND KEEP YOU WARM?
SHE'S DRUNK, ISN'T SHE?
THAT LOOKS FUN.
WWAAAH!!
UM, I MADE SOME RICE PORRIDGE FOR YOU.
ガシャーン
I'M SO SORRY FOR INTERRUPTING!
SHINOBU, IT'S NOT LIKE THAT!!
ダッ
HMM?
I CAN'T BELIEVE THIS.
ド!!
ALRIGHT, ALL OF YOU!!
THAT'S ABOUT ENOUGH!!

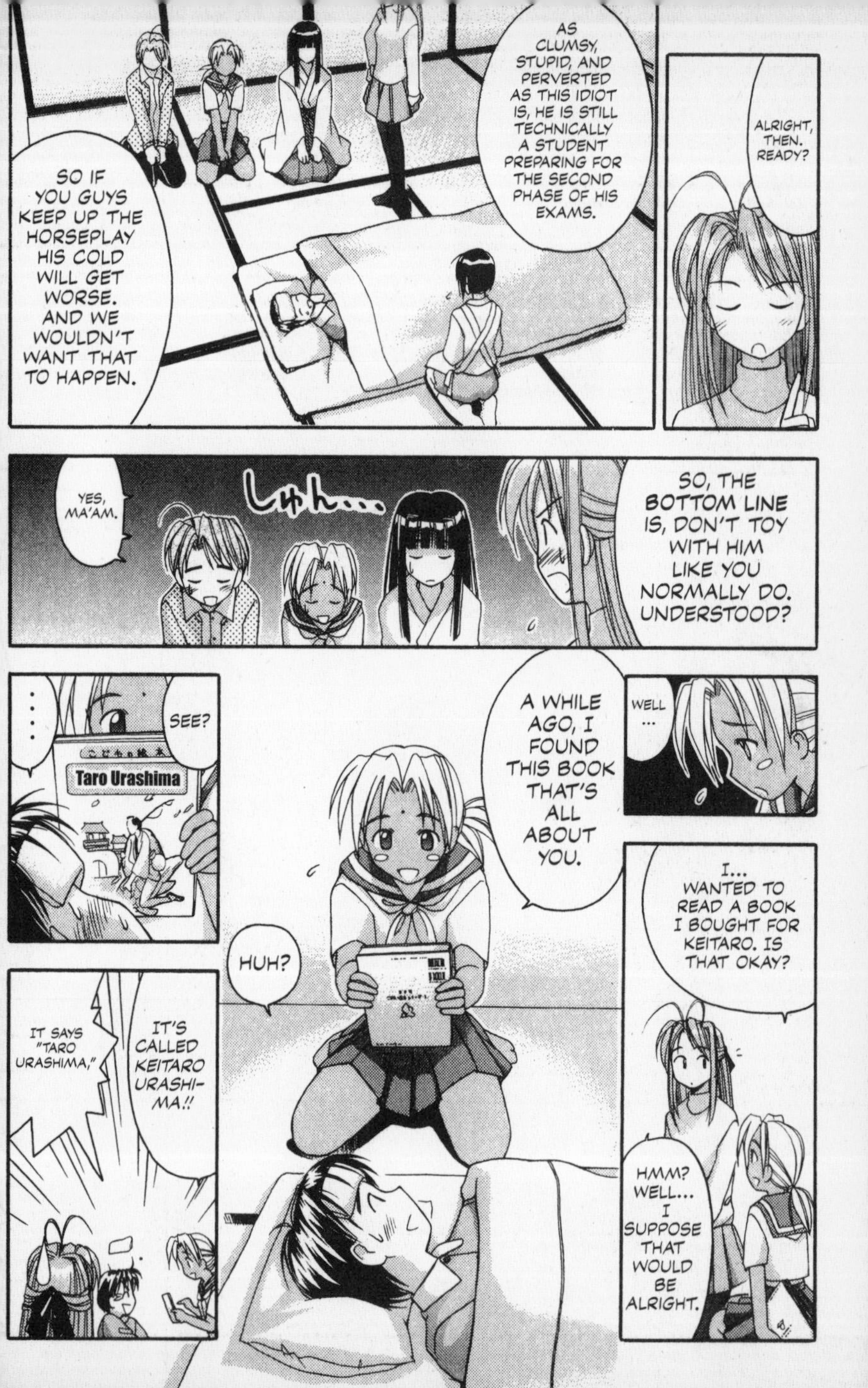
ALRIGHT, THEN. READY?
AS CLUMSY, STUPID, AND PERVERTED AS THIS IDIOT IS, HE IS STILL TECHNICALLY A STUDENT PREPARING FOR THE SECOND PHASE OF HIS EXAMS.
SO IF YOU GUYS KEEP UP THE HORSEPLAY HIS COLD WILL GET WORSE. AND WE WOULDN'T WANT THAT TO HAPPEN.
SO, THE BOTTOM LINE IS, DON'T TOY WITH HIM LIKE YOU NORMALLY DO. UNDERSTOOD?
しゅん...
YES, MA'AM.
WELL ...
I... WANTED TO READ A BOOK I BOUGHT FOR KEITARO. IS THAT OKAY?
HMM? WELL... I SUPPOSE THAT WOULD BE ALRIGHT.
A WHILE AGO, I FOUND THIS BOOK THAT'S ALL ABOUT YOU.
HUH?
SEE?
.....
Taro Urashima
IT'S CALLED KEITARO URASHIMA!!
IT SAYS "TARO URASHIMA,"

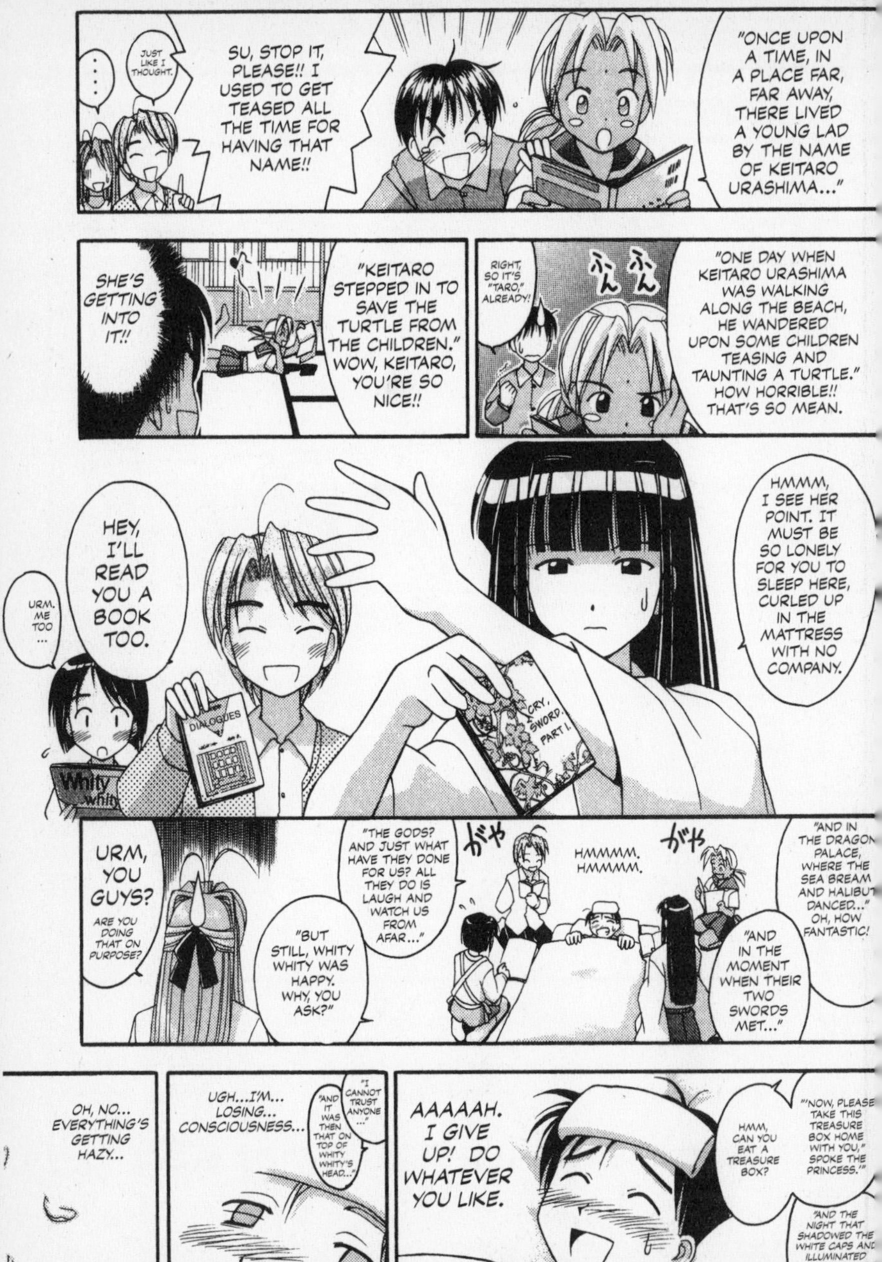
"ONCE UPON A TIME, IN A PLACE FAR, FAR AWAY, THERE LIVED A YOUNG LAD BY THE NAME OF KEITARO URASHIMA..."
SU, STOP IT, PLEASE!! I USED TO GET TEASED ALL THE TIME FOR HAVING THAT NAME!!
JUST LIKE I THOUGHT.
....
"ONE DAY WHEN KEITARO URASHIMA WAS WALKING ALONG THE BEACH, HE WANDERED UPON SOME CHILDREN TEASING AND TAUNTING A TURTLE." HOW HORRIBLE!! THAT'S SO MEAN.
ふん ふん
RIGHT, SO IT'S "TARO," ALREADY!
"KEITARO STEPPED IN TO SAVE THE TURTLE FROM THE CHILDREN." WOW, KEITARO, YOU'RE SO NICE!!
SHE'S GETTING INTO IT!!
HMMM, I SEE HER POINT. IT MUST BE SO LONELY FOR YOU TO SLEEP HERE, CURLED UP IN THE MATTRESS WITH NO COMPANY.
CRY, SWORD. PART I.
HEY, I'LL READ YOU A BOOK TOO.
DIALOGUES
URM. ME TOO ...
Whity
"AND IN THE DRAGON PALACE, WHERE THE SEA BREAM AND HALIBUT DANCED..." OH, HOW FANTASTIC!
"AND IN THE MOMENT WHEN THEIR TWO SWORDS MET..."
がや
HMMMM. HMMMM.
がや
"THE GODS? AND JUST WHAT HAVE THEY DONE FOR US? ALL THEY DO IS LAUGH AND WATCH US FROM AFAR..."
"BUT STILL, WHITY WHITY WAS HAPPY. WHY, YOU ASK?"
URM, YOU GUYS?
ARE YOU DOING THAT ON PURPOSE?
"'NOW, PLEASE TAKE THIS TREASURE BOX HOME WITH YOU,' SPOKE THE PRINCESS.'"
HMM, CAN YOU EAT A TREASURE BOX?
"AND THE NIGHT THAT SHADOWED THE WHITE CAPS AND ILLUMINATED COLDLY AGAINST THE WAVES FADED SLOWLY INTO..."
AAAAAH. I GIVE UP! DO WHATEVER YOU LIKE.
"I CANNOT TRUST ANYONE ..."
"AND IT WAS THEN THAT ON TOP OF WHITY WHITY'S HEAD..."
UGH...I'M... LOSING... CONSCIOUSNESS...
OH, NO... EVERYTHING'S GETTING HAZY...

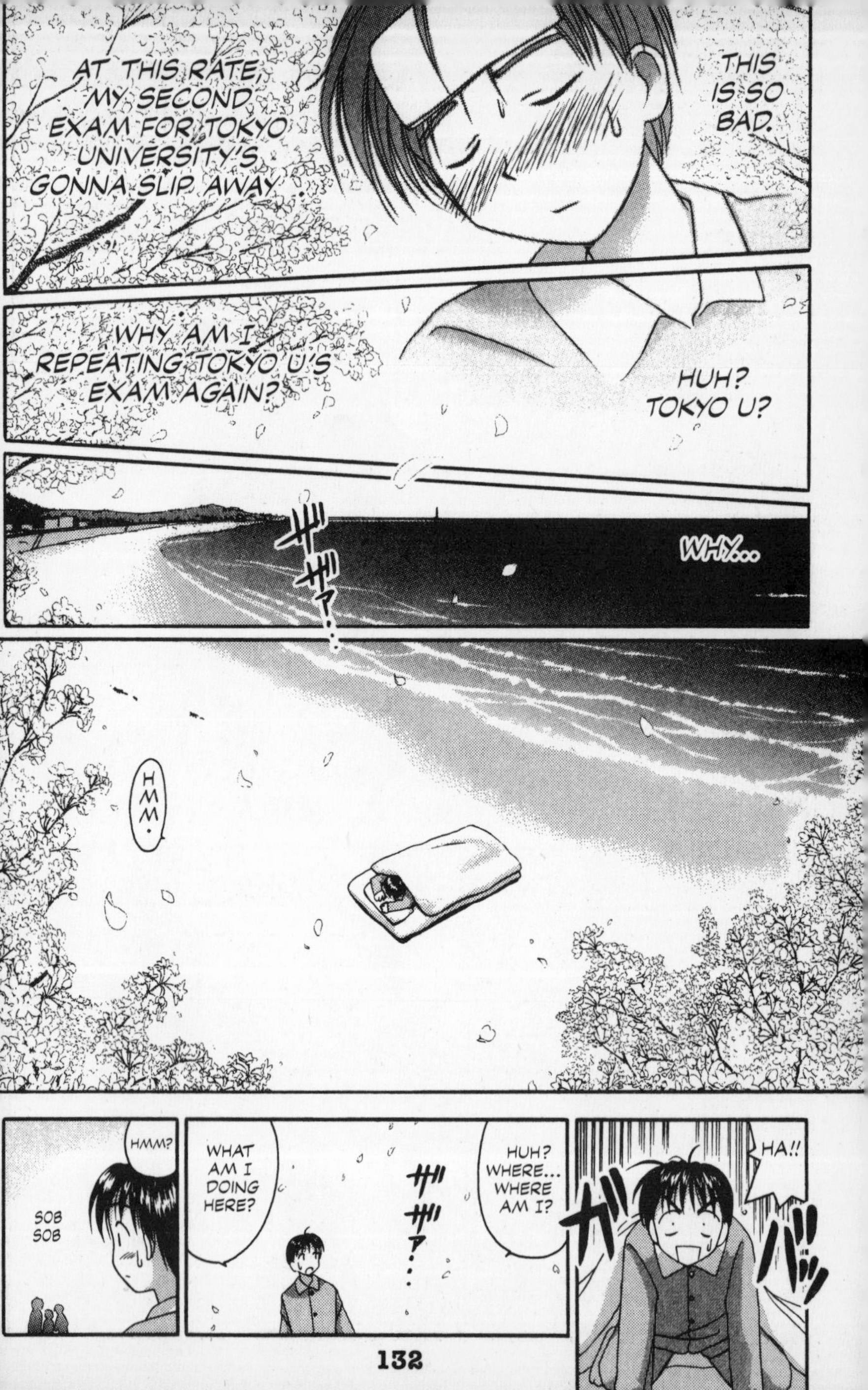
THIS IS SO BAD.
AT THIS RATE, MY SECOND EXAM FOR TOKYO UNIVERSITY'S GONNA SLIP AWAY.
WHY AM I REPEATING TOKYO U'S EXAM AGAIN?
HUH? TOKYO U?
WHY...
ザザァ...
HMM.
HA!!
ガバッ
HUH? WHERE... WHERE AM I?
ザザァ...
WHAT AM I DOING HERE?
HMM?
SOB SOB

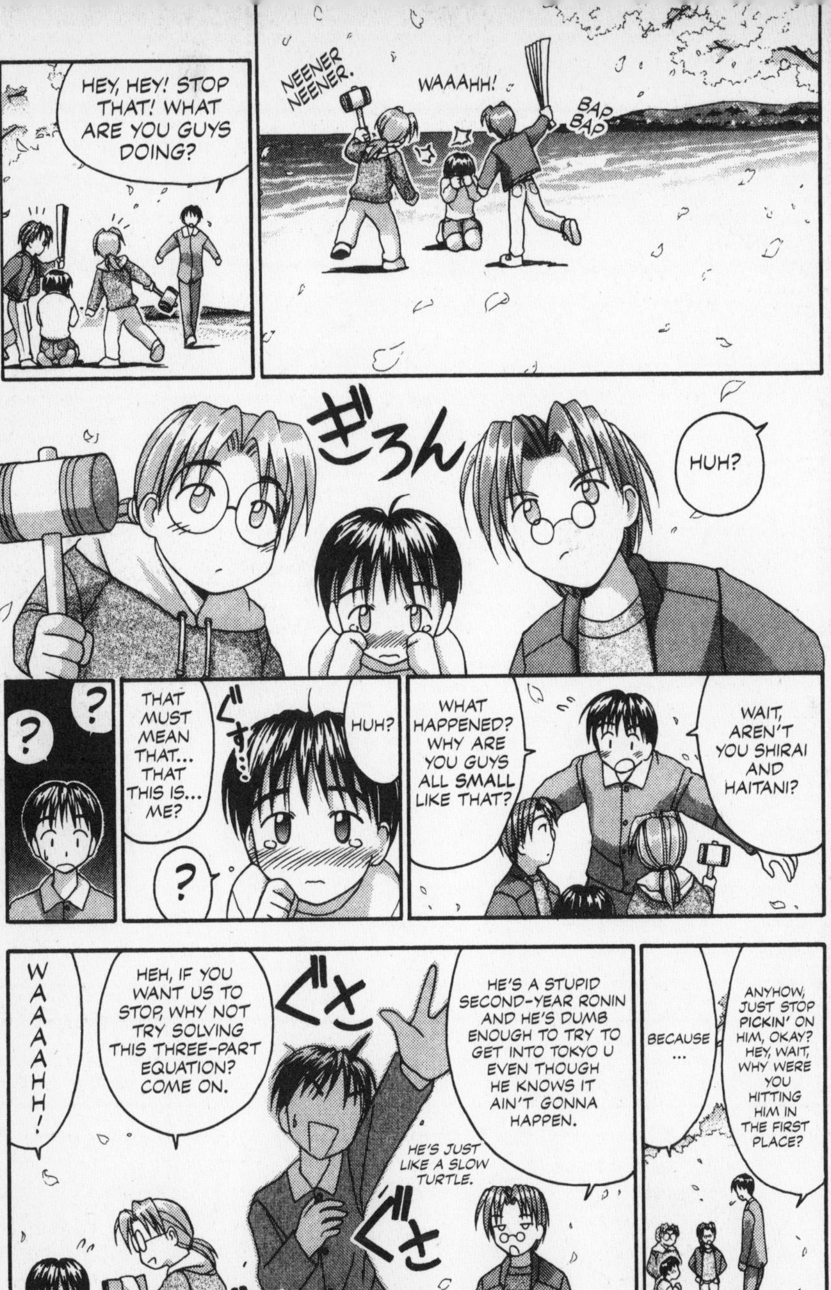
BAP BAP
WAAAHH!
NEENER NEENER.
HEY, HEY! STOP THAT! WHAT ARE YOU GUYS DOING?
HUH?
ぎろん
WAIT, AREN'T YOU SHIRAI AND HAITANI?
WHAT HAPPENED? WHY ARE YOU GUYS ALL SMALL LIKE THAT?
HUH?
ぐす...
THAT MUST MEAN THAT... THAT THIS IS... ME?
?
?
?
ANYHOW, JUST STOP PICKIN' ON HIM, OKAY? HEY, WAIT, WHY WERE YOU HITTING HIM IN THE FIRST PLACE?
BECAUSE ...
HE'S A STUPID SECOND-YEAR RONIN AND HE'S DUMB ENOUGH TO TRY TO GET INTO TOKYO U EVEN THOUGH HE KNOWS IT AIN'T GONNA HAPPEN.
ぐさ
HEH, IF YOU WANT US TO STOP, WHY NOT TRY SOLVING THIS THREE-PART EQUATION? COME ON.
WAAAAAHH!
HE'S JUST LIKE A SLOW TURTLE.
ぐさ
ぐさっ

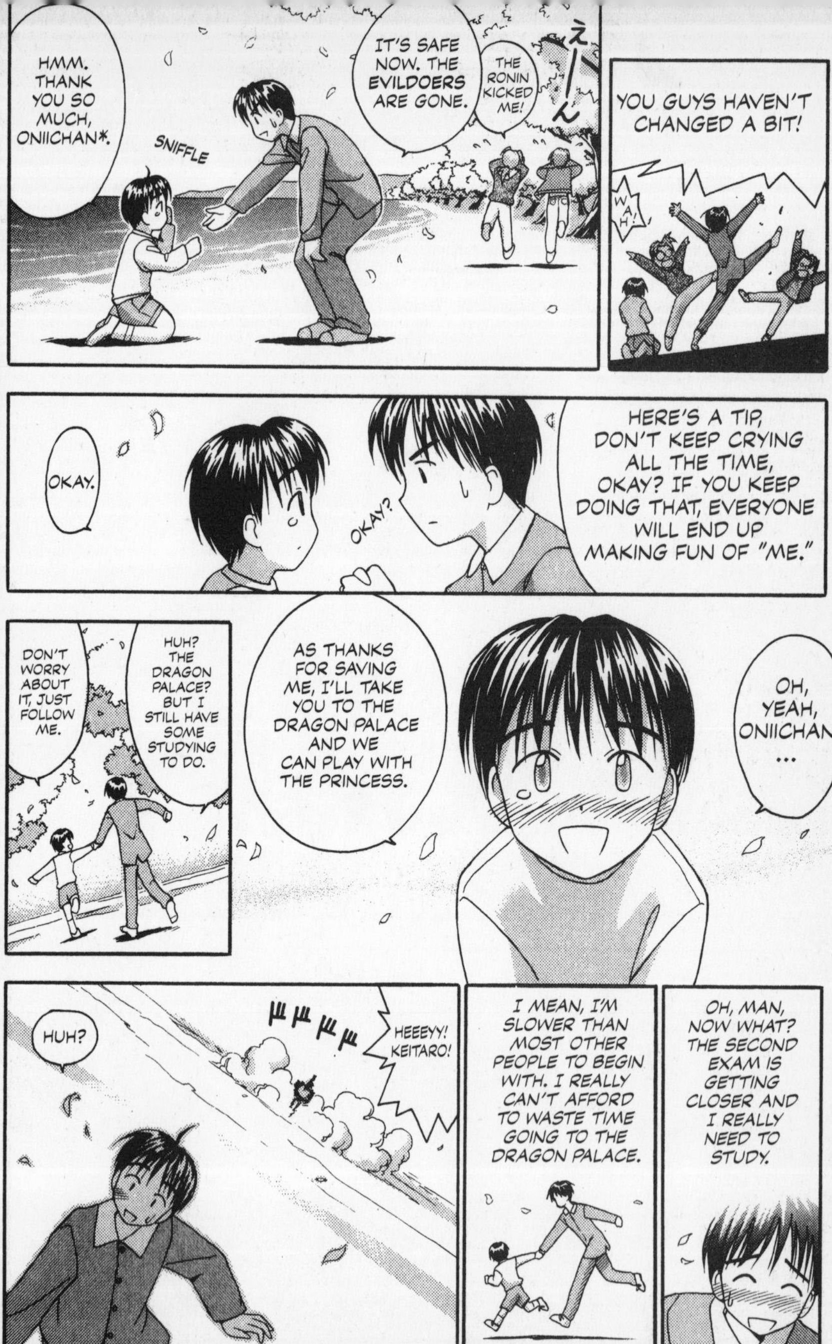
YOU GUYS HAVEN'T CHANGED A BIT!
WAH!
えーん
THE RONIN KICKED ME!
IT'S SAFE NOW. THE EVILDOERS ARE GONE.
SNIFFLE
HMM. THANK YOU SO MUCH, ONIICHAN*.
HERE'S A TIP, DON'T KEEP CRYING ALL THE TIME, OKAY? IF YOU KEEP DOING THAT, EVERYONE WILL END UP MAKING FUN OF "ME."
OKAY?
OKAY.
OH, YEAH, ONIICHAN...
AS THANKS FOR SAVING ME, I'LL TAKE YOU TO THE DRAGON PALACE AND WE CAN PLAY WITH THE PRINCESS.
HUH? THE DRAGON PALACE? BUT I STILL HAVE SOME STUDYING TO DO.
DON'T WORRY ABOUT IT, JUST FOLLOW ME.
OH, MAN, NOW WHAT? THE SECOND EXAM IS GETTING CLOSER AND I REALLY NEED TO STUDY.
I MEAN, I'M SLOWER THAN MOST OTHER PEOPLE TO BEGIN WITH. I REALLY CAN'T AFFORD TO WASTE TIME GOING TO THE DRAGON PALACE.
HEEEYY! KEITARO!
HUH?

*ONIICHAN - A WORD USED BY YOUNGER SIBLINGS AND CHILDREN WHICH MEANS "BIG BROTHER."

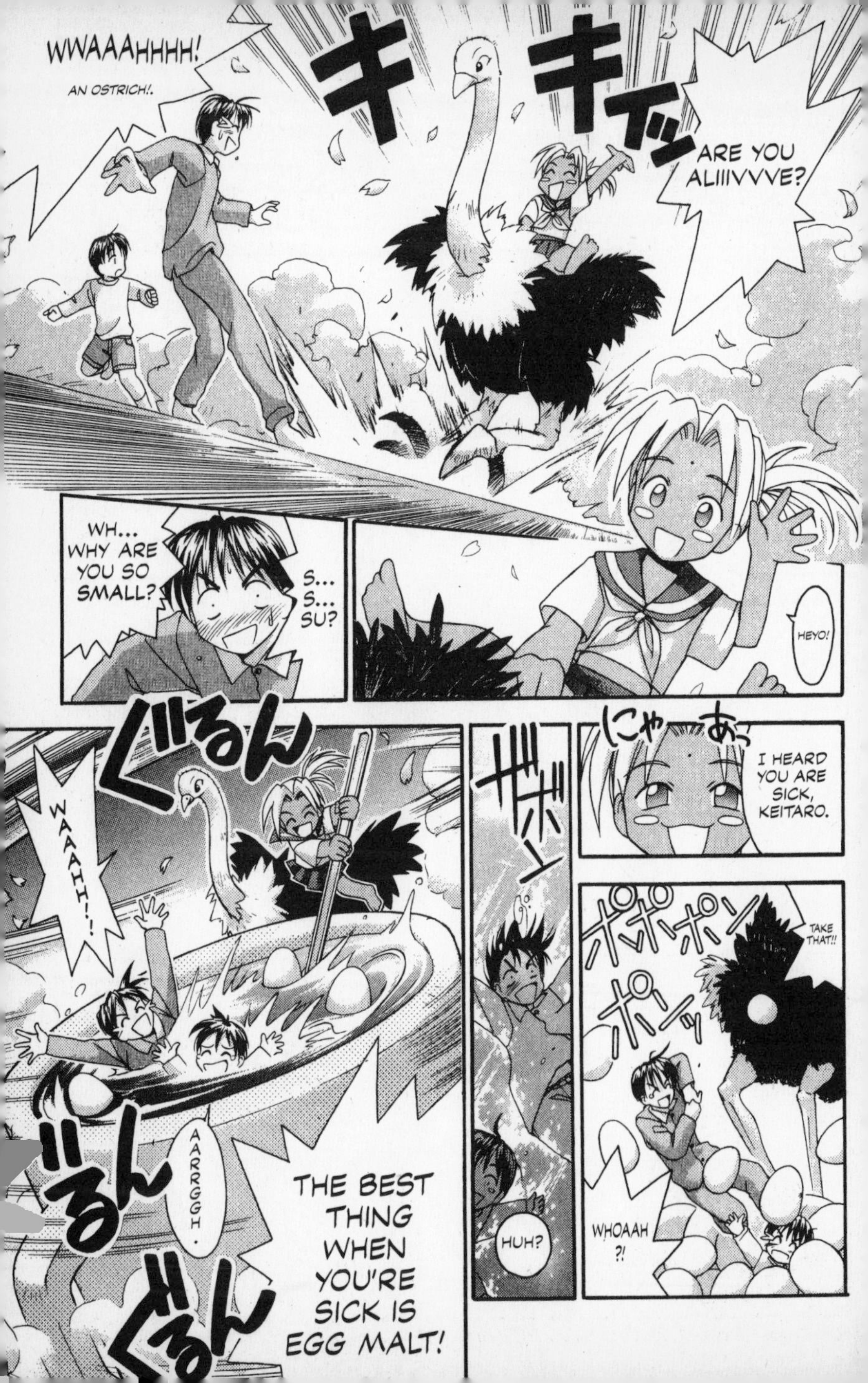
キキィッ
ARE YOU ALIIIVVVE?
WWAAAHHHH!
AN OSTRICH!.
HEYO!
S... S... SU?
WH... WHY ARE YOU SO SMALL?
にゃーあっ
I HEARD YOU ARE SICK, KEITARO.
TAKE THAT!!
WHOAAH ?!
HUH?
ぐるん
WAAAHH!!
AARRGGH.
THE BEST THING WHEN YOU'RE SICK IS EGG MALT!
ぐるん
ぐるん

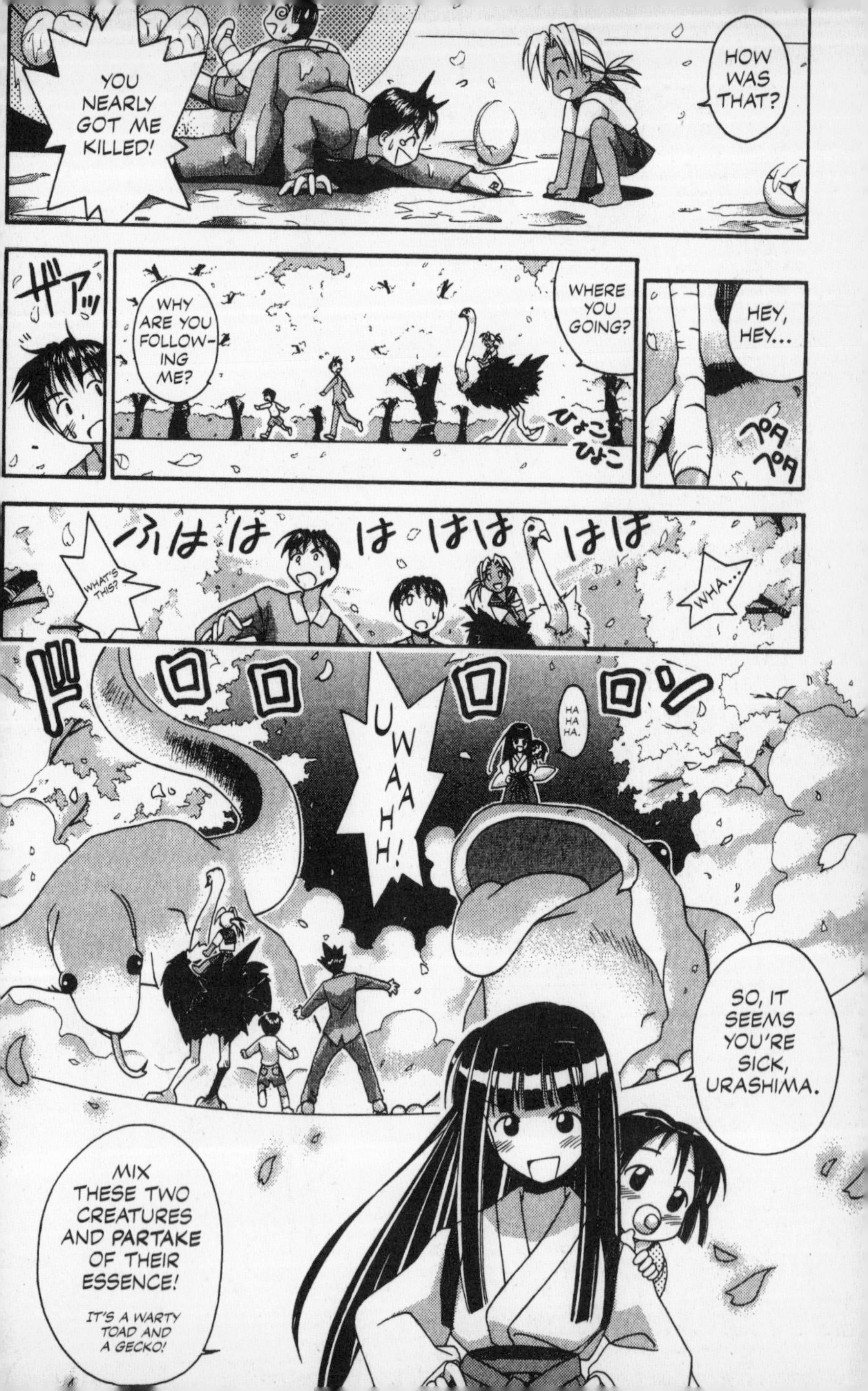
HOW WAS THAT?
YOU NEARLY GOT ME KILLED!
HEY, HEY...
ペタペタ
WHERE YOU GOING?
ひょこひょこ
WHY ARE YOU FOLLOWING ME?
ザアッ
WHA...
ふははははははは
WHAT'S THIS?
ドロロロロン
HA HA HA.
UWAAHH!
SO, IT SEEMS YOU'RE SICK, URASHIMA.
MIX THESE TWO CREATURES AND PARTAKE OF THEIR ESSENCE!
IT'S A WARTY TOAD AND A GECKO!

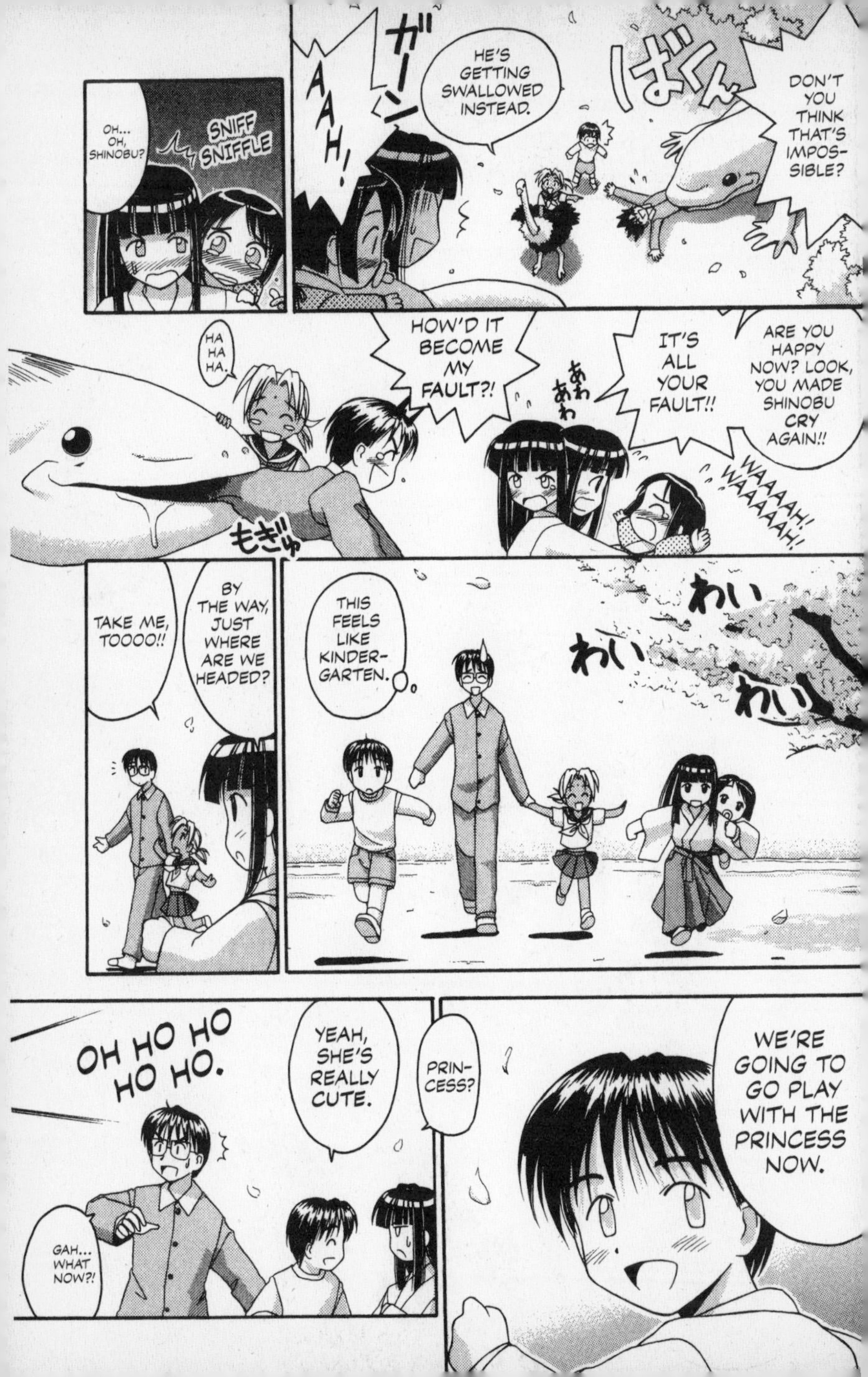
ばくん
DON'T YOU THINK THAT'S IMPOS-SIBLE?
HE'S GETTING SWALLOWED INSTEAD.
ガーン
AAH!
OH... OH, SHINOBU?
SNIFF SNIFFLE
ARE YOU HAPPY NOW? LOOK, YOU MADE SHINOBU CRY AGAIN!!
IT'S ALL YOUR FAULT!!
あわあわ
WAAAAAH! WAAAAAAH!
HOW'D IT BECOME MY FAULT?!
HA HA HA.
もぎゅ
わい
わい
わい
THIS FEELS LIKE KINDER-GARTEN.
BY THE WAY, JUST WHERE ARE WE HEADED?
TAKE ME, TOOOO!!
WE'RE GOING TO GO PLAY WITH THE PRINCESS NOW.
PRIN-CESS?
YEAH, SHE'S REALLY CUTE.
OH HO HO HO HO.
GAH... WHAT NOW?!

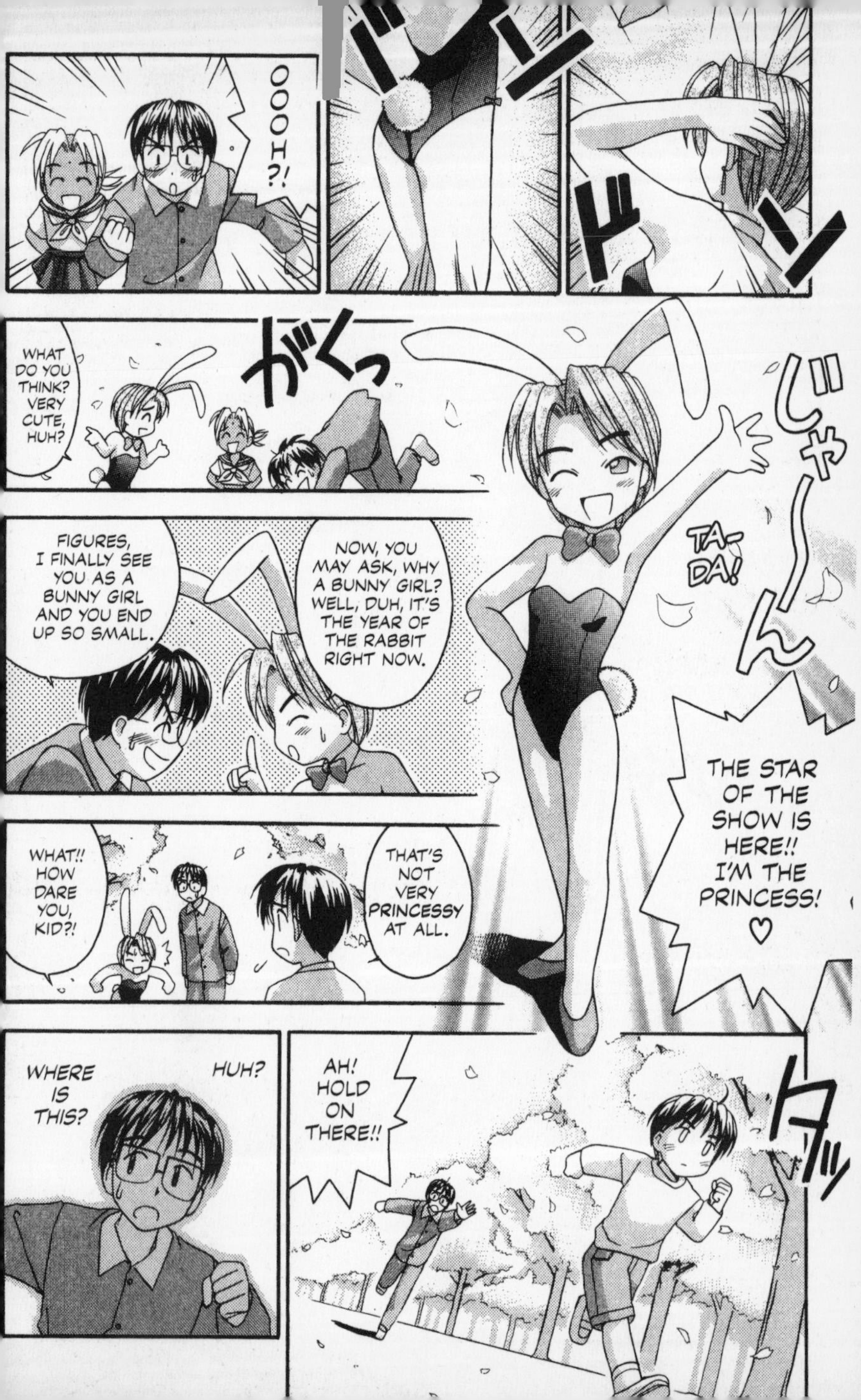
ドン
ドン
OOOOH?!
じゃーん
TA-DA!
THE STAR OF THE SHOW IS HERE!! I'M THE PRINCESS! ♡
がくっ
WHAT DO YOU THINK? VERY CUTE, HUH?
NOW, YOU MAY ASK, WHY A BUNNY GIRL? WELL, DUH, IT'S THE YEAR OF THE RABBIT RIGHT NOW.
FIGURES, I FINALLY SEE YOU AS A BUNNY GIRL AND YOU END UP SO SMALL.
THAT'S NOT VERY PRINCESSY AT ALL.
WHAT!! HOW DARE YOU, KID?!
ダッ
AH! HOLD ON THERE!!
HUH?
WHERE IS THIS?

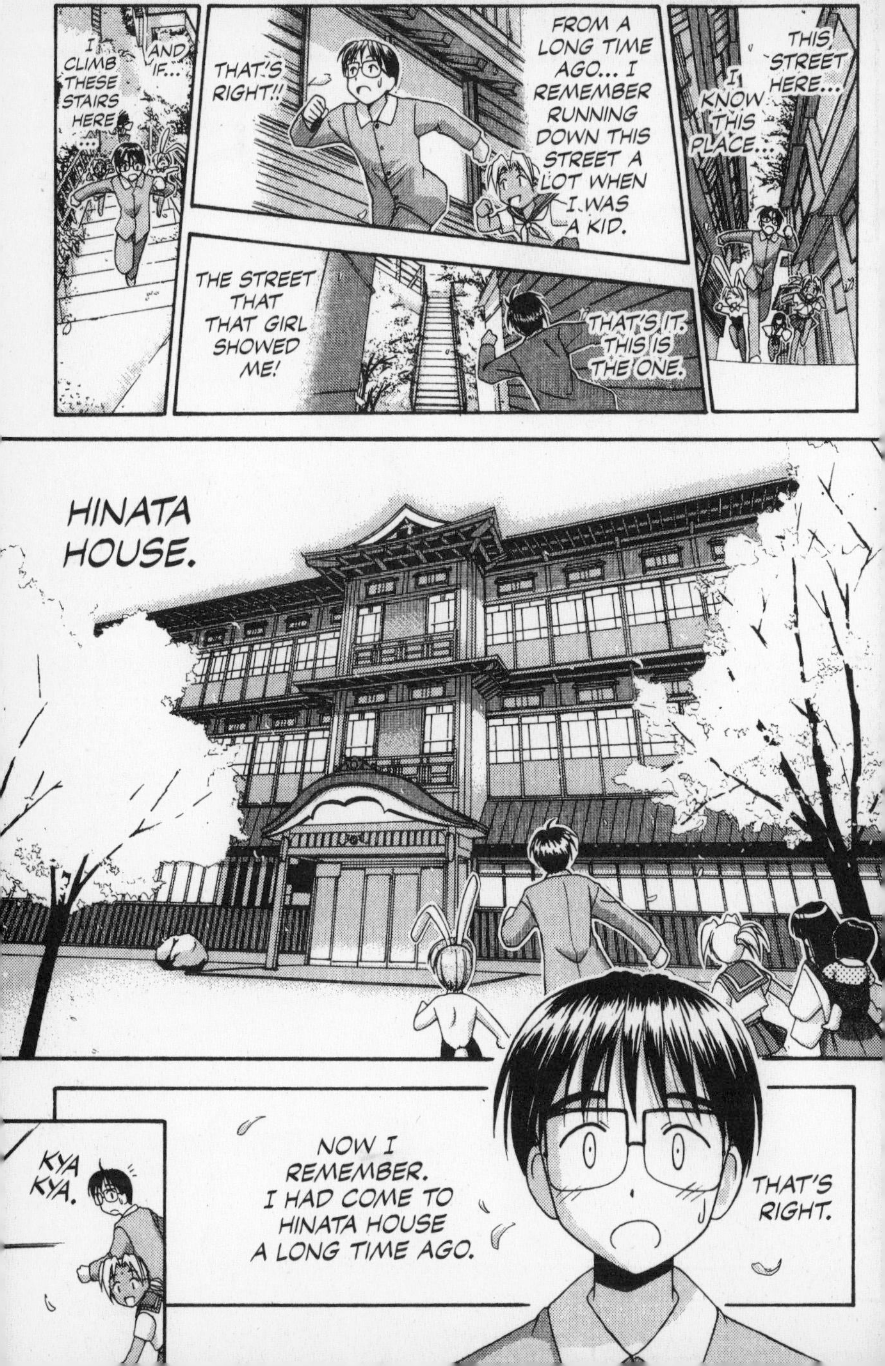
THIS STREET HERE...
I KNOW THIS PLACE...
FROM A LONG TIME AGO... I REMEMBER RUNNING DOWN THIS STREET A LOT WHEN I WAS A KID.
THAT'S RIGHT!!
THAT'S IT. THIS IS THE ONE.
THE STREET THAT THAT GIRL SHOWED ME!
AND IF...
I CLIMB THESE STAIRS HERE...
HINATA HOUSE.
THAT'S RIGHT.
NOW I REMEMBER. I HAD COME TO HINATA HOUSE A LONG TIME AGO.
KYA KYA.

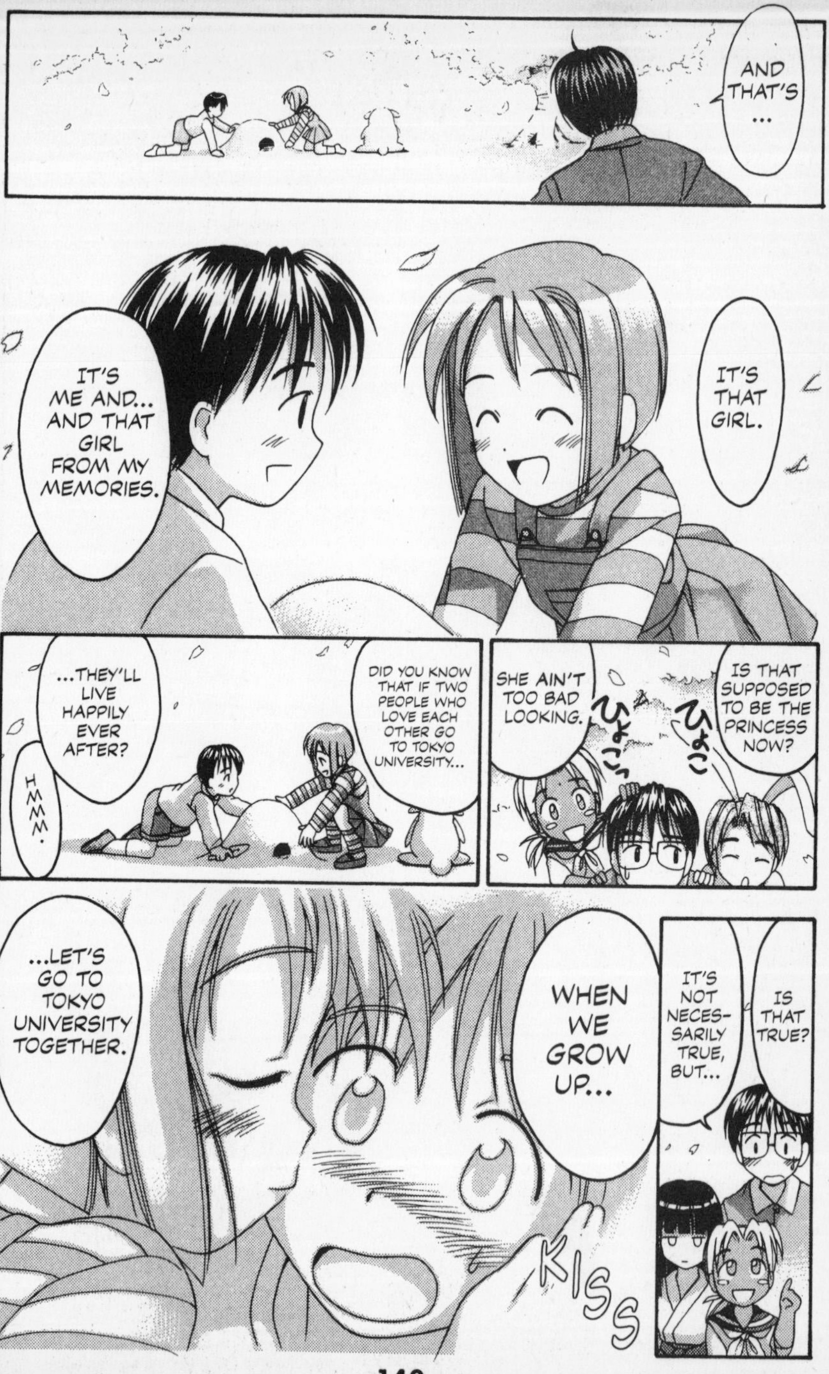
AND THAT'S ...
IT'S THAT GIRL.
IT'S ME AND... AND THAT GIRL FROM MY MEMORIES.
IS THAT SUPPOSED TO BE THE PRINCESS NOW?
ひょこ
ひょこっ
SHE AIN'T TOO BAD LOOKING.
DID YOU KNOW THAT IF TWO PEOPLE WHO LOVE EACH OTHER GO TO TOKYO UNIVERSITY...
...THEY'LL LIVE HAPPILY EVER AFTER?
HMMM.
IS THAT TRUE?
IT'S NOT NECES-SARILY TRUE, BUT...
WHEN WE GROW UP...
...LET'S GO TO TOKYO UNIVERSITY TOGETHER.
KISS

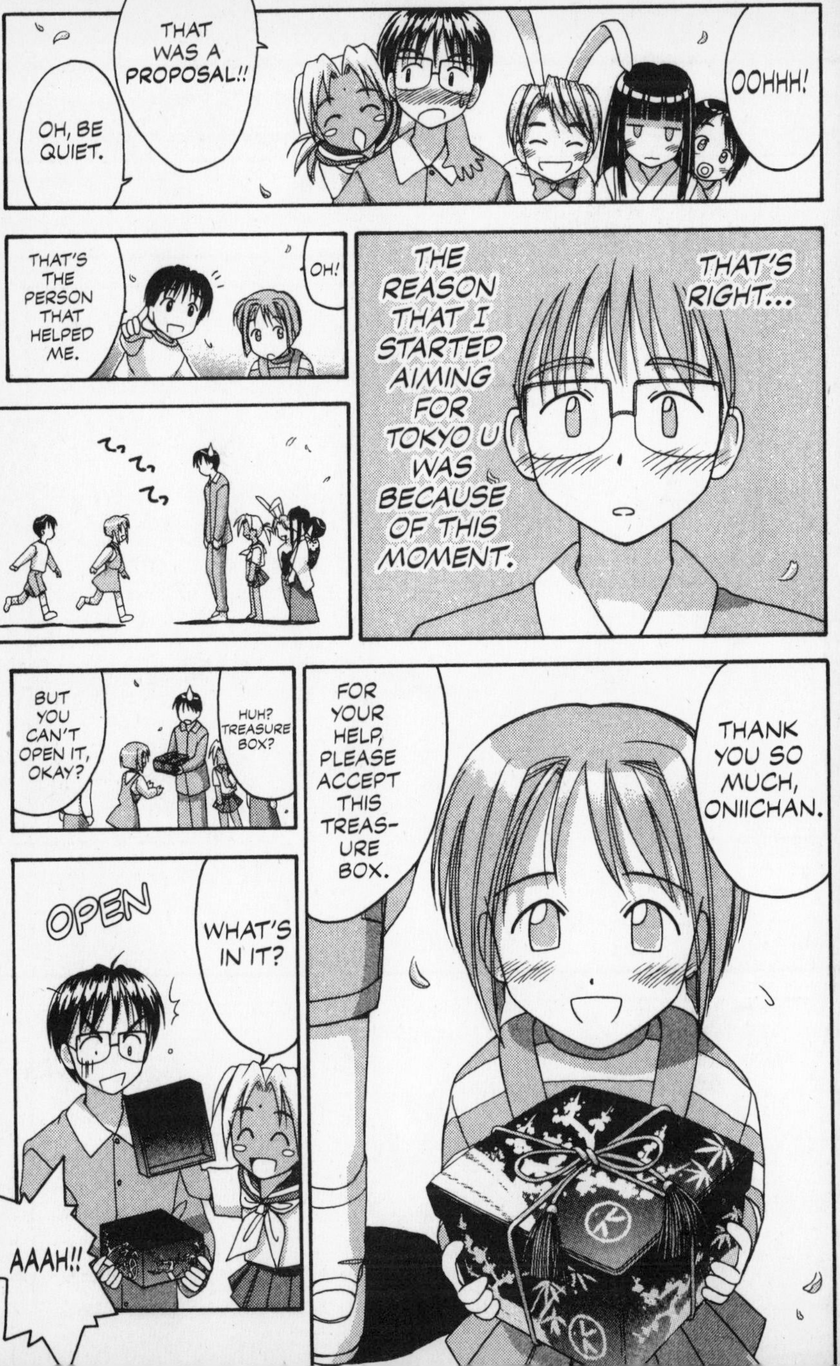
OOHHH!
THAT WAS A PROPOSAL!!
OH, BE QUIET.
THAT'S RIGHT...
THE REASON THAT I STARTED AIMING FOR TOKYO U WAS BECAUSE OF THIS MOMENT.
OH!
THAT'S THE PERSON THAT HELPED ME.
THANK YOU SO MUCH, ONIICHAN.
FOR YOUR HELP, PLEASE ACCEPT THIS TREAS-URE BOX.
HUH? TREASURE BOX?
BUT YOU CAN'T OPEN IT, OKAY?
WHAT'S IN IT?
OPEN
AAAH!!

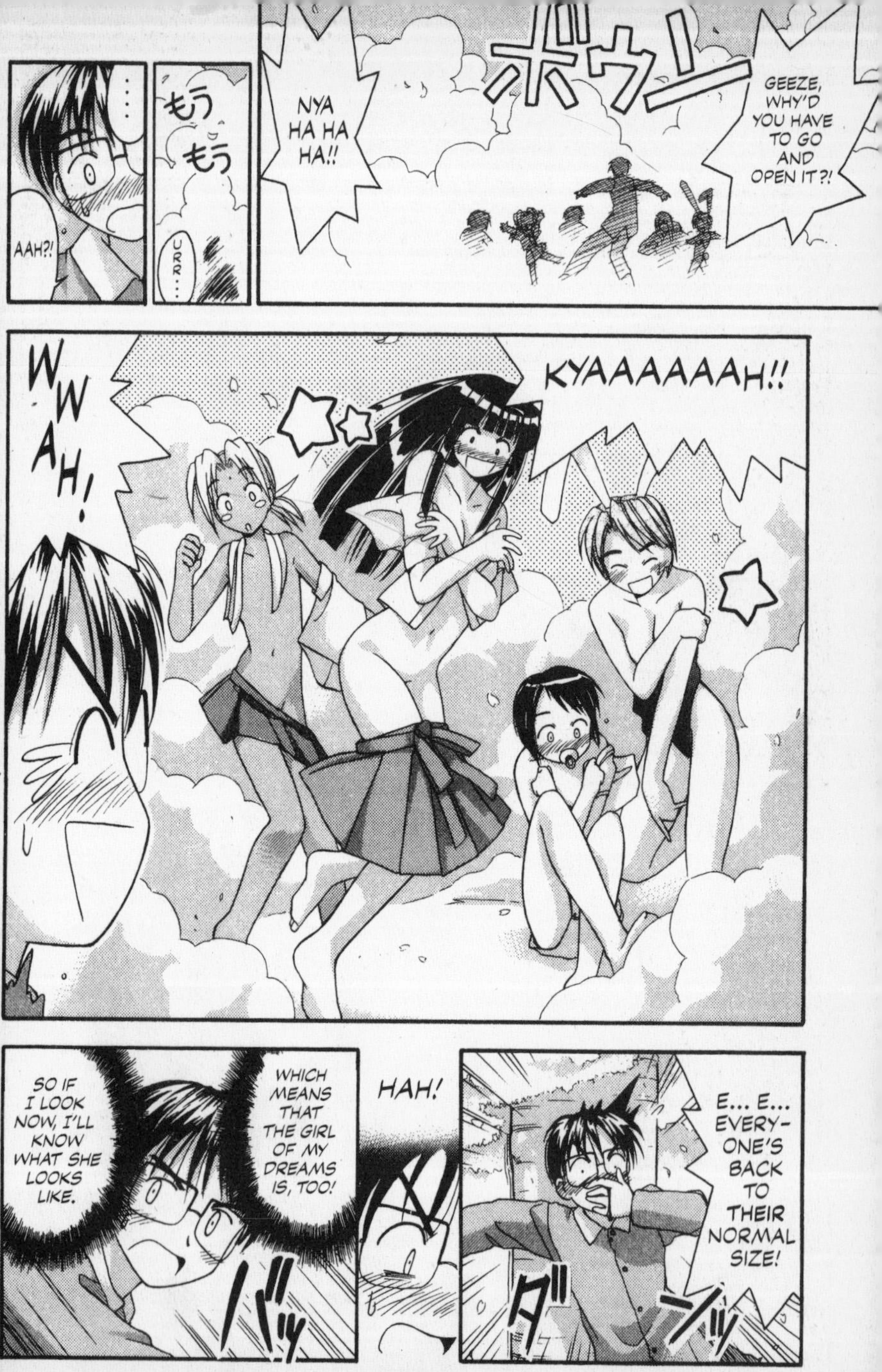
ボウン
GEEZE, WHY'D YOU HAVE TO GO AND OPEN IT?!
NYA HA HA HA!!
もう もう
URR...
...
AAH?!
KYAAAAAAH!!
WWAH!
E... E... EVERY-ONE'S BACK TO THEIR NORMAL SIZE!
ダッ
HAH!
WHICH MEANS THAT THE GIRL OF MY DREAMS IS, TOO!
SO IF I LOOK NOW, I'LL KNOW WHAT SHE LOOKS LIKE.
バッ

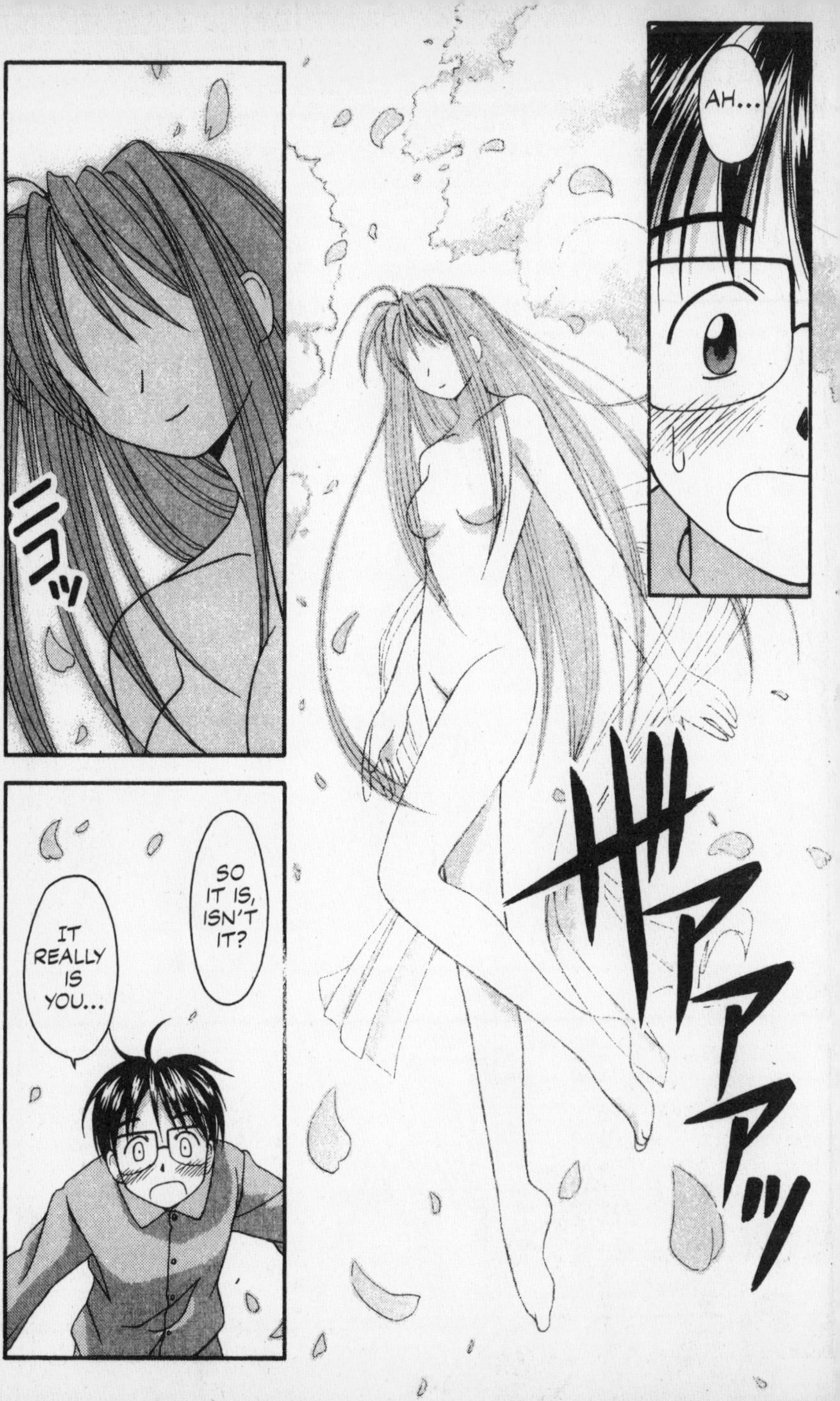
AH...
ザァアアッ
ニコッ
SO IT IS, ISN'T IT?
IT REALLY IS YOU...

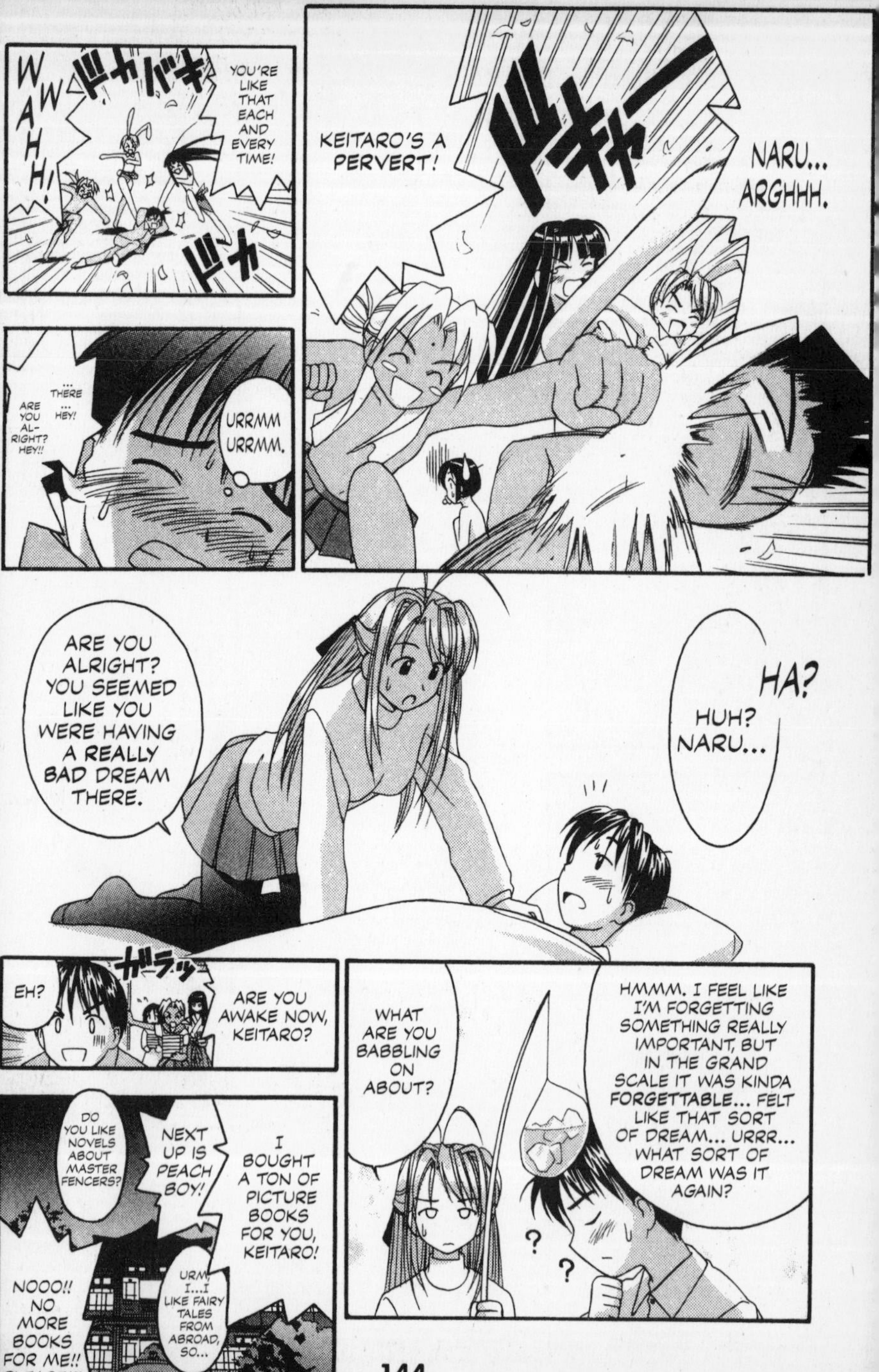
NARU... ARGHHH.
ドキャー
KEITARO'S A PERVERT!
YOU'RE LIKE THAT EACH AND EVERY TIME!
ドカバキ
WAWAHH!
ドカ
URRMM URRMM.
... THERE ... HEY!
ARE YOU AL-RIGHT? HEY!!
HA?
HUH? NARU...
ARE YOU ALRIGHT? YOU SEEMED LIKE YOU WERE HAVING A REALLY BAD DREAM THERE.
HMMM. I FEEL LIKE I'M FORGETTING SOMETHING REALLY IMPORTANT, BUT IN THE GRAND SCALE IT WAS KINDA FORGETTABLE... FELT LIKE THAT SORT OF DREAM... URRR... WHAT SORT OF DREAM WAS IT AGAIN?
WHAT ARE YOU BABBLING ON ABOUT?
ガラッ
ARE YOU AWAKE NOW, KEITARO?
EH?
I BOUGHT A TON OF PICTURE BOOKS FOR YOU, KEITARO!
NEXT UP IS PEACH BOY!
DO YOU LIKE NOVELS ABOUT MASTER FENCERS?
URM, I...I LIKE FAIRY TALES FROM ABROAD, SO...
NOOO!! NO MORE BOOKS FOR ME!! PLEASE!!!

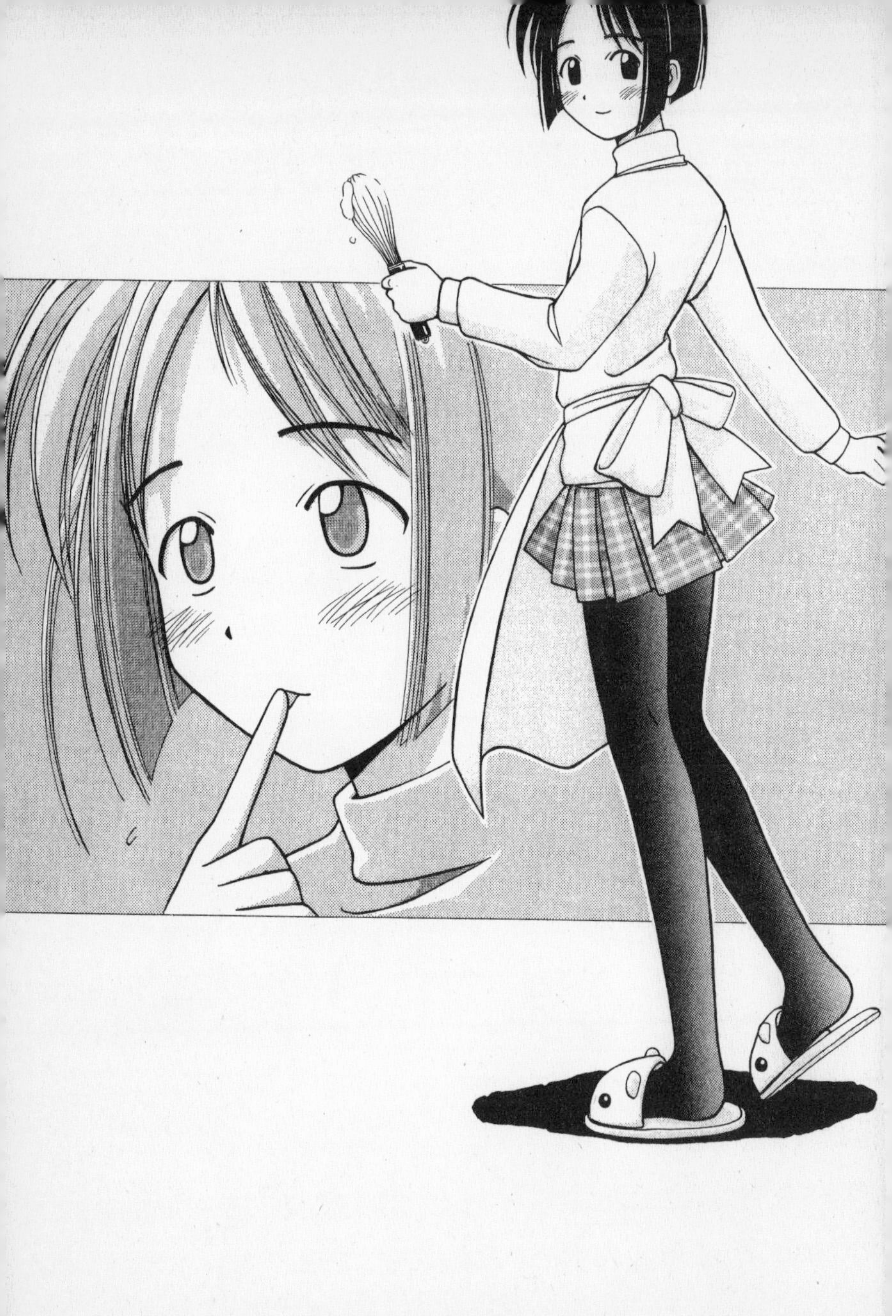

HINATA. 14 I Hate Valentine's Day!

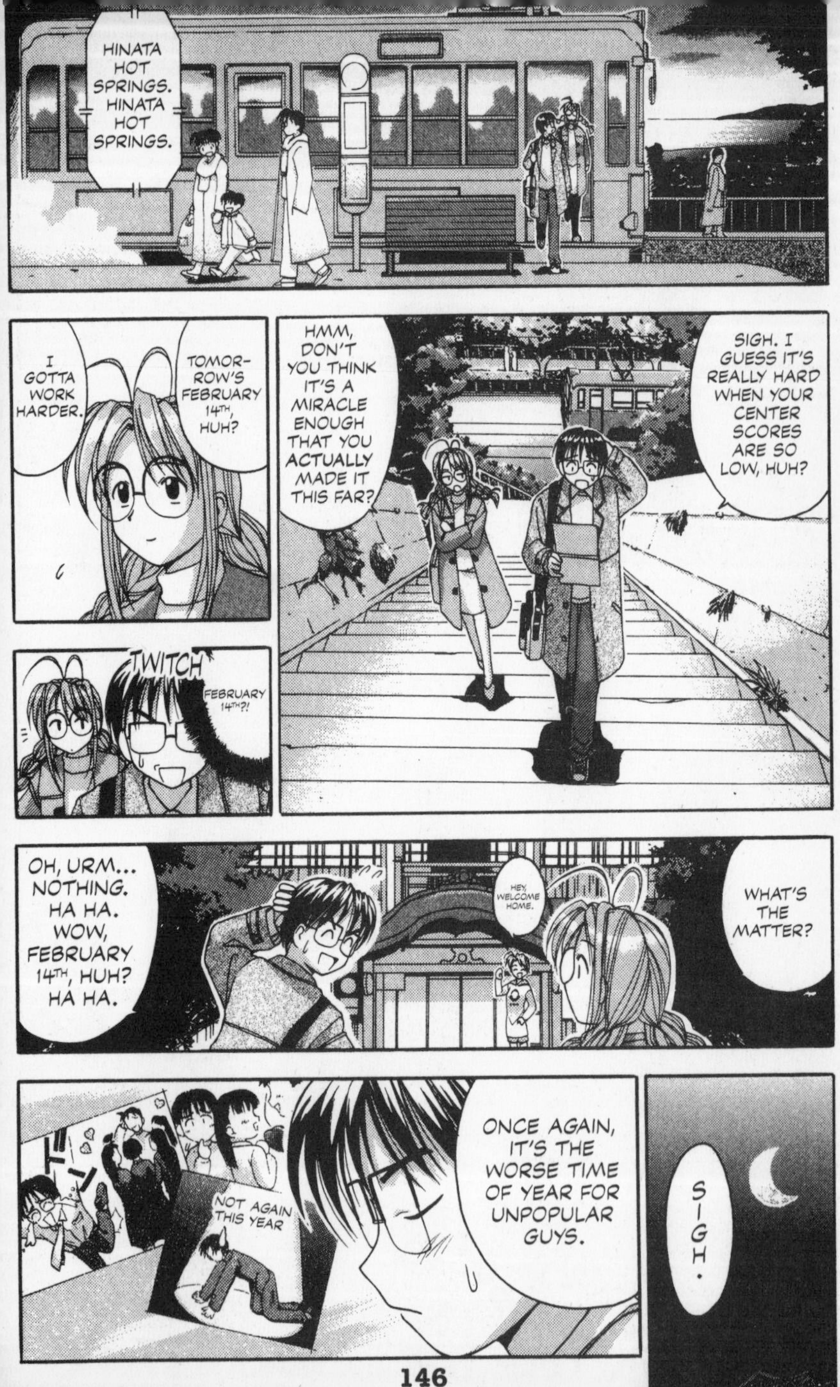
HINATA HOT SPRINGS. HINATA HOT SPRINGS.
SIGH. I GUESS IT'S REALLY HARD WHEN YOUR CENTER SCORES ARE SO LOW, HUH?
HMM, DON'T YOU THINK IT'S A MIRACLE ENOUGH THAT YOU ACTUALLY MADE IT THIS FAR?
TOMORROW'S FEBRUARY 14TH, HUH?
I GOTTA WORK HARDER.
TWITCH
FEBRUARY 14TH?!
WHAT'S THE MATTER?
HEY, WELCOME HOME.
OH, URM... NOTHING. HA HA. WOW, FEBRUARY 14TH, HUH? HA HA.
SIGH.
ONCE AGAIN, IT'S THE WORSE TIME OF YEAR FOR UNPOPULAR GUYS.
NOT AGAIN THIS YEAR

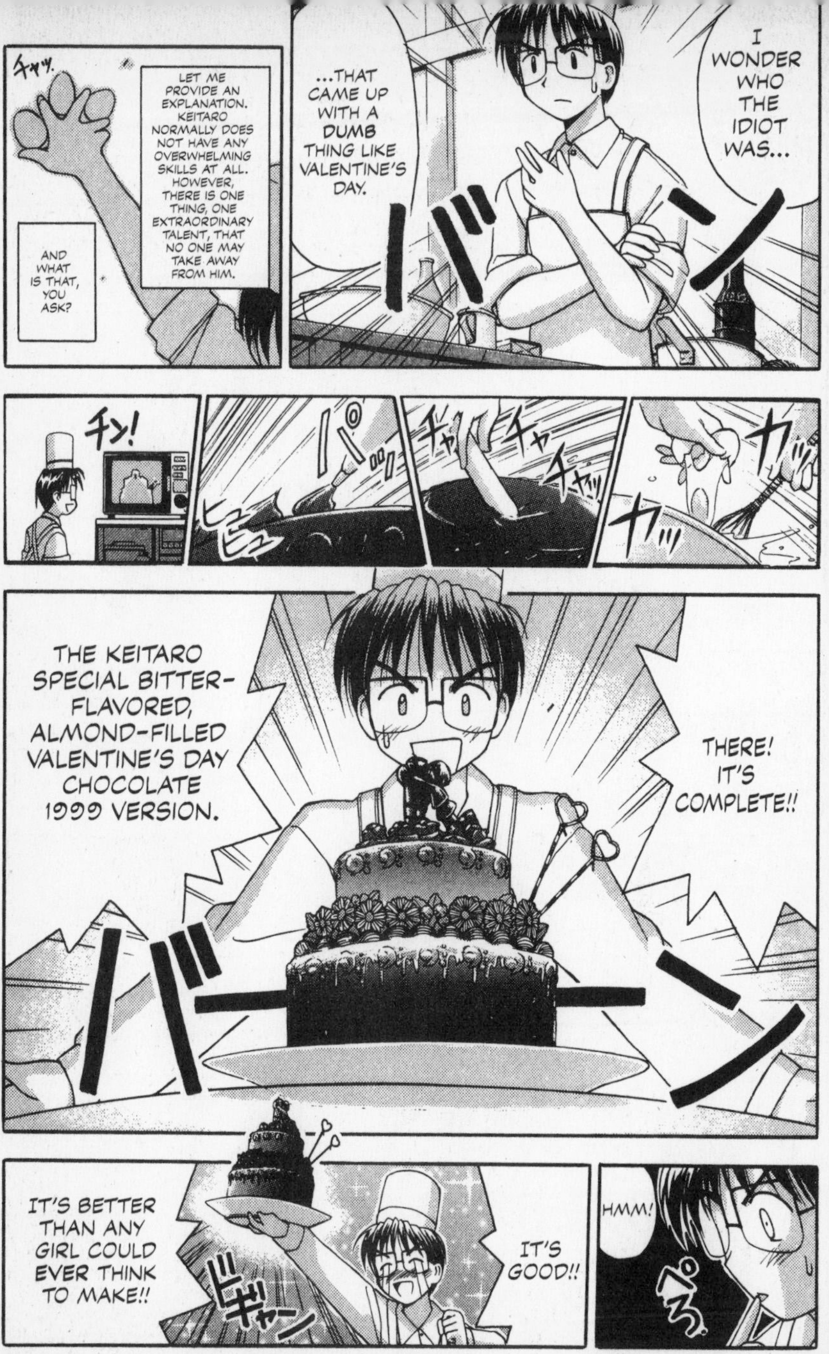
I WONDER WHO THE IDIOT WAS...
...THAT CAME UP WITH A DUMB THING LIKE VALENTINE'S DAY.
LET ME PROVIDE AN EXPLANATION. KEITARO NORMALLY DOES NOT HAVE ANY OVERWHELMING SKILLS AT ALL. HOWEVER, THERE IS ONE THING, ONE EXTRAORDINARY TALENT, THAT NO ONE MAY TAKE AWAY FROM HIM.
AND WHAT IS THAT, YOU ASK?
チン!
THERE! IT'S COMPLETE!!
THE KEITARO SPECIAL BITTER-FLAVORED, ALMOND-FILLED VALENTINE'S DAY CHOCOLATE 1999 VERSION.
HMM!
IT'S GOOD!!
IT'S BETTER THAN ANY GIRL COULD EVER THINK TO MAKE!!

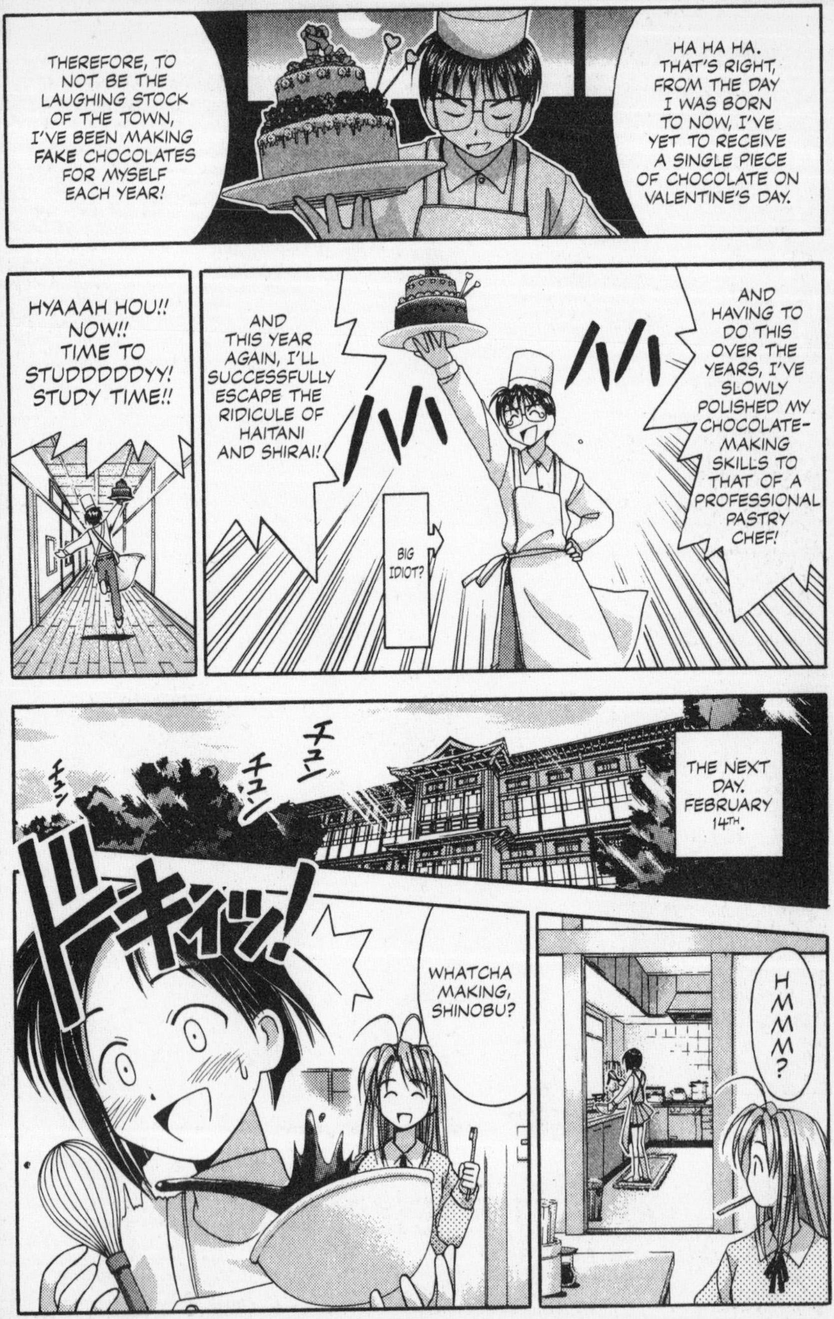
HA HA HA. THAT'S RIGHT, FROM THE DAY I WAS BORN TO NOW, I'VE YET TO RECEIVE A SINGLE PIECE OF CHOCOLATE ON VALENTINE'S DAY.
THEREFORE, TO NOT BE THE LAUGHING STOCK OF THE TOWN, I'VE BEEN MAKING FAKE CHOCOLATES FOR MYSELF EACH YEAR!
AND HAVING TO DO THIS OVER THE YEARS, I'VE SLOWLY POLISHED MY CHOCOLATE-MAKING SKILLS TO THAT OF A PROFESSIONAL PASTRY CHEF!
AND THIS YEAR AGAIN, I'LL SUCCESSFULLY ESCAPE THE RIDICULE OF HAITANI AND SHIRAI!
BIG IDIOT?
HYAAAH HOU!! NOW!! TIME TO STUDDDDDYY! STUDY TIME!!
THE NEXT DAY. FEBRUARY 14TH.
チュン
チュン
チュン
HMMMM?
ドキィッ!
WHATCHA MAKING, SHINOBU?

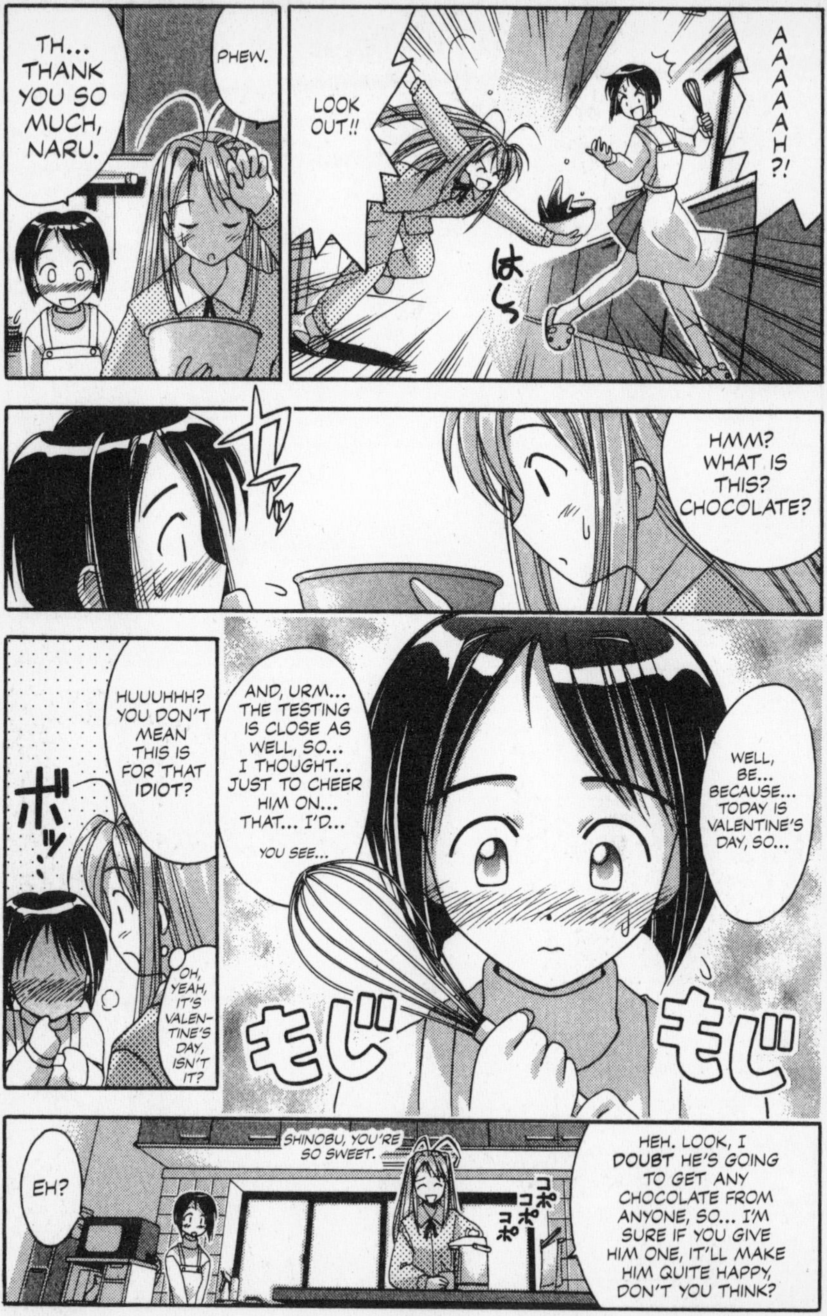
AAAAAAH?!
LOOK OUT!!
PHEW.
TH... THANK YOU SO MUCH, NARU.
HMM? WHAT IS THIS? CHOCOLATE?
WELL, BE... BECAUSE... TODAY IS VALENTINE'S DAY, SO...
AND, URM... THE TESTING IS CLOSE AS WELL, SO... I THOUGHT... JUST TO CHEER HIM ON... THAT... I'D...
YOU SEE...
もじ
もじ
HUUUHHH? YOU DON'T MEAN THIS IS FOR THAT IDIOT?
ボッ
OH, YEAH, IT'S VALENTINE'S DAY, ISN'T IT?
HEH. LOOK, I DOUBT HE'S GOING TO GET ANY CHOCOLATE FROM ANYONE, SO... I'M SURE IF YOU GIVE HIM ONE, IT'LL MAKE HIM QUITE HAPPY, DON'T YOU THINK?
コポ
コポ
コポ
SHINOBU, YOU'RE SO SWEET.
EH?

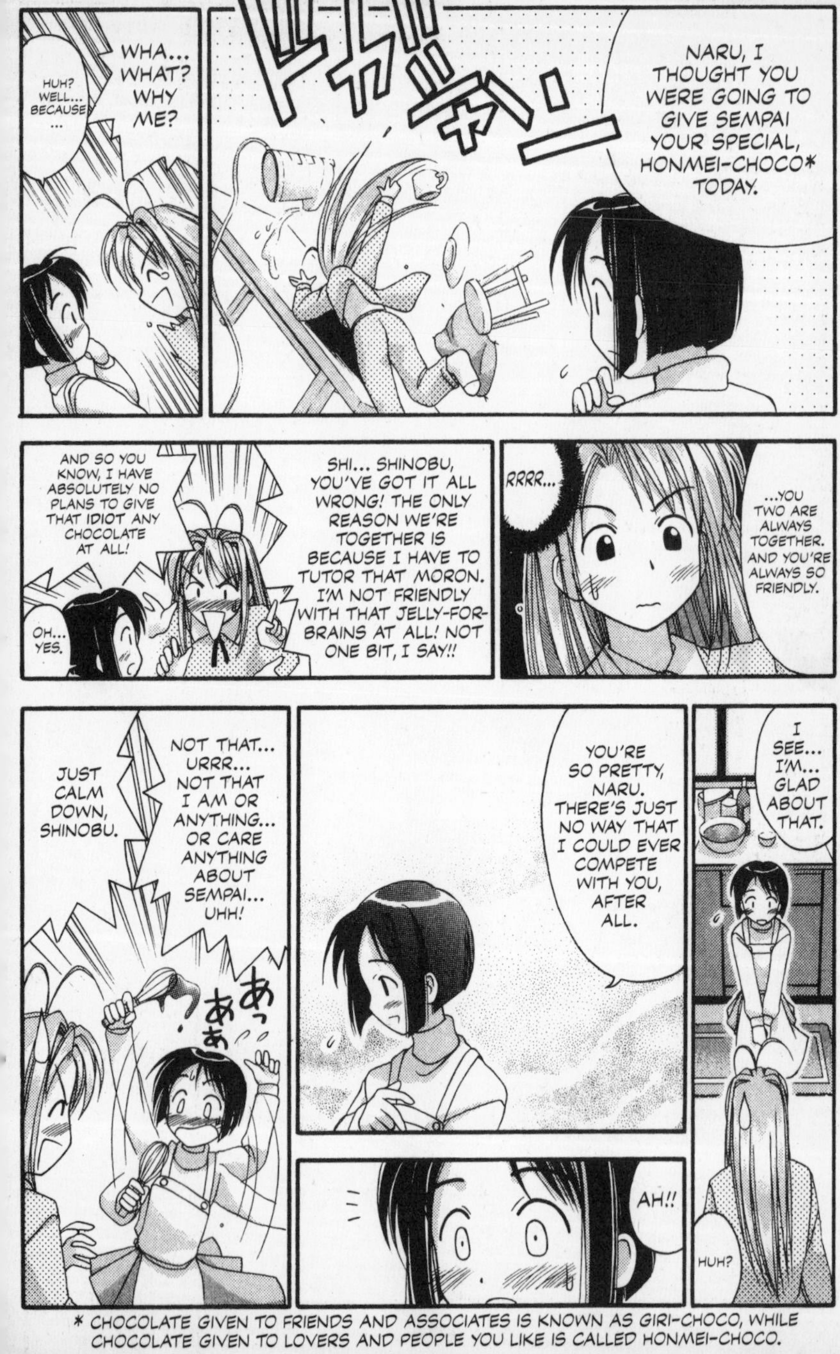
ドカ!!
NARU, I THOUGHT YOU WERE GOING TO GIVE SEMPAI YOUR SPECIAL, HONMEI-CHOCO* TODAY.
WHA... WHAT? WHY ME?
HUH? WELL... BECAUSE ...
...YOU TWO ARE ALWAYS TOGETHER. AND YOU'RE ALWAYS SO FRIENDLY.
RRRR...
SHI... SHINOBU, YOU'VE GOT IT ALL WRONG! THE ONLY REASON WE'RE TOGETHER IS BECAUSE I HAVE TO TUTOR THAT MORON. I'M NOT FRIENDLY WITH THAT JELLY-FOR-BRAINS AT ALL! NOT ONE BIT, I SAY!!
AND SO YOU KNOW, I HAVE ABSOLUTELY NO PLANS TO GIVE THAT IDIOT ANY CHOCOLATE AT ALL!
OH... YES.
I SEE... I'M... GLAD ABOUT THAT.
HUH?
YOU'RE SO PRETTY, NARU. THERE'S JUST NO WAY THAT I COULD EVER COMPETE WITH YOU, AFTER ALL.
AH!!
NOT THAT... URRR... NOT THAT I AM OR ANYTHING... OR CARE ANYTHING ABOUT SEMPAI... UHH!
JUST CALM DOWN, SHINOBU.
あっ
あぁ

* CHOCOLATE GIVEN TO FRIENDS AND ASSOCIATES IS KNOWN AS GIRI-CHOCO, WHILE CHOCOLATE GIVEN TO LOVERS AND PEOPLE YOU LIKE IS CALLED HONMEI-CHOCO.

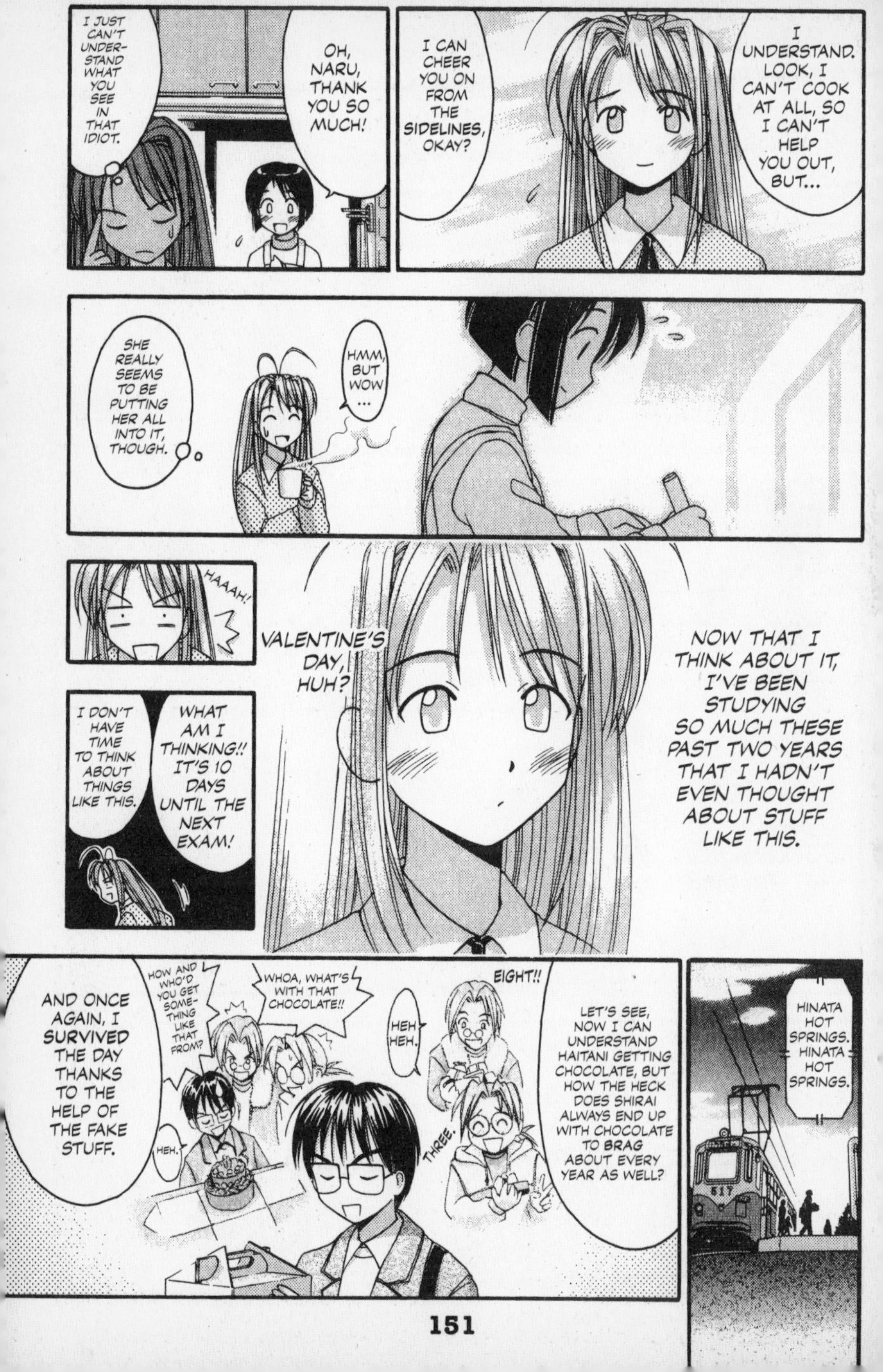

I UNDERSTAND. LOOK, I CAN'T COOK AT ALL, SO I CAN'T HELP YOU OUT, BUT...
I CAN CHEER YOU ON FROM THE SIDELINES, OKAY?
OH, NARU, THANK YOU SO MUCH!
I JUST CAN'T UNDER-STAND WHAT YOU SEE IN THAT IDIOT.
HMM, BUT WOW ...
SHE REALLY SEEMS TO BE PUTTING HER ALL INTO IT, THOUGH.
NOW THAT I THINK ABOUT IT, I'VE BEEN STUDYING SO MUCH THESE PAST TWO YEARS THAT I HADN'T EVEN THOUGHT ABOUT STUFF LIKE THIS.
VALENTINE'S DAY, HUH?
HAAAAH!
WHAT AM I THINKING!! IT'S 10 DAYS UNTIL THE NEXT EXAM!
I DON'T HAVE TIME TO THINK ABOUT THINGS LIKE THIS.
HINATA HOT SPRINGS. HINATA HOT SPRINGS.
LET'S SEE, NOW I CAN UNDERSTAND HAITANI GETTING CHOCOLATE, BUT HOW THE HECK DOES SHIRAI ALWAYS END UP WITH CHOCOLATE TO BRAG ABOUT EVERY YEAR AS WELL?
EIGHT!!
HEH HEH.
THREE.
WHOA, WHAT'S WITH THAT CHOCOLATE!!
HOW AND WHO'D YOU GET SOME-THING LIKE THAT FROM?
HEH.
AND ONCE AGAIN, I SURVIVED THE DAY THANKS TO THE HELP OF THE FAKE STUFF.

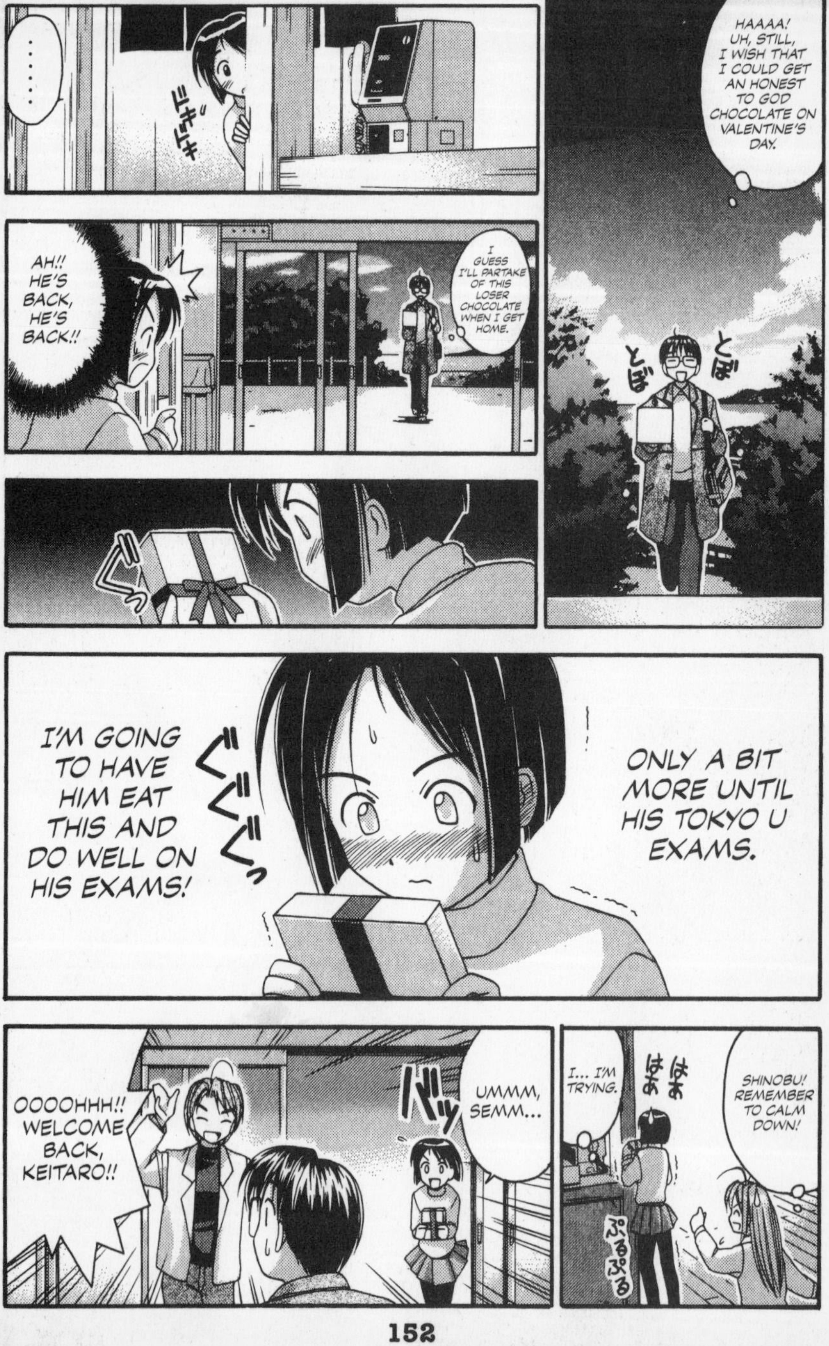
HAAAA! UH, STILL, I WISH THAT I COULD GET AN HONEST TO GOD CHOCOLATE ON VALENTINE'S DAY.
とぼとぼ
......
ドキドキ
I GUESS I'LL PARTAKE OF THIS LOSER CHOCOLATE WHEN I GET HOME.
AH!! HE'S BACK, HE'S BACK!!
ONLY A BIT MORE UNTIL HIS TOKYO U EXAMS.
ぐぐぐっ
I'M GOING TO HAVE HIM EAT THIS AND DO WELL ON HIS EXAMS!
SHINOBU! REMEMBER TO CALM DOWN!
はあはあ
I... I'M TRYING.
ぷるぷる
UMMM, SEMM...
バッ
OOOOHHH!! WELCOME BACK, KEITARO!!

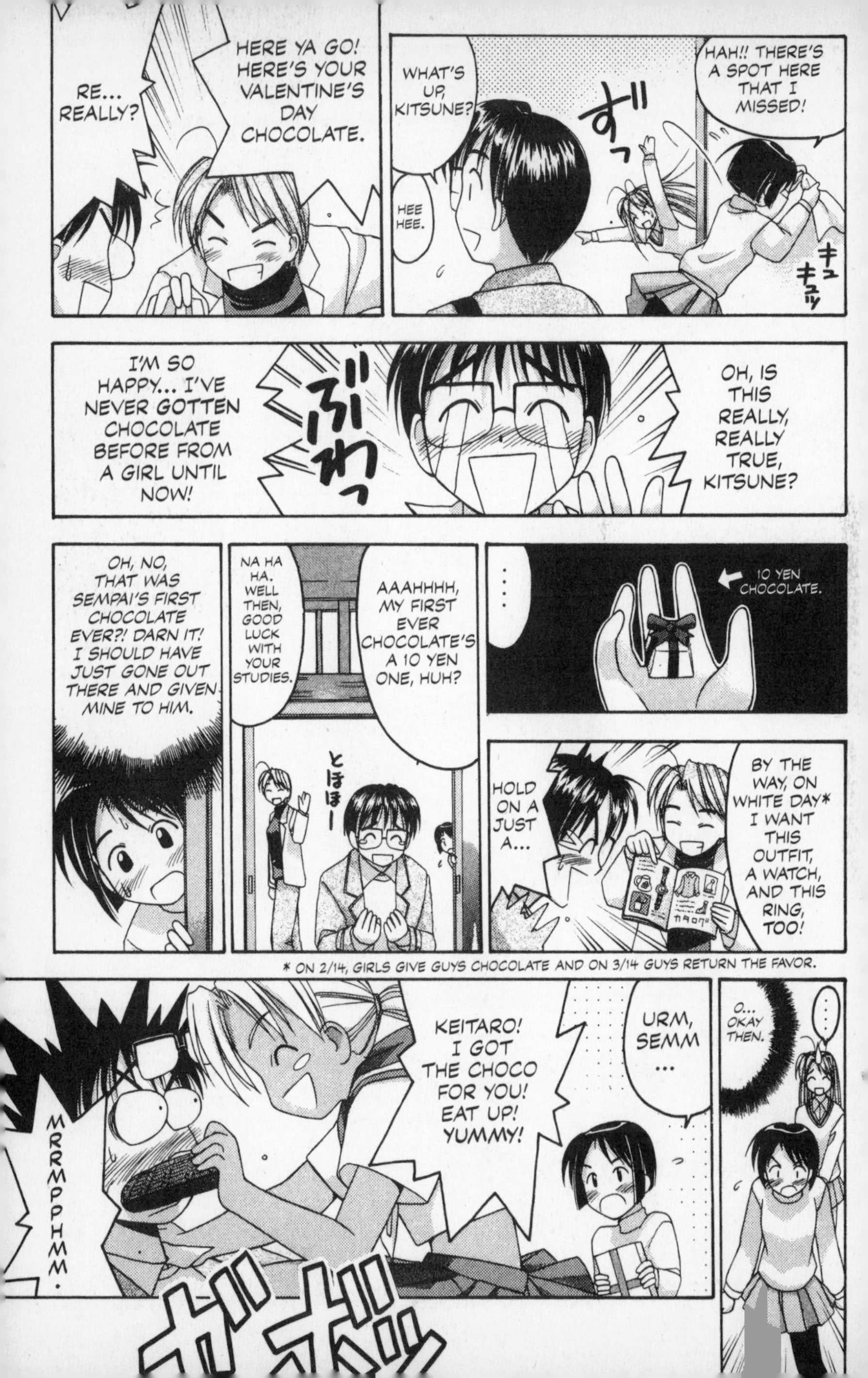
HAH!! THERE'S A SPOT HERE THAT I MISSED!
ずっ
WHAT'S UP, KITSUNE?
キュキュッ
HEE HEE.
HERE YA GO! HERE'S YOUR VALENTINE'S DAY CHOCOLATE.
RE... REALLY?
OH, IS THIS REALLY, REALLY TRUE, KITSUNE?
ぶわっ
I'M SO HAPPY... I'VE NEVER GOTTEN CHOCOLATE BEFORE FROM A GIRL UNTIL NOW!
10 YEN CHOCOLATE.
....
BY THE WAY, ON WHITE DAY* I WANT THIS OUTFIT, A WATCH, AND THIS RING, TOO!
HOLD ON A JUST A...
AAAHHHH, MY FIRST EVER CHOCOLATE'S A 10 YEN ONE, HUH?
NA HA HA. WELL THEN, GOOD LUCK WITH YOUR STUDIES.
とほほー
OH, NO, THAT WAS SEMPAI'S FIRST CHOCOLATE EVER?! DARN IT! I SHOULD HAVE JUST GONE OUT THERE AND GIVEN MINE TO HIM.
* ON 2/14, GIRLS GIVE GUYS CHOCOLATE AND ON 3/14 GUYS RETURN THE FAVOR.
....
O... OKAY THEN.
URM, SEMM ...
KEITARO! I GOT THE CHOCO FOR YOU! EAT UP! YUMMY!
MRRMPPHMM.
ガボッ

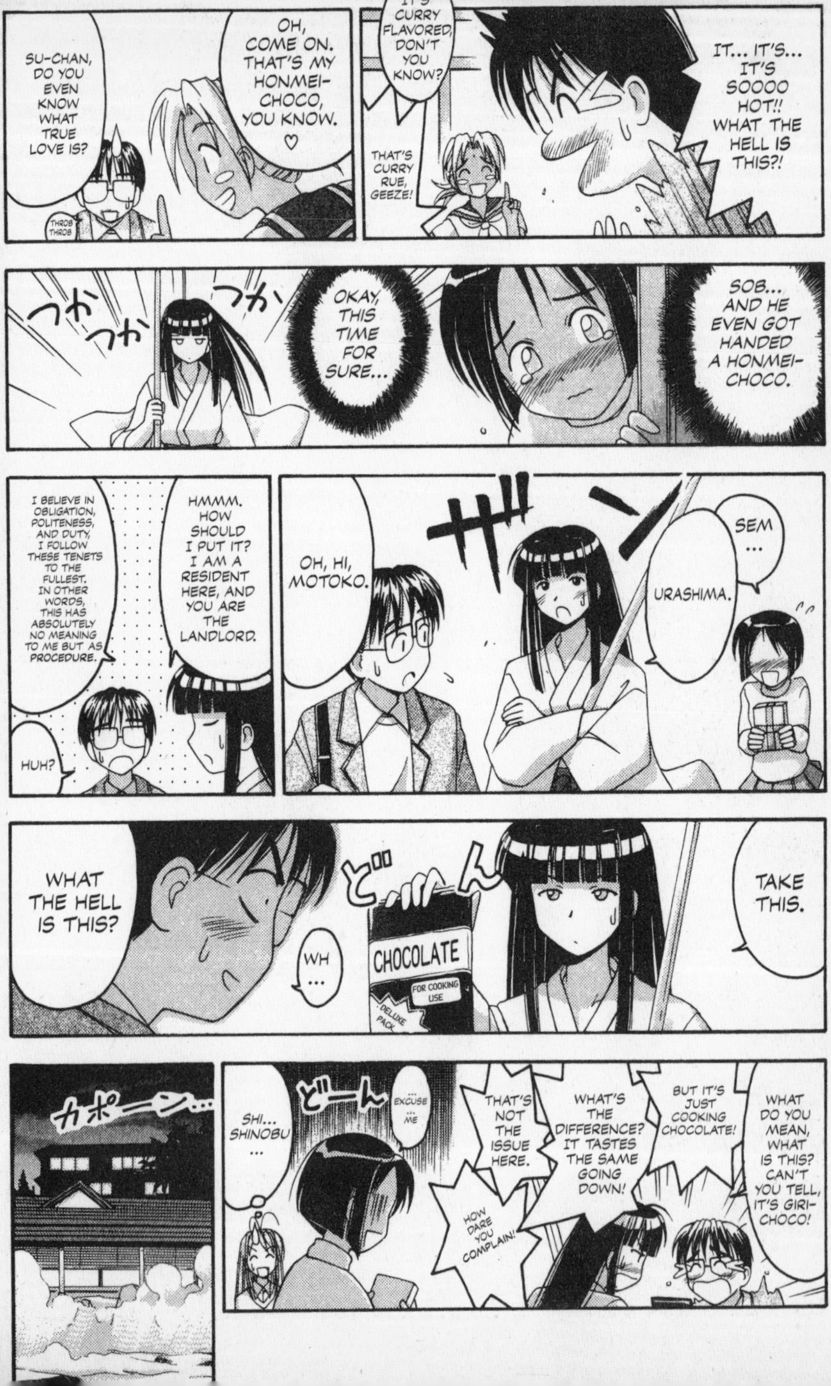

IT... IT'S... IT'S SOOOO HOT!! WHAT THE HELL IS THIS?!
IT'S CURRY FLAVORED, DON'T YOU KNOW?
THAT'S CURRY RUE, GEEZE!
OH, COME ON. THAT'S MY HONMEI-CHOCO, YOU KNOW. ♡
SU-CHAN, DO YOU EVEN KNOW WHAT TRUE LOVE IS?
THROB THROB
SOB... AND HE EVEN GOT HANDED A HONMEI-CHOCO.
OKAY, THIS TIME FOR SURE...
つかつかつか
SEM ...
URASHIMA.
ザン
OH, HI, MOTOKO.
HMMM. HOW SHOULD I PUT IT? I AM A RESIDENT HERE, AND YOU ARE THE LANDLORD.
I BELIEVE IN OBLIGATION, POLITENESS, AND DUTY, I FOLLOW THESE TENETS TO THE FULLEST. IN OTHER WORDS, THIS HAS ABSOLUTELY NO MEANING TO ME BUT AS PROCEDURE.
HUH?
TAKE THIS.
どん
CHOCOLATE
FOR COOKING USE
DELUXE PACK
WH ...
WHAT THE HELL IS THIS?
WHAT DO YOU MEAN, WHAT IS THIS? CAN'T YOU TELL, IT'S GIRI-CHOCO!
BUT IT'S JUST COOKING CHOCOLATE!
WHAT'S THE DIFFERENCE? IT TASTES THE SAME GOING DOWN!
THAT'S NOT THE ISSUE HERE.
HOW DARE YOU COMPLAIN!
... EXCUSE ... ME
どーん
SHI... SHINOBU ...
カポーン...

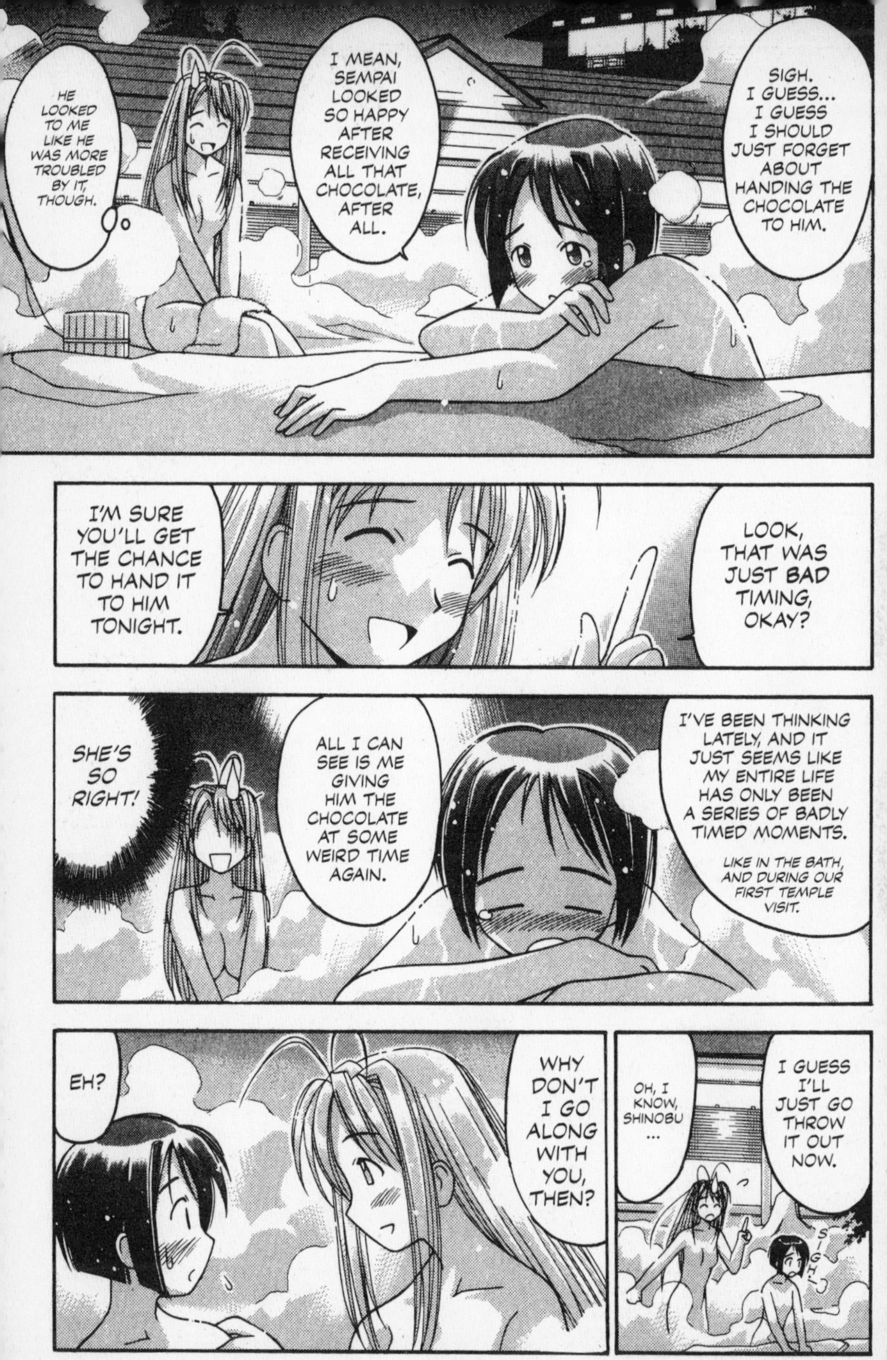
SIGH. I GUESS... I GUESS I SHOULD JUST FORGET ABOUT HANDING THE CHOCOLATE TO HIM.
I MEAN, SEMPAI LOOKED SO HAPPY AFTER RECEIVING ALL THAT CHOCOLATE, AFTER ALL.
HE LOOKED TO ME LIKE HE WAS MORE TROUBLED BY IT, THOUGH.
LOOK, THAT WAS JUST BAD TIMING, OKAY?
I'M SURE YOU'LL GET THE CHANCE TO HAND IT TO HIM TONIGHT.
I'VE BEEN THINKING LATELY, AND IT JUST SEEMS LIKE MY ENTIRE LIFE HAS ONLY BEEN A SERIES OF BADLY TIMED MOMENTS.
LIKE IN THE BATH, AND DURING OUR FIRST TEMPLE VISIT.
ALL I CAN SEE IS ME GIVING HIM THE CHOCOLATE AT SOME WEIRD TIME AGAIN.
SHE'S SO RIGHT!
I GUESS I'LL JUST GO THROW IT OUT NOW.
SIGH~
OH, I KNOW, SHINOBU ...
WHY DON'T I GO ALONG WITH YOU, THEN?
EH?

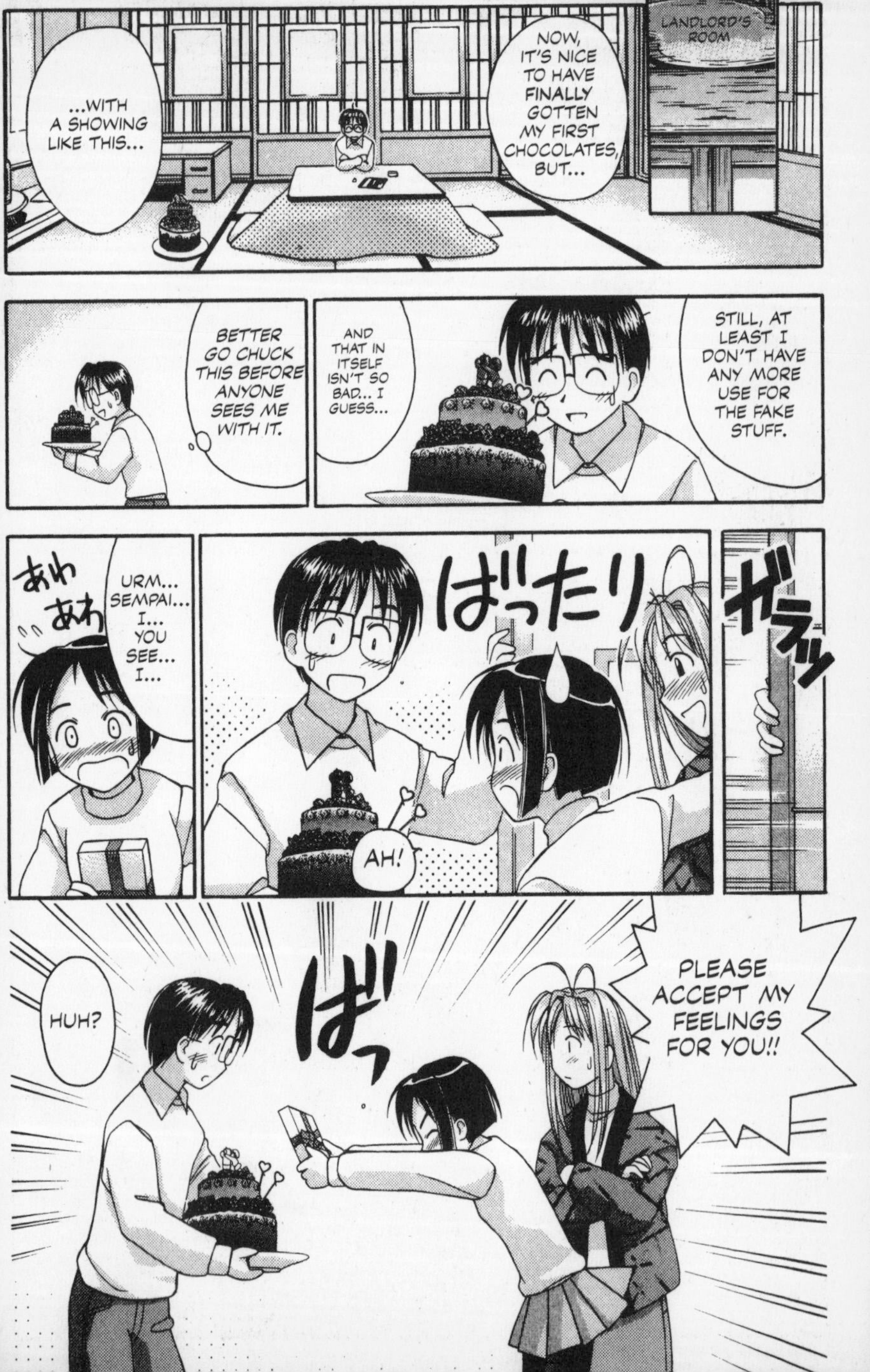
LANDLORD'S ROOM
NOW, IT'S NICE TO HAVE FINALLY GOTTEN MY FIRST CHOCOLATES, BUT...
...WITH A SHOWING LIKE THIS...
STILL, AT LEAST I DON'T HAVE ANY MORE USE FOR THE FAKE STUFF.
AND THAT IN ITSELF ISN'T SO BAD... I GUESS...
BETTER GO CHUCK THIS BEFORE ANYONE SEES ME WITH IT.
ガラッ
ばったり
AH!
あわあわ
URM... SEMPAI... I... YOU SEE... I...
PLEASE ACCEPT MY FEELINGS FOR YOU!!
ばっ
HUH?

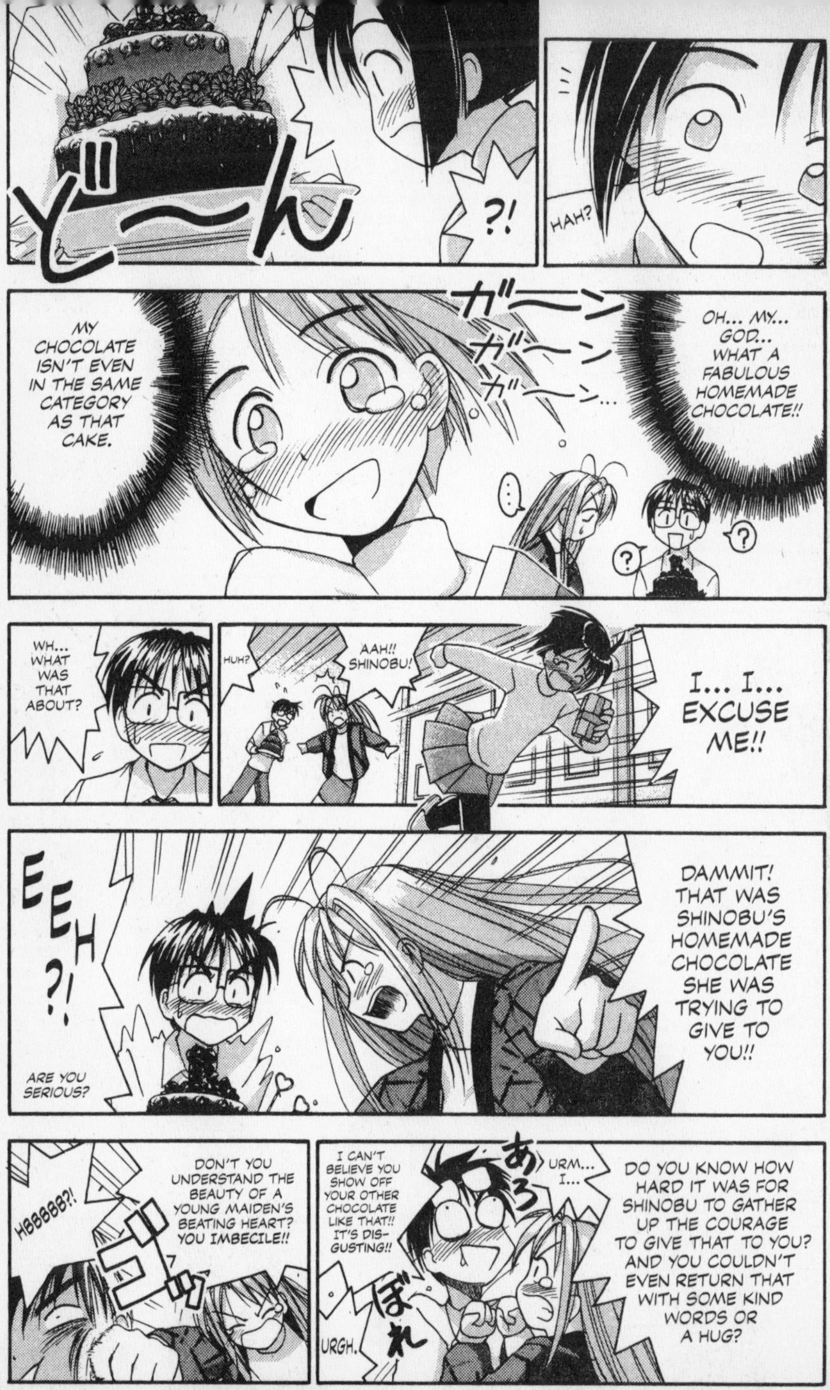
HAH?
どーん
?!
OH... MY... GOD... WHAT A FABULOUS HOMEMADE CHOCOLATE!!
ガーン
ガーン
ガーン...
MY CHOCOLATE ISN'T EVEN IN THE SAME CATEGORY AS THAT CAKE.
...
?
?
I... I... EXCUSE ME!!
AAH!! SHINOBU!
HUH?
WH... WHAT WAS THAT ABOUT?
DAMMIT! THAT WAS SHINOBU'S HOMEMADE CHOCOLATE SHE WAS TRYING TO GIVE TO YOU!!
EEH?!
ARE YOU SERIOUS?
DO YOU KNOW HOW HARD IT WAS FOR SHINOBU TO GATHER UP THE COURAGE TO GIVE THAT TO YOU? AND YOU COULDN'T EVEN RETURN THAT WITH SOME KIND WORDS OR A HUG?
URM... I...
あろ
I CAN'T BELIEVE YOU SHOW OFF YOUR OTHER CHOCOLATE LIKE THAT!! IT'S DIS-GUSTING!!
ぽれ
URGH.
DON'T YOU UNDERSTAND THE BEAUTY OF A YOUNG MAIDEN'S BEATING HEART? YOU IMBECILE!!
HBBBBB?!

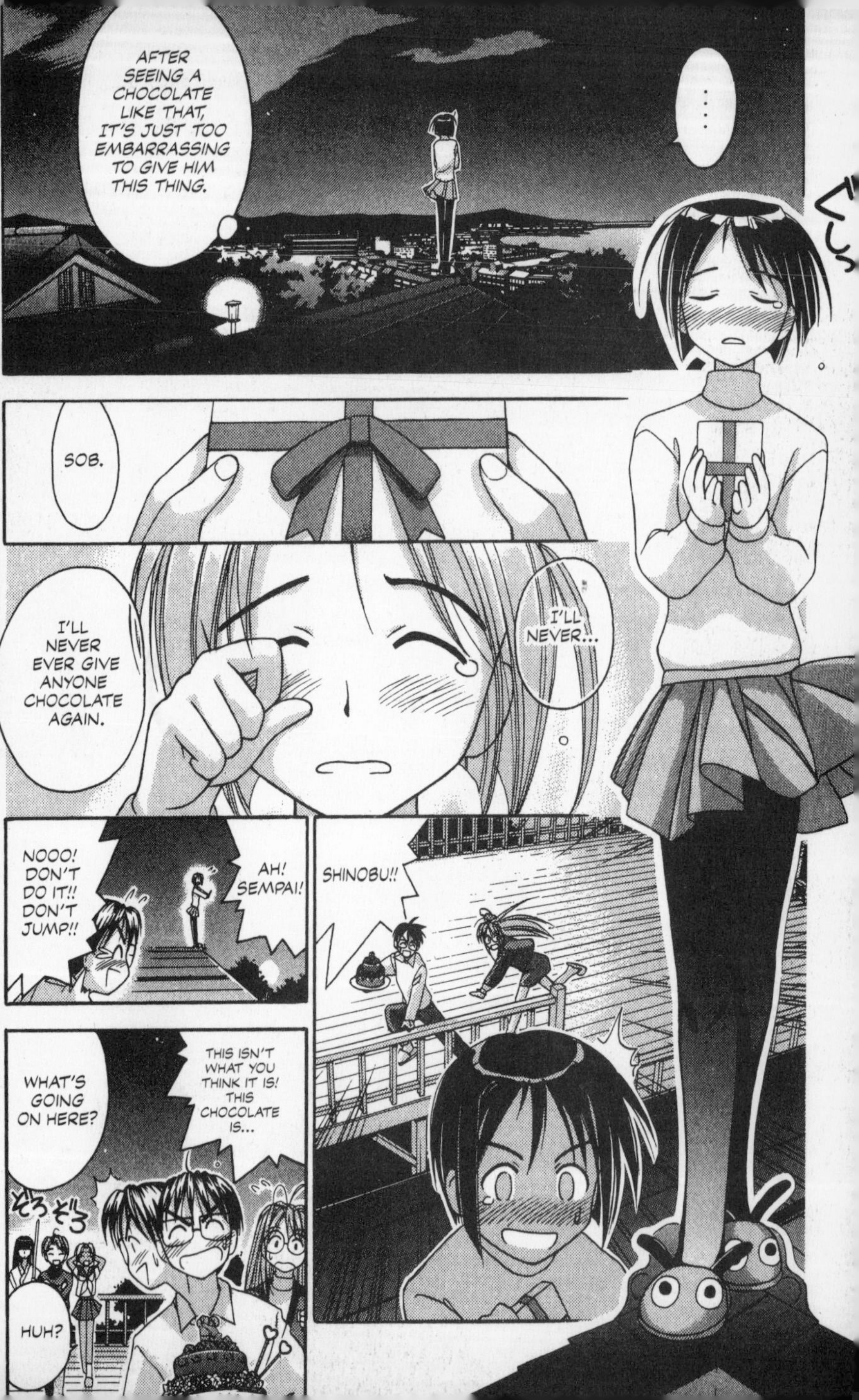
......
AFTER SEEING A CHOCOLATE LIKE THAT, IT'S JUST TOO EMBARRASSING TO GIVE HIM THIS THING.
ぐしっ
SOB.
I'LL NEVER...
I'LL NEVER EVER GIVE ANYONE CHOCOLATE AGAIN.
SHINOBU!!
AH! SEMPAI!
NOOO! DON'T DO IT!! DON'T JUMP!!
THIS ISN'T WHAT YOU THINK IT IS! THIS CHOCOLATE IS...
WHAT'S GOING ON HERE?
そろ そろ
HUH?

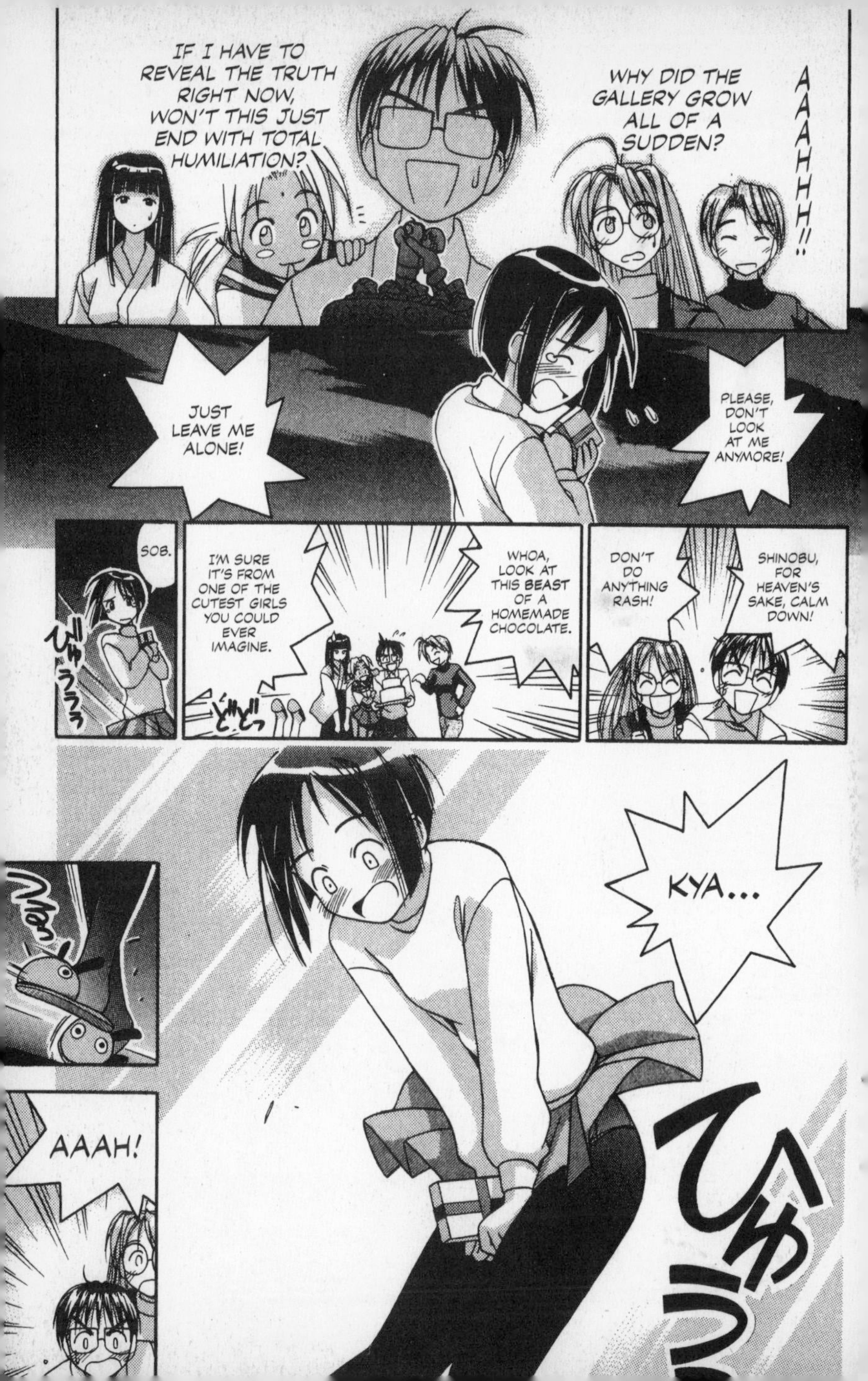
AAAAHHH!!
WHY DID THE GALLERY GROW ALL OF A SUDDEN?
IF I HAVE TO REVEAL THE TRUTH RIGHT NOW, WON'T THIS JUST END WITH TOTAL HUMILIATION?
PLEASE, DON'T LOOK AT ME ANYMORE!
JUST LEAVE ME ALONE!
SHINOBU, FOR HEAVEN'S SAKE, CALM DOWN!
DON'T DO ANYTHING RASH!
WHOA, LOOK AT THIS BEAST OF A HOMEMADE CHOCOLATE.
I'M SURE IT'S FROM ONE OF THE CUTEST GIRLS YOU COULD EVER IMAGINE.
SOB.
KYA...
AAAH!

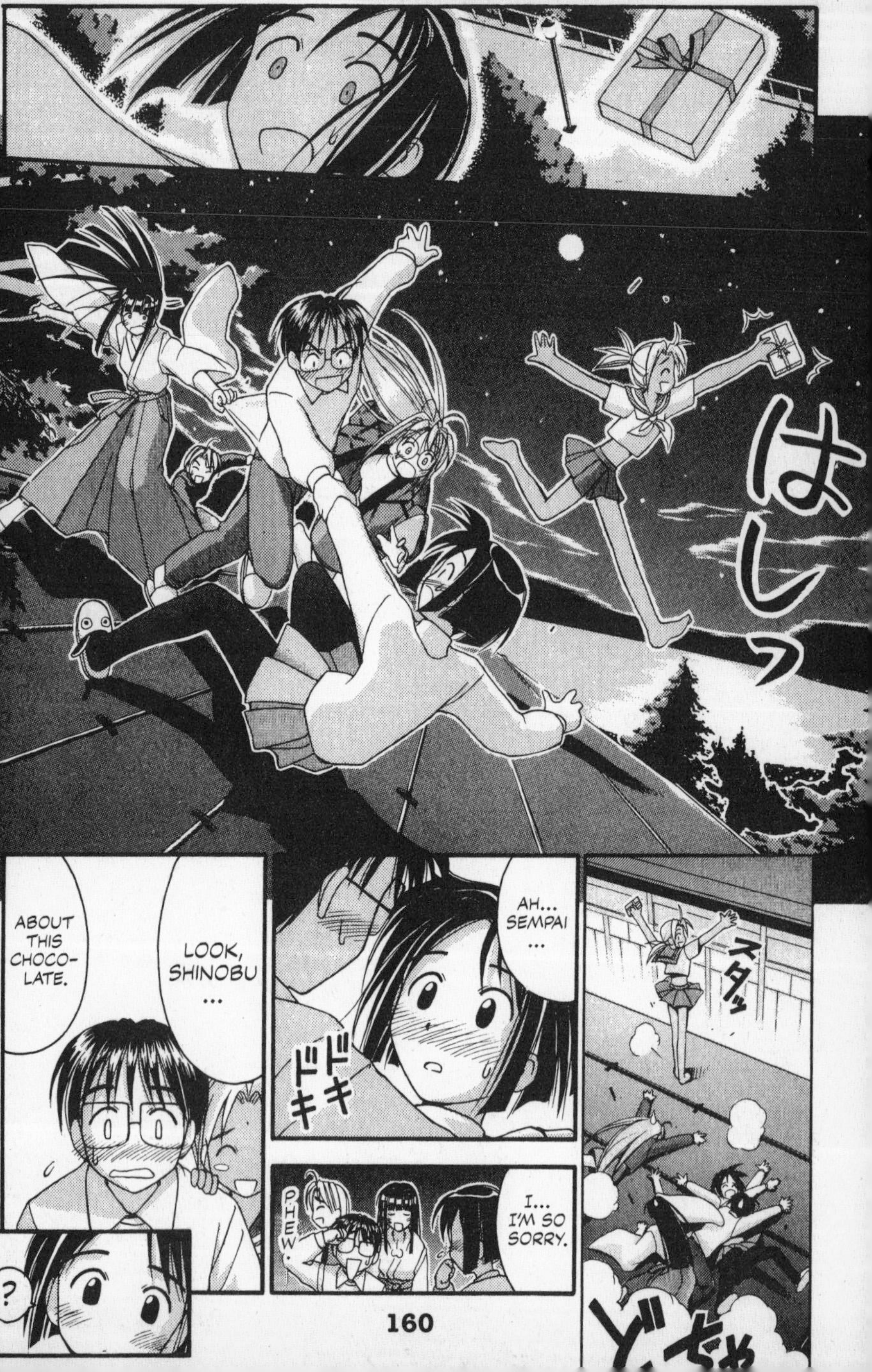
はしっ
スタッ
AH... SEMPAI ...
ドキドキ
I... I'M SO SORRY.
PHEW.
LOOK, SHINOBU ...
ABOUT THIS CHOCO-LATE.
?

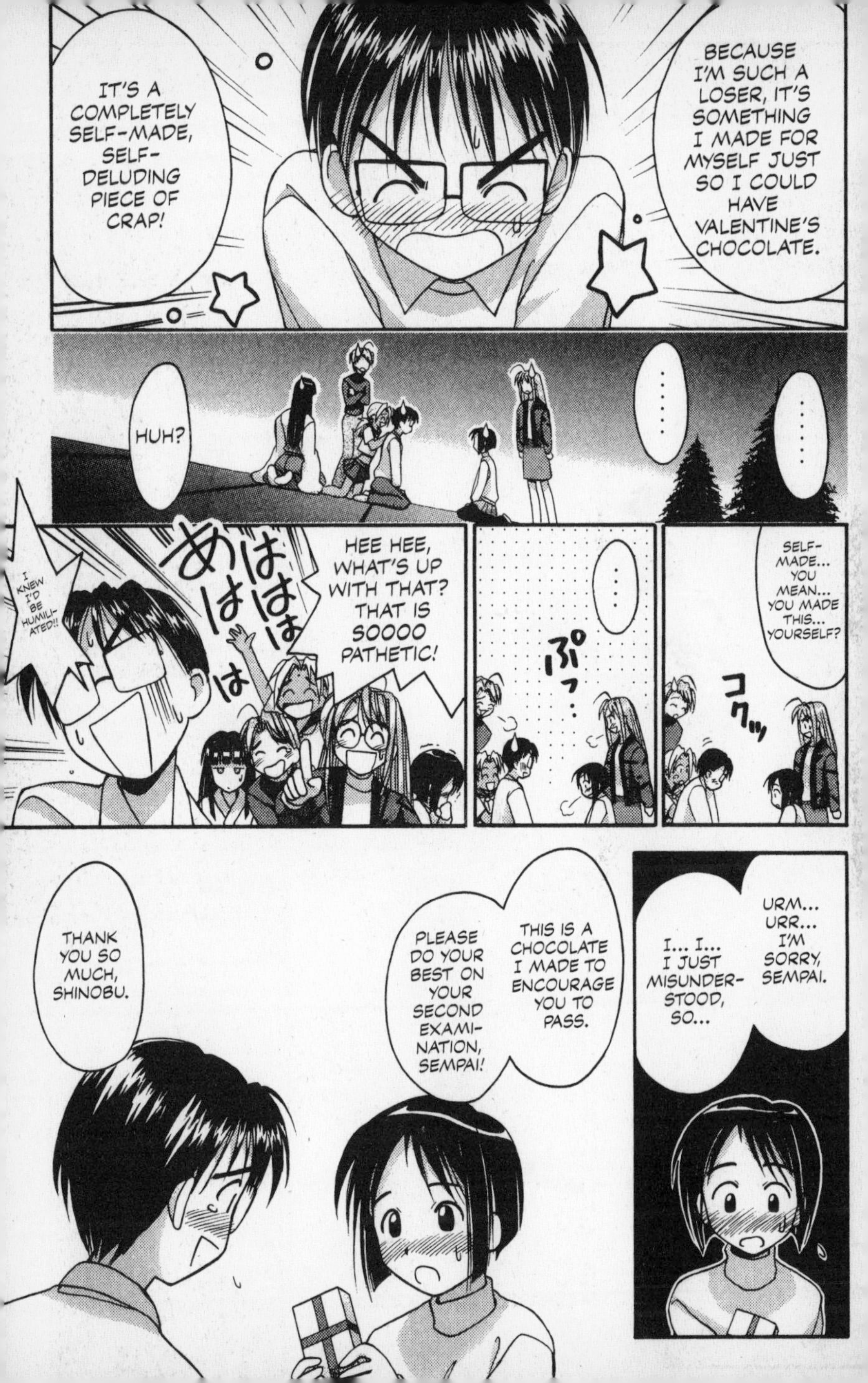

BECAUSE I'M SUCH A LOSER, IT'S SOMETHING I MADE FOR MYSELF JUST SO I COULD HAVE VALENTINE'S CHOCOLATE.
IT'S A COMPLETELY SELF-MADE, SELF-DELUDING PIECE OF CRAP!
......
.....
HUH?
SELF-MADE... YOU MEAN... YOU MADE THIS... YOURSELF?
コクッ
....
ぷっ...
HEE HEE, WHAT'S UP WITH THAT? THAT IS SOOOO PATHETIC!
あははは
は
I KNEW I'D BE HUMILIATED!!
URM... URR... I'M SORRY, SEMPAI.
I... I... I JUST MISUNDERSTOOD, SO...
THIS IS A CHOCOLATE I MADE TO ENCOURAGE YOU TO PASS.
PLEASE DO YOUR BEST ON YOUR SECOND EXAMINATION, SEMPAI!
THANK YOU SO MUCH, SHINOBU.

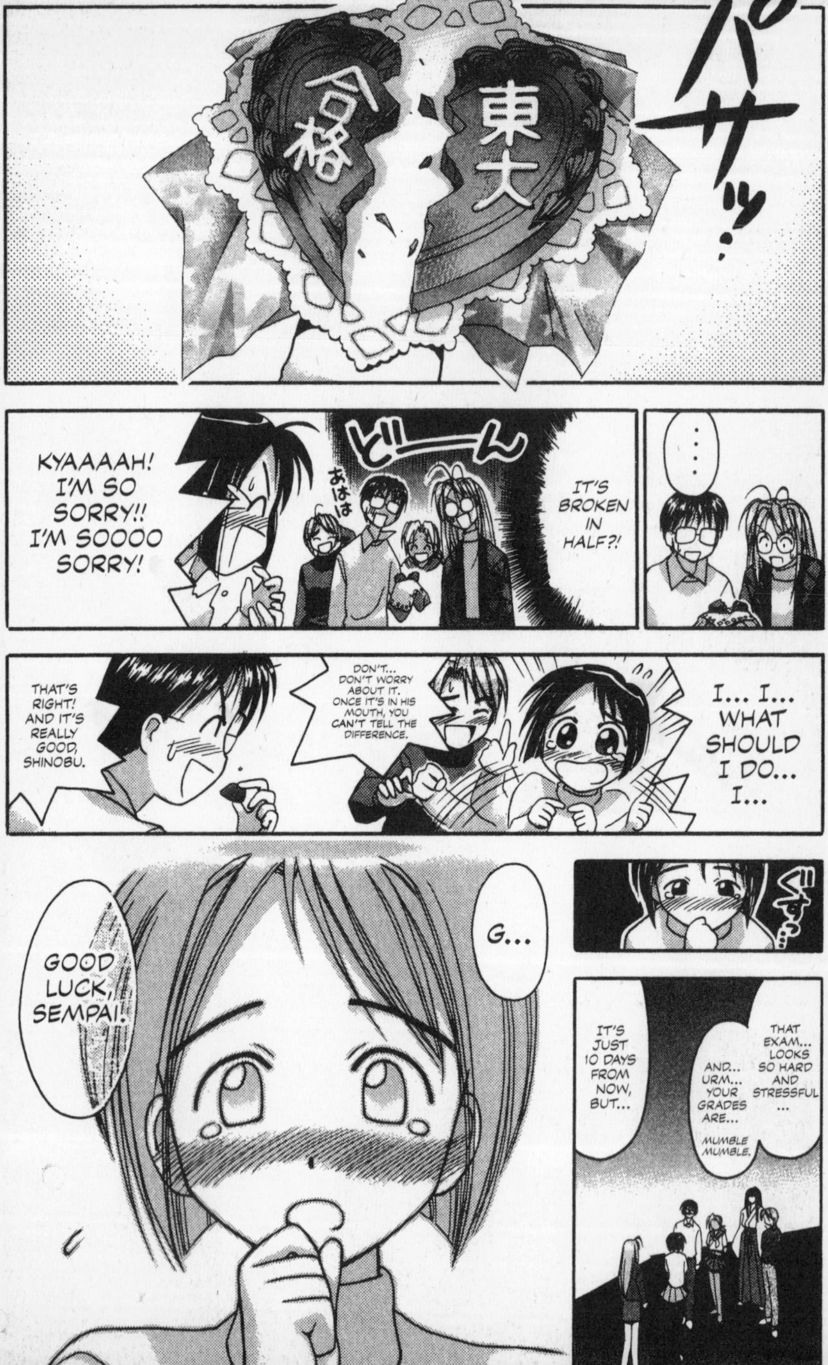
パサッ
東大
合格
. . . .
IT'S BROKEN IN HALF?!
どーん
あはは
KYAAAAH! I'M SO SORRY!! I'M SOOOO SORRY!
I... I... WHAT SHOULD I DO... I...
DON'T... DON'T WORRY ABOUT IT. ONCE IT'S IN HIS MOUTH, YOU CAN'T TELL THE DIFFERENCE.
THAT'S RIGHT! AND IT'S REALLY GOOD, SHINOBU.
ぐすっ..
THAT EXAM... LOOKS SO HARD AND STRESSFUL...
AND... URM... YOUR GRADES ARE...
MUMBLE MUMBLE.
IT'S JUST 10 DAYS FROM NOW, BUT...
G...
GOOD LUCK, SEMPAI!

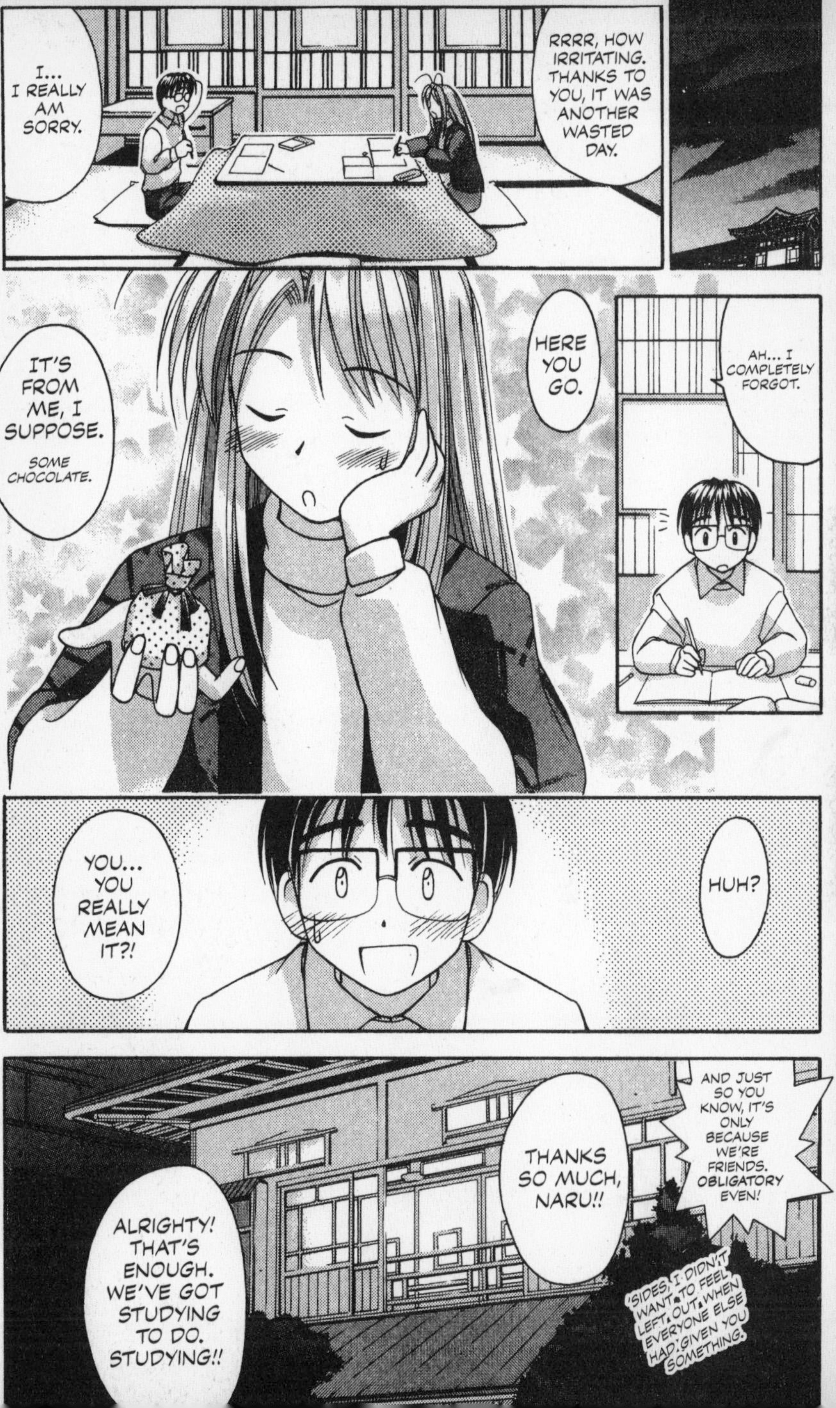
RRRR, HOW IRRITATING. THANKS TO YOU, IT WAS ANOTHER WASTED DAY.
I... I REALLY AM SORRY.
AH... I COMPLETELY FORGOT.
HERE YOU GO.
IT'S FROM ME, I SUPPOSE. SOME CHOCOLATE.
HUH?
YOU... YOU REALLY MEAN IT?!
AND JUST SO YOU KNOW, IT'S ONLY BECAUSE WE'RE FRIENDS. OBLIGATORY EVEN!
THANKS SO MUCH, NARU!!
'SIDES, I DIDN'T WANT TO FEEL LEFT OUT WHEN EVERYONE ELSE HAD GIVEN YOU SOMETHING.
ALRIGHTY! THAT'S ENOUGH. WE'VE GOT STUDYING TO DO. STUDYING!!

GRAB

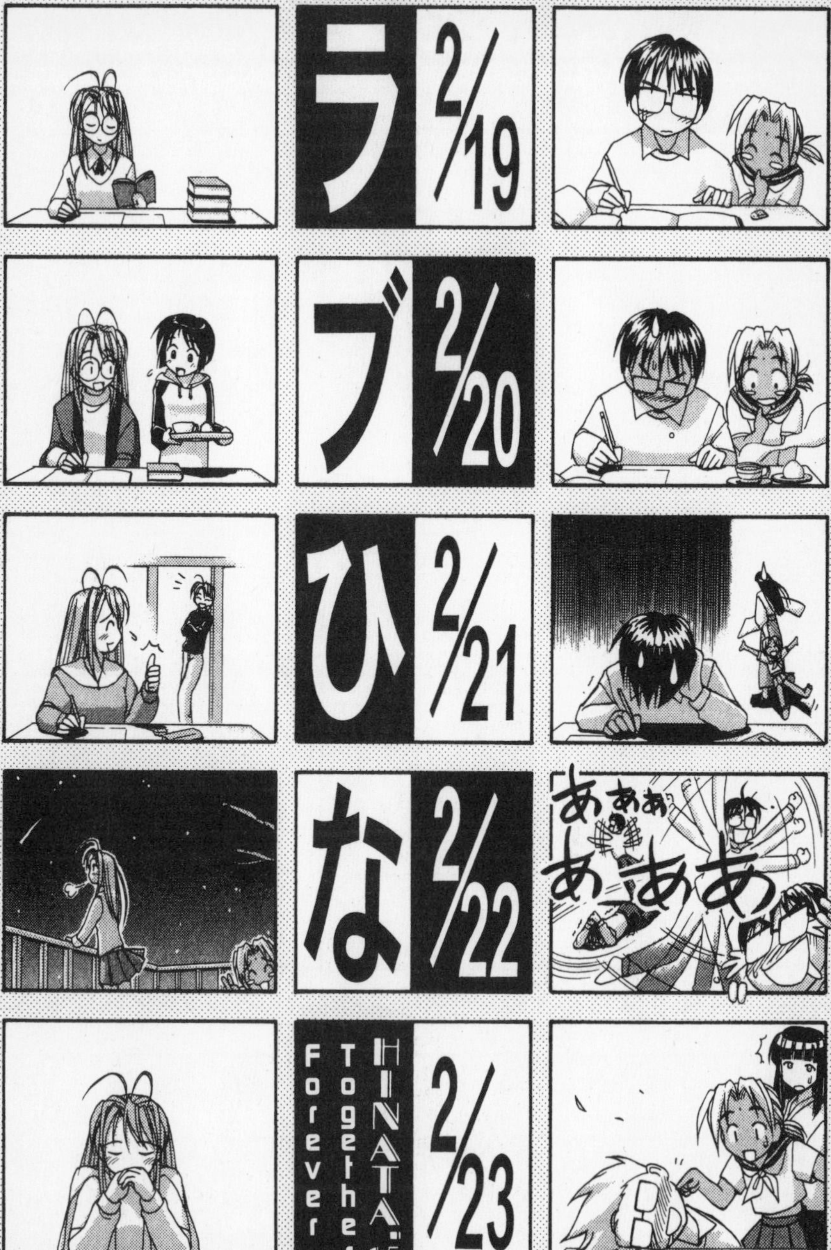

ラ
2/19
ブ
2/20
ひ
2/21
あああ
あああ
な
2/22
2/23
HINATA. 15
Together
Forever

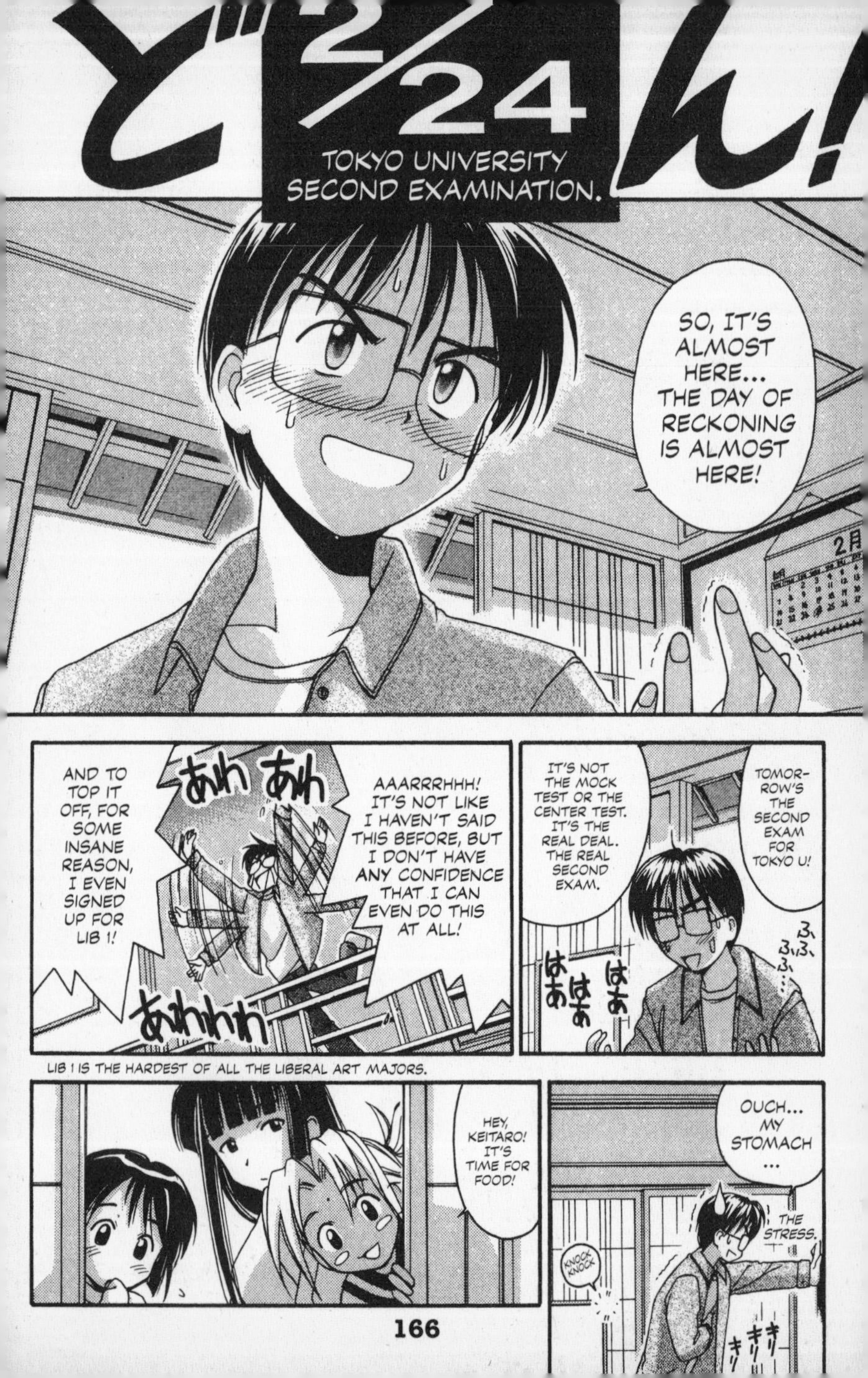

どーん!
2/24
TOKYO UNIVERSITY SECOND EXAMINATION.
SO, IT'S ALMOST HERE... THE DAY OF RECKONING IS ALMOST HERE!
2月
TOMORROW'S THE SECOND EXAM FOR TOKYO U!
IT'S NOT THE MOCK TEST OR THE CENTER TEST. IT'S THE REAL DEAL. THE REAL SECOND EXAM.
ふふふ...
はあはあはあ
AAARRRHHH! IT'S NOT LIKE I HAVEN'T SAID THIS BEFORE, BUT I DON'T HAVE ANY CONFIDENCE THAT I CAN EVEN DO THIS AT ALL!
AND TO TOP IT OFF, FOR SOME INSANE REASON, I EVEN SIGNED UP FOR LIB 1!
あわあわ
あわわわ
LIB 1 IS THE HARDEST OF ALL THE LIBERAL ART MAJORS.
OUCH... MY STOMACH ...
THE STRESS.
KNOCK KNOCK
きりきりきり
HEY, KEITARO! IT'S TIME FOR FOOD!

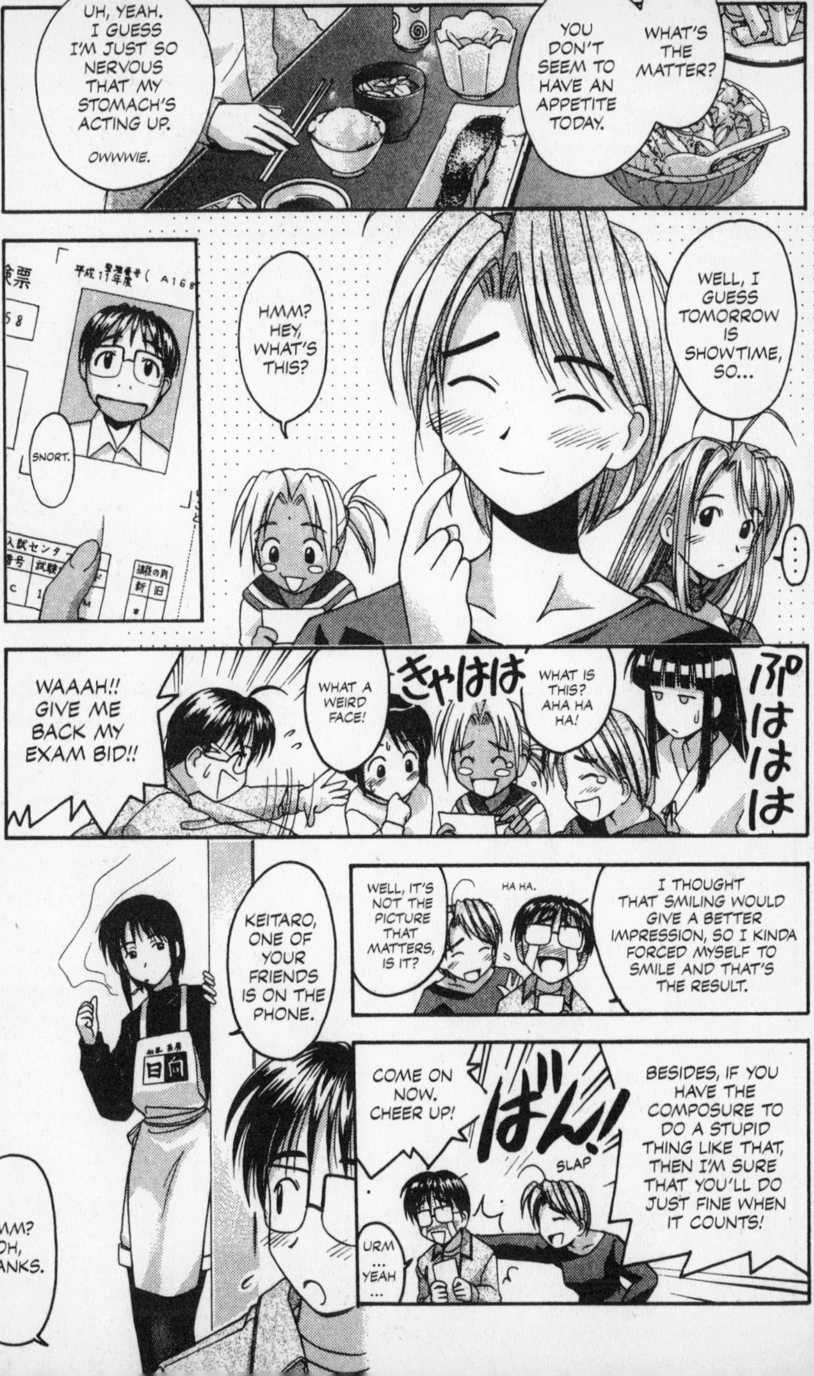
WHAT'S THE MATTER?
YOU DON'T SEEM TO HAVE AN APPETITE TODAY.
UH, YEAH. I GUESS I'M JUST SO NERVOUS THAT MY STOMACH'S ACTING UP.
OWWWIE.
WELL, I GUESS TOMORROW IS SHOWTIME, SO...
...
HMM? HEY, WHAT'S THIS?
SNORT.
ぷははは
WHAT IS THIS? AHA HA HA!
きゃはは
WHAT A WEIRD FACE!
WAAAH!! GIVE ME BACK MY EXAM BID!!
I THOUGHT THAT SMILING WOULD GIVE A BETTER IMPRESSION, SO I KINDA FORCED MYSELF TO SMILE AND THAT'S THE RESULT.
HA HA.
WELL, IT'S NOT THE PICTURE THAT MATTERS, IS IT?
BESIDES, IF YOU HAVE THE COMPOSURE TO DO A STUPID THING LIKE THAT, THEN I'M SURE THAT YOU'LL DO JUST FINE WHEN IT COUNTS!
SLAP
ぱん!
COME ON NOW. CHEER UP!
URM ... YEAH ...
KEITARO, ONE OF YOUR FRIENDS IS ON THE PHONE.
HMM? OH, THANKS.

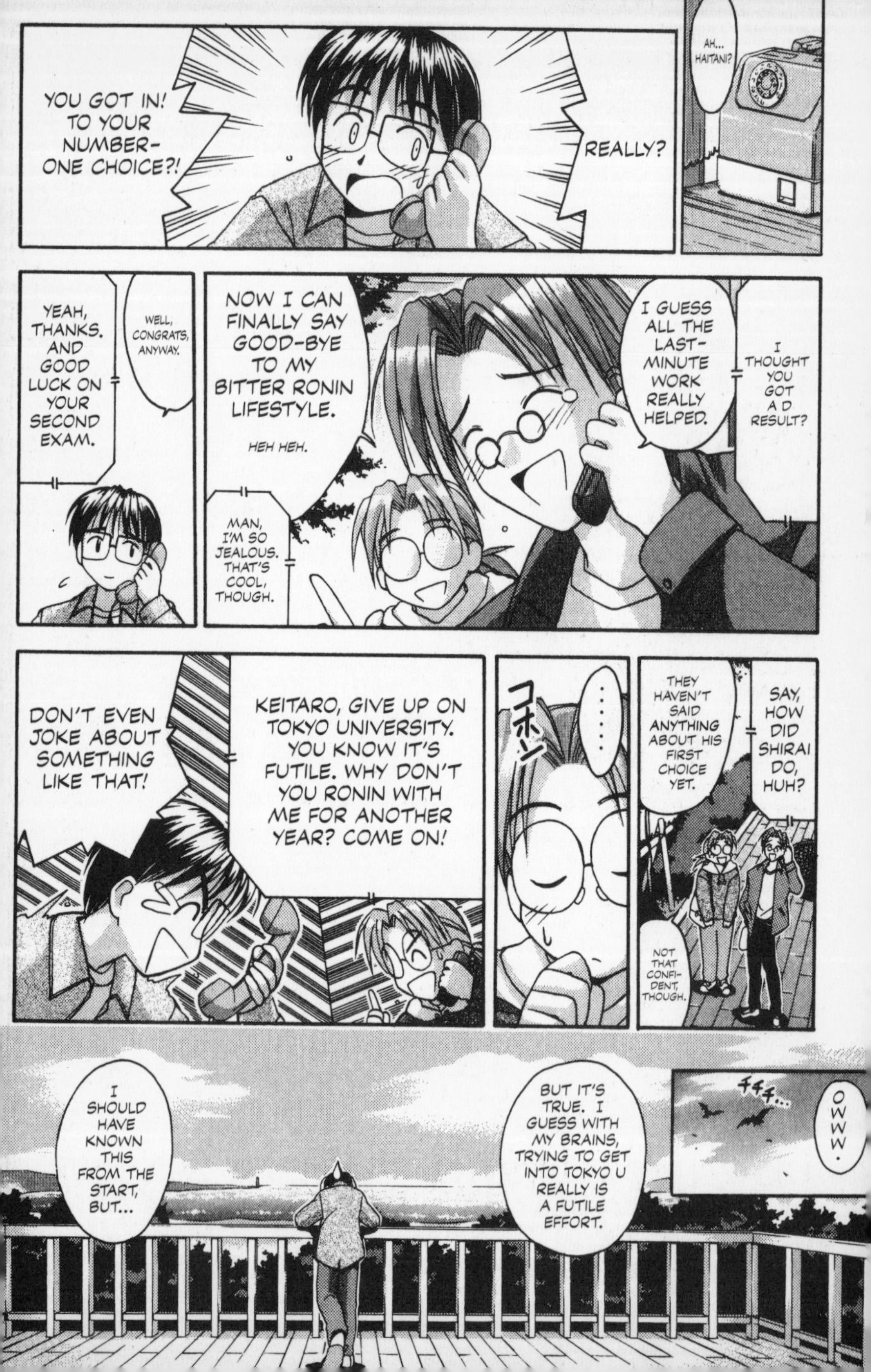
AH... HAITANI?
REALLY?
YOU GOT IN! TO YOUR NUMBER-ONE CHOICE?!
I THOUGHT YOU GOT A D RESULT?
I GUESS ALL THE LAST-MINUTE WORK REALLY HELPED.
NOW I CAN FINALLY SAY GOOD-BYE TO MY BITTER RONIN LIFESTYLE.
HEH HEH.
MAN, I'M SO JEALOUS. THAT'S COOL, THOUGH.
WELL, CONGRATS, ANYWAY.
YEAH, THANKS. AND GOOD LUCK ON YOUR SECOND EXAM.
SAY, HOW DID SHIRAI DO, HUH?
THEY HAVEN'T SAID ANYTHING ABOUT HIS FIRST CHOICE YET.
NOT THAT CONFIDENT, THOUGH.
......
コホン
KEITARO, GIVE UP ON TOKYO UNIVERSITY. YOU KNOW IT'S FUTILE. WHY DON'T YOU RONIN WITH ME FOR ANOTHER YEAR? COME ON!
DON'T EVEN JOKE ABOUT SOMETHING LIKE THAT!
OWWW.
チチチ...
BUT IT'S TRUE. I GUESS WITH MY BRAINS, TRYING TO GET INTO TOKYO U REALLY IS A FUTILE EFFORT.
I SHOULD HAVE KNOWN THIS FROM THE START, BUT...

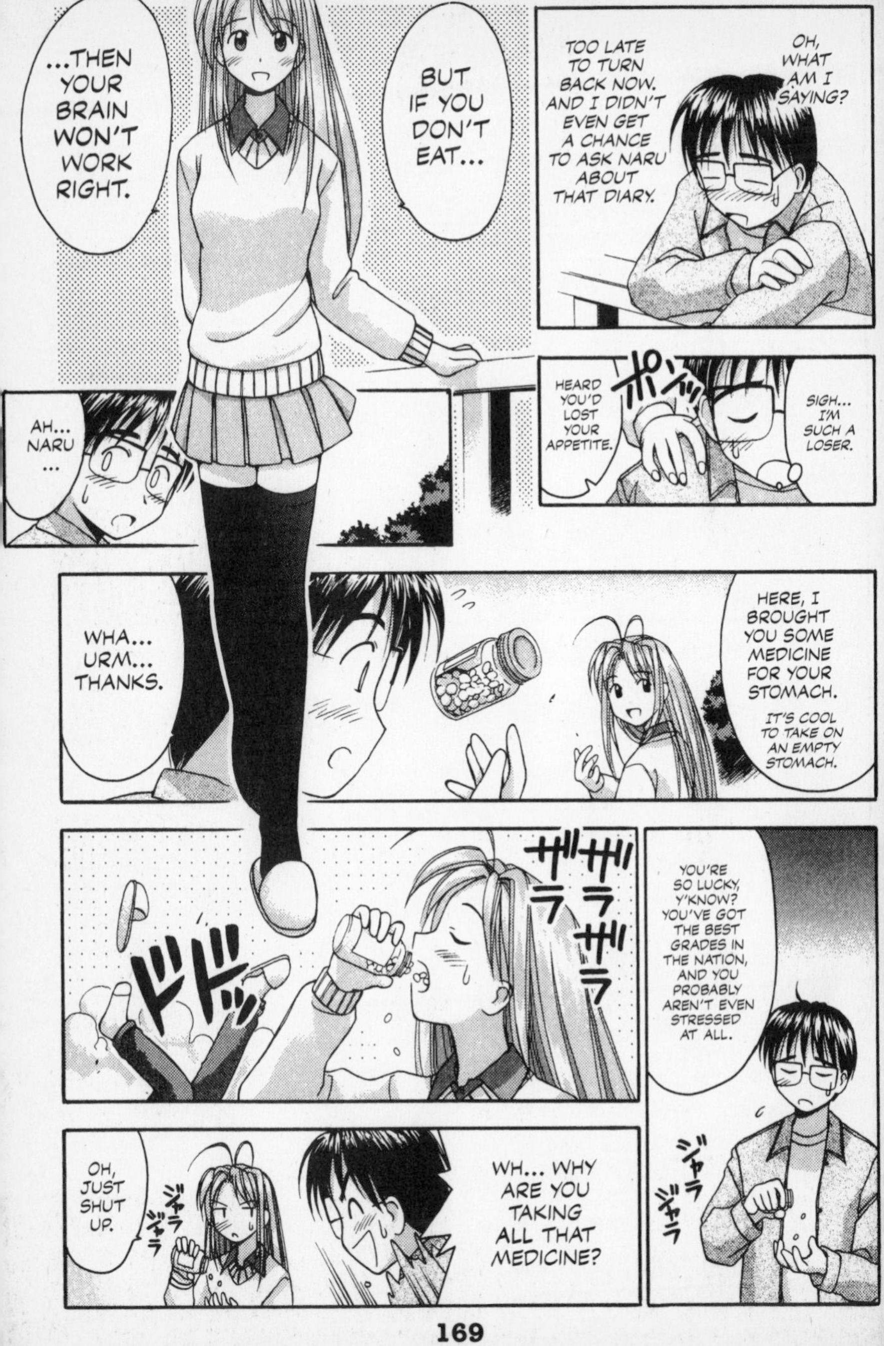
OH, WHAT AM I SAYING?
TOO LATE TO TURN BACK NOW. AND I DIDN'T EVEN GET A CHANCE TO ASK NARU ABOUT THAT DIARY.
SIGH... I'M SUCH A LOSER.
ポンッ
HEARD YOU'D LOST YOUR APPETITE.
BUT IF YOU DON'T EAT...
...THEN YOUR BRAIN WON'T WORK RIGHT.
AH... NARU ...
HERE, I BROUGHT YOU SOME MEDICINE FOR YOUR STOMACH.
IT'S COOL TO TAKE ON AN EMPTY STOMACH.
WHA... URM... THANKS.
YOU'RE SO LUCKY, Y'KNOW? YOU'VE GOT THE BEST GRADES IN THE NATION, AND YOU PROBABLY AREN'T EVEN STRESSED AT ALL.
ジャラ ジャラ
ザラ ザラ ザラ
ドドッ
WH... WHY ARE YOU TAKING ALL THAT MEDICINE?
ジャラ ジャラ
OH, JUST SHUT UP.

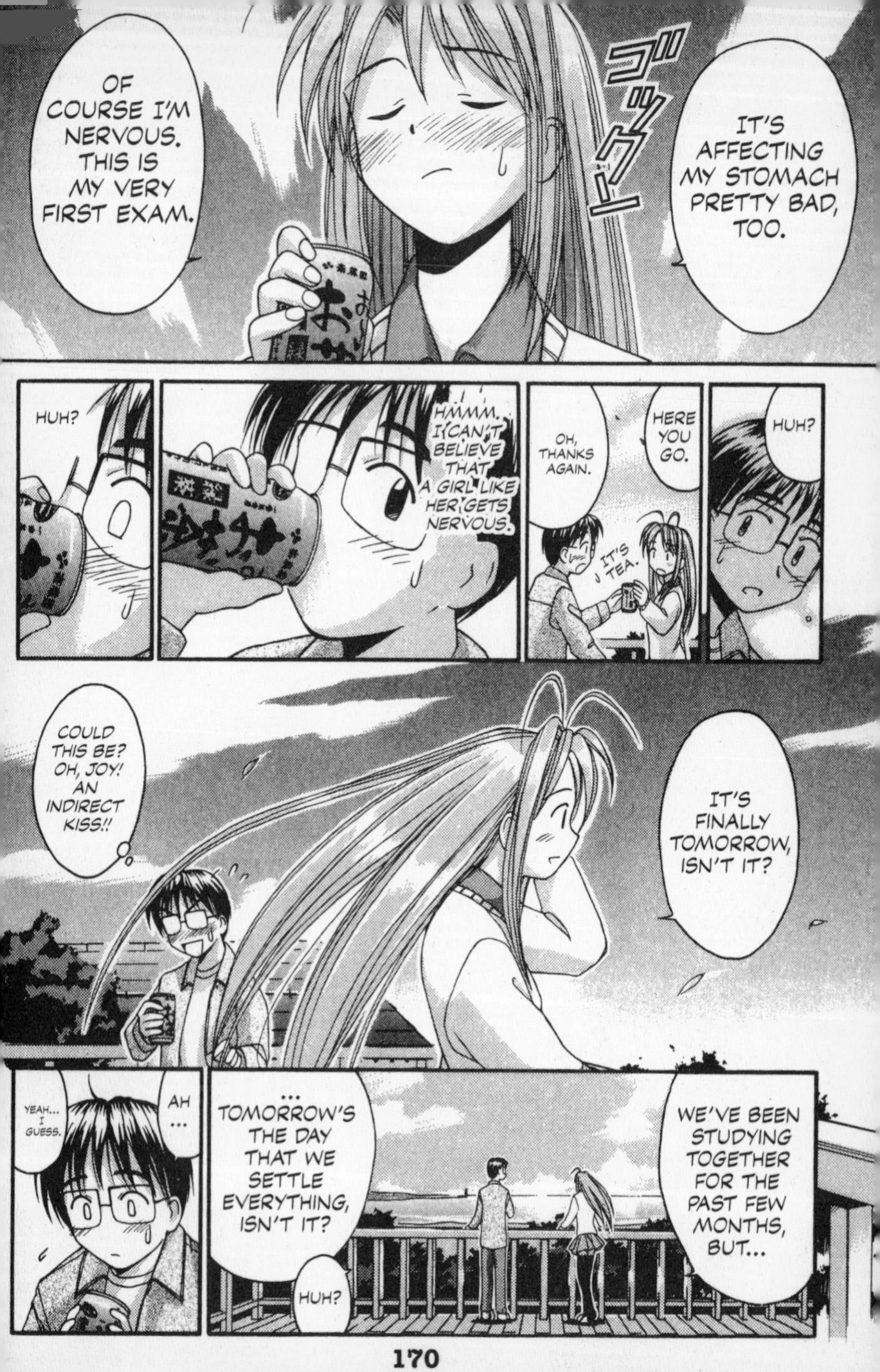
ゴックン
IT'S AFFECTING MY STOMACH PRETTY BAD, TOO.
OF COURSE I'M NERVOUS. THIS IS MY VERY FIRST EXAM.
HUH?
HERE YOU GO.
OH, THANKS AGAIN.
IT'S TEA.
HMMM. I CAN'T BELIEVE THAT A GIRL LIKE HER GETS NERVOUS.
HUH?
IT'S FINALLY TOMORROW, ISN'T IT?
COULD THIS BE? OH, JOY! AN INDIRECT KISS!!
WE'VE BEEN STUDYING TOGETHER FOR THE PAST FEW MONTHS, BUT...
... TOMORROW'S THE DAY THAT WE SETTLE EVERYTHING, ISN'T IT?
HUH?
AH ...
YEAH... I GUESS.

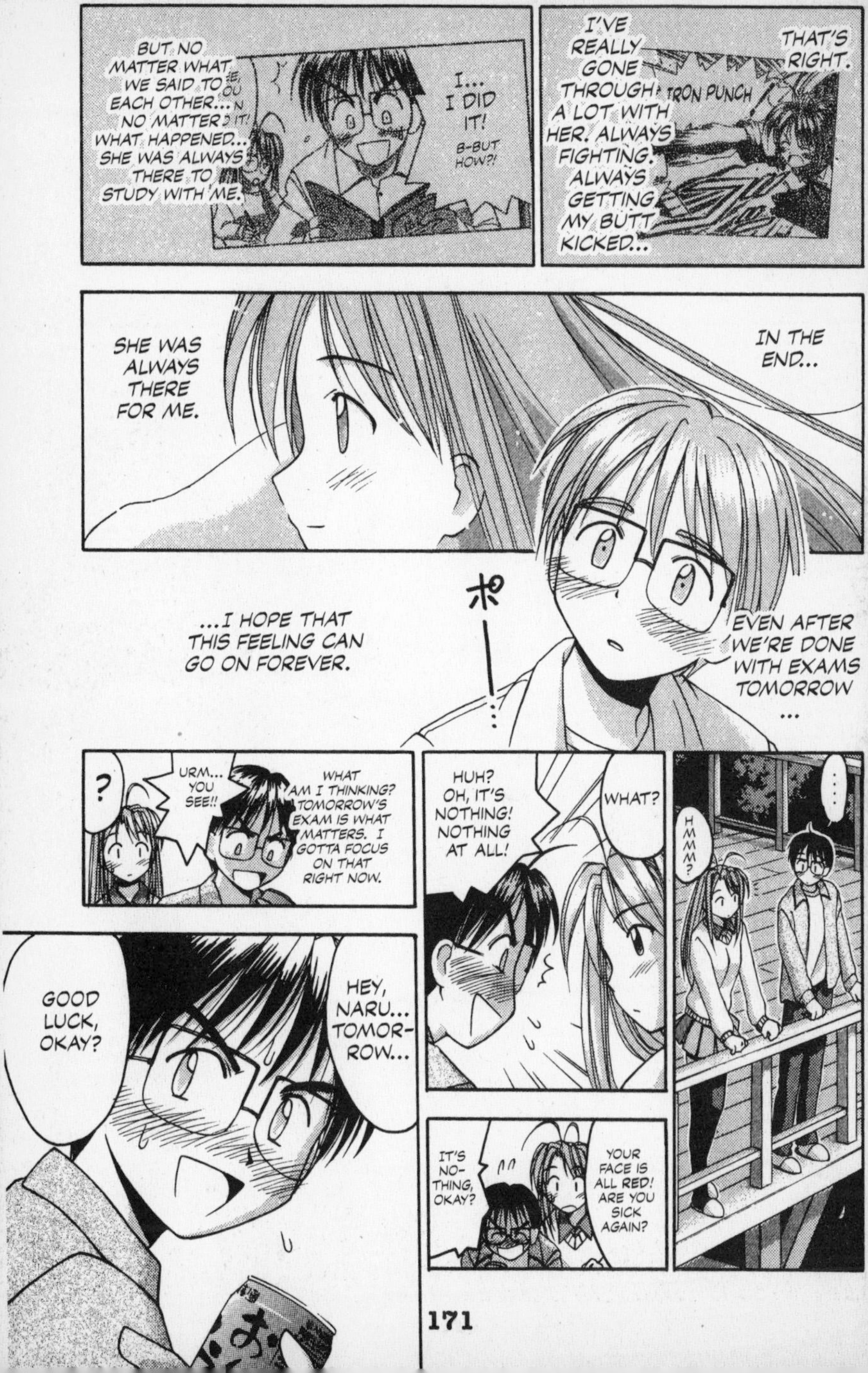
THAT'S RIGHT.
I'VE REALLY GONE THROUGH A LOT WITH HER. ALWAYS FIGHTING. ALWAYS GETTING MY BUTT KICKED...
I... I DID IT!
B-BUT HOW?!
BUT NO MATTER WHAT WE SAID TO EACH OTHER... NO MATTER WHAT HAPPENED... SHE WAS ALWAYS THERE TO STUDY WITH ME.
IN THE END...
SHE WAS ALWAYS THERE FOR ME.
EVEN AFTER WE'RE DONE WITH EXAMS TOMORROW ...
ポー…
...I HOPE THAT THIS FEELING CAN GO ON FOREVER.
...
HMMM?
WHAT?
HUH? OH, IT'S NOTHING! NOTHING AT ALL!
YOUR FACE IS ALL RED! ARE YOU SICK AGAIN?
IT'S NO-THING, OKAY?
WHAT AM I THINKING? TOMORROW'S EXAM IS WHAT MATTERS. I GOTTA FOCUS ON THAT RIGHT NOW.
URM... YOU SEE!!
?
HEY, NARU... TOMOR-ROW...
GOOD LUCK, OKAY?

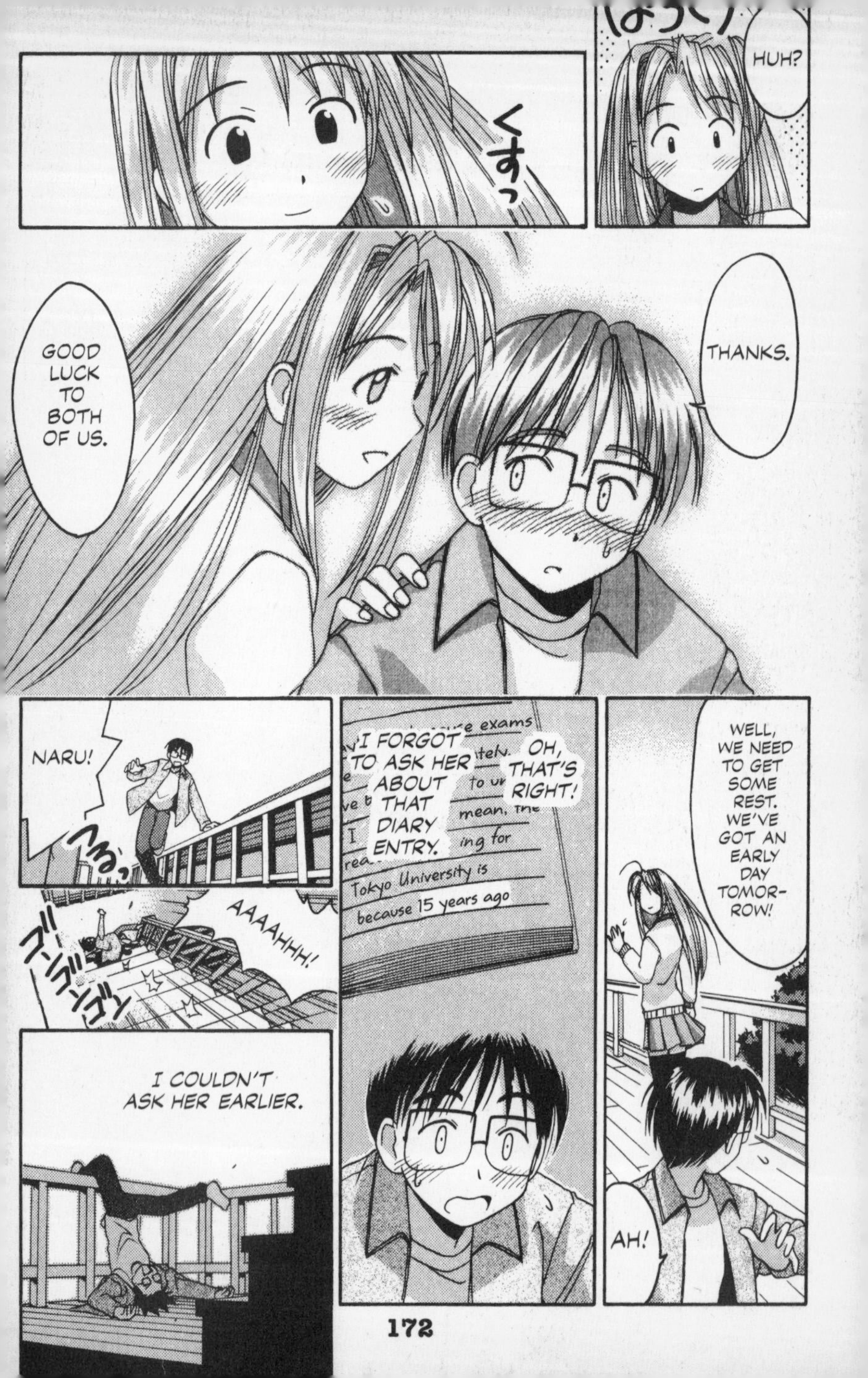
HUH?
くすっ
THANKS.
GOOD LUCK TO BOTH OF US.
WELL, WE NEED TO GET SOME REST. WE'VE GOT AN EARLY DAY TOMOR-ROW!
AH!
OH, THAT'S RIGHT!
I FORGOT TO ASK HER ABOUT THAT DIARY ENTRY.
Tokyo University is
because 15 years ago
NARU!
つるっ
AAAAHHH!
I COULDN'T ASK HER EARLIER.

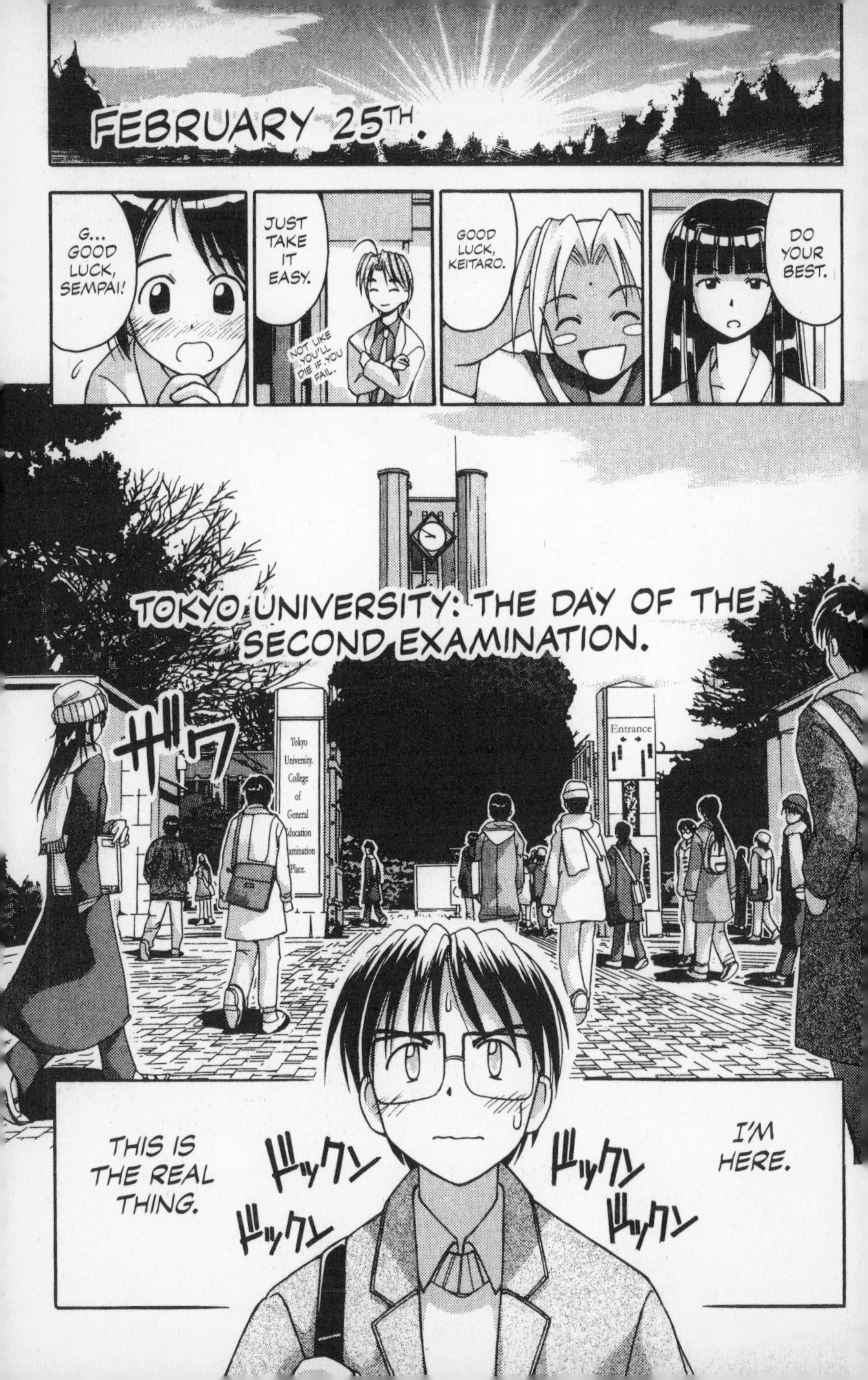
FEBRUARY 25TH.
DO YOUR BEST.
GOOD LUCK, KEITARO.
JUST TAKE IT EASY.
NOT LIKE YOU'LL DIE IF YOU FAIL.
G... GOOD LUCK, SEMPAI!
TOKYO UNIVERSITY: THE DAY OF THE SECOND EXAMINATION.
Entrance
Tokyo University. College of General
I'M HERE.
ドックン
ドックン
ドックン
ドックン
THIS IS THE REAL THING.

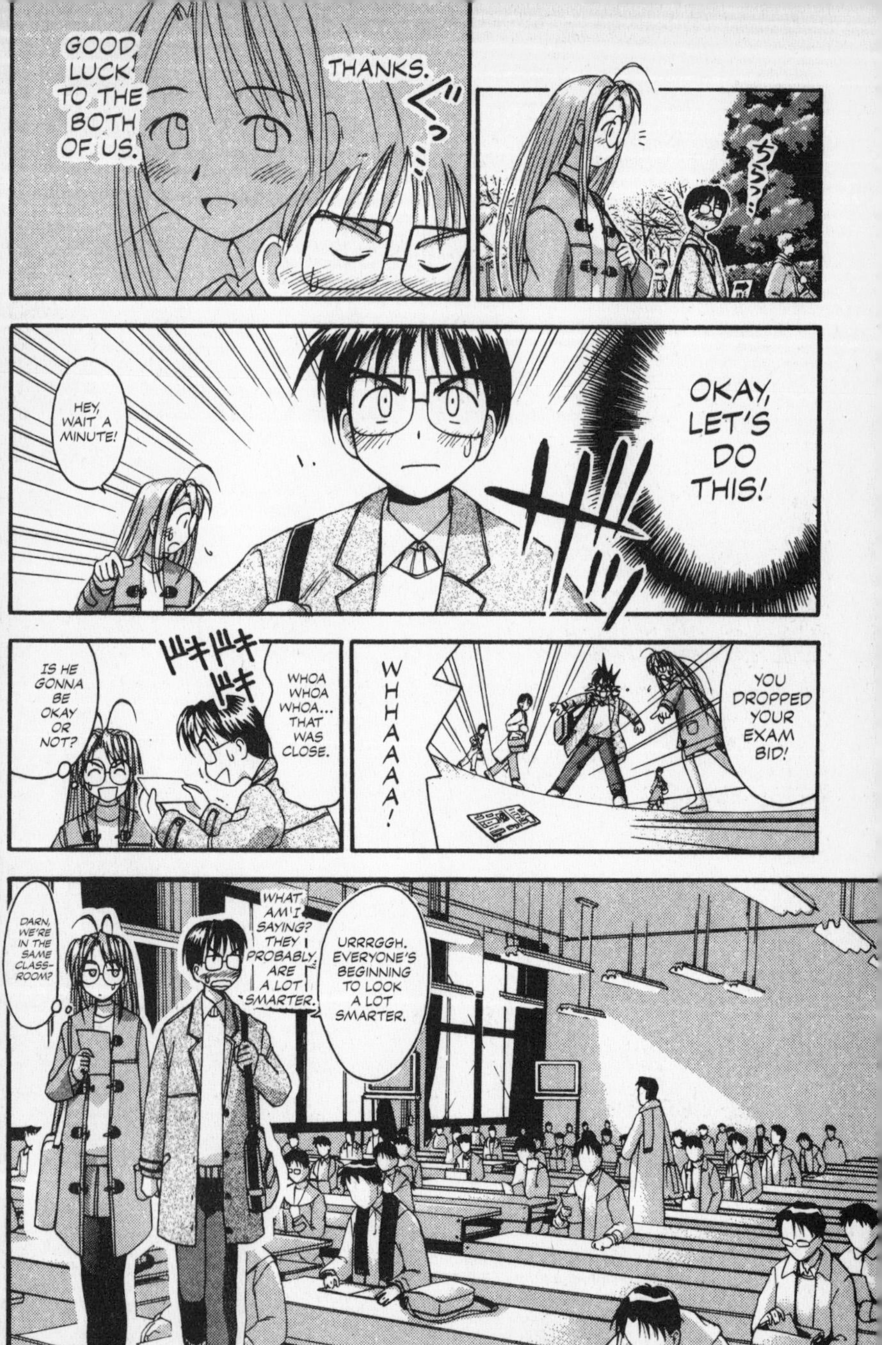
ちらっ…
GOOD LUCK TO THE BOTH OF US.
THANKS.
ぐっ…
OKAY, LET'S DO THIS!
HEY, WAIT A MINUTE!
YOU DROPPED YOUR EXAM BID!
WHHAAAAA!
WHOA WHOA WHOA... THAT WAS CLOSE.
ドキドキドキ
IS HE GONNA BE OKAY OR NOT?
URRRGGH. EVERYONE'S BEGINNING TO LOOK A LOT SMARTER.
WHAT AM I SAYING? THEY PROBABLY ARE A LOT SMARTER.
DARN, WE'RE IN THE SAME CLASSROOM?

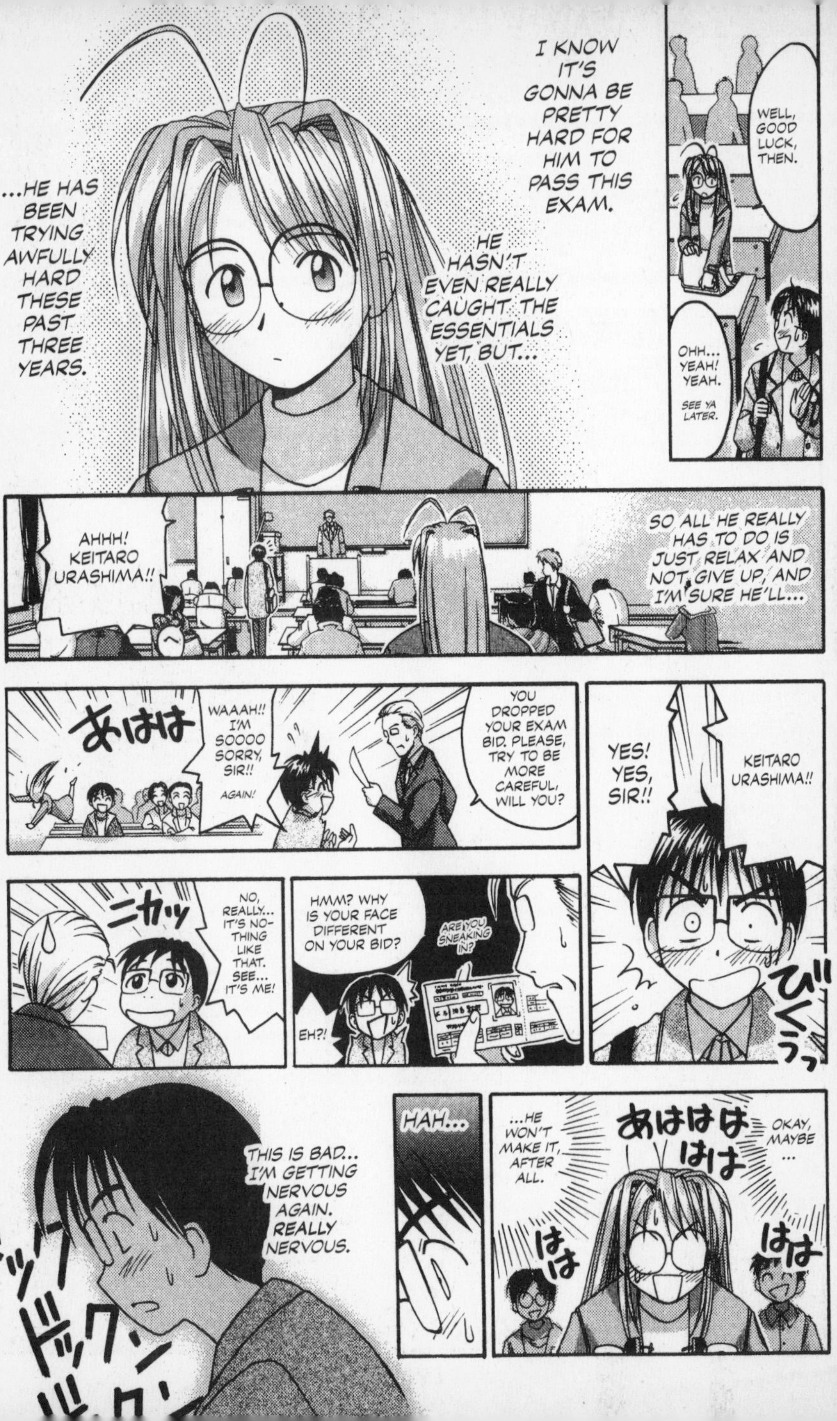
WELL, GOOD LUCK, THEN.
OHH... YEAH! YEAH.
SEE YA LATER.
I KNOW IT'S GONNA BE PRETTY HARD FOR HIM TO PASS THIS EXAM.
HE HASN'T EVEN REALLY CAUGHT THE ESSENTIALS YET, BUT...
...HE HAS BEEN TRYING AWFULLY HARD THESE PAST THREE YEARS.
SO ALL HE REALLY HAS TO DO IS JUST RELAX AND NOT GIVE UP, AND I'M SURE HE'LL...
AHHH! KEITARO URASHIMA!!
KEITARO URASHIMA!!
YES! YES, SIR!!
びくぅっ
YOU DROPPED YOUR EXAM BID. PLEASE, TRY TO BE MORE CAREFUL, WILL YOU?
WAAAH!! I'M SOOOO SORRY, SIR!!
AGAIN!
あはは
HMM? WHY IS YOUR FACE DIFFERENT ON YOUR BID?
ARE YOU SNEAKING IN?
EH?!
ニカッ
NO, REALLY... IT'S NOTHING LIKE THAT. SEE... IT'S ME!
OKAY, MAYBE ...
あはははははは
...HE WON'T MAKE IT, AFTER ALL.
はは
はは
HAH...
THIS IS BAD... I'M GETTING NERVOUS AGAIN. REALLY NERVOUS.
ドッドクンドクン

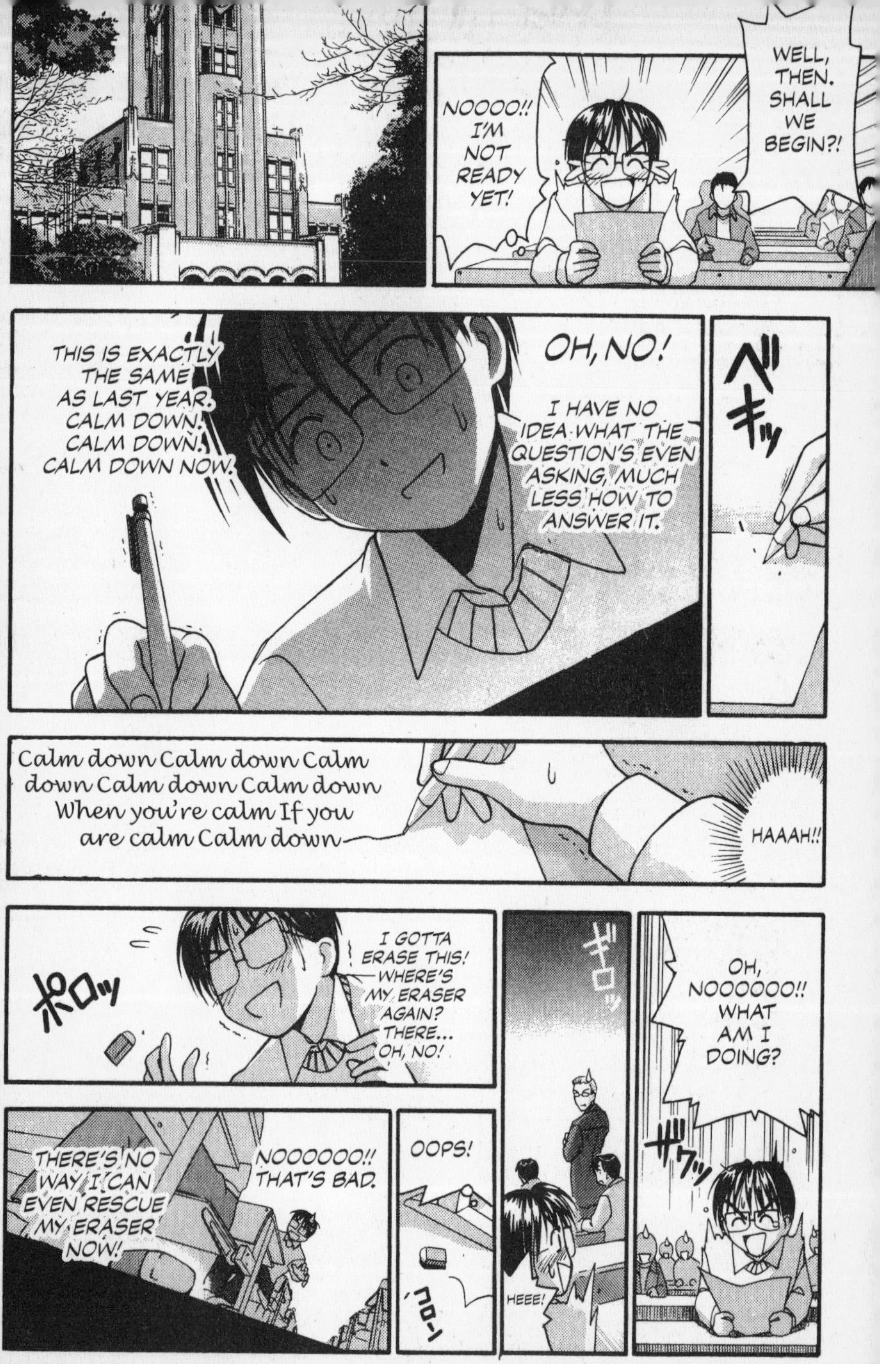
WELL, THEN. SHALL WE BEGIN?!
NOOOO!! I'M NOT READY YET!
ベキッ
OH, NO!
I HAVE NO IDEA WHAT THE QUESTION'S EVEN ASKING, MUCH LESS HOW TO ANSWER IT.
THIS IS EXACTLY THE SAME AS LAST YEAR. CALM DOWN. CALM DOWN. CALM DOWN NOW.
Calm down Calm down Calm down Calm down Calm down When you're calm If you are calm Calm down
HAAAH!!
OH, NOOOOOO!! WHAT AM I DOING?
ザワッ
ギロッ
HEEE!
I GOTTA ERASE THIS! WHERE'S MY ERASER AGAIN? THERE... OH, NO!
ポロッ
OOPS!
コローン
NOOOOOO!! THAT'S BAD.
THERE'S NO WAY I CAN EVEN RESCUE MY ERASER NOW!

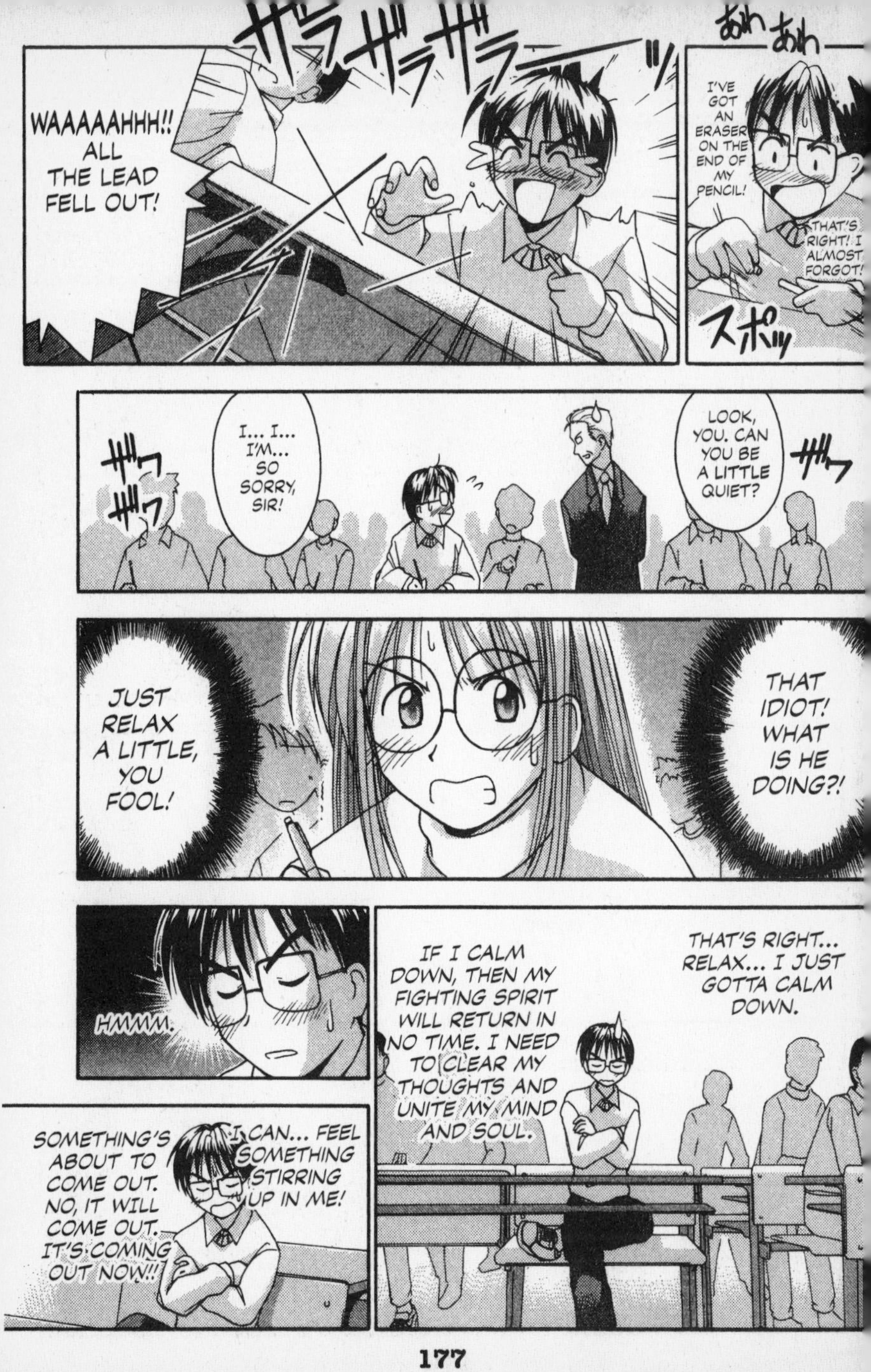
あれ あれ
I'VE GOT AN ERASER ON THE END OF MY PENCIL!
THAT'S RIGHT! I ALMOST FORGOT!
スポッ
ザラザラザラ
WAAAAAHHH!! ALL THE LEAD FELL OUT!
ザワ
LOOK, YOU. CAN YOU BE A LITTLE QUIET?
I... I... I'M... SO SORRY, SIR!
ザワ ザワ
THAT IDIOT! WHAT IS HE DOING?!
JUST RELAX A LITTLE, YOU FOOL!
THAT'S RIGHT... RELAX... I JUST GOTTA CALM DOWN.
IF I CALM DOWN, THEN MY FIGHTING SPIRIT WILL RETURN IN NO TIME. I NEED TO CLEAR MY THOUGHTS AND UNITE MY MIND AND SOUL.
HMMM.
I CAN... FEEL SOMETHING STIRRING UP IN ME!
SOMETHING'S ABOUT TO COME OUT. NO, IT WILL COME OUT. IT'S COMING OUT NOW!!

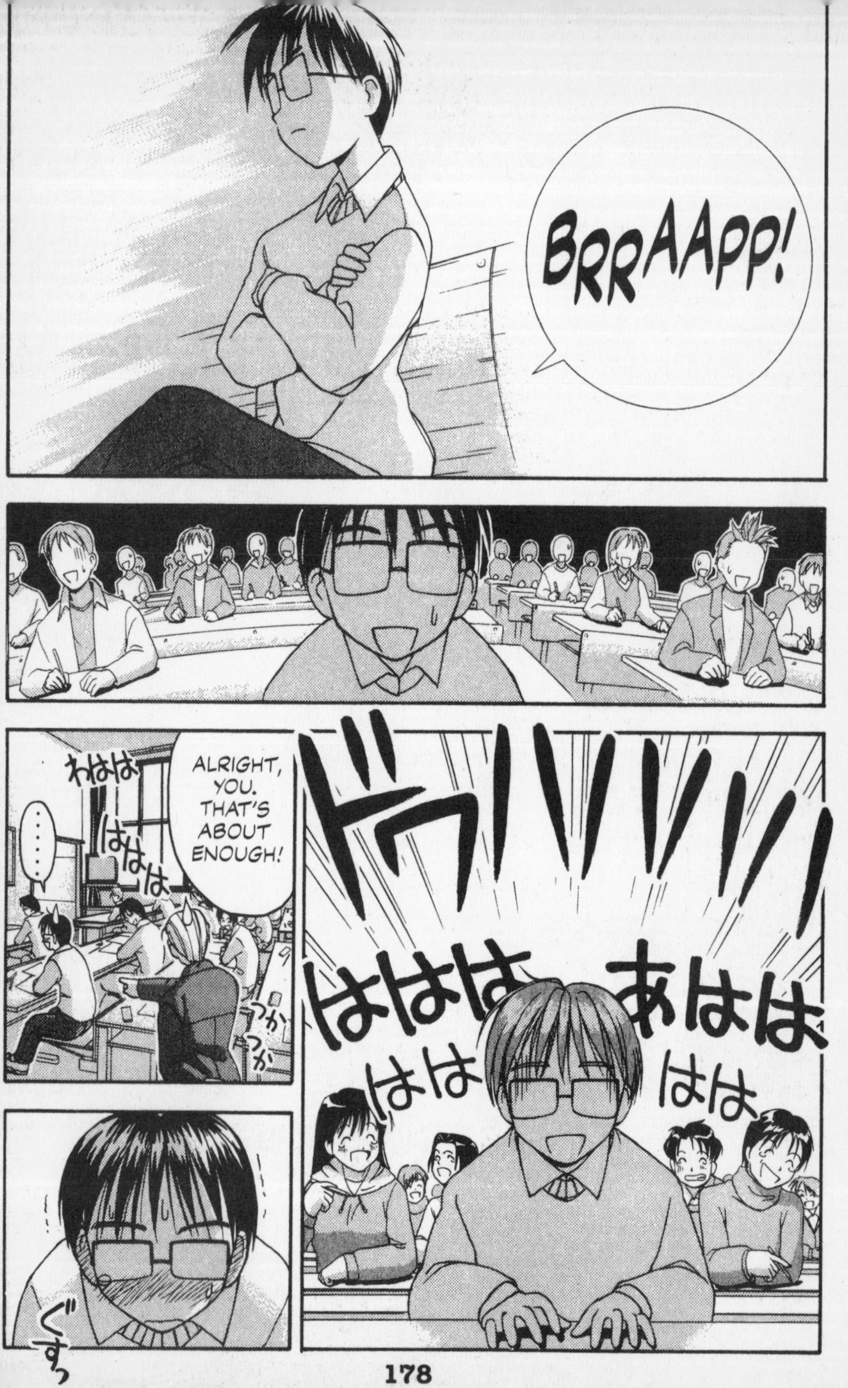

BRRAAPP!
ドワッ!!!!
ははは
あはは
はは
はは
ALRIGHT, YOU. THAT'S ABOUT ENOUGH!
わははははは
……
つかつか
ぐすっ

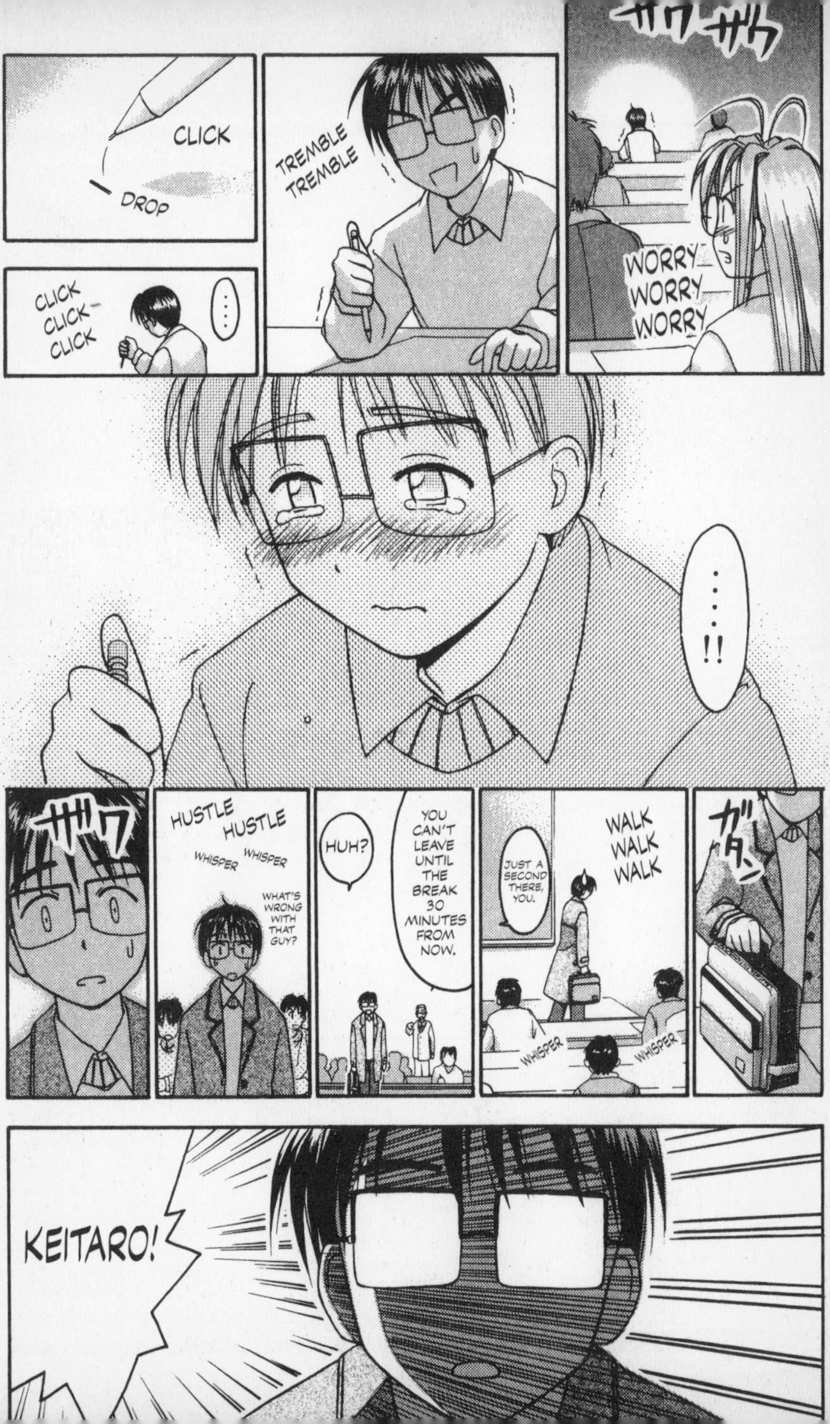
ザワ ザワ
WORRY WORRY WORRY
TREMBLE TREMBLE
CLICK
DROP
CLICK CLICK CLICK
....
.....!!
ガタン
WALK WALK WALK
JUST A SECOND THERE, YOU.
WHISPER
WHISPER
YOU CAN'T LEAVE UNTIL THE BREAK 30 MINUTES FROM NOW.
HUH?
HUSTLE HUSTLE
WHISPER
WHISPER
WHAT'S WRONG WITH THAT GUY?
ザワ
KEITARO!

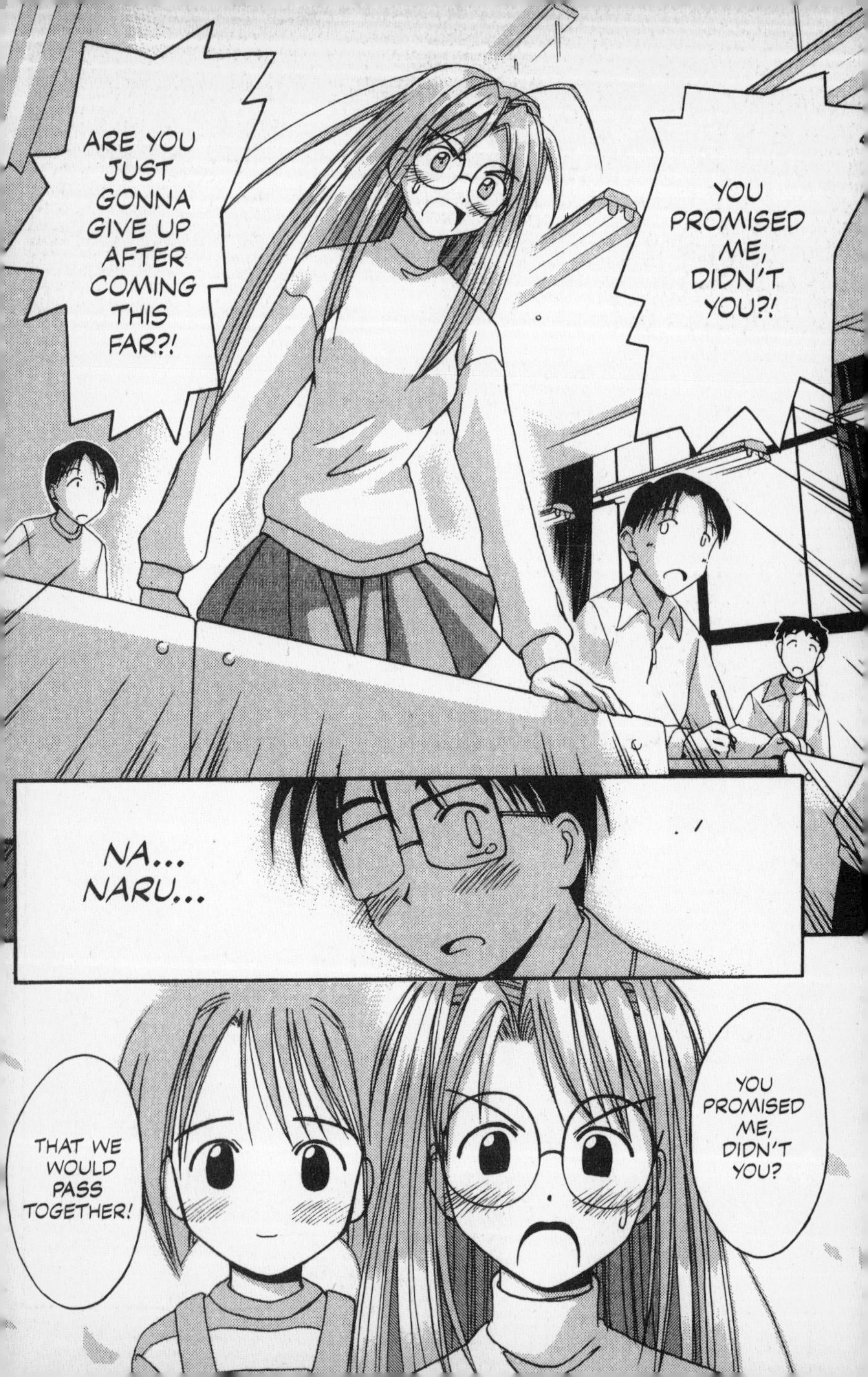
YOU PROMISED ME, DIDN'T YOU?!
ARE YOU JUST GONNA GIVE UP AFTER COMING THIS FAR?!
NA... NARU...
YOU PROMISED ME, DIDN'T YOU?
THAT WE WOULD PASS TOGETHER!

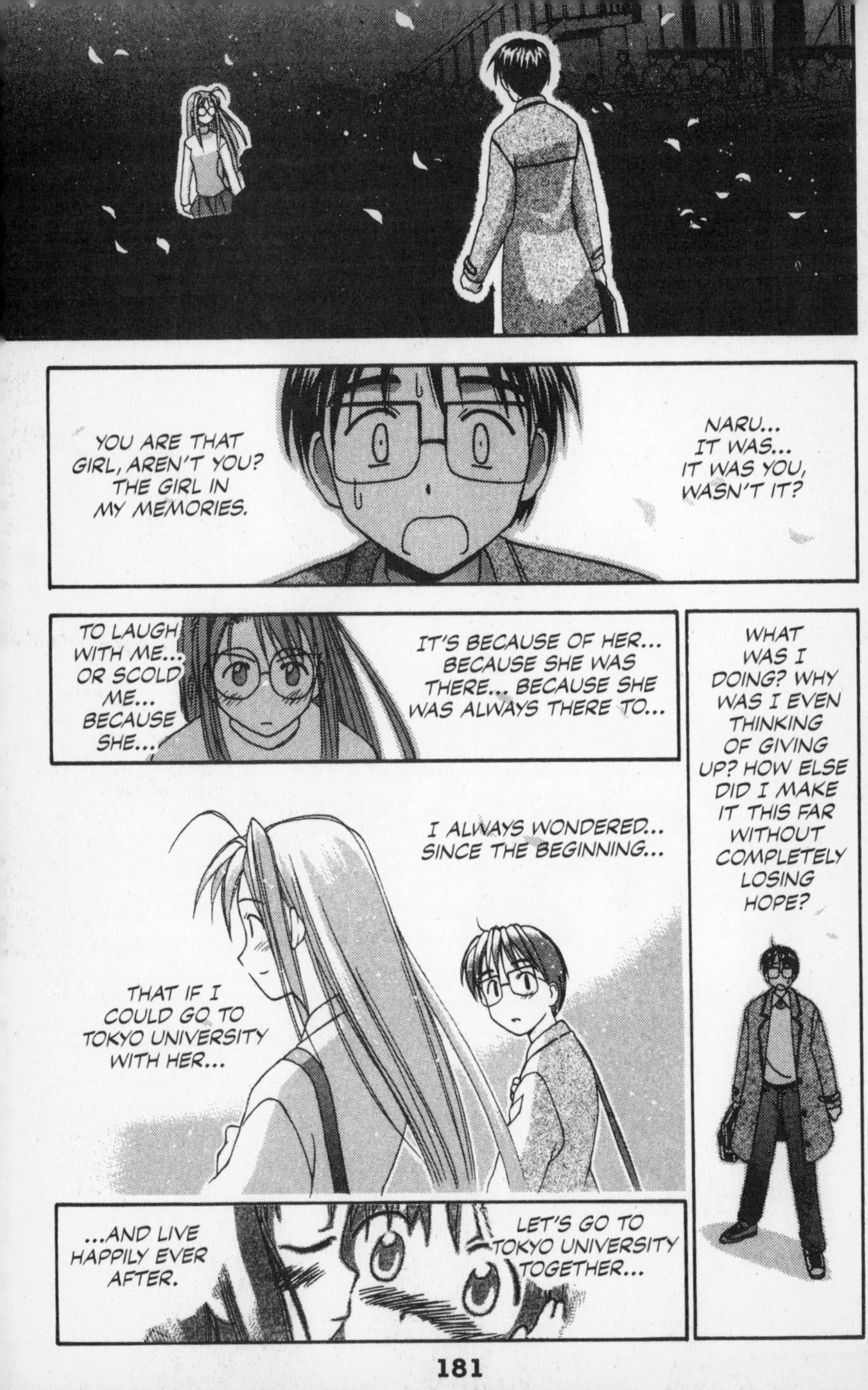
NARU... IT WAS... IT WAS YOU, WASN'T IT?
YOU ARE THAT GIRL, AREN'T YOU? THE GIRL IN MY MEMORIES.
WHAT WAS I DOING? WHY WAS I EVEN THINKING OF GIVING UP? HOW ELSE DID I MAKE IT THIS FAR WITHOUT COMPLETELY LOSING HOPE?
IT'S BECAUSE OF HER... BECAUSE SHE WAS THERE... BECAUSE SHE WAS ALWAYS THERE TO...
TO LAUGH WITH ME... OR SCOLD ME... BECAUSE SHE...
I ALWAYS WONDERED... SINCE THE BEGINNING...
THAT IF I COULD GO TO TOKYO UNIVERSITY WITH HER...
LET'S GO TO TOKYO UNIVERSITY TOGETHER...
...AND LIVE HAPPILY EVER AFTER.

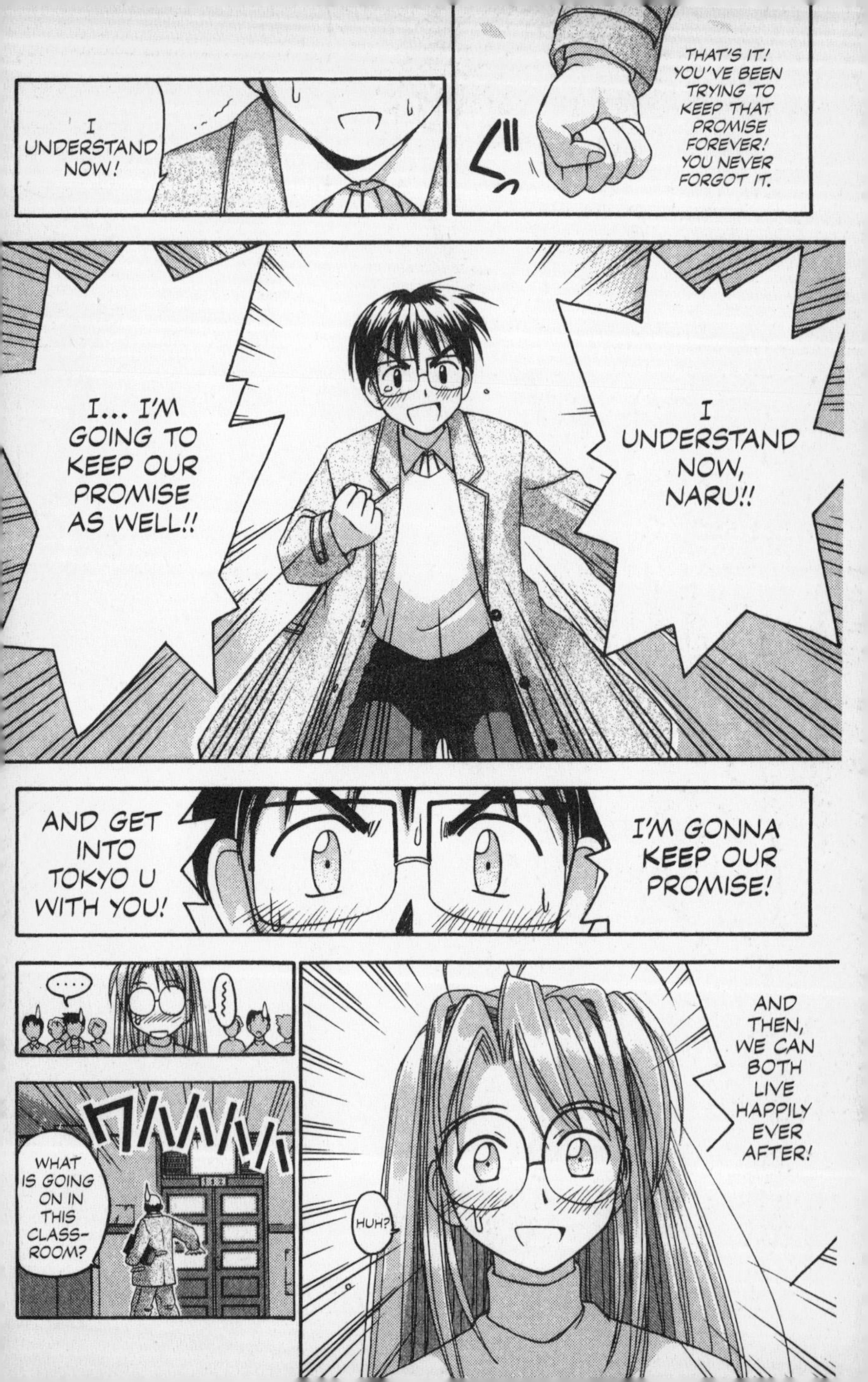
THAT'S IT! YOU'VE BEEN TRYING TO KEEP THAT PROMISE FOREVER! YOU NEVER FORGOT IT.
I UNDERSTAND NOW!
I UNDERSTAND NOW, NARU!!
I... I'M GOING TO KEEP OUR PROMISE AS WELL!!
I'M GONNA KEEP OUR PROMISE!
AND GET INTO TOKYO U WITH YOU!
AND THEN, WE CAN BOTH LIVE HAPPILY EVER AFTER!
HUH?
....
WHAT IS GOING ON IN THIS CLASS-ROOM?

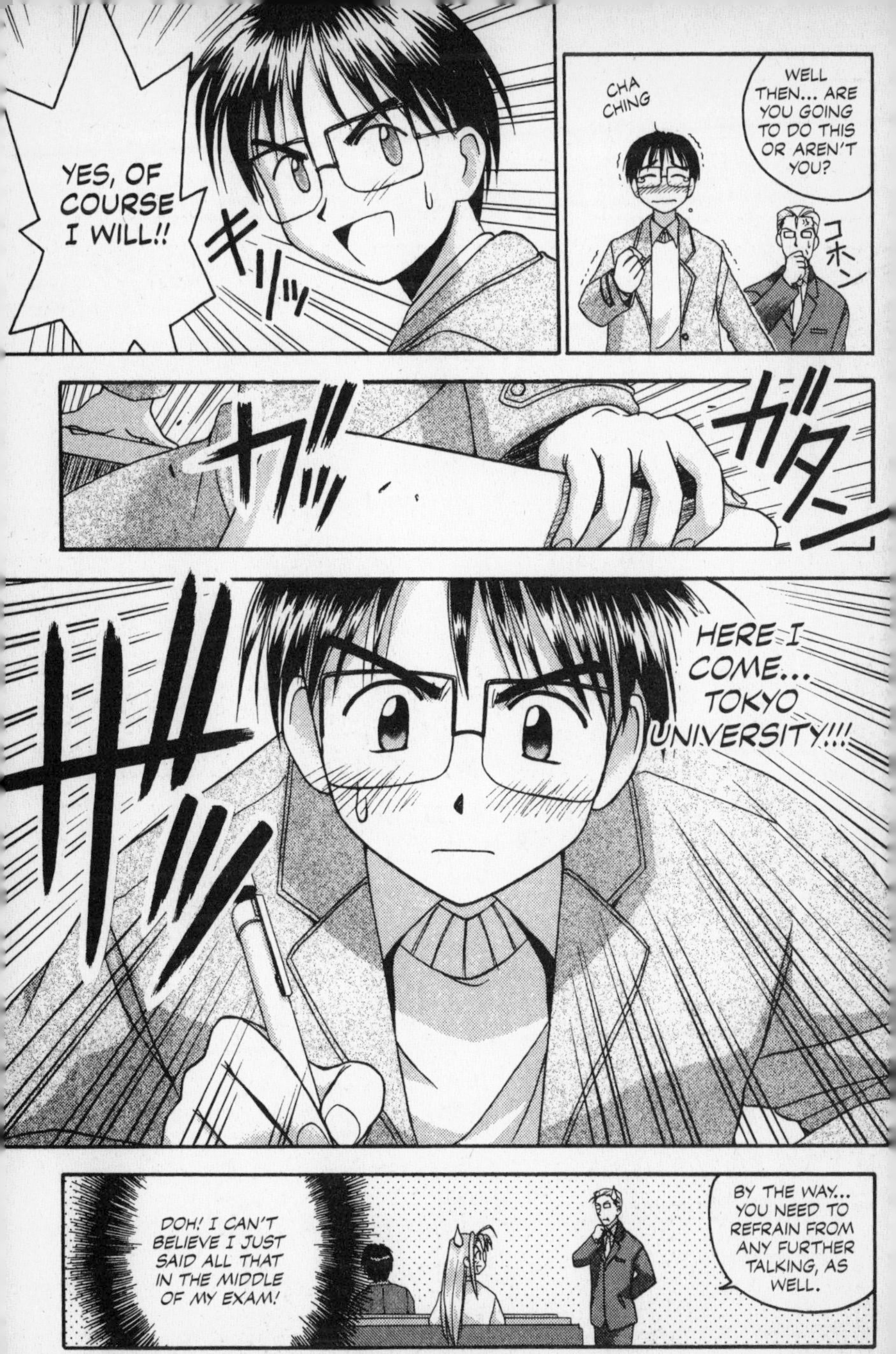
WELL THEN... ARE YOU GOING TO DO THIS OR AREN'T YOU?
CHA CHING
コホン
YES, OF COURSE I WILL!!
キリッ
ガタン
ガッ
HERE I COME... TOKYO UNIVERSITY!!!
ザッ
BY THE WAY... YOU NEED TO REFRAIN FROM ANY FURTHER TALKING, AS WELL.
DOH! I CAN'T BELIEVE I JUST SAID ALL THAT IN THE MIDDLE OF MY EXAM!

Volume 2: The End.

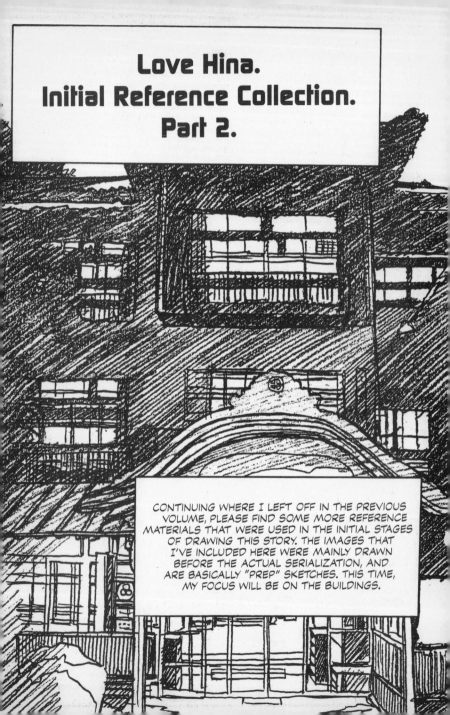

Love Hina.
Initial Reference Collection.
Part 2.

CONTINUING WHERE I LEFT OFF IN THE PREVIOUS
VOLUME, PLEASE FIND SOME MORE REFERENCE
MATERIALS THAT WERE USED IN THE INITIAL STAGES
OF DRAWING THIS STORY. THE IMAGES THAT
I'VE INCLUDED HERE WERE MAINLY DRAWN
BEFORE THE ACTUAL SERIALIZATION, AND
ARE BASICALLY "PREP" SKETCHES. THIS TIME,
MY FOCUS WILL BE ON THE BUILDINGS.

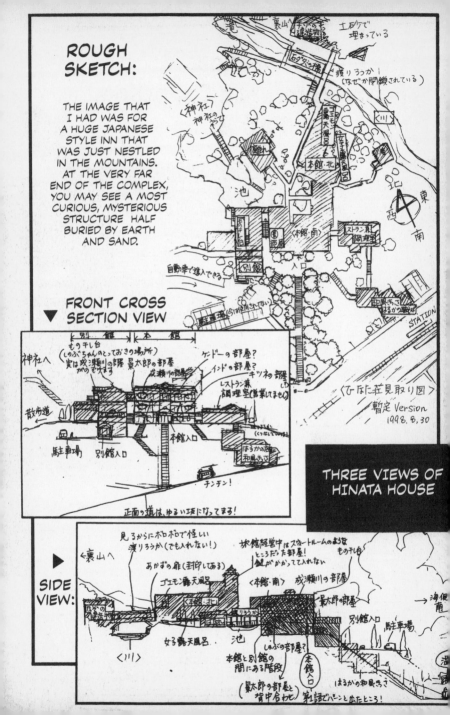

ROUGH SKETCH:

THE IMAGE THAT I HAD WAS FOR A HUGE JAPANESE STYLE INN THAT WAS JUST NESTLED IN THE MOUNTAINS. AT THE VERY FAR END OF THE COMPLEX, YOU MAY SEE A MOST CURIOUS, MYSTERIOUS STRUCTURE HALF BURIED BY EARTH AND SAND.

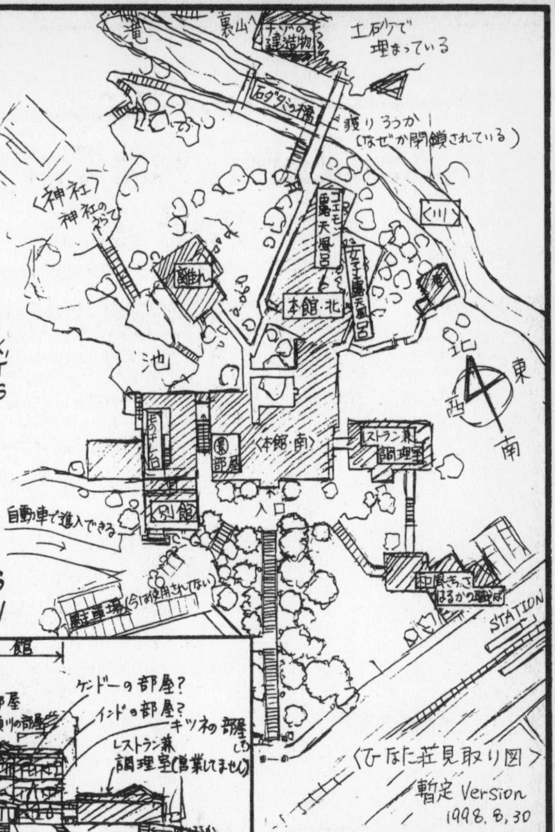

滝
裏山へ
ナゾの建造物
土砂で埋まっている
石ダタミの橋
渡りろうか
(なぜか閉鎖されている)
〈神社へ〉
神社のやしろ
離れ
ゴエモン露天風呂
女子露天風呂
本館・北
〈川〉
池
〈本館・南〉
レストラン兼調理室
北
東
西
南
入口
別館
自動車で進入できる
駐車場(今は使用されてない)
和風きっさはるかの店
STATION
〈ひなた荘見取り図〉
暫定 Version
1998.8.30

▼ FRONT CROSS SECTION VIEW

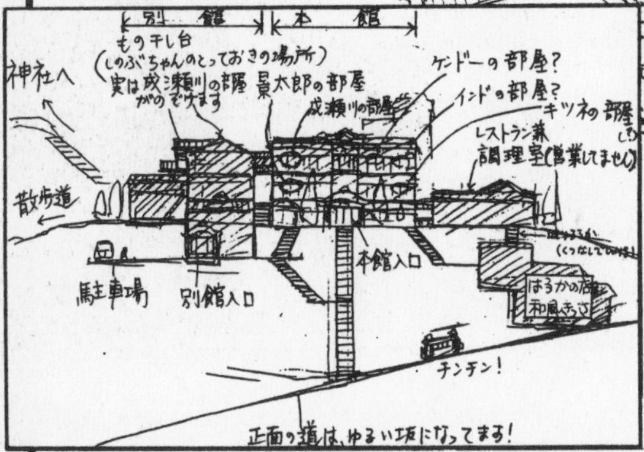

別館
本館
もの干し台
(しのぶちゃんのとっておきの場所)
実は成瀬川の部屋 景太郎の部屋がのぞけます
神社へ
ケンドーの部屋?
インドの部屋?
成瀬川の部屋
キツネの部屋
レストラン兼
調理室(営業してません)
散歩道
本館入口
駐車場
別館入口
はるかの店
和風きっさ
チンチン!
正面の道は、ゆるい坂になってます!

THREE VIEWS OF HINATA HOUSE

▶ SIDE VIEW:

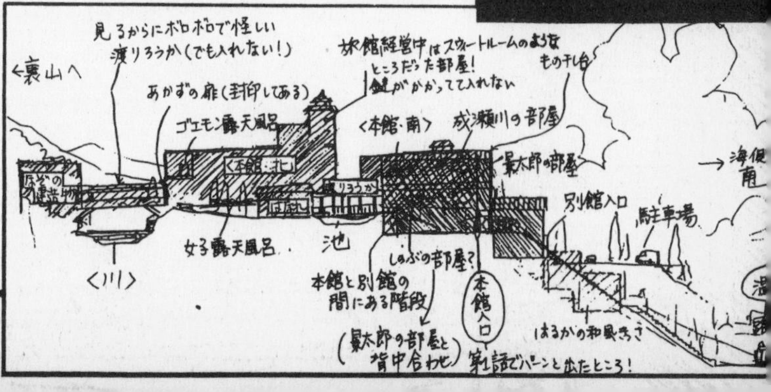

見るからにボロボロで怪しい
渡りろうか(でも入れない!)
<裏山へ
あかずの扉(封印してある)
旅館経営中はスウィートルームのような
ところだった部屋!
鍵がかかって入れない
もの干し台
ゴエモン露天風呂
〈本館・南〉
成瀬川の部屋
〈本館・北〉
景太郎の部屋
海側
南
渡りろうか
別館入口
駐車場
女子露天風呂
池
〈川〉
しのぶの部屋?
本館と別館の間にある階段
本館入口
(景太郎の部屋と背中合わせ)
はるかの和風きっさ
第1話でバーンと出たところ!

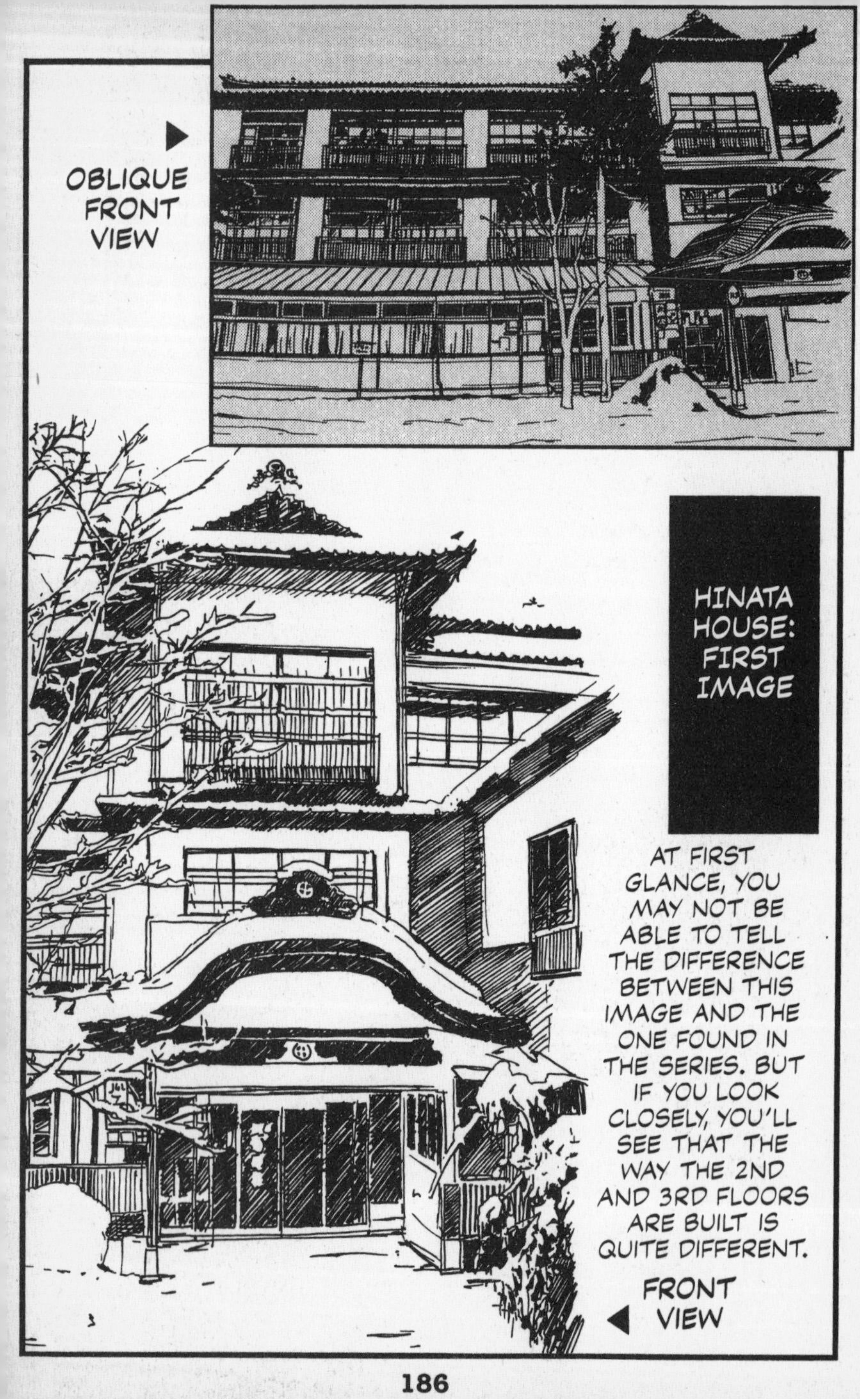
OBLIQUE FRONT VIEW
HINATA HOUSE: FIRST IMAGE
AT FIRST GLANCE, YOU MAY NOT BE ABLE TO TELL THE DIFFERENCE BETWEEN THIS IMAGE AND THE ONE FOUND IN THE SERIES. BUT IF YOU LOOK CLOSELY, YOU'LL SEE THAT THE WAY THE 2ND AND 3RD FLOORS ARE BUILT IS QUITE DIFFERENT.
FRONT VIEW

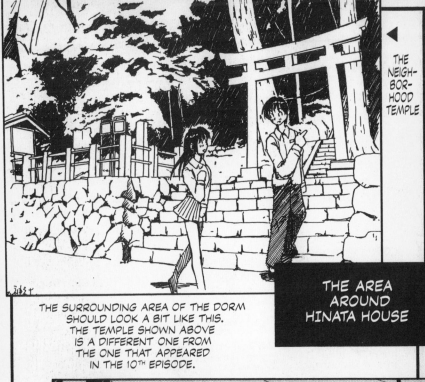

THE AREA AROUND HINATA HOUSE

THE NEIGHBORHOOD TEMPLE

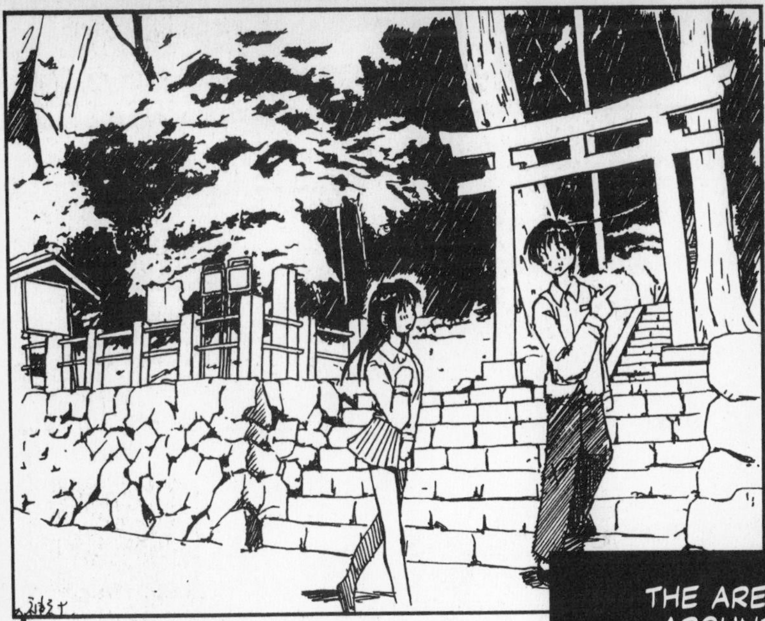

THE SURROUNDING AREA OF THE DORM SHOULD LOOK A BIT LIKE THIS. THE TEMPLE SHOWN ABOVE IS A DIFFERENT ONE FROM THE ONE THAT APPEARED IN THE 10TH EPISODE.

THE BACK VIEW (RIVER)

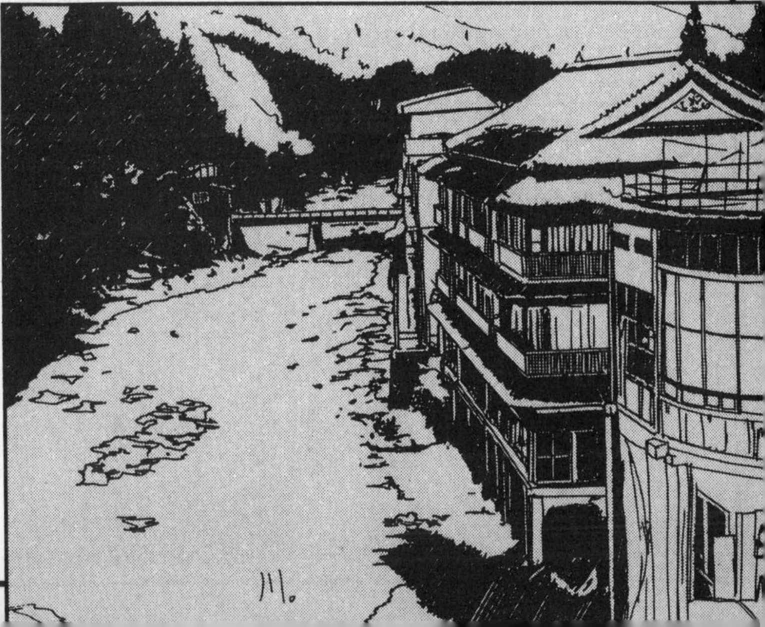
川。

THE BATHS

UNLIKE THE ACTUAL STORY, THE OPEN-AIR BATH WAS ORIGINALLY IN THE COURTYARD (INNER GARDEN). AS FOR KEITARO'S BATH, THE INSTANT HOT WATER MACHINE KINDA INVITES TEARS, DOESN'T IT? (LAUGH)

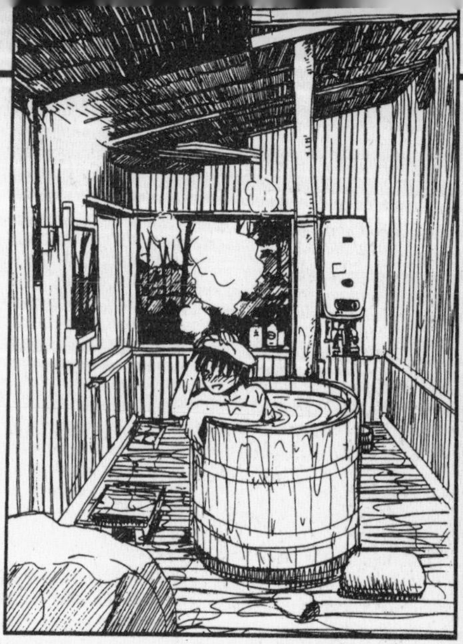

KEITARO'S BATH ▶

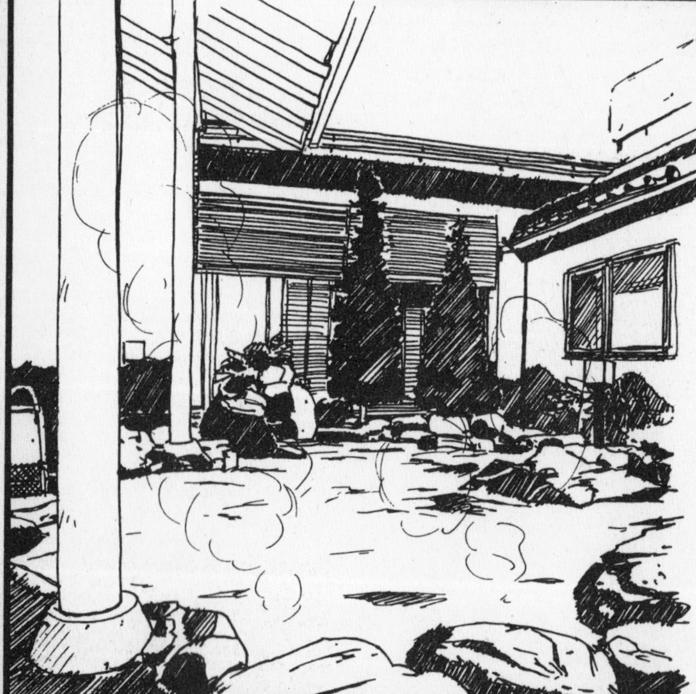

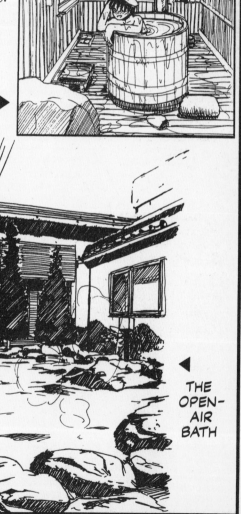

◀ THE OPEN-AIR BATH

HINATA HOUSE: ANNEX DETAILS

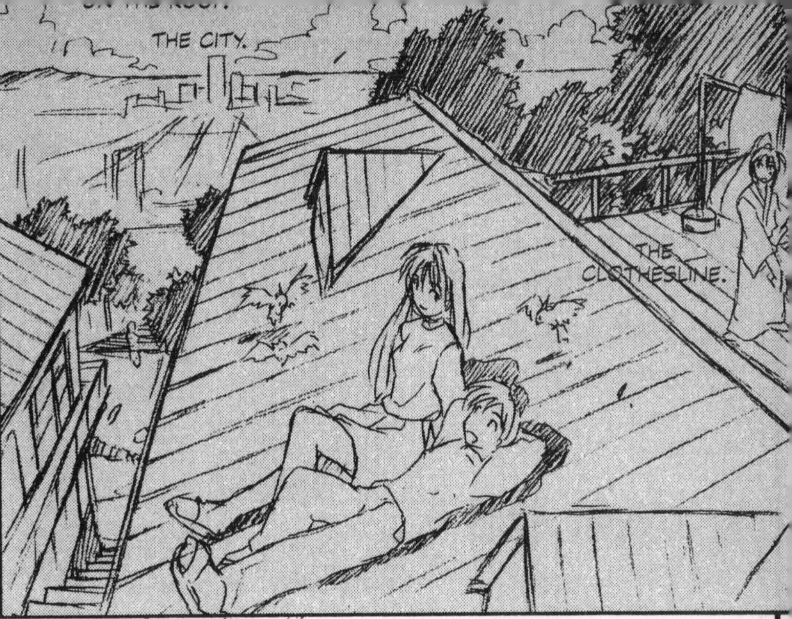
THE CITY.
THE CLOTHESLINE.

▲ THE ROOF OF THE ANNEX (PLACE FOR DRYING LAUNDRY)

◀ THE WALKWAY TO THE ANNEX

THE BUILDING WHICH HOUSES TWO OF SHINOBU'S "SPECIAL SPOTS" IS CALLED THE ANNEX. THESE TWO AREAS ARE USED PRETTY MUCH "AS IS" IN THE SERIES.

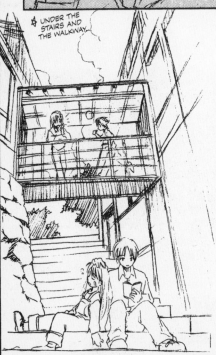

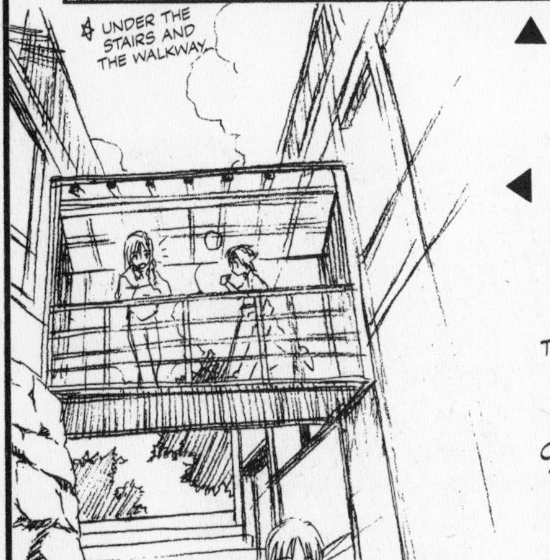
UNDER THE STAIRS AND THE WALKWAY

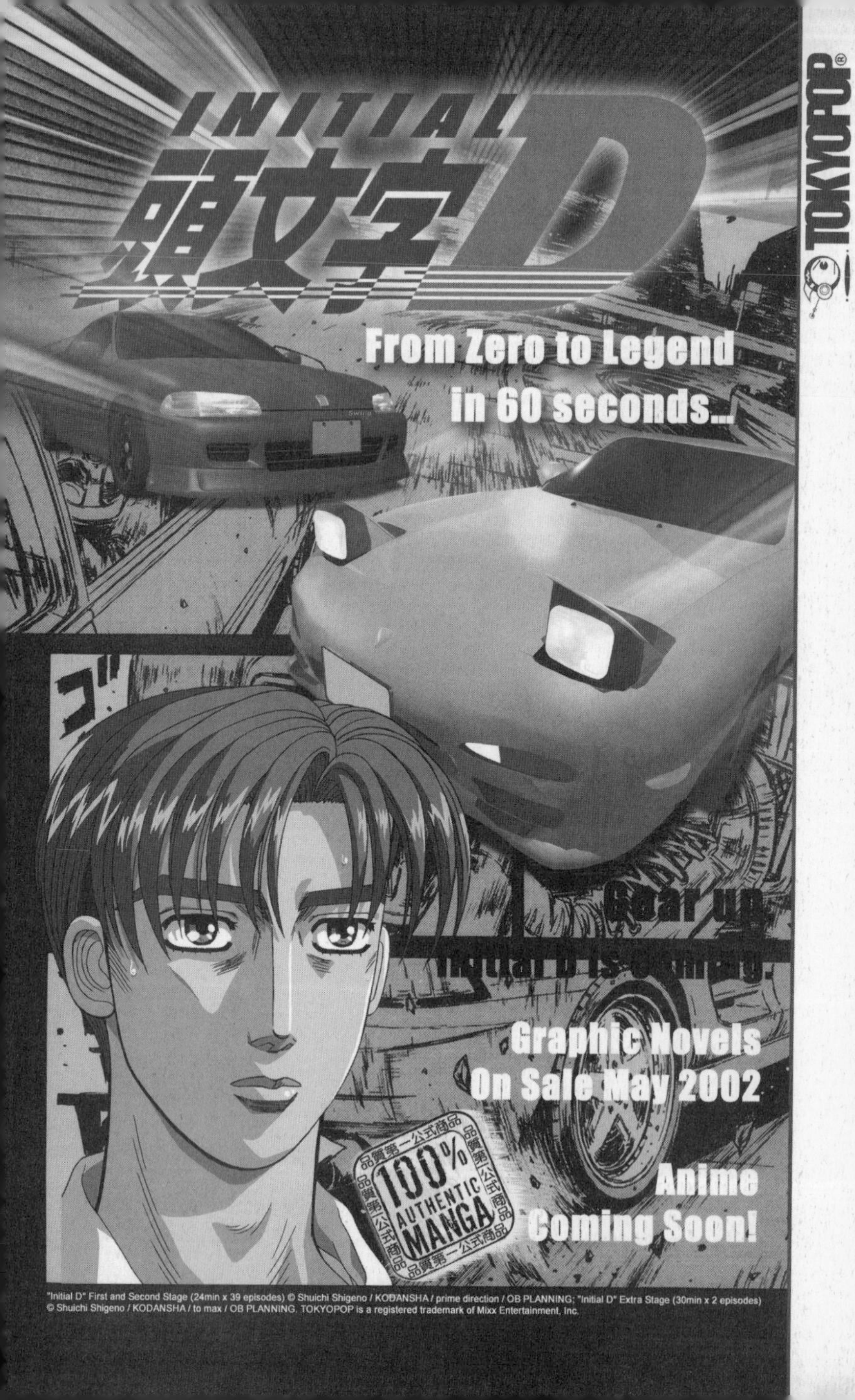
INITIAL
頭文字D
From Zero to Legend
in 60 seconds...
ゴ
Gear up.
Initial D is Coming.
Graphic Novels
On Sale May 2002
Anime
Coming Soon!
100% AUTHENTIC MANGA
品質第一公式商品

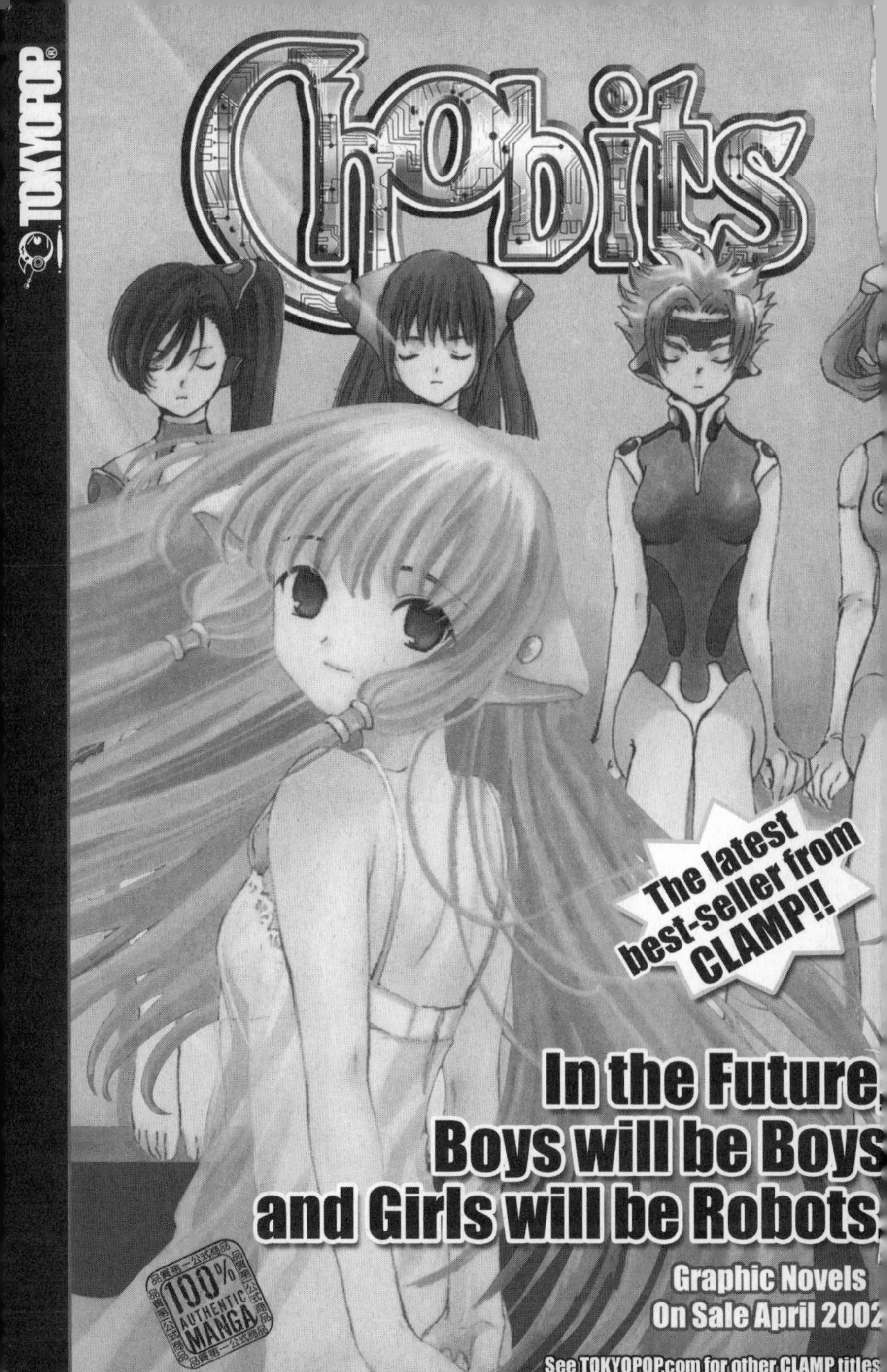
TOKYOPOP®
Chobits
The latest best-seller from CLAMP!!
In the Future, Boys will be Boys and Girls will be Robots.
100% AUTHENTIC MANGA
Graphic Novels
On Sale April 2002
See TOKYOPOP.com for other CLAMP titles

STOP!

This is the back of the book.
You wouldn't want to spoil a great ending!

This book is printed "manga-style," in the authentic Japanese right-to-left format. Since none of the artwork has been flipped or altered, readers get to experience the story just as the creator intended. You've been asking for it, so TOKYOPOP® delivered: authentic, hot-off-the-press, and far more fun!

DIRECTIONS

If this is your first time reading manga-style, here's a quick guide to help you understand how it works.

It's easy... just start in the top right panel and follow the numbers. Have fun, and look for more 100% authentic manga from TOKYOPOP®!